Sports Illustrated

Sports Illustrated

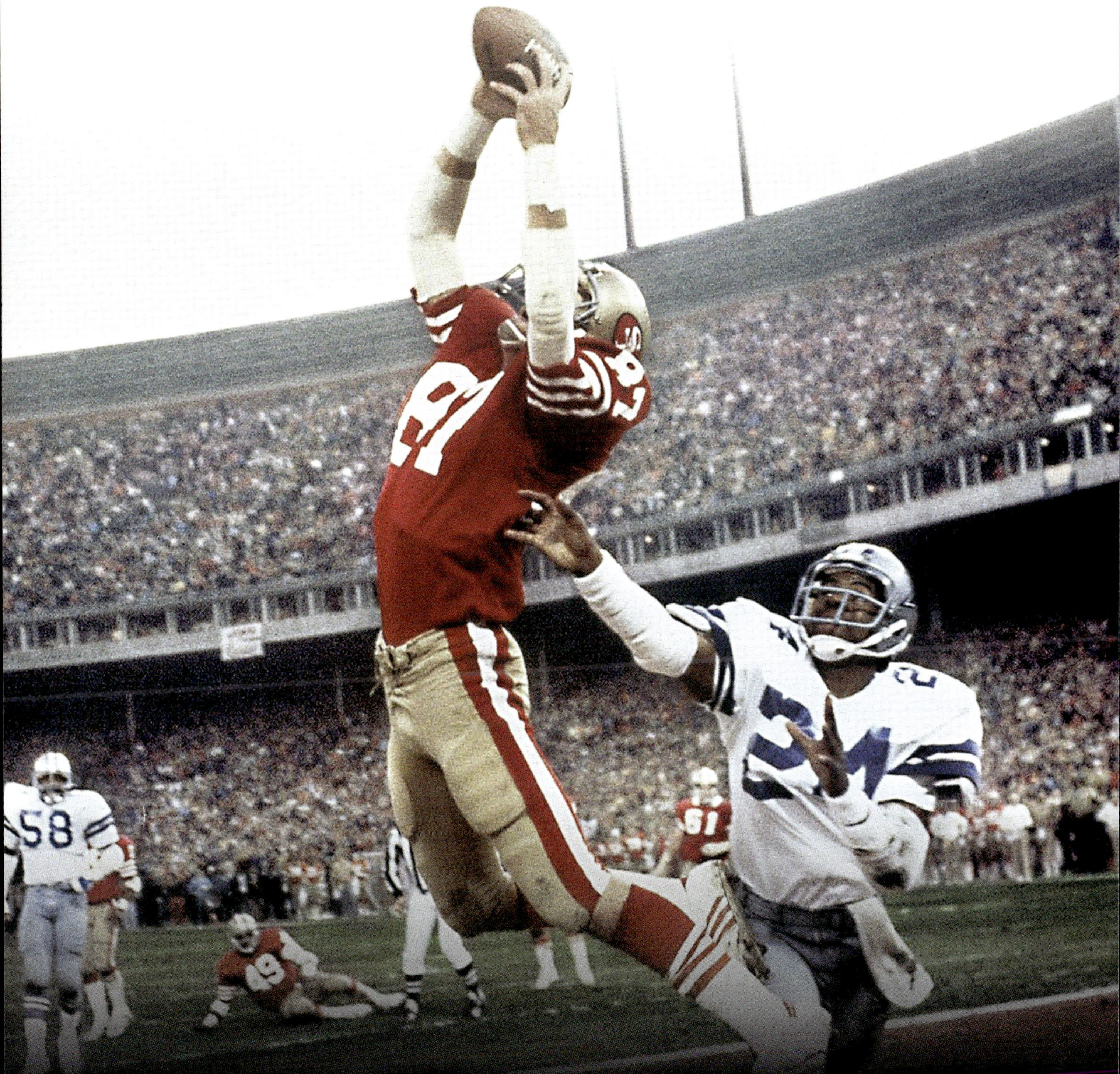

THE SAN FRANCISCO 49ERS AT 75

CELEBRATING THE HISTORY OF 49ERS FOOTBALL

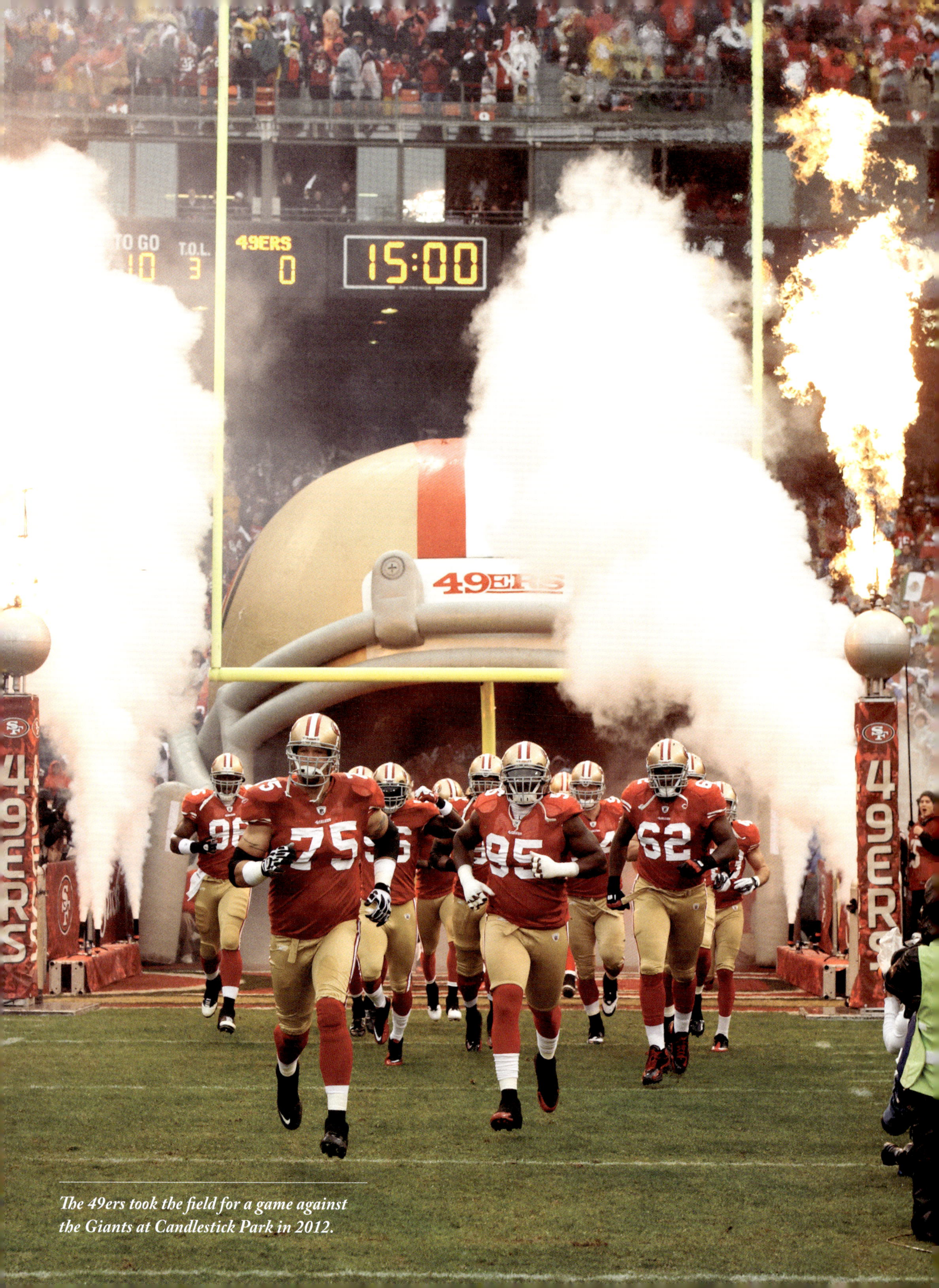

The 49ers took the field for a game against the Giants at Candlestick Park in 2012.

CONTENTS

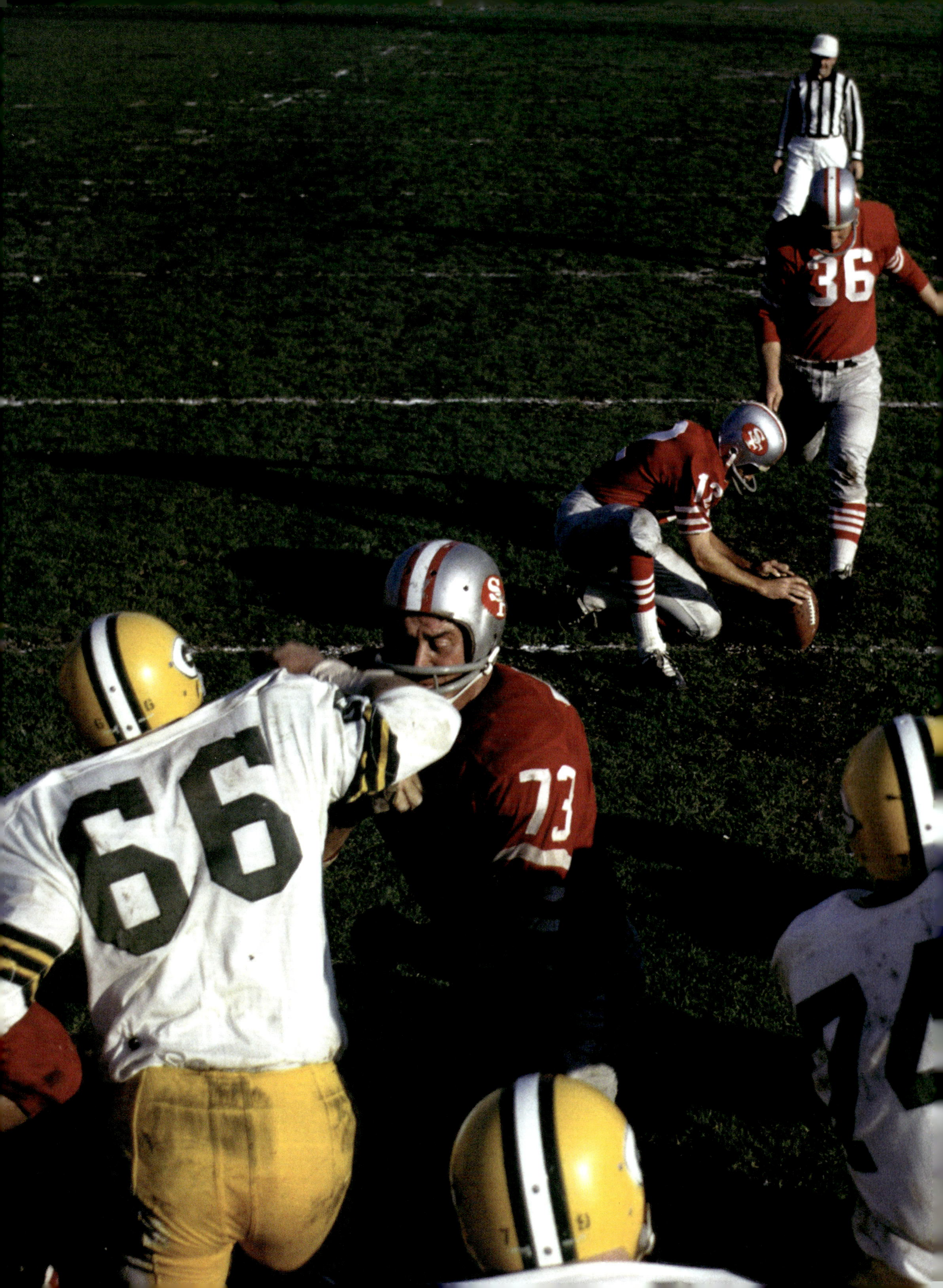

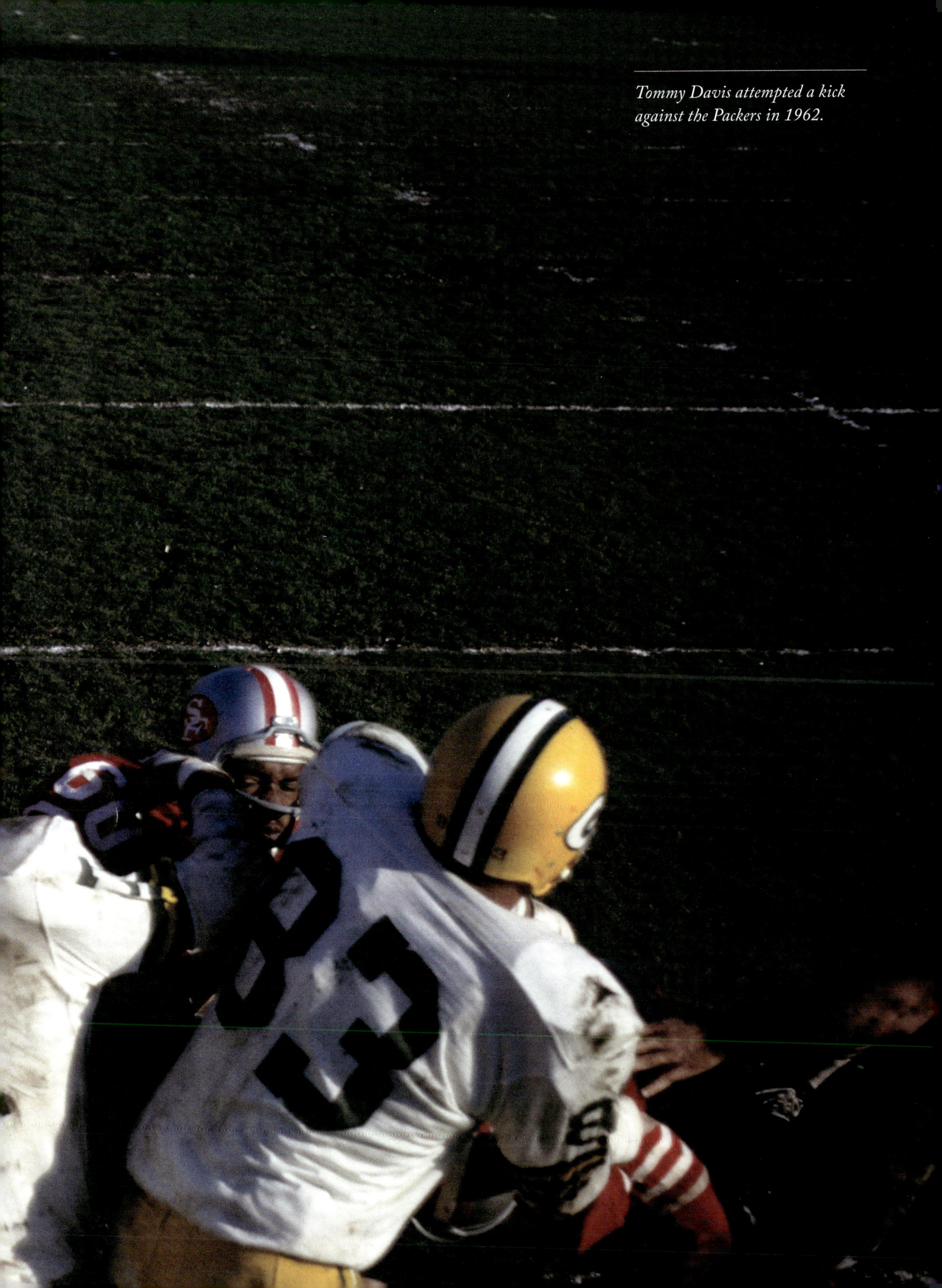

Tommy Davis attempted a kick against the Packers in 1962.

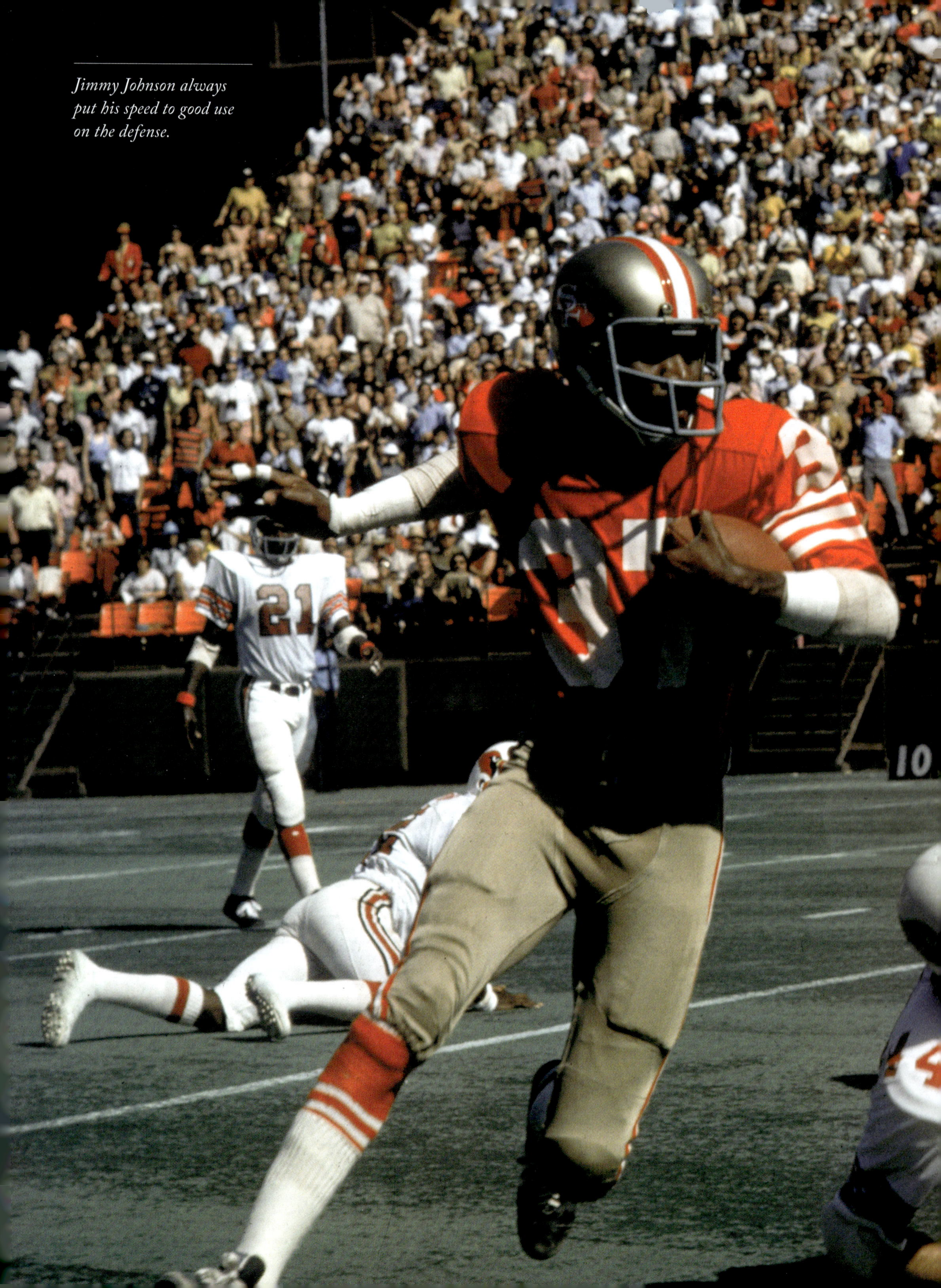

Jimmy Johnson always put his speed to good use on the defense.

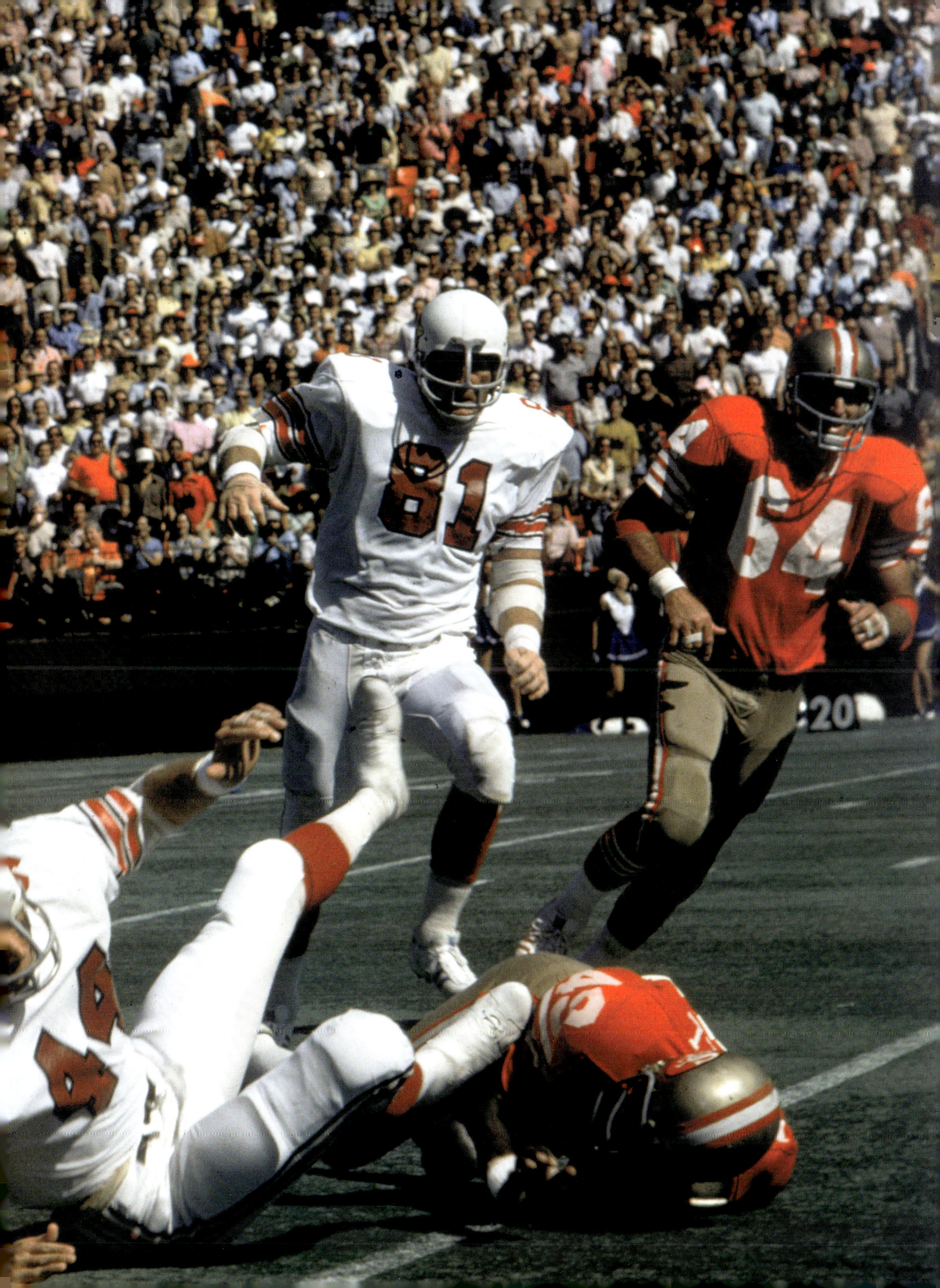

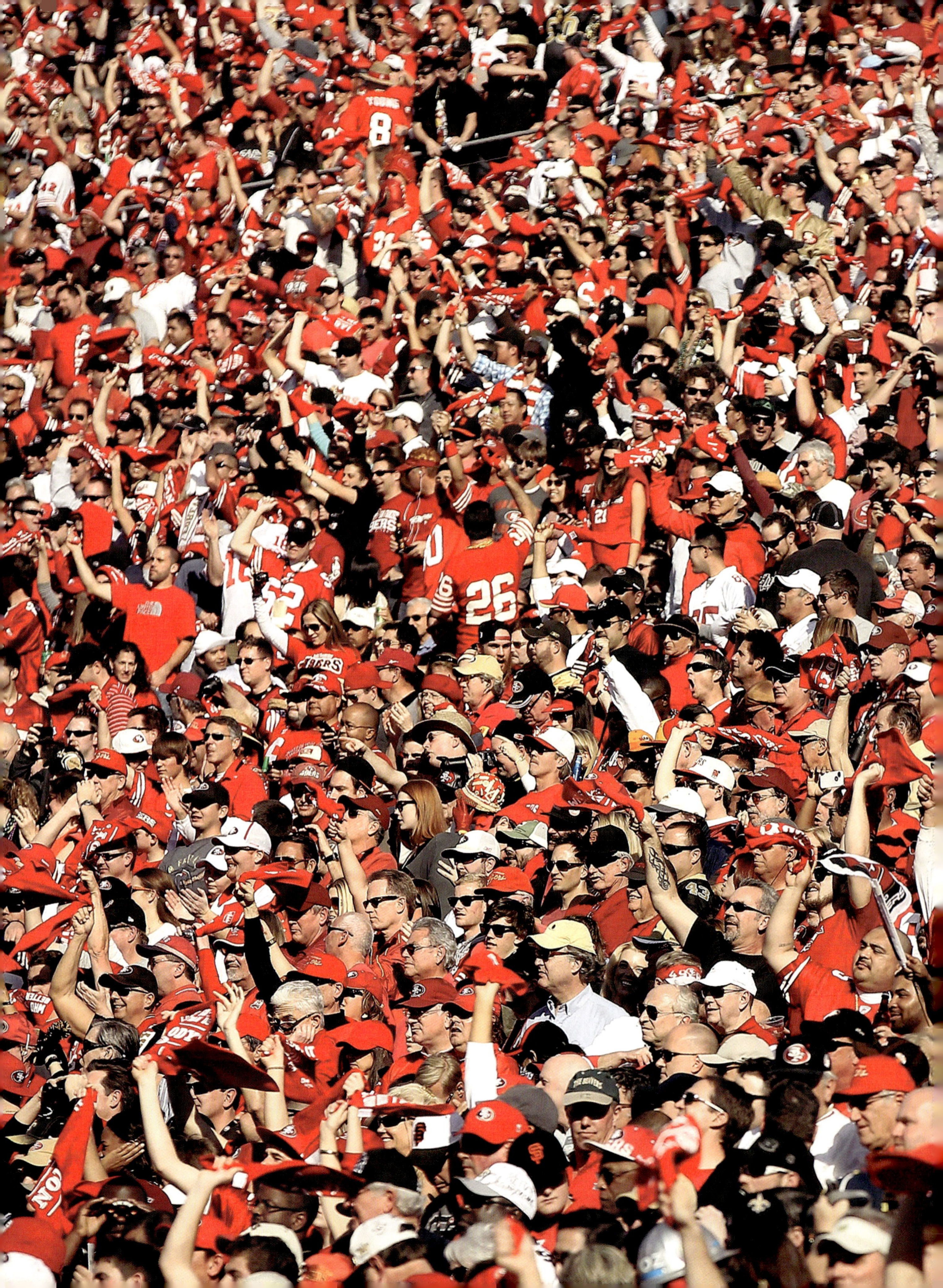
YOUNG
8
26

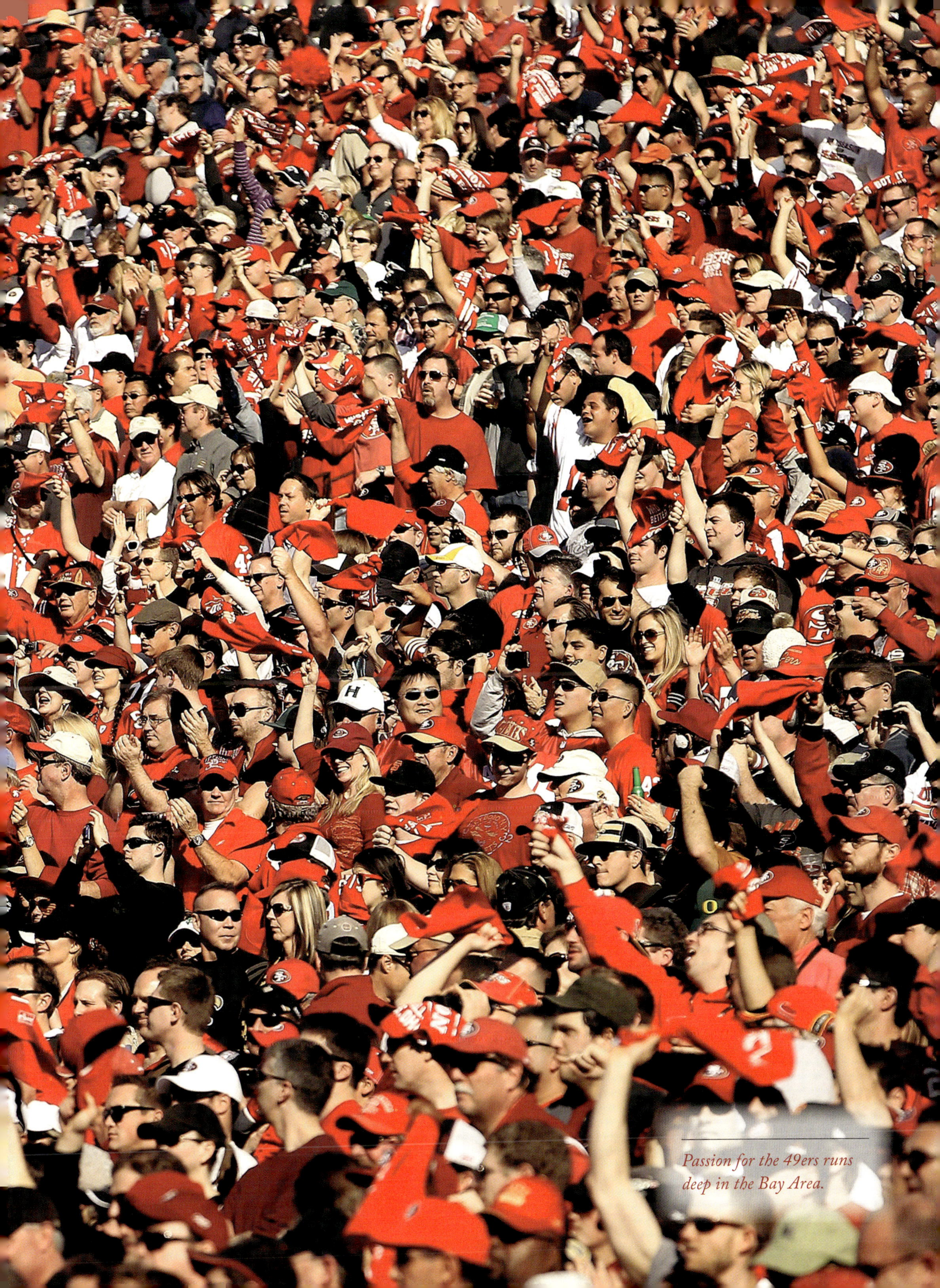

Passion for the 49ers runs deep in the Bay Area.

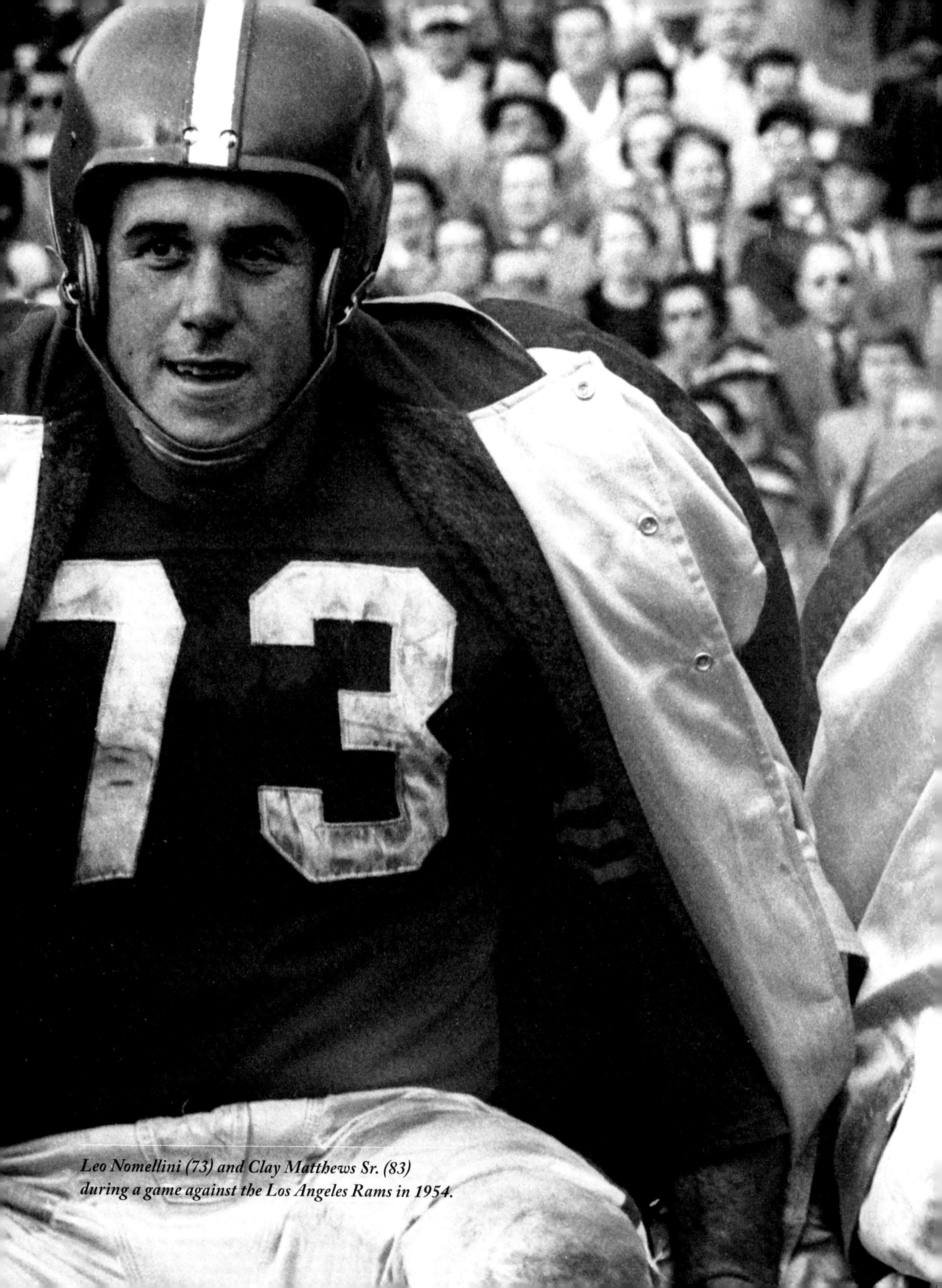

Leo Nomellini (73) and Clay Matthews Sr. (83) during a game against the Los Angeles Rams in 1954.

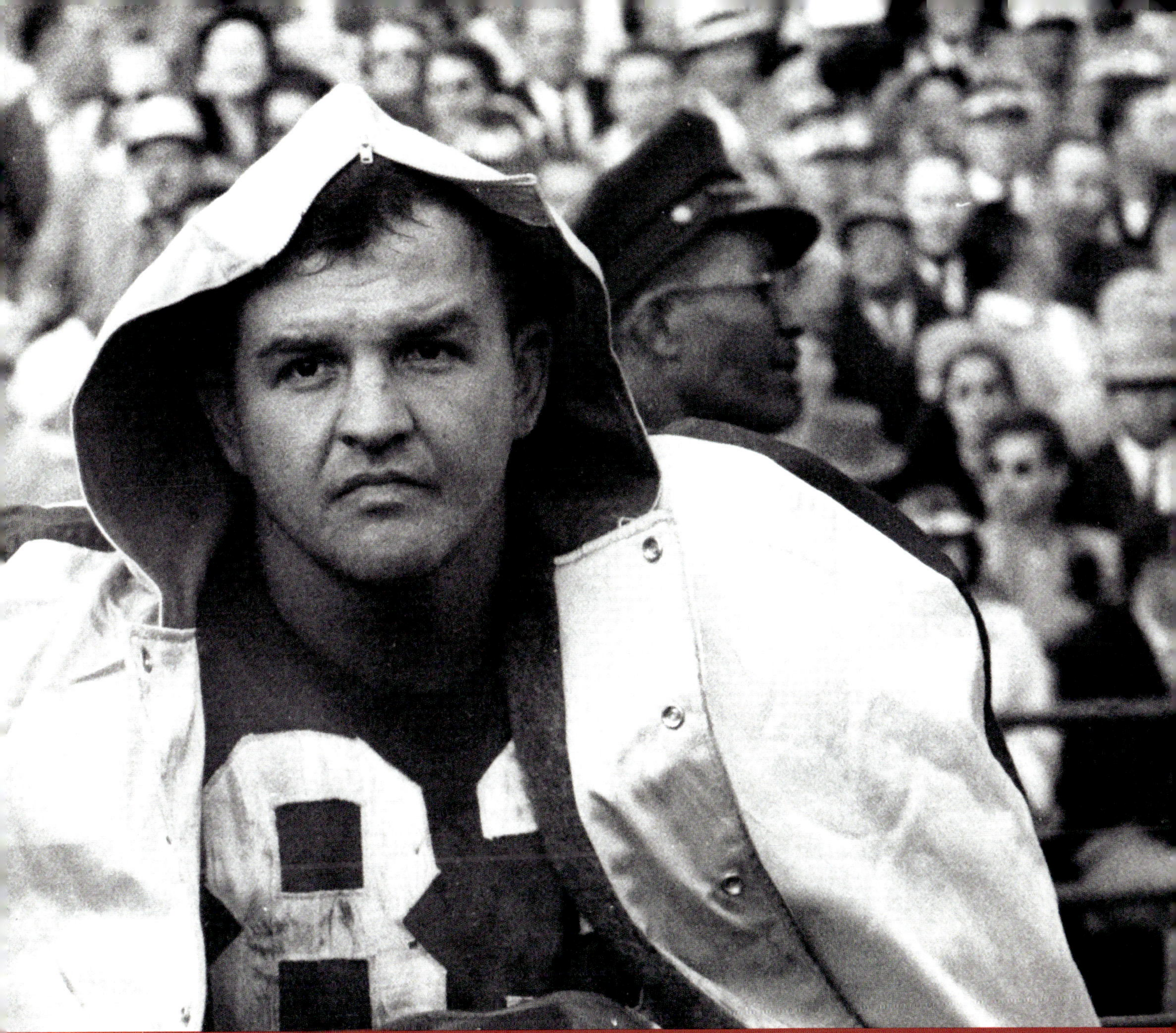

THE PLAYERS

Beginning with their inaugural NFL season in 1950, a succession of stars helped turn the 49ers into one of the league's premier franchises

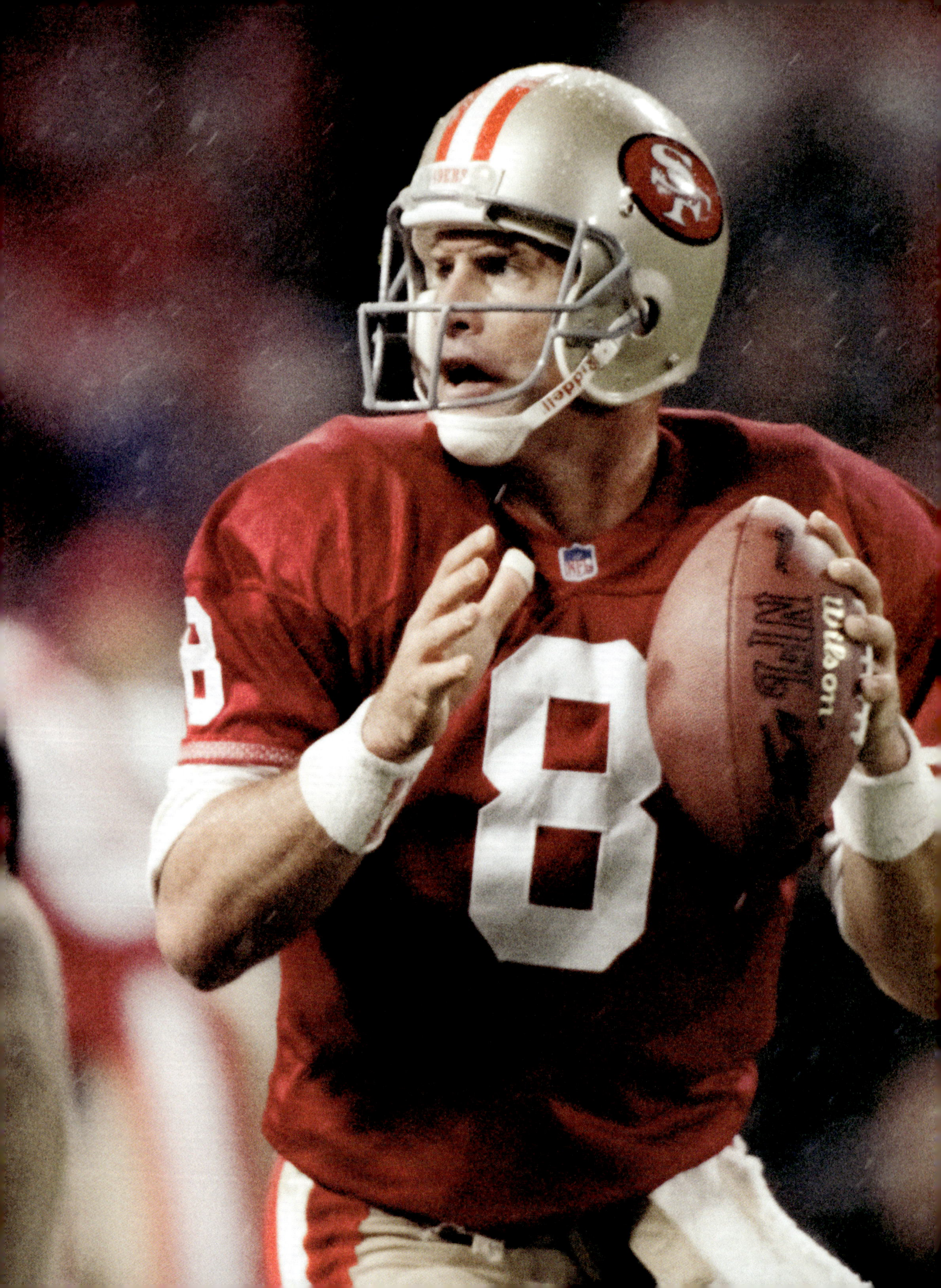
Wilson

STEVE YOUNG

- » Quarterback 1987–1999
- » Three-time Super Bowl champion
- » Two-time NFL MVP
- » Three-time All-Pro
- » Seven-time Pro Bowl selection
- » Pro Football Hall of Fame 2005
- » San Francisco jersey #8 retired 2008

Once the eighth-string quarterback at Brigham Young University, Steve Young began his professional career in the USFL before joining the Tampa Bay Buccaneers in 1985. A trade to the 49ers offered Young a fresh start, but he found himself backing up Joe Montana for four seasons. Young finally got his chance in 1991, then won the NFL MVP award in 1992 and again in 1994, the same season he led the Niners to victory in Super Bowl XXIX.

When finally given the chance to start for the Niners, Young made the most of it.

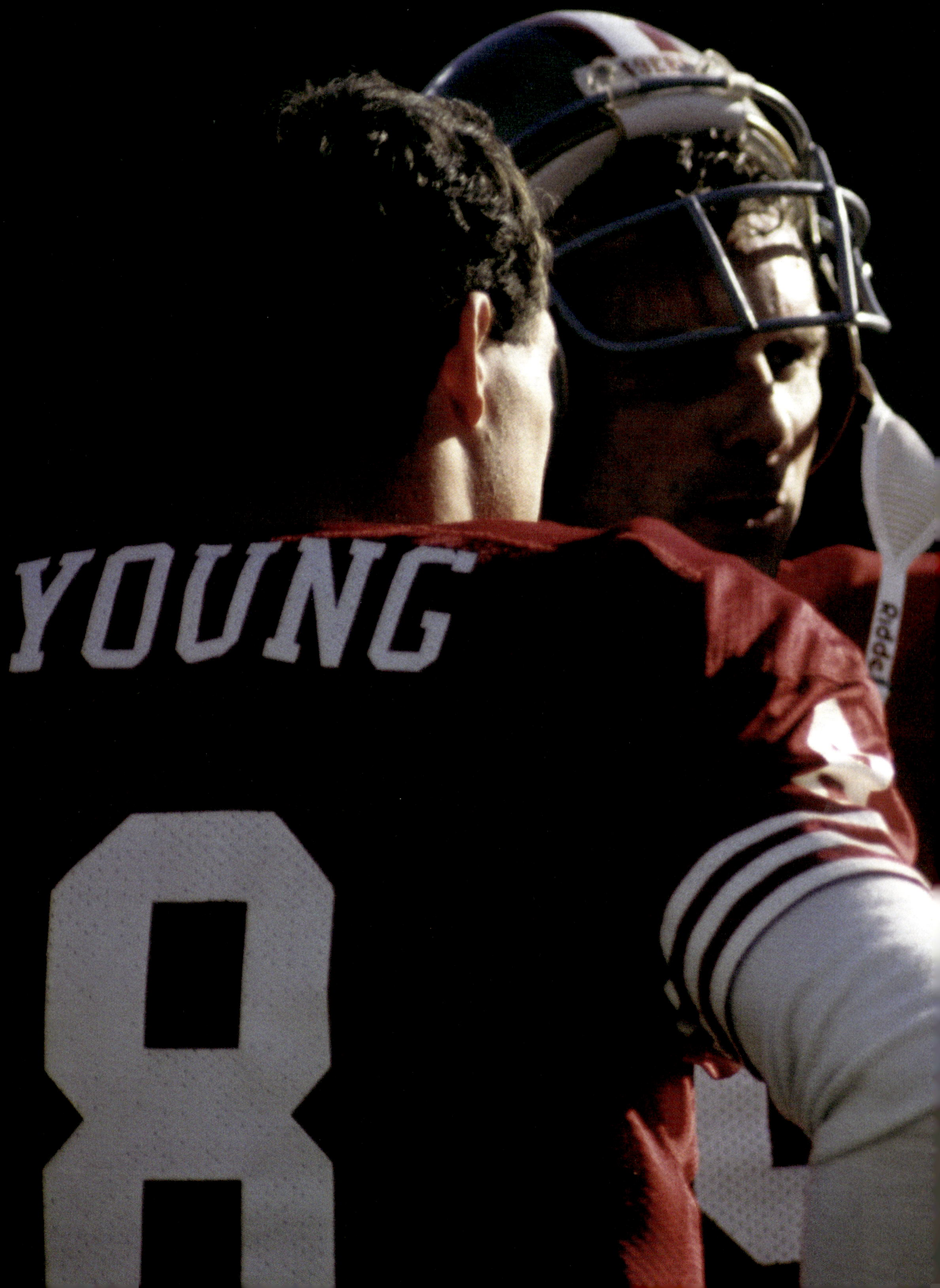
YOUNG
8

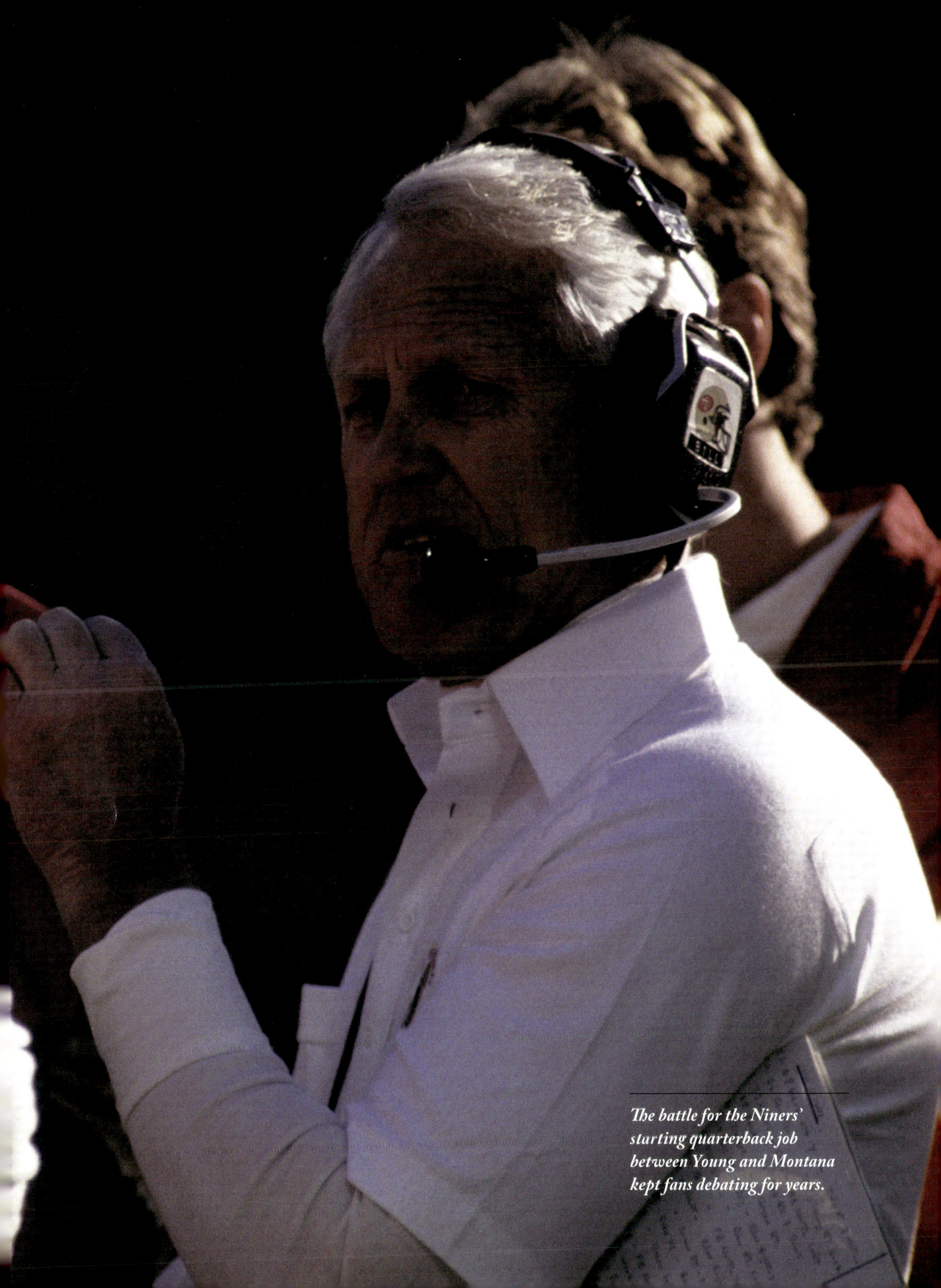

The battle for the Niners' starting quarterback job between Young and Montana kept fans debating for years.

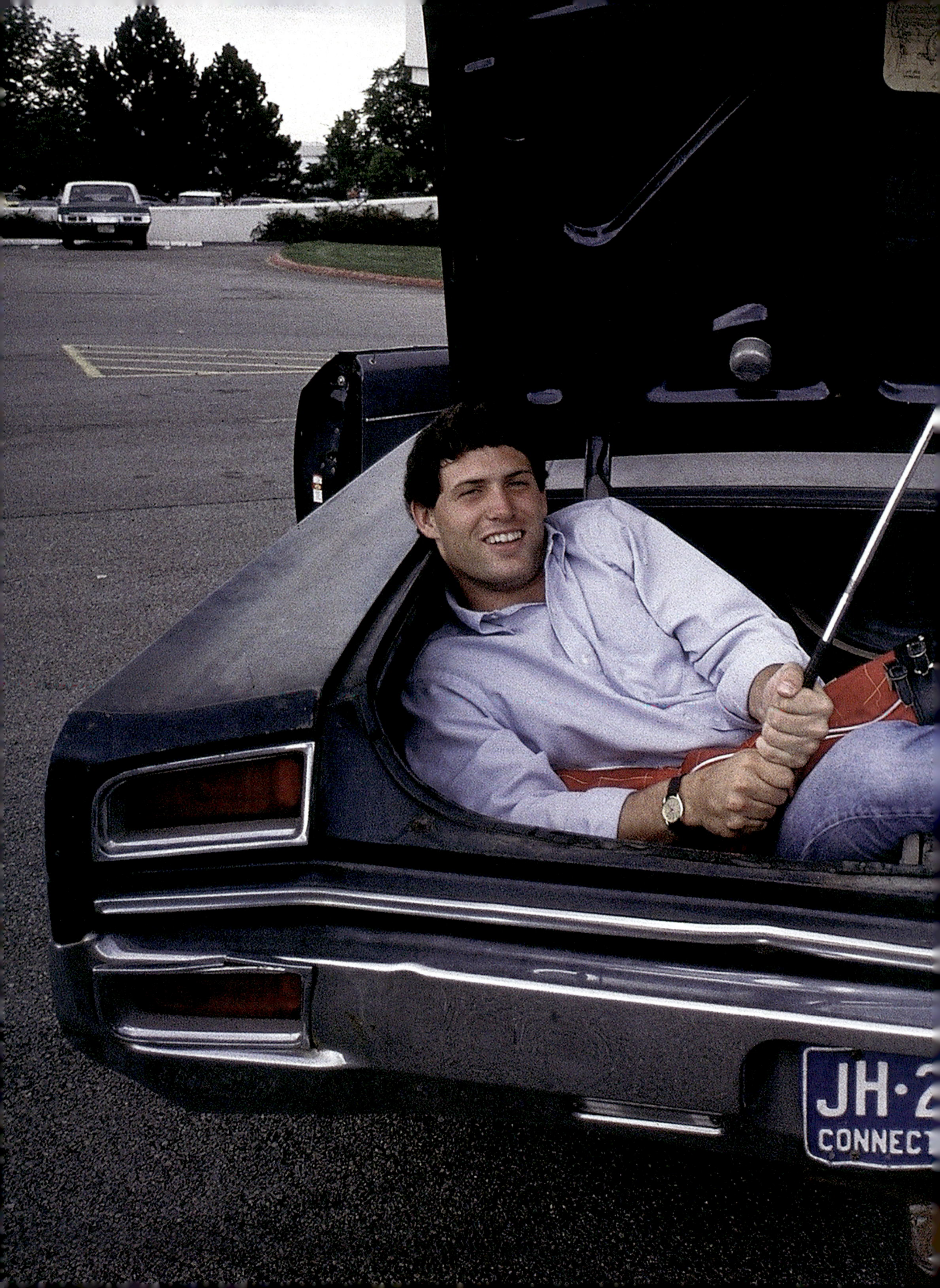
JH·2
CONNECT

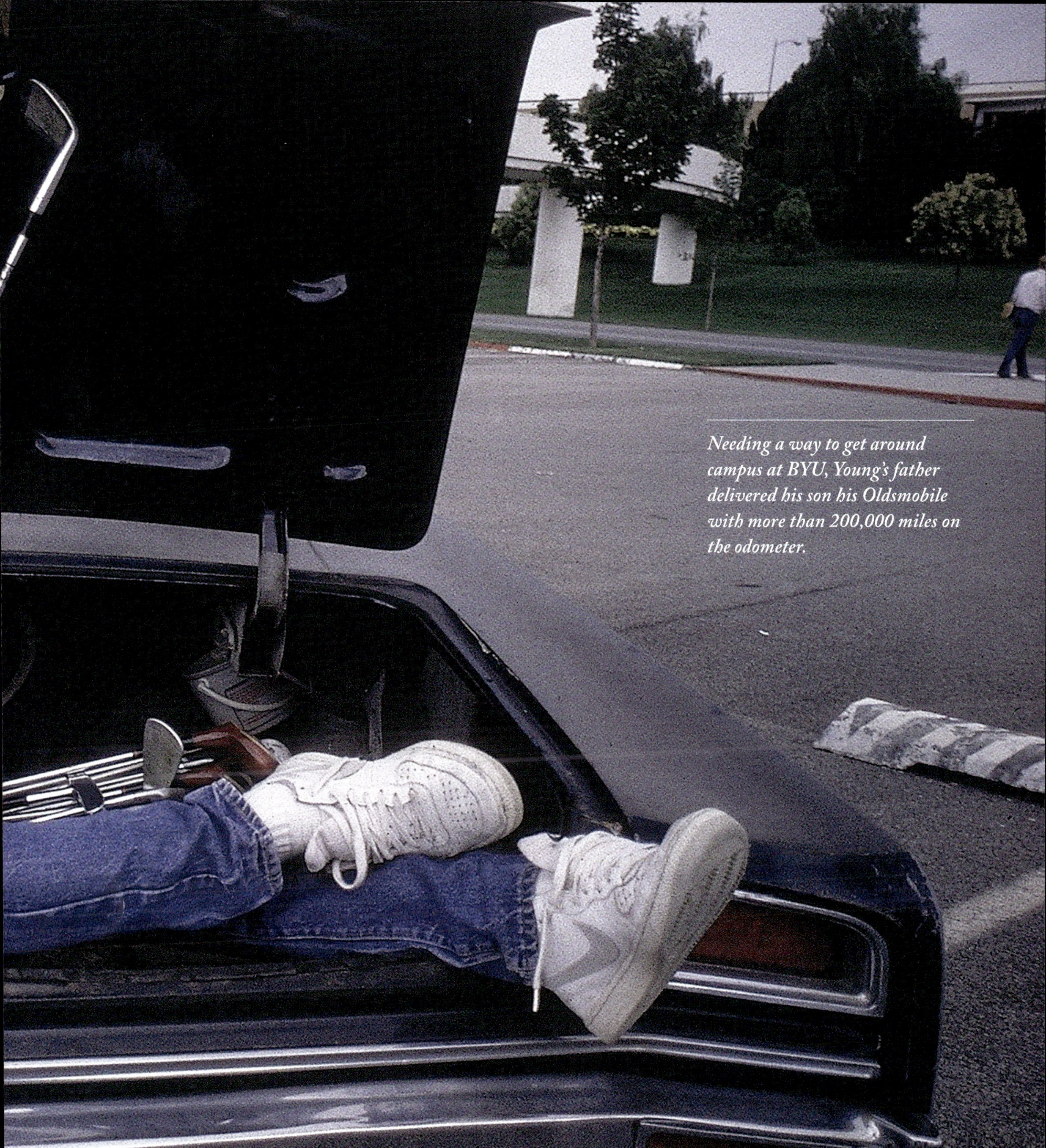

Needing a way to get around campus at BYU, Young's father delivered his son his Oldsmobile with more than 200,000 miles on the odometer.

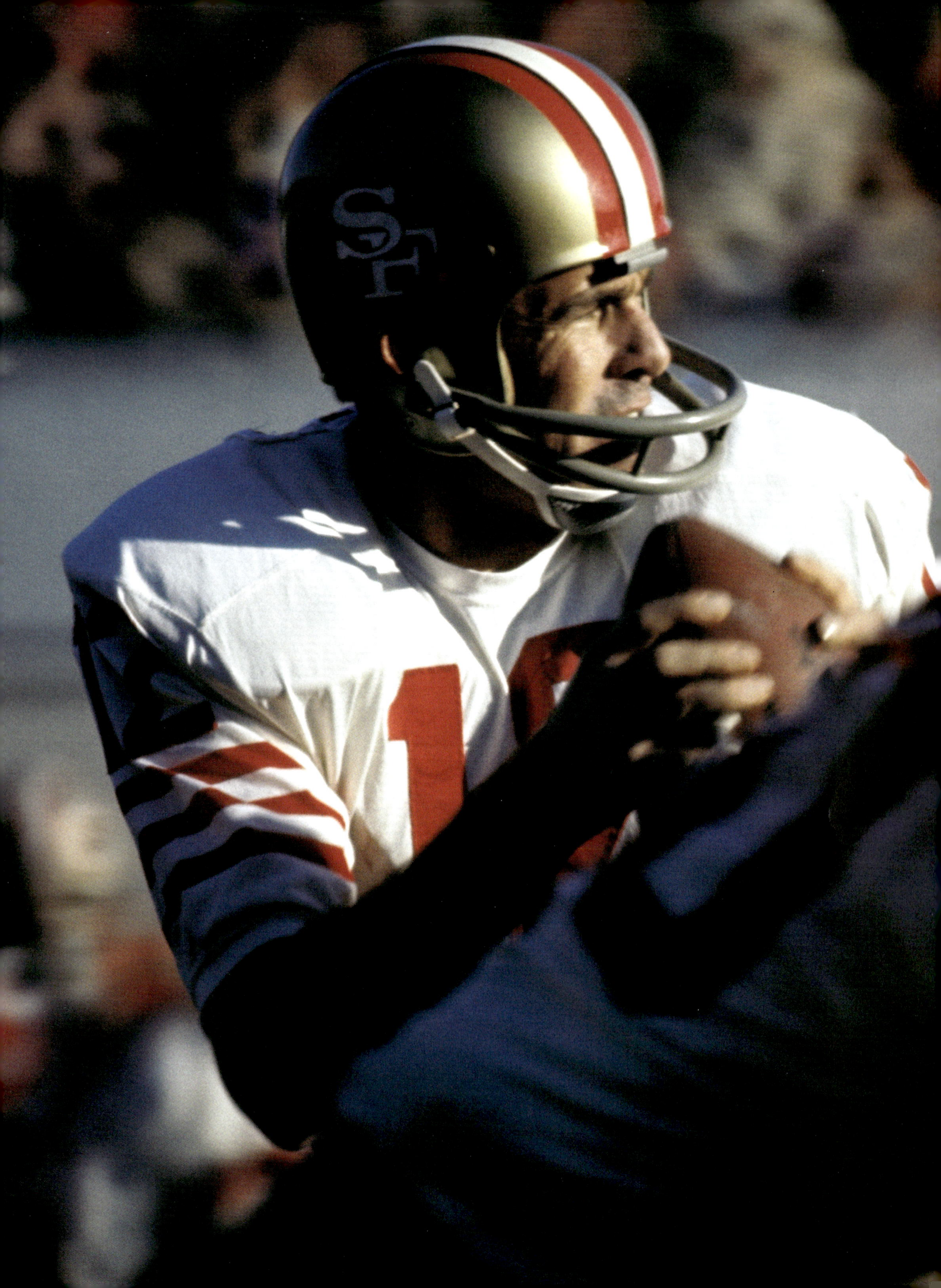

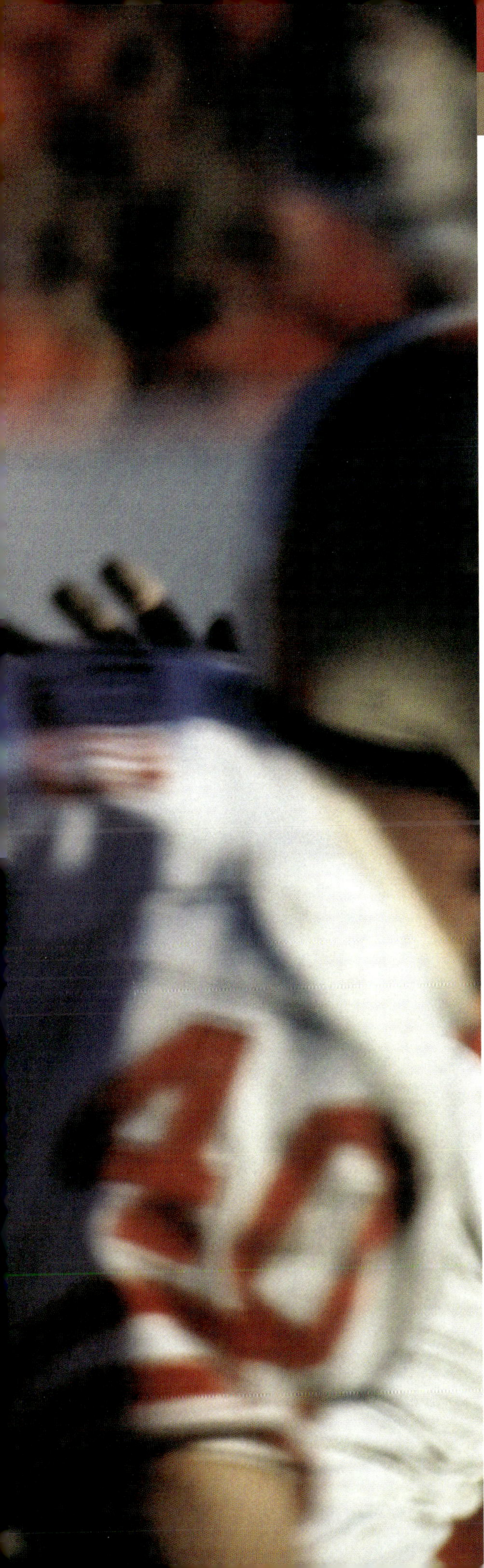

JOHN BRODIE

- **Quarterback 1957–1973**
- **NFL MVP 1970**
- **All-Pro 1970**
- **Two-time Pro Bowl selection**
- **San Francisco jersey #12 retired 1973**

John Brodie is the longest-tenured player in team history; his 201 games as quarterback far outpace Joe Montana (167) and Steve Young (150). An Oakland native who played college football at Stanford, Brodie joined the Niners in 1957 and became the starting quarterback in 1961 after Y.A. Tittle was traded to the New York Giants. Though the team missed the playoffs from 1958 to 1969, Brodie was a steadying presence and became the first Niner to win the NFL MVP award in 1970. He retired third in NFL history in passing yards, trailing only Johnny Unitas and Fran Tarkenton.

Brodie's ascendancy led partly to the Niners' trading Y.A. Tittle to the New York Giants.

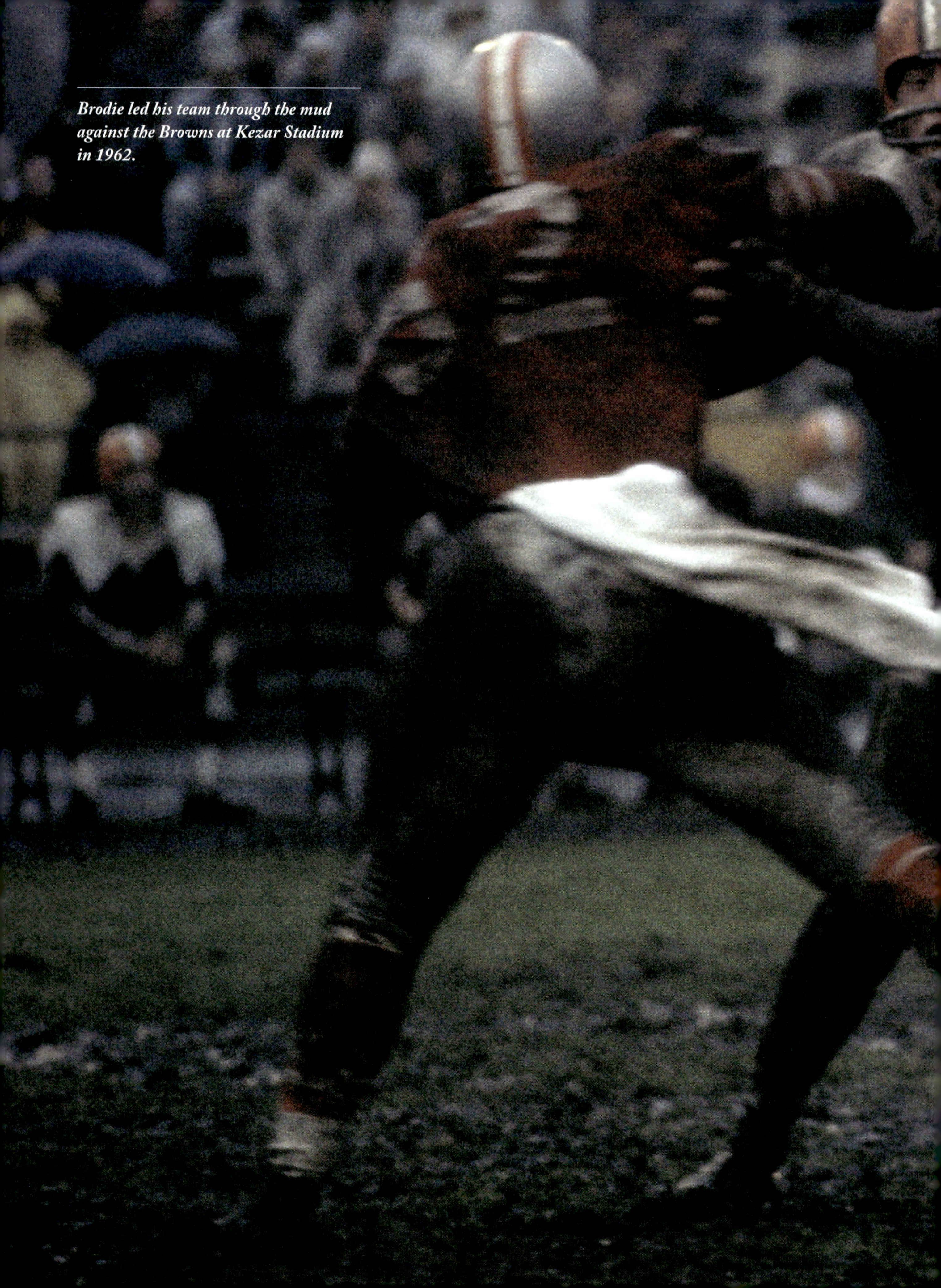

Brodie led his team through the mud against the Browns at Kezar Stadium in 1962.

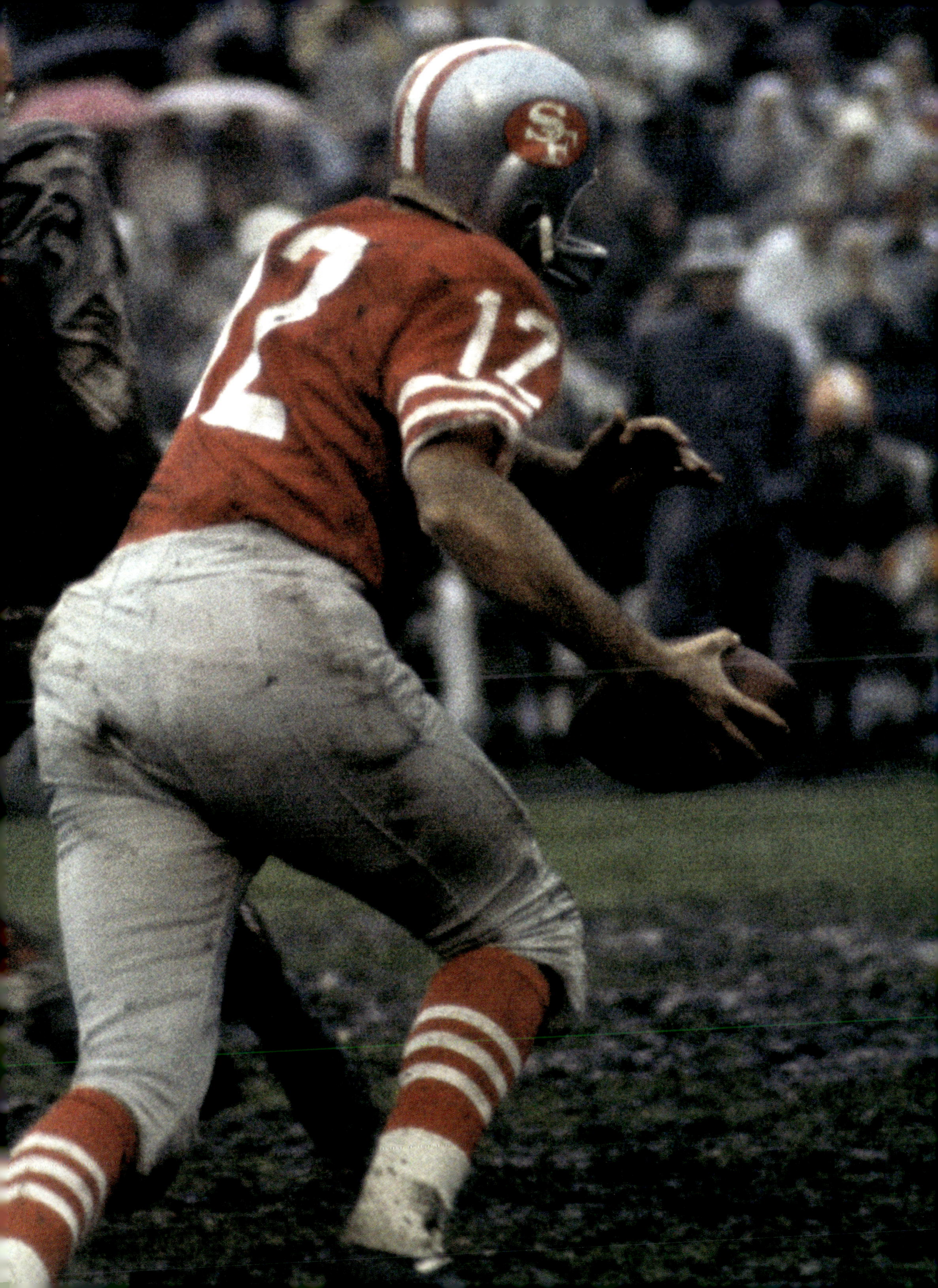

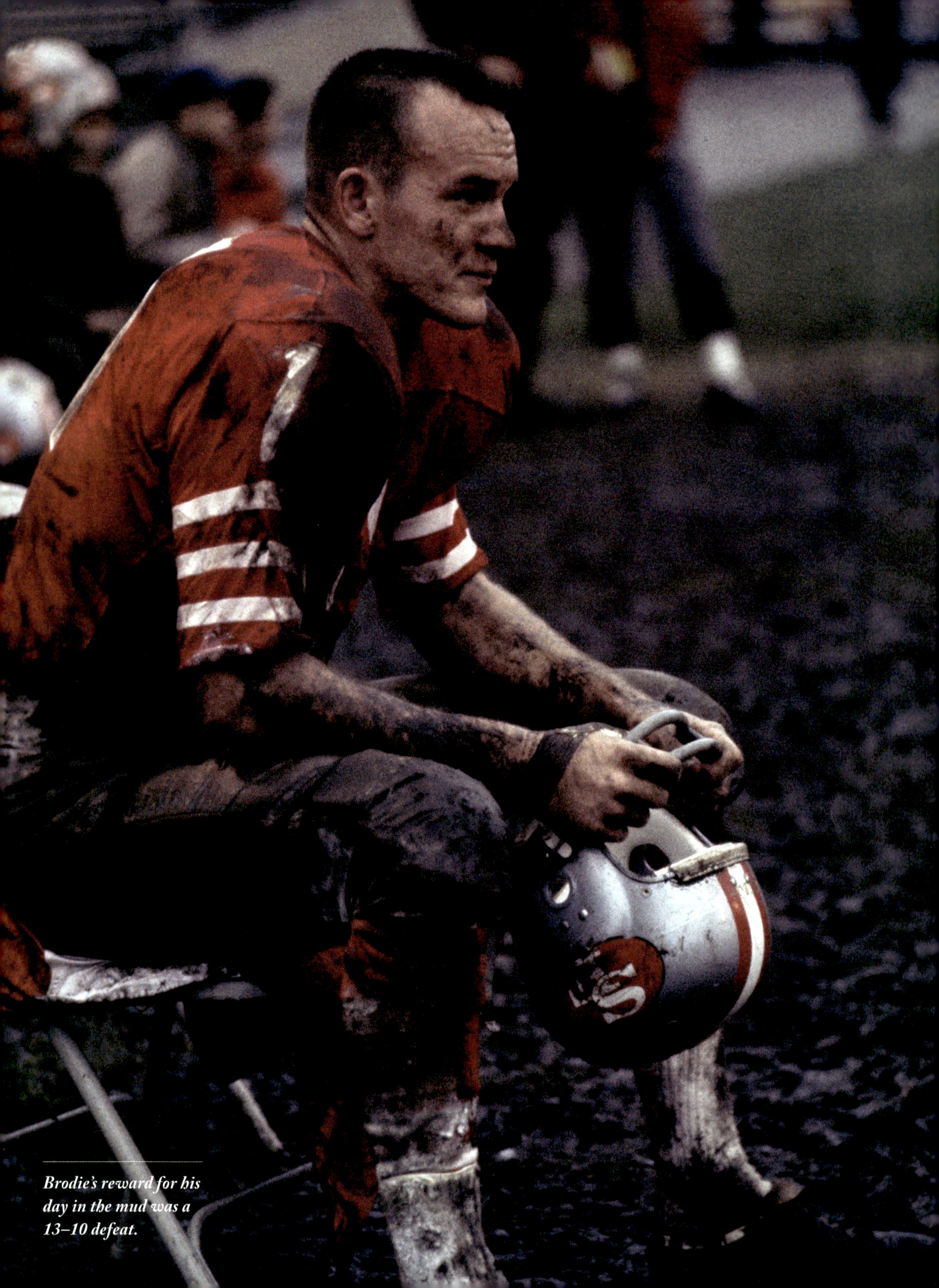

Brodie's reward for his day in the mud was a 13–10 defeat.

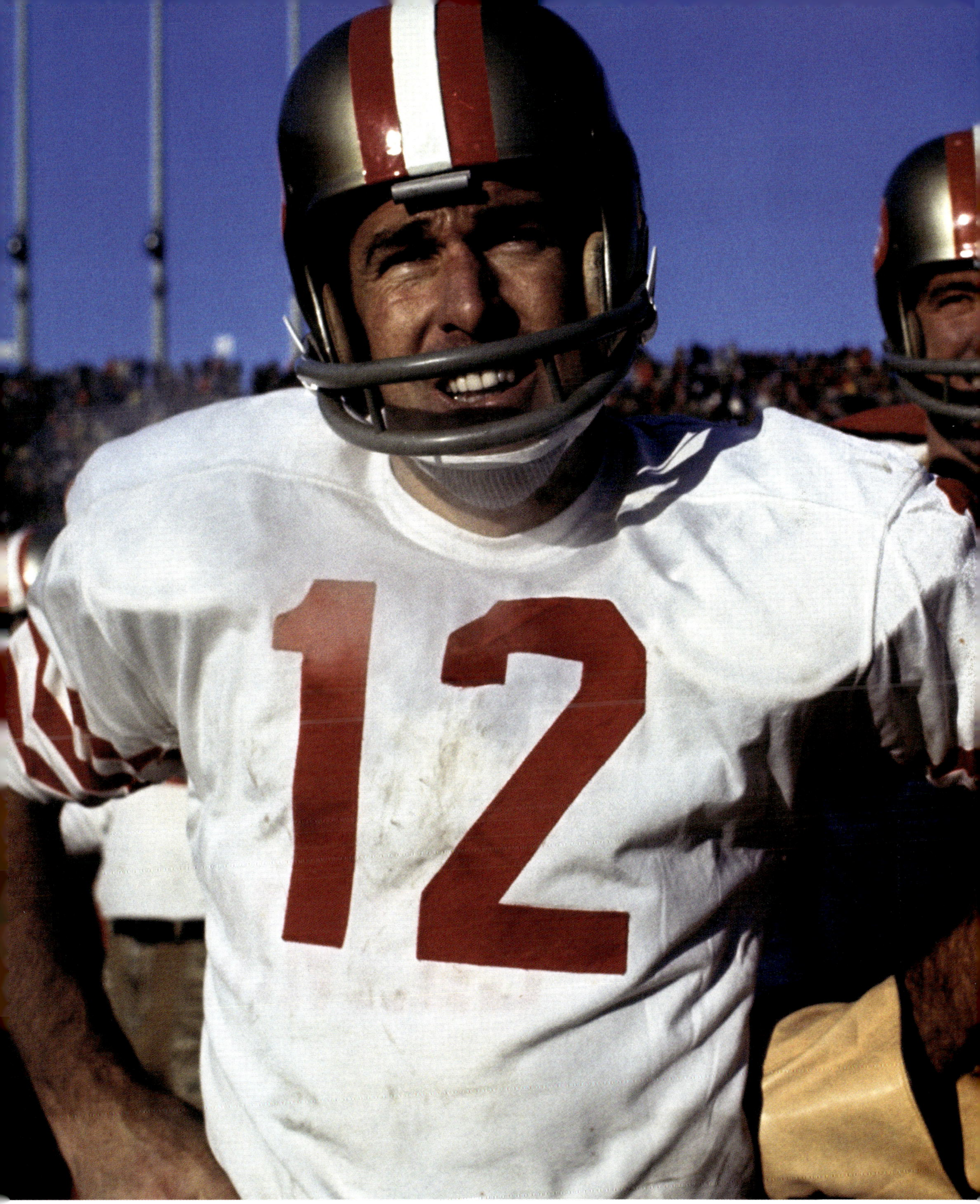

Brodie spent 17 seasons in San Francisco, amassing a 74–76–8 record as a starting quarterback.

Y.A. TITTLE

- **Quarterback 1951–1960**
- **NFL MVP 1963**
- **Three-time All-Pro**
- **Seven-time Pro Bowl selection**
- **Pro Football Hall of Fame 1971**

Yelberton Abraham Tittle Jr. set school passing records at LSU before starting his professional career with the Baltimore Colts in the AAFC. He joined the Niners in 1951 and by 1953 was part of the so-called Million Dollar Backfield, composed of four eventual Hall of Famers. Believing Tittle to be past his prime and looking to make John Brodie the starter, the team traded the 34-year-old quarterback to the New York Giants in 1961, where he led his new team to three NFC Championship Games and broke his own single-season record for touchdown passes in 1963.

Tittle was drafted by the Niners after the Colts folded following the 1950 NFL season.

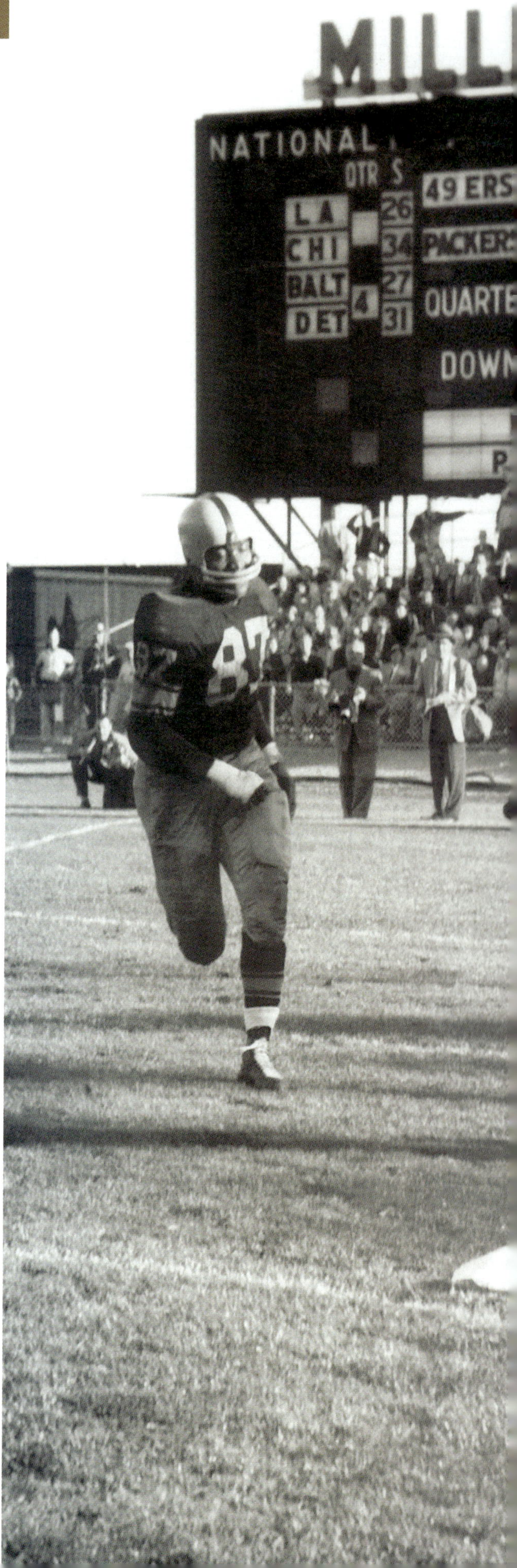

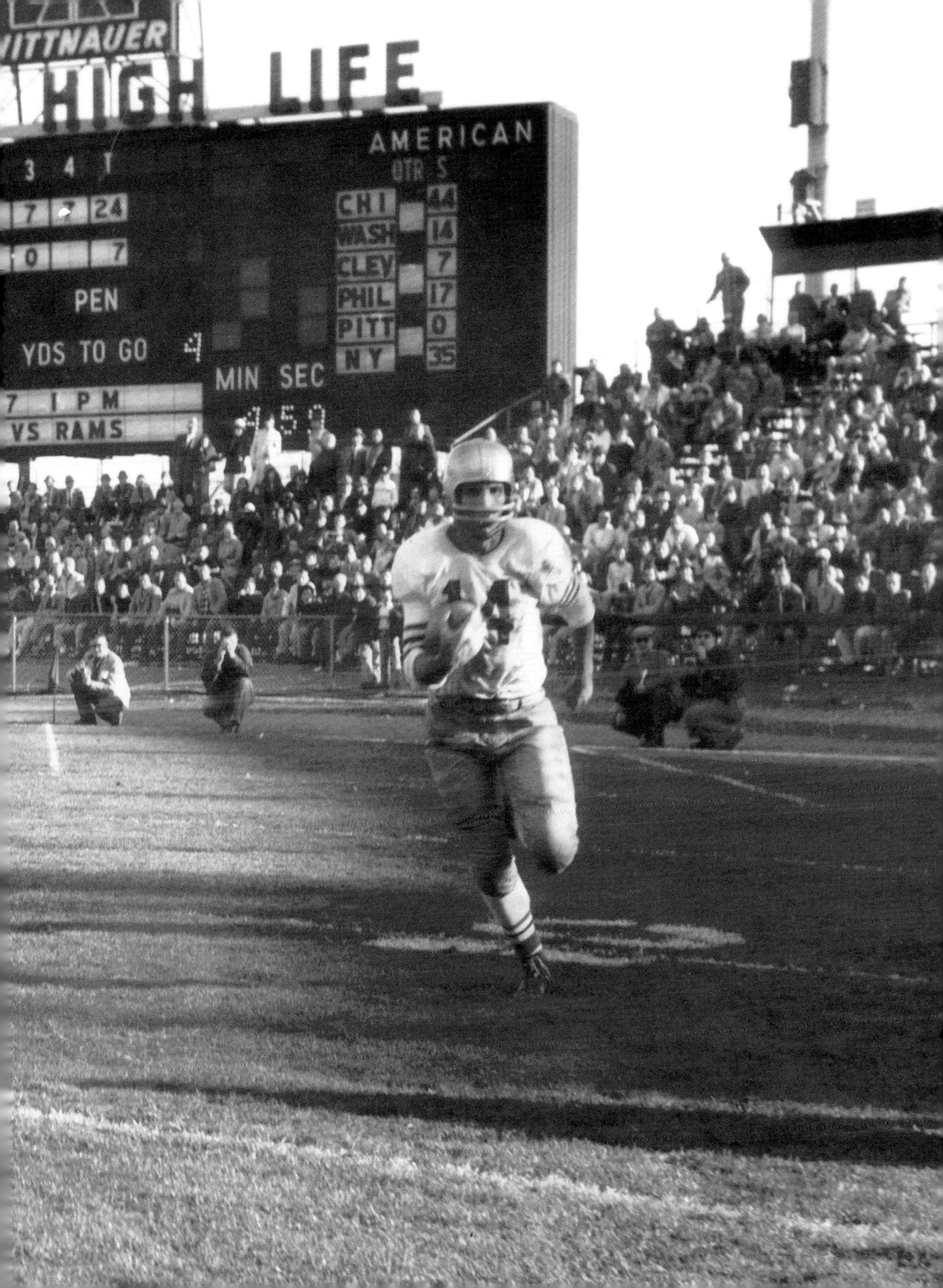
HIGH LIFE
AMERICAN
CHI 44
WASH 14
CLEV 7
PHIL 17
PITT 0
NY 35
PEN
YDS TO GO 4
MIN SEC
VS RAMS

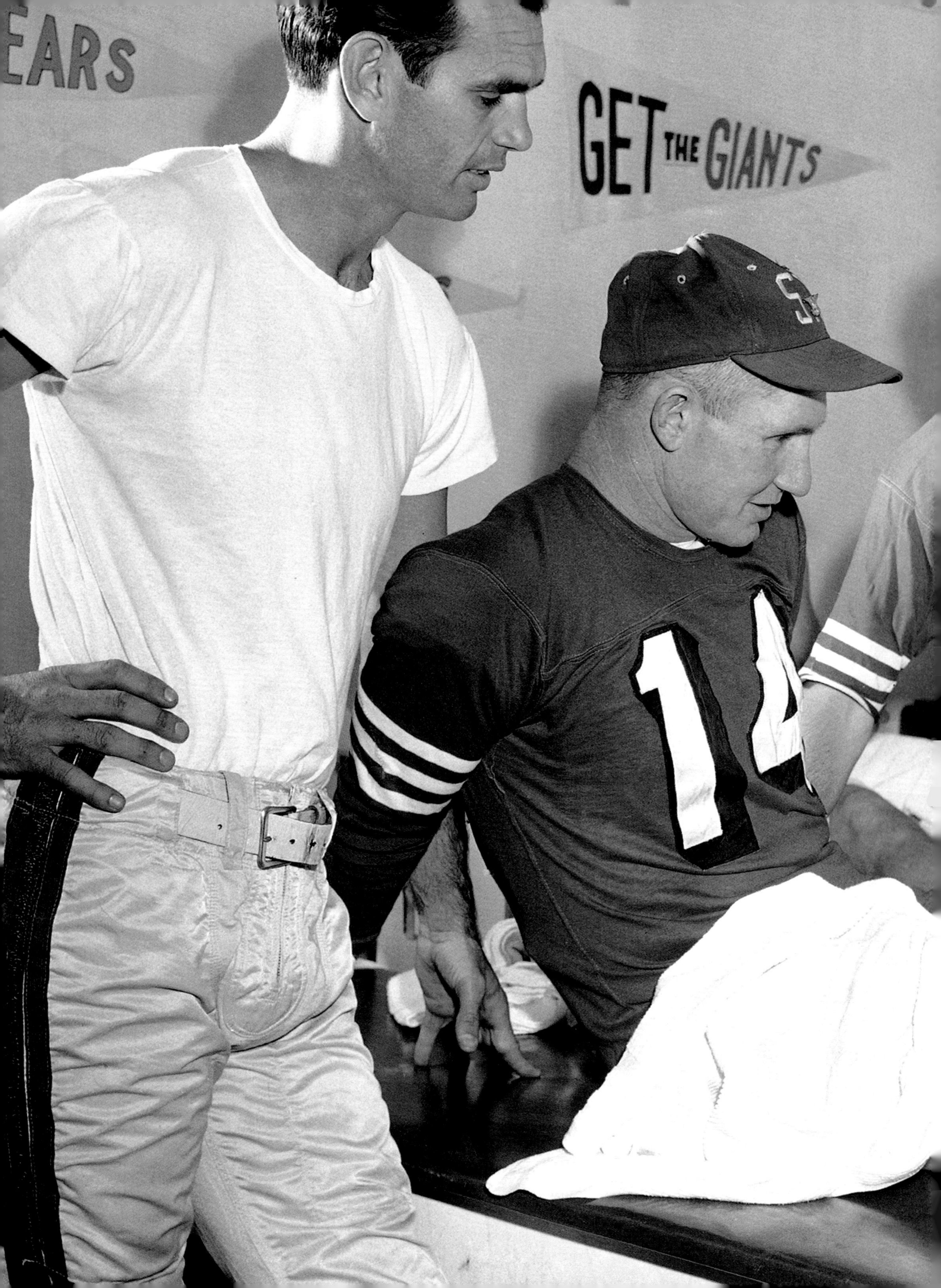
EARS
GET THE GIANTS

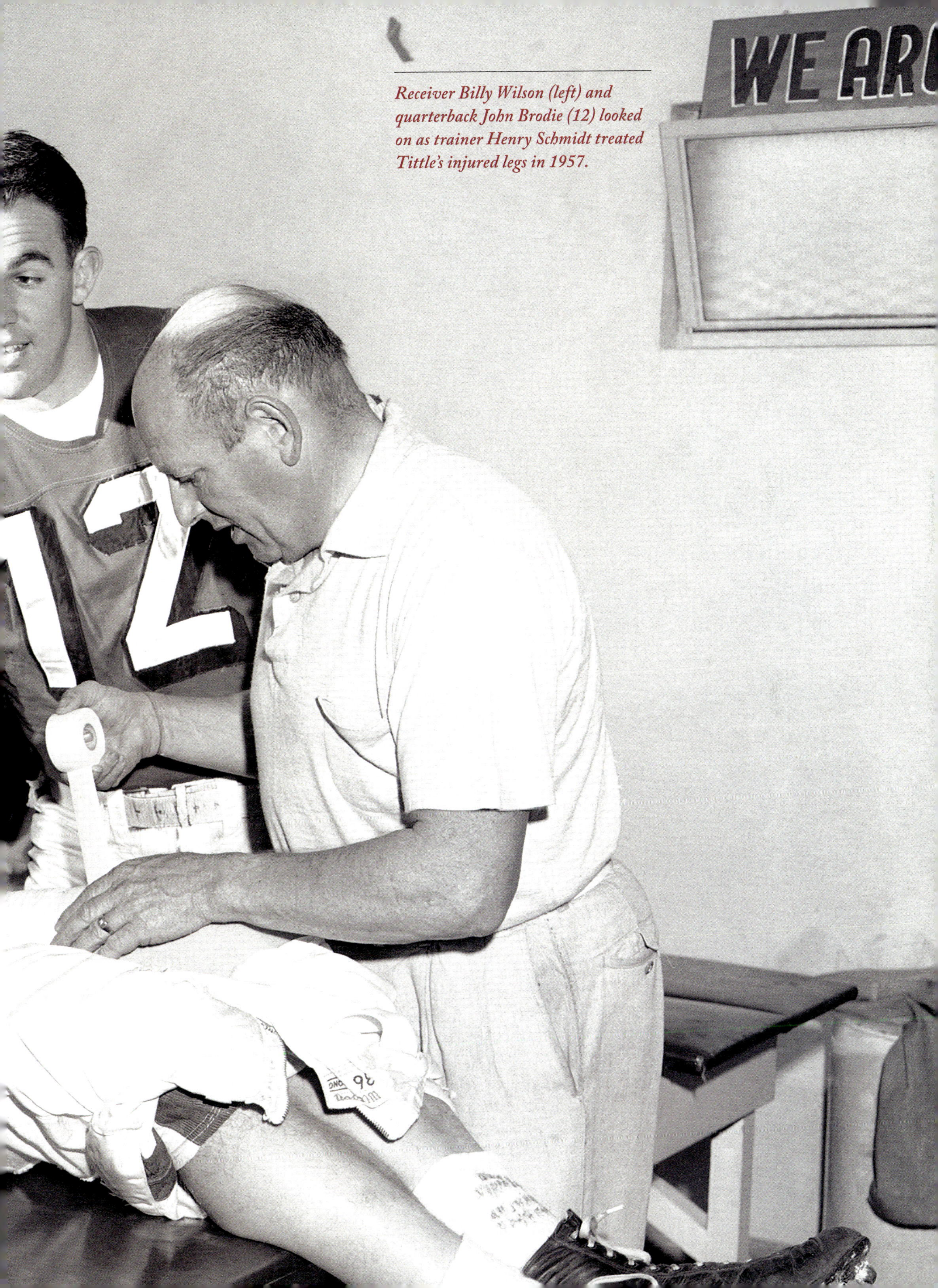

Receiver Billy Wilson (left) and quarterback John Brodie (12) looked on as trainer Henry Schmidt treated Tittle's injured legs in 1957.

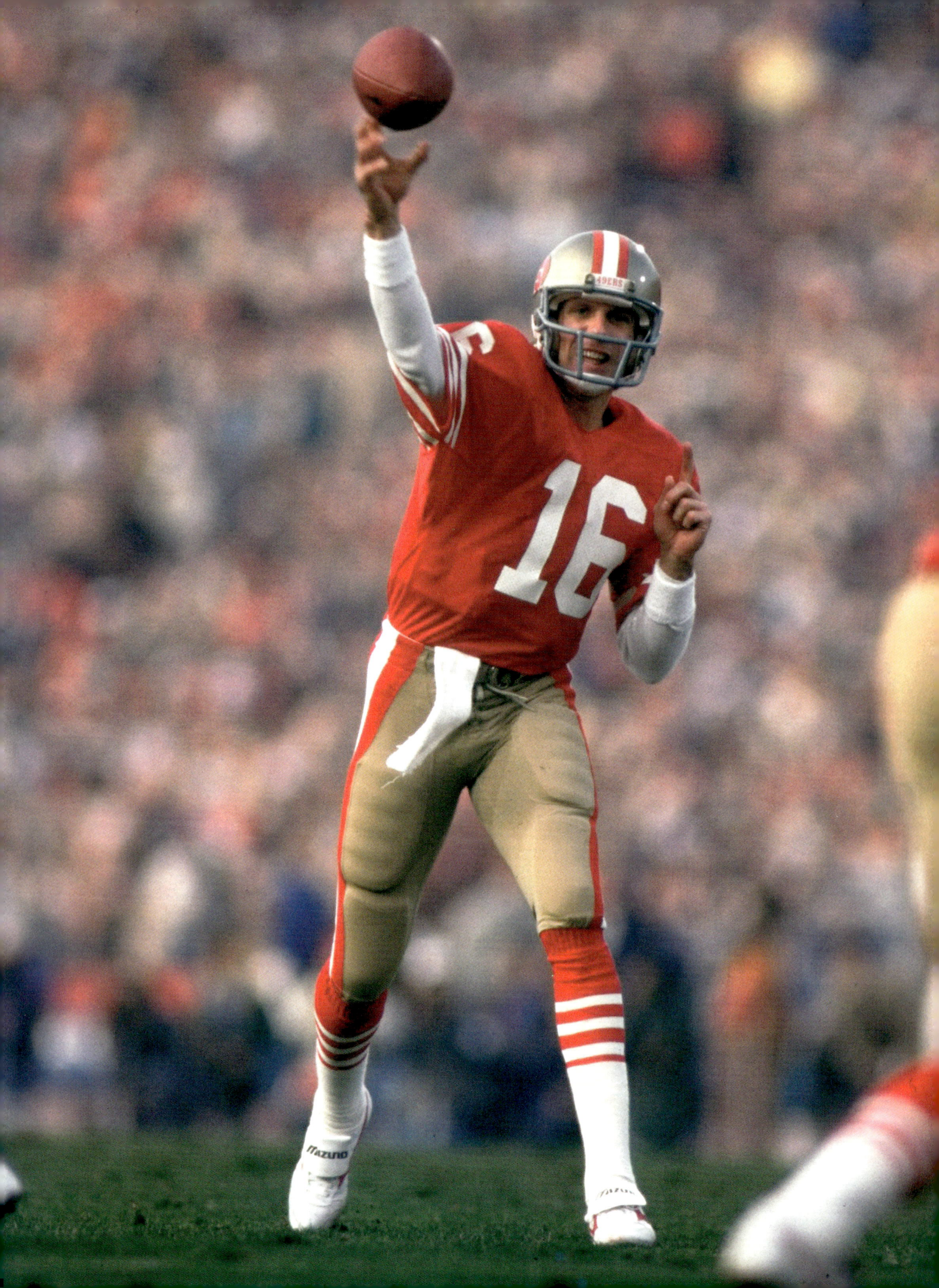
49ERS
16

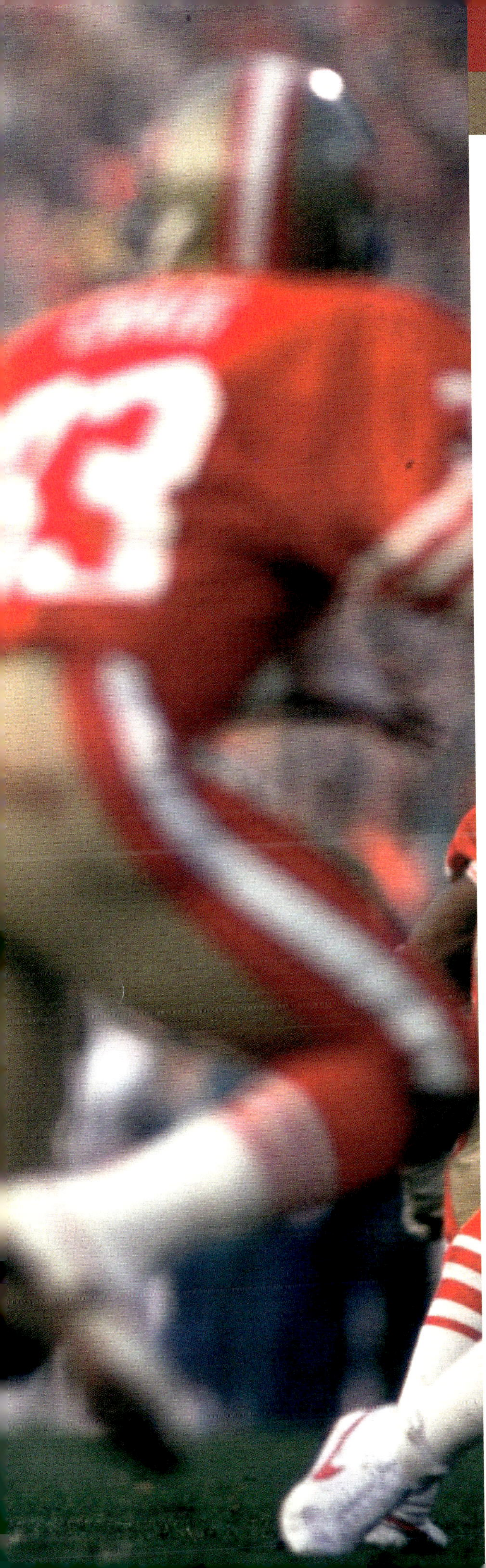

JOE MONTANA

- » Quarterback 1979–1992
- » Four-time Super Bowl champion
- » Three-time Super Bowl MVP
- » Two-time NFL MVP
- » Five-time All-Pro
- » Eight-time Pro Bowl selection
- » Pro Football Hall of Fame 2000
- » San Francisco jersey #16 retired 1997

Joe Montana's case as the greatest quarterback in NFL history is simple: a 4–0 record in the Super Bowl, three Super Bowl MVPs, and the championship game's all-time highest passer rating (127.8), which included 11 touchdown passes and zero interceptions. Over 14 seasons in San Francisco, "Joe Cool" teamed with head coach Bill Walsh to revolutionize the NFL with their West Coast offensive system.

Montana's regular-season record as San Francisco's quarterback was 100–39.

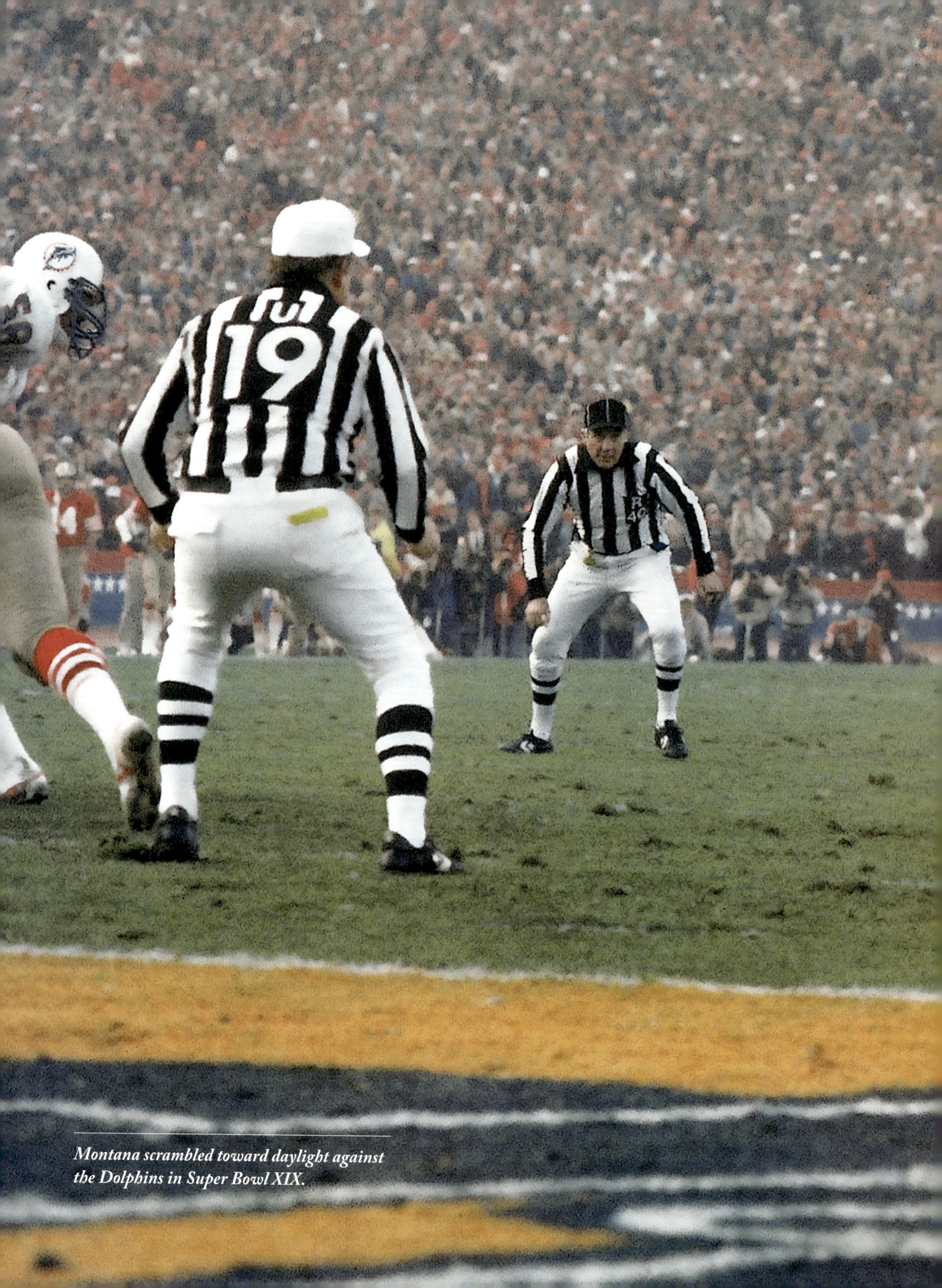

Montana scrambled toward daylight against the Dolphins in Super Bowl XIX.

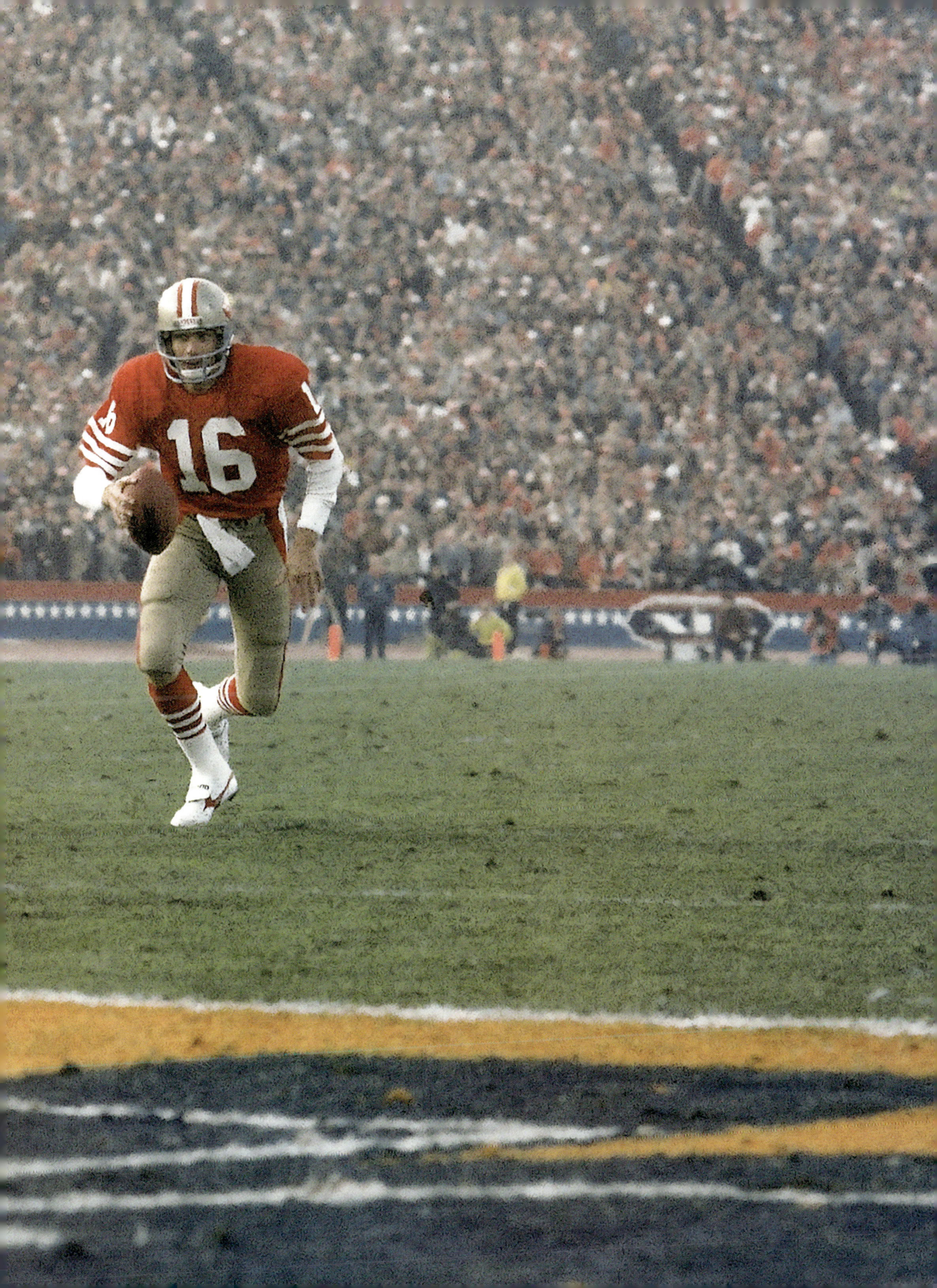

JOE PERRY

- Running Back 1948–1960, 1963
- Two-time All-Pro
- Three-time Pro Bowl selection
- Pro Football Hall of Fame 1969
- San Francisco jersey #34 retired 1971

The first Black player in Niners history, Joe "The Jet" Perry was the first NFL runner to record back-to-back 1,000-yard rushing seasons. He spent 14 years in San Francisco, and his 8,689 career rushing yards remain second on the franchise's all-time list, behind only Frank Gore; he remains the franchise leader in rushing touchdowns, with 68. When Perry retired in 1963, he was the league's all-time leading rusher, and was the first member of the Million Dollar Backfield to be inducted into the Pro Football Hall of Fame, in 1969.

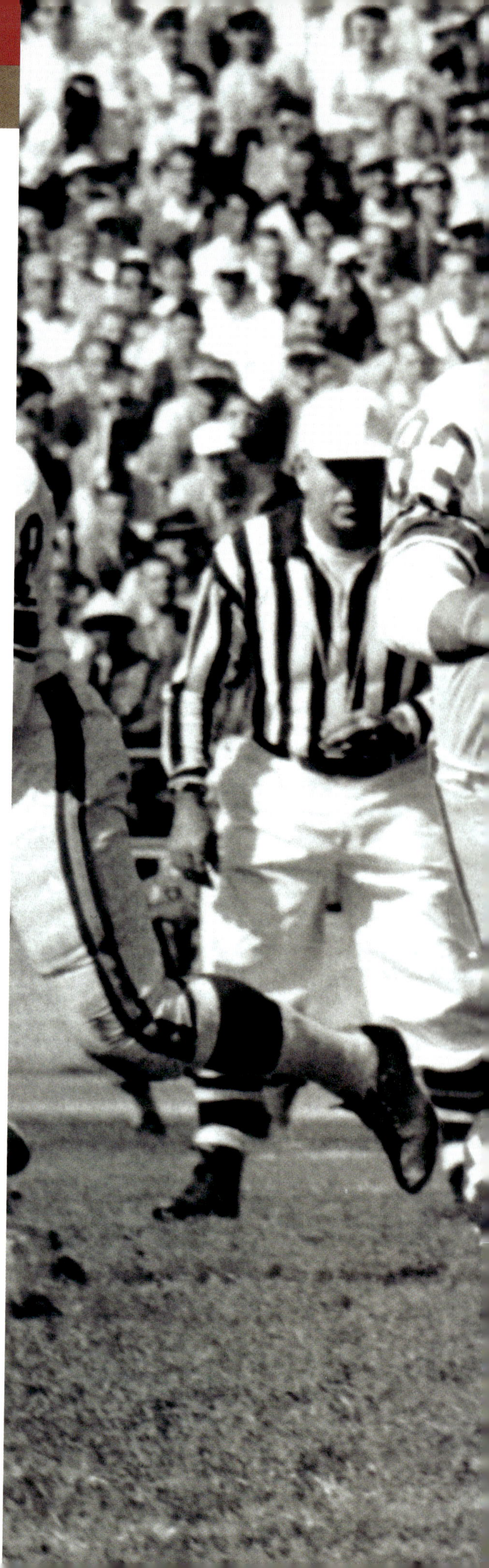

No Niners running back scored more touchdowns than Joe Perry.

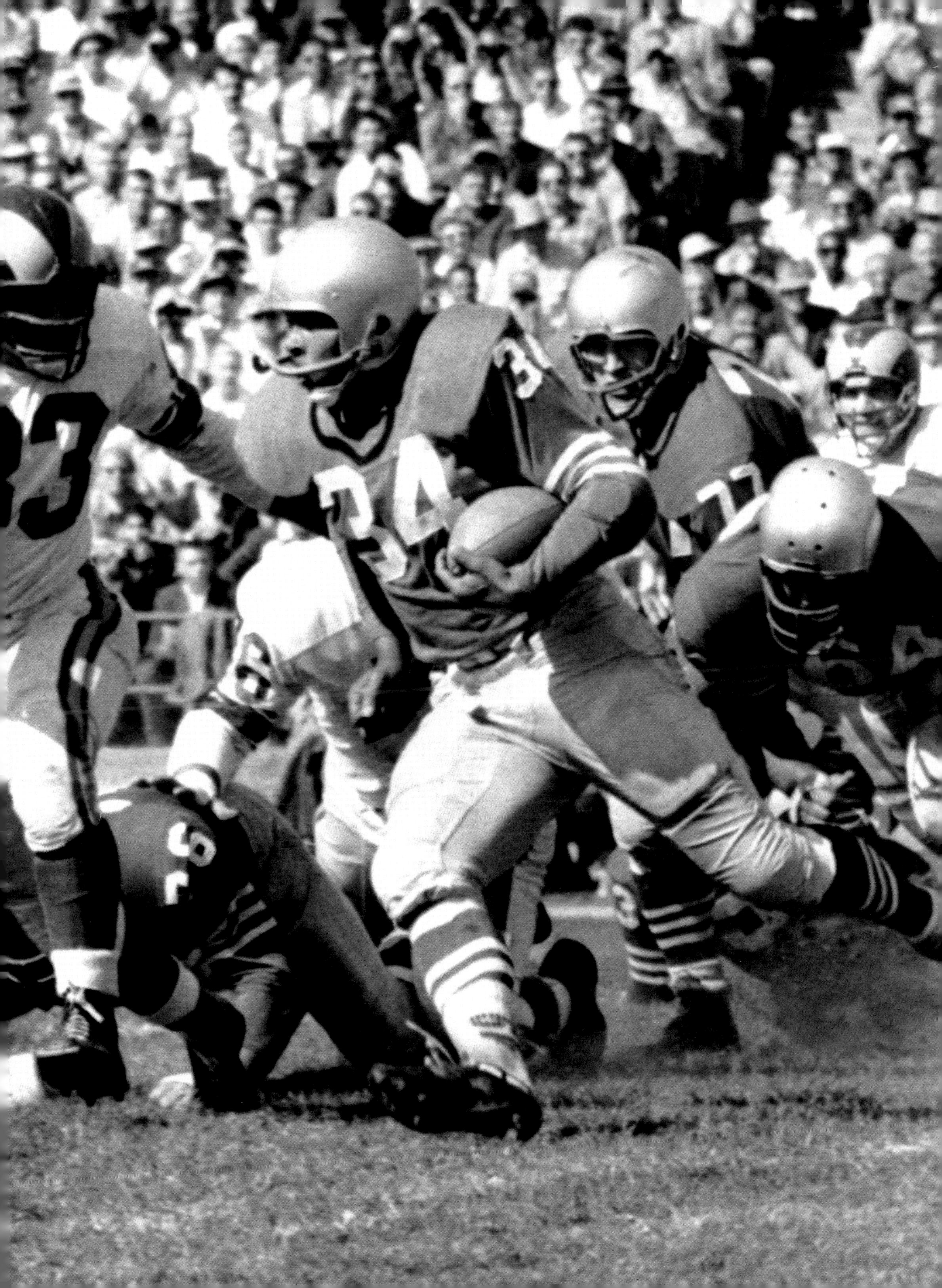

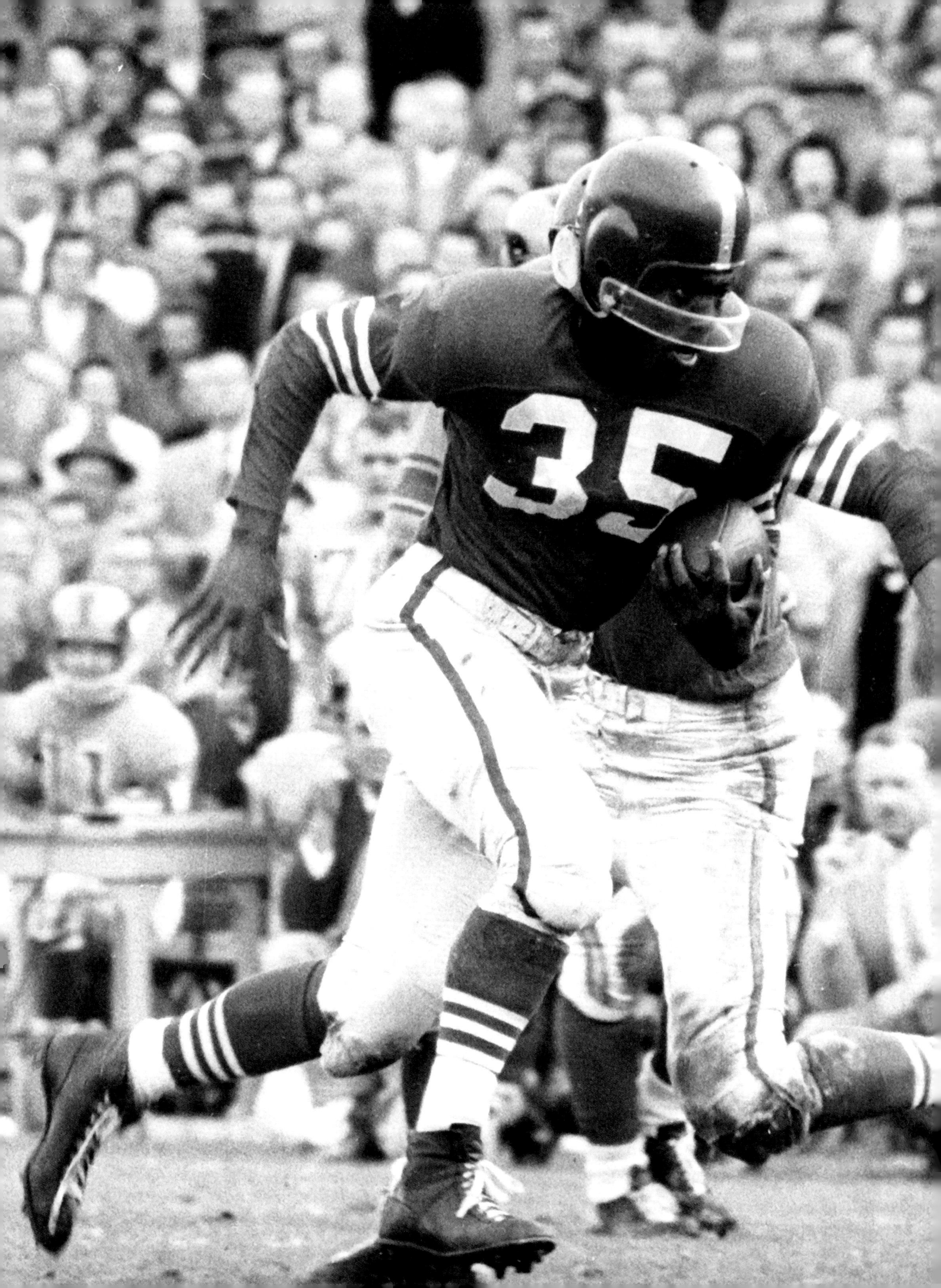

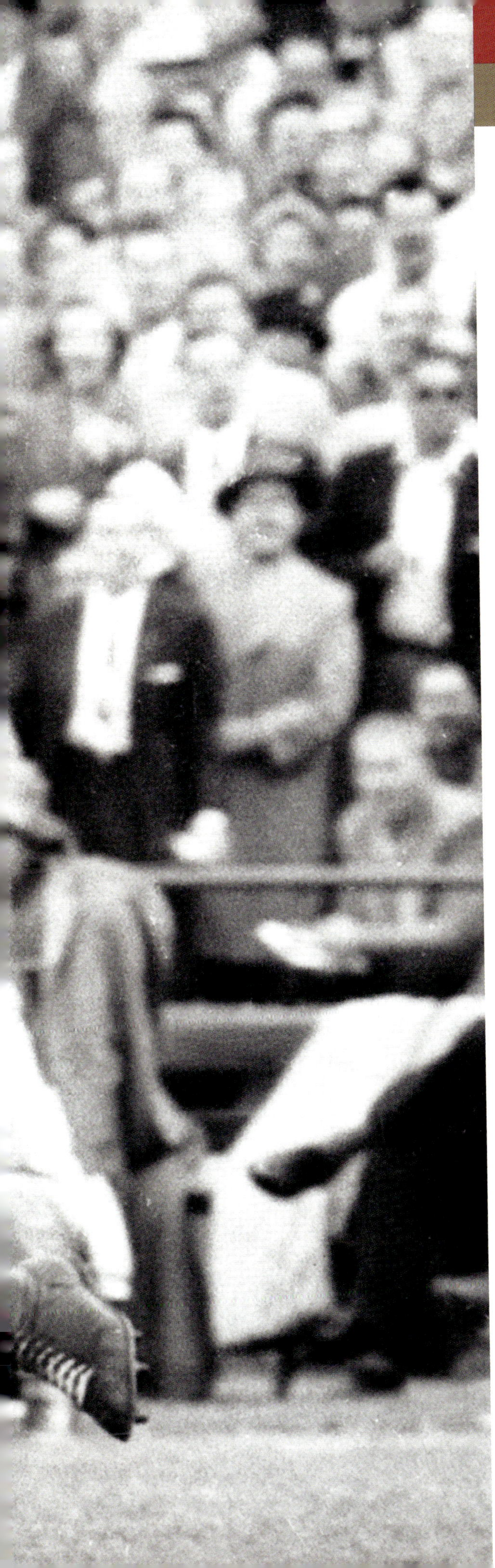

JOHN HENRY JOHNSON

- » Running Back 1954–1956
- » NFL champion 1957
- » Two-time All-Pro
- » Four-time Pro Bowl selection
- » Pro Football Hall of Fame 1987

Perhaps the most rugged member of the Million Dollar Backfield, John Henry Johnson made his impact felt during his three seasons with the Niners. Born in Louisiana, Johnson played high school football at Pittsburg in Contra County before going to college at St. Mary's and later Arizona State. In 1954, he finished second in the NFL in rushing behind Joe Perry, for whom he served as a primary blocker. "Football was like a combat zone," Johnson said. "I was always told that you carry the impact to the opponent. If you wait for it, the impact will be on you."

Johnson rushed for 12 touchdowns during his three seasons in San Francisco.

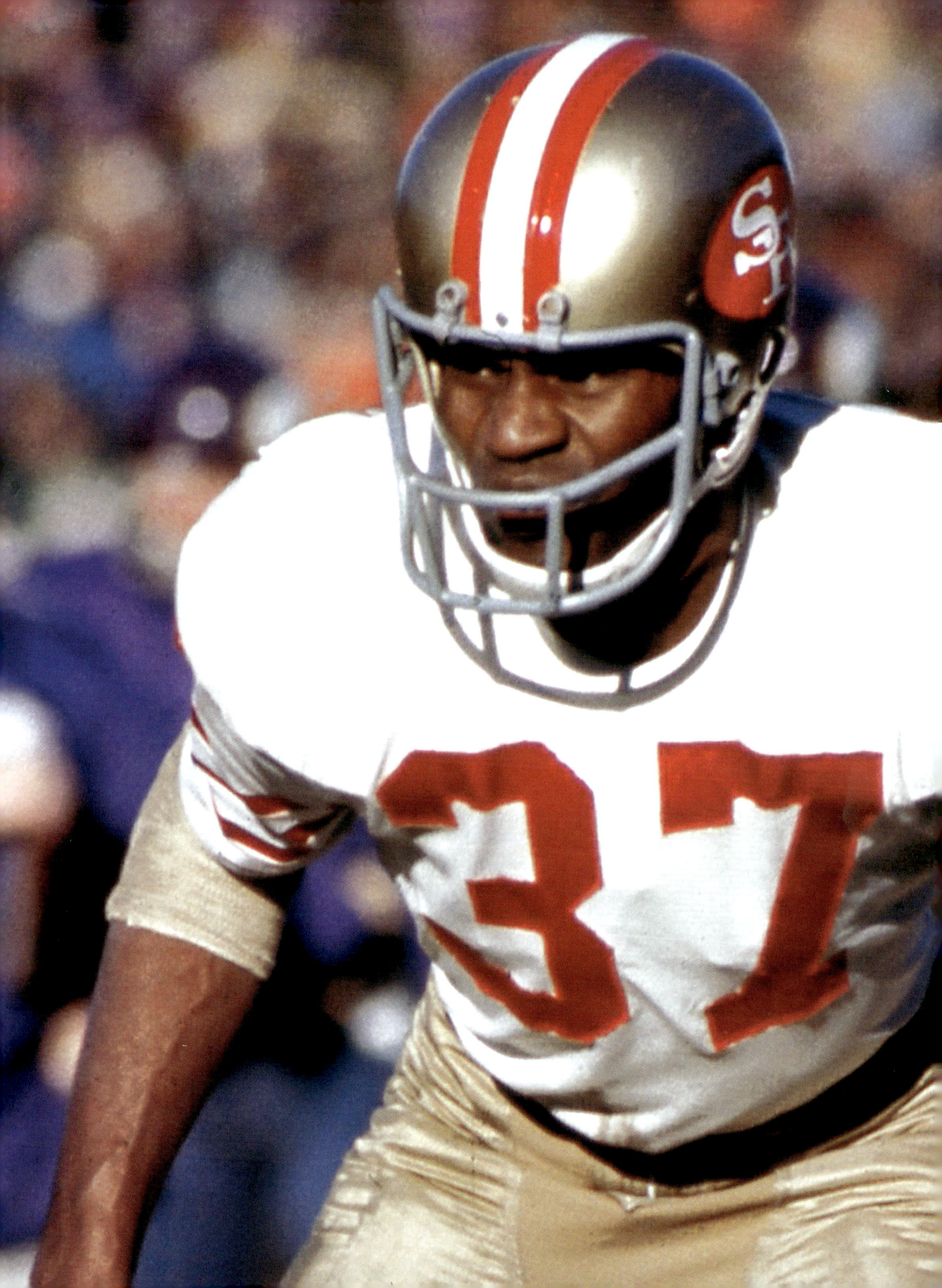

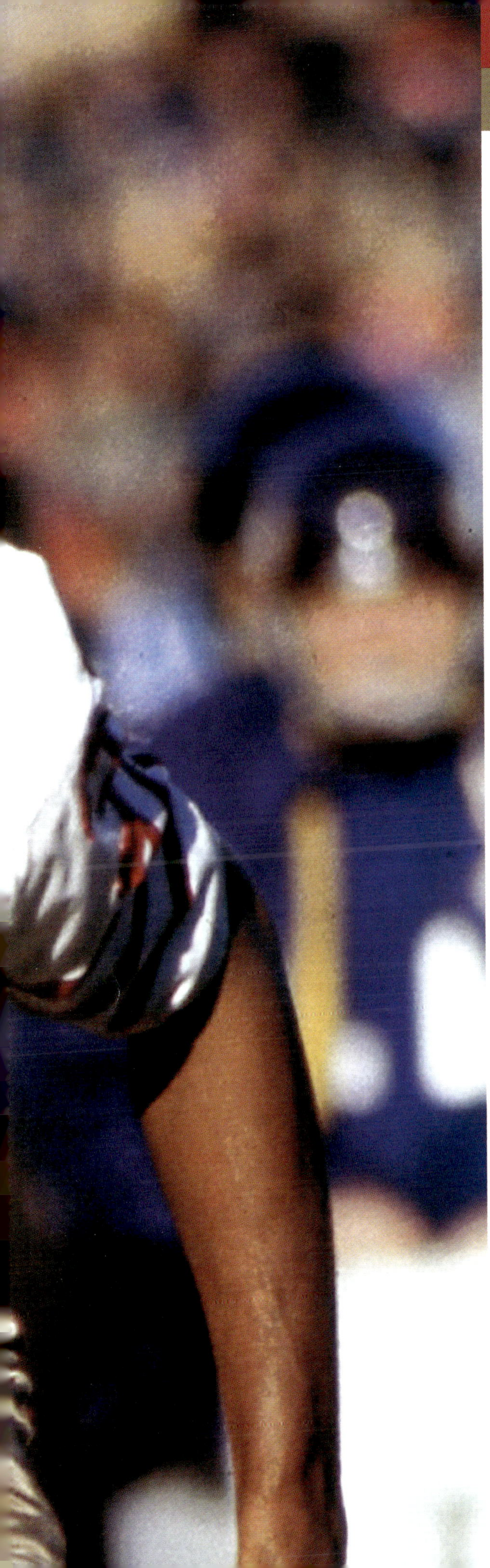

JIMMY JOHNSON

- » **Cornerback/Wide Receiver 1961–1976**
- » **Eight-time All-Pro**
- » **Five-time Pro Bowl selection**
- » **Pro Football Hall of Fame 1994**
- » **San Francisco jersey #37 retired 1977**

A track star at UCLA, Jimmy Johnson had no plans to become a professional football player. But once he began receiving invitations to collegiate all-star games and was seen by NFL scouts, his future suddenly became clear. Johnson used his speed on both sides of the ball during his 16-year NFL career. He played both wide receiver and cornerback during his first two seasons in San Francisco before staying on defense for good beginning in 1963. He appeared in 213 games with the Niners, second in franchise history behind Jerry Rice (238).

Johnson caught 40 passes on offense and intercepted 47 on defense as a Niner.

HUGH McELHENNY

- Running Back 1952–1960
- Five-time All-Pro
- Six-time Pro Bowl selection
- Pro Football Hall of Fame 1970
- San Francisco jersey #39 retired 1971

Born and raised in Los Angeles, Hugh McElhenny made a great first impression after being drafted by the Niners in 1952. On his very first play as a professional, he ran for 40 yards and a touchdown. Later in his rookie season, he recorded the longest run from scrimmage (89 yards), the longest punt return (94 yards) and the highest rushing average (7.0). Another member of the Million Dollar Backfield, McElhenny spent nine seasons in San Francisco before being selected by the Minnesota Vikings in the 1961 expansion draft.

McElhenny was reportedly nicknamed "The King" by Niners teammate Frankie Albert.

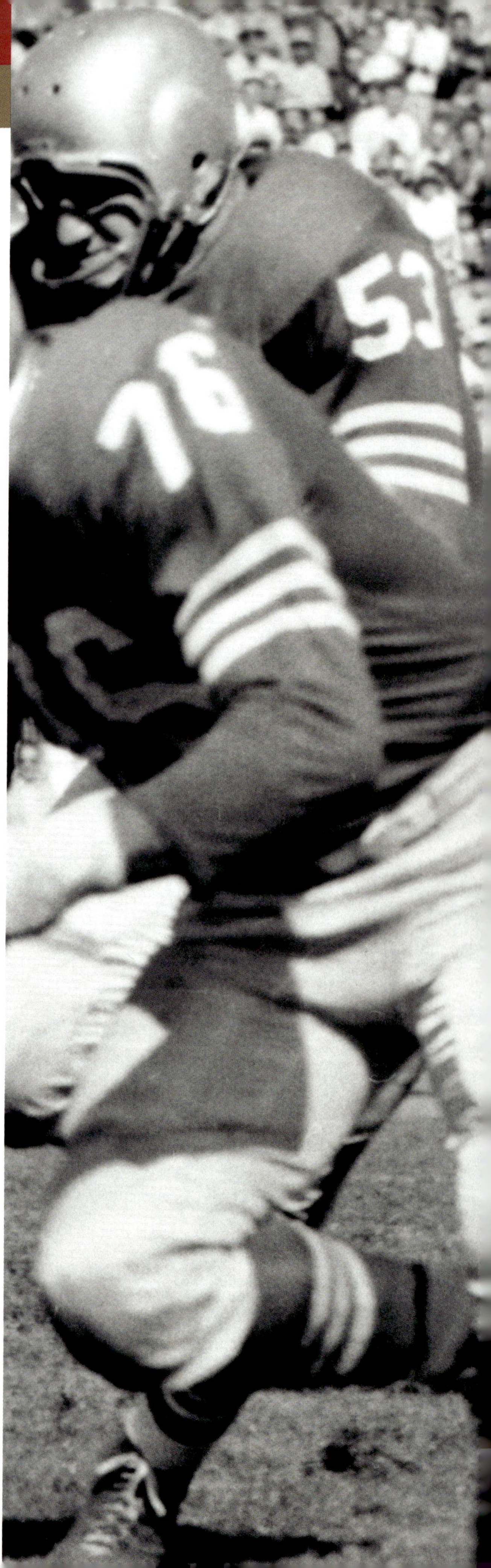

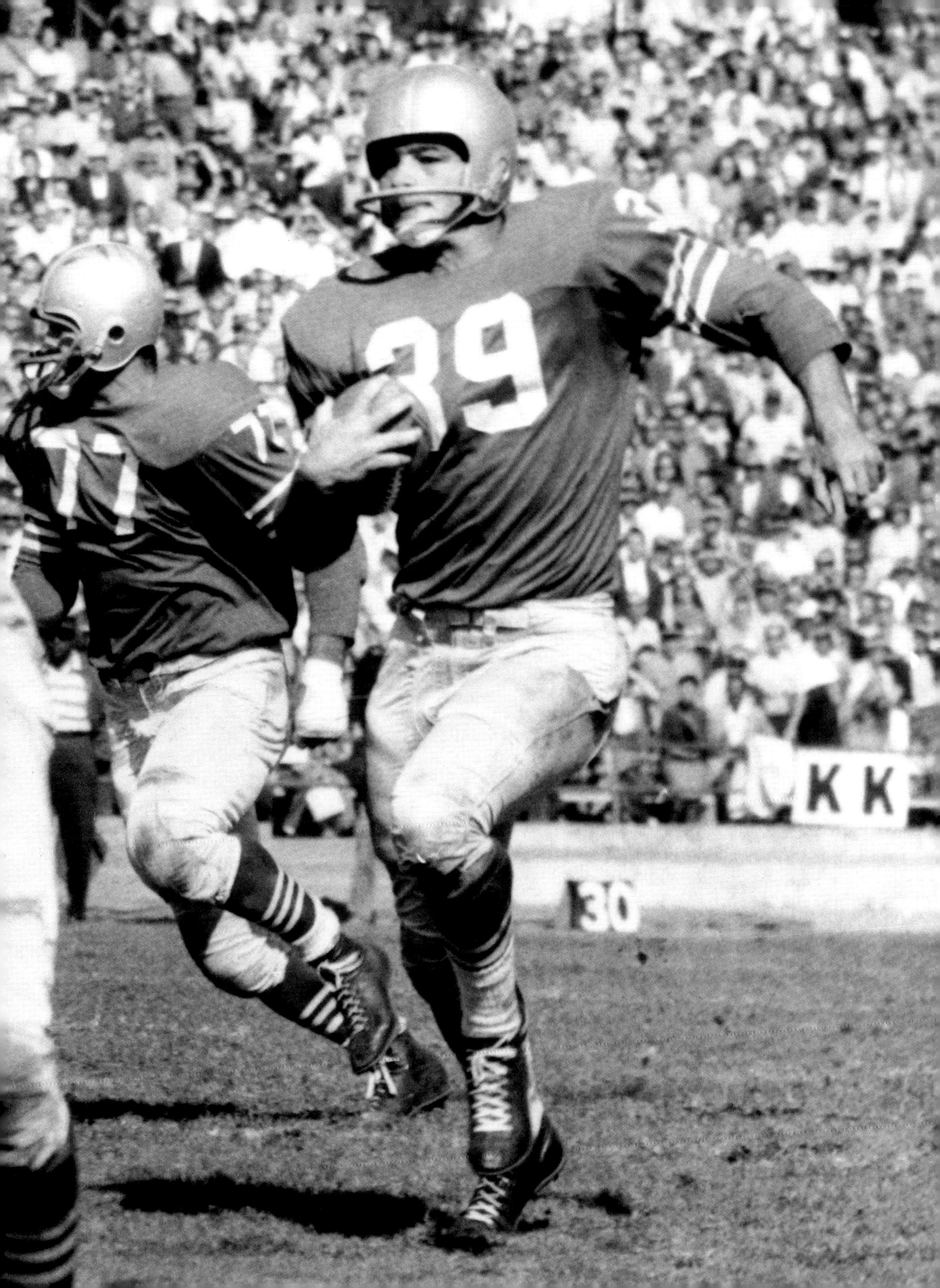
39
KK
30

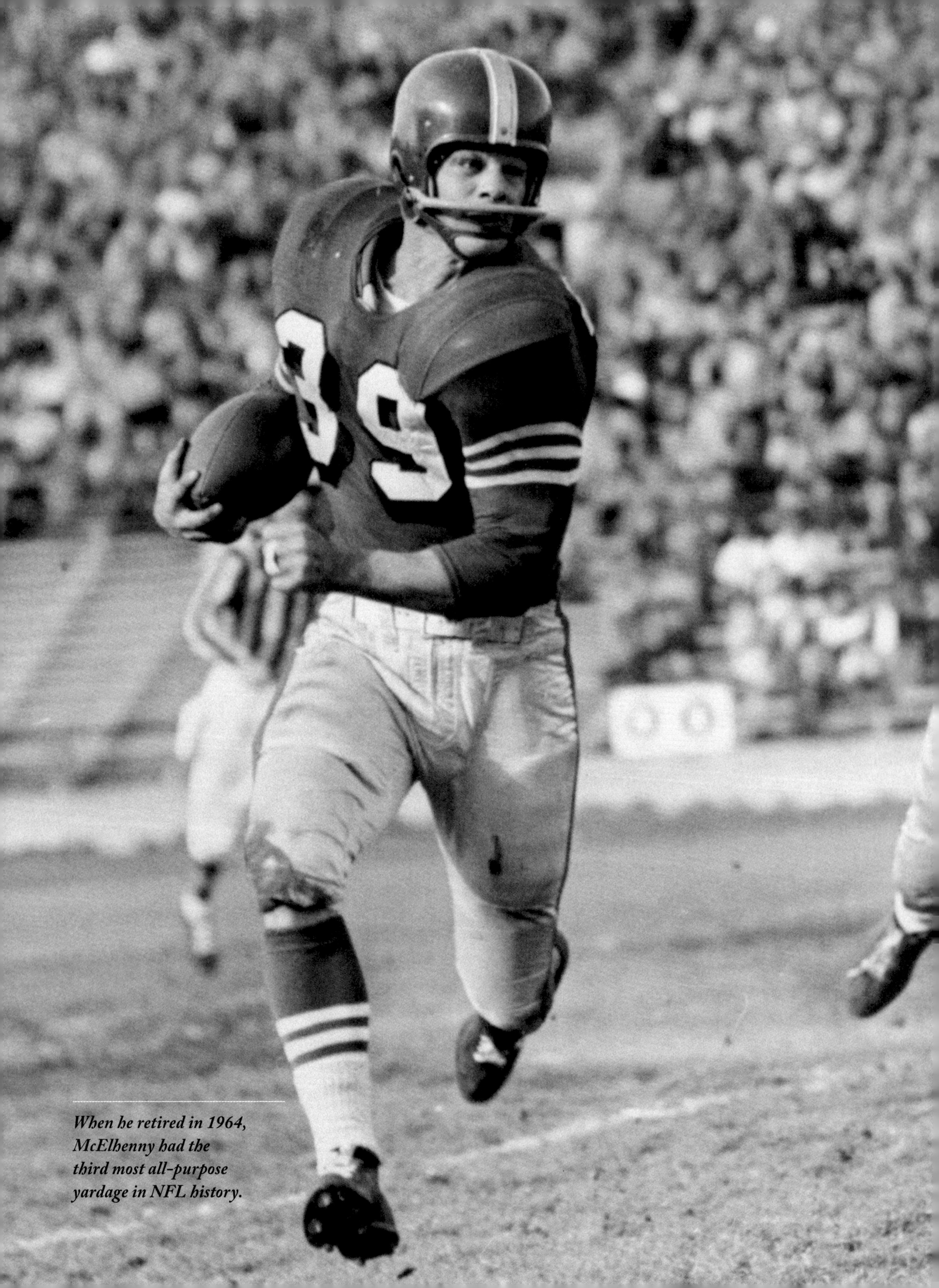

When he retired in 1964, McElhenny had the third most all-purpose yardage in NFL history.

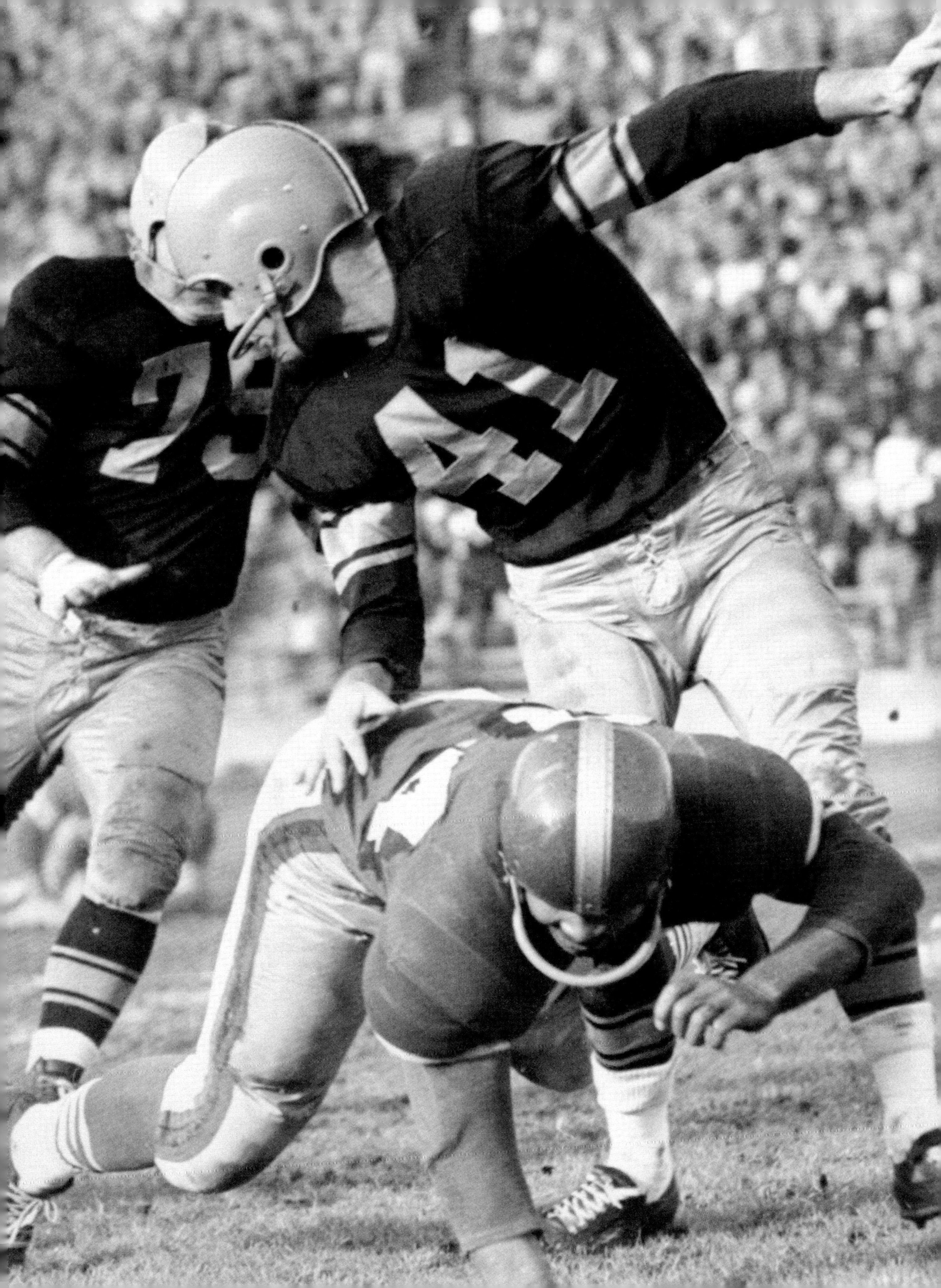

RONNIE LOTT

- » Safety/Cornerback 1981–1990
- » Four-time Super Bowl champion
- » Eight-time All-Pro
- » 10-time Pro Bowl selection
- » Pro Football Hall of Fame 2000
- » San Francisco jersey #42 retired 2003

One of the most fearsome defenders in NFL history, Ronnie Lott is one of only five players to appear on all four of the Niners' Super Bowl champions during the 1980s. His greatness was evident from the beginning: in his rookie season, he picked off seven passes, returning three of them for touchdowns, and helped lead San Francisco to victory in Super Bowl XVI. As a sign of his consistent excellence, he was named to the NFL's All-Decade Team for the 1980s and the 1990s.

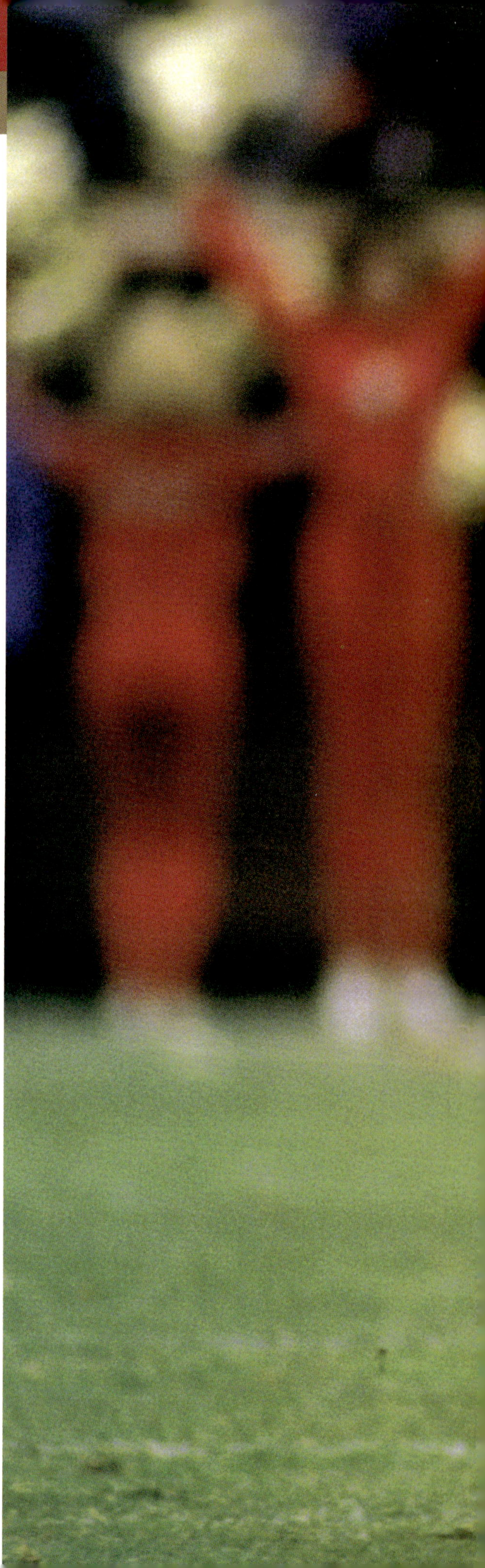

Lott picked off 51 passes during his 10 seasons in San Francisco.

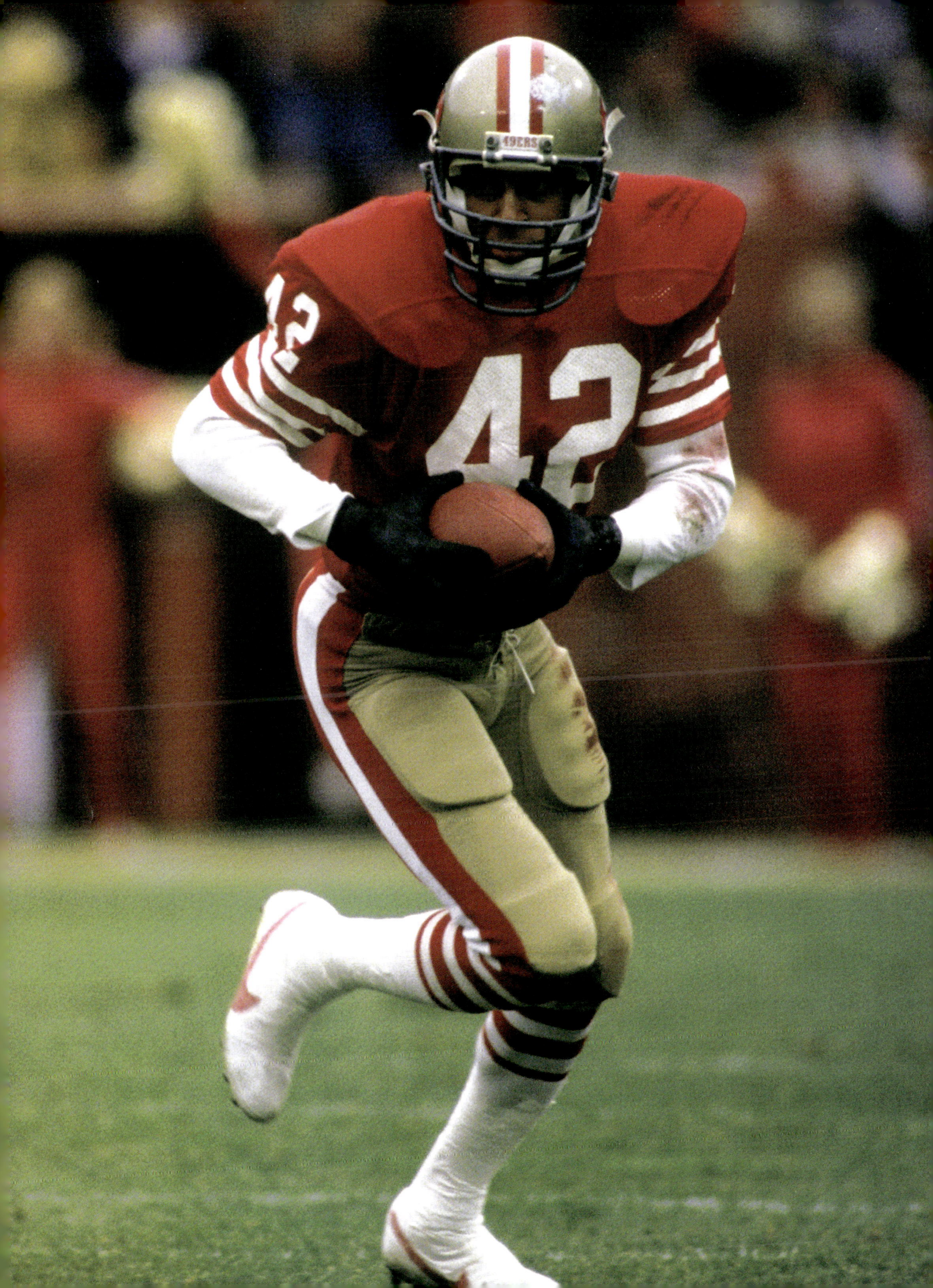
49ERS
42

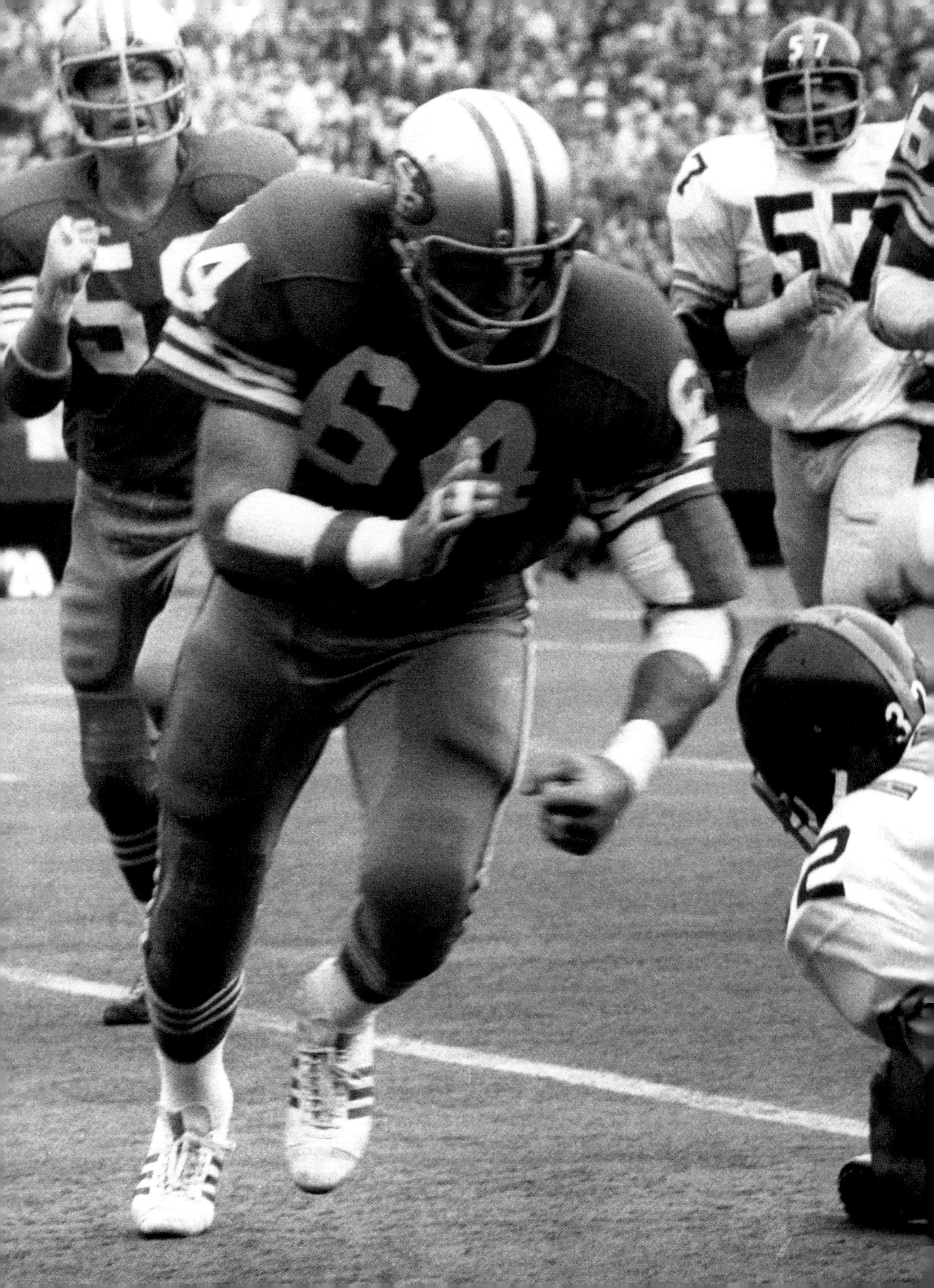
64
57

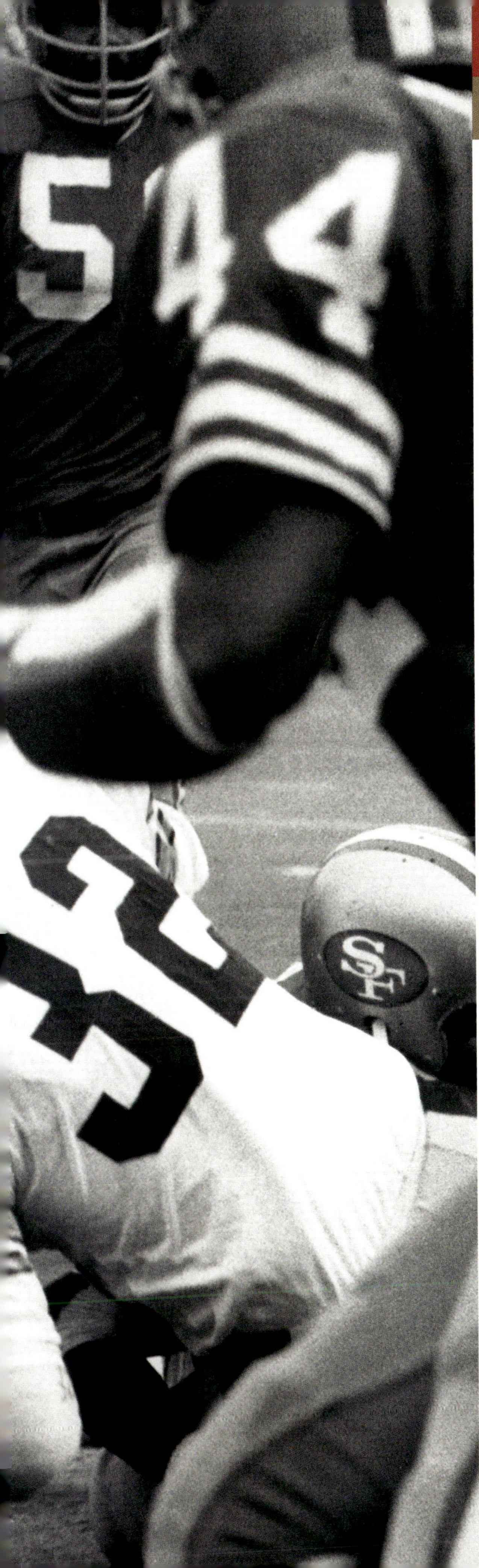

DAVE WILCOX

- **Linebacker 1964–1974**
- **Four-time All-Pro**
- **Seven-time Pro Bowl selection**
- **Pro Football Hall of Fame 2000**

Nicknamed "The Intimidator," Dave Wilcox spent his entire 11-season career with the Niners, missing only one game during that span due to injury. A lineman in college at the University of Oregon, he was converted to linebacker in San Francisco and proceeded to make difficult the lives of tight ends and would-be blockers. In 1973, Wilcox recorded 104 solo tackles, four forced fumbles and 13 tackles for loss. Each season, the team would grade the players on a numerical scale. An average score for a linebacker was 750; in 1973, Wilcox measured 1,306.

Wilcox was an iron man during his years as a 49er.

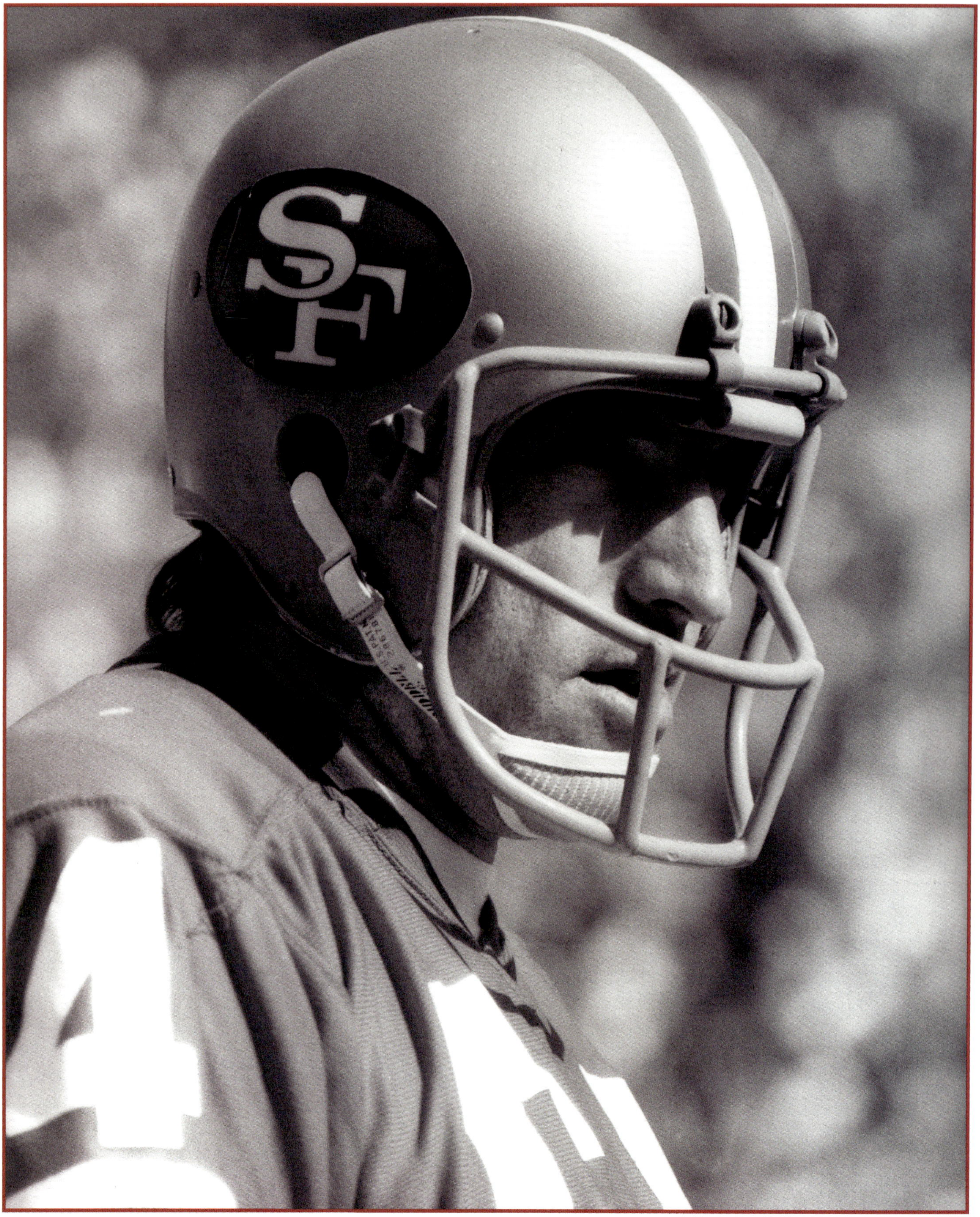

Wilcox once said, "I just hate to be blocked." (Right) He and teammate Cedric Hardman (86) certainly were not on this tackle of Atlanta's Pat Sullivan.

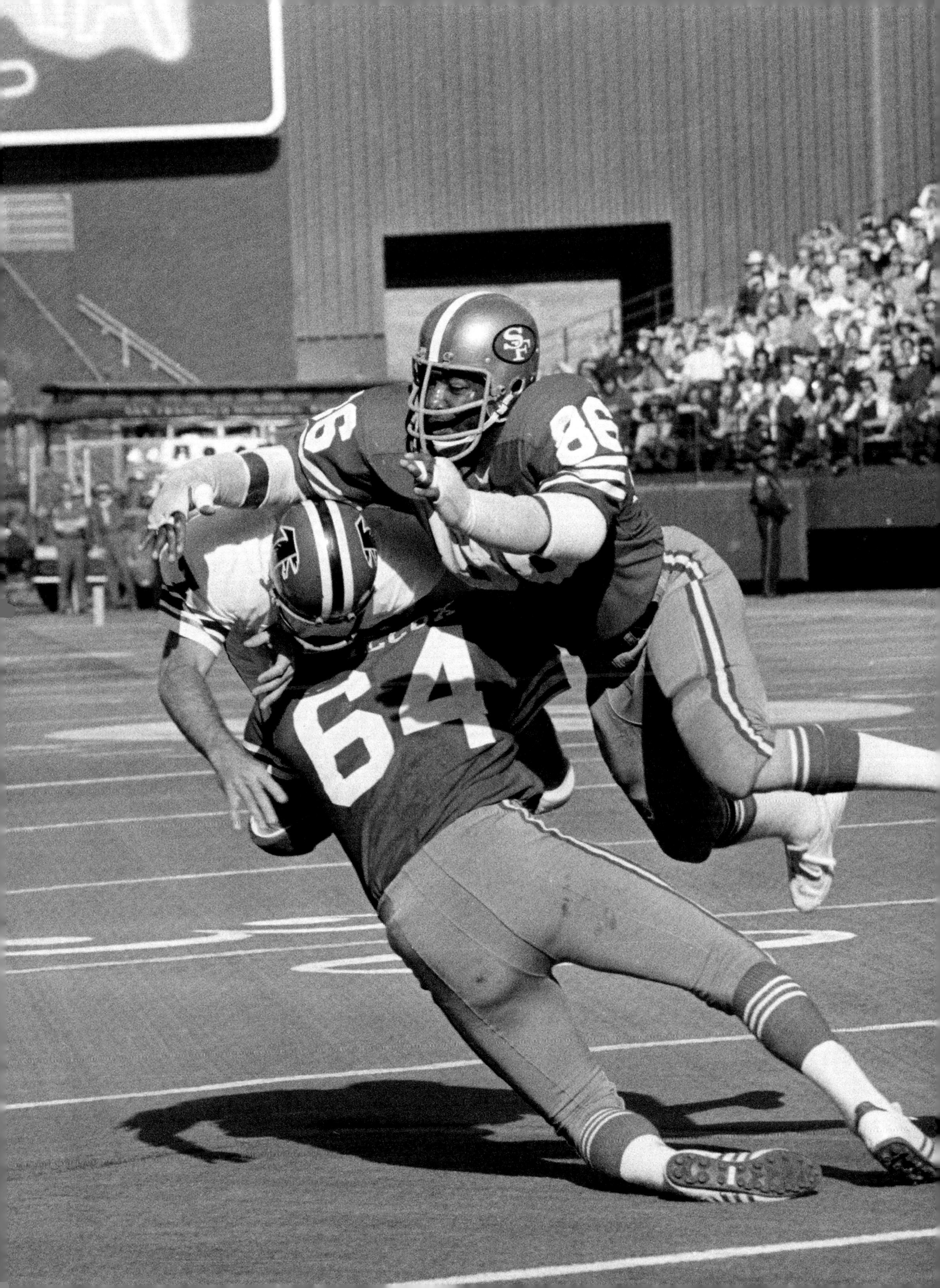

CHARLIE KRUEGER

- **Defensive Lineman 1959–1973**
- **Two-time All-Pro**
- **Two-time Pro Bowl selection**
- **San Francisco jersey #70 retired 1974**

Charlie Krueger spent all 15 seasons of his NFL career with the 49ers, fourth-most in team history, and played more games at defensive tackle than anyone other than Bryant Young. Born and raised in Texas, Krueger played for Bear Bryant at Texas A&M before joining the Niners in 1958. In a 1973 Sports Illustrated story, it was noted the Dallas Cowboys ran 90 percent of their plays away from Krueger in the 1971 NFC title game. "No one is able to gain running at Charlie Krueger," Cowboys coach Tom Landry said, "and we were not about to experiment."

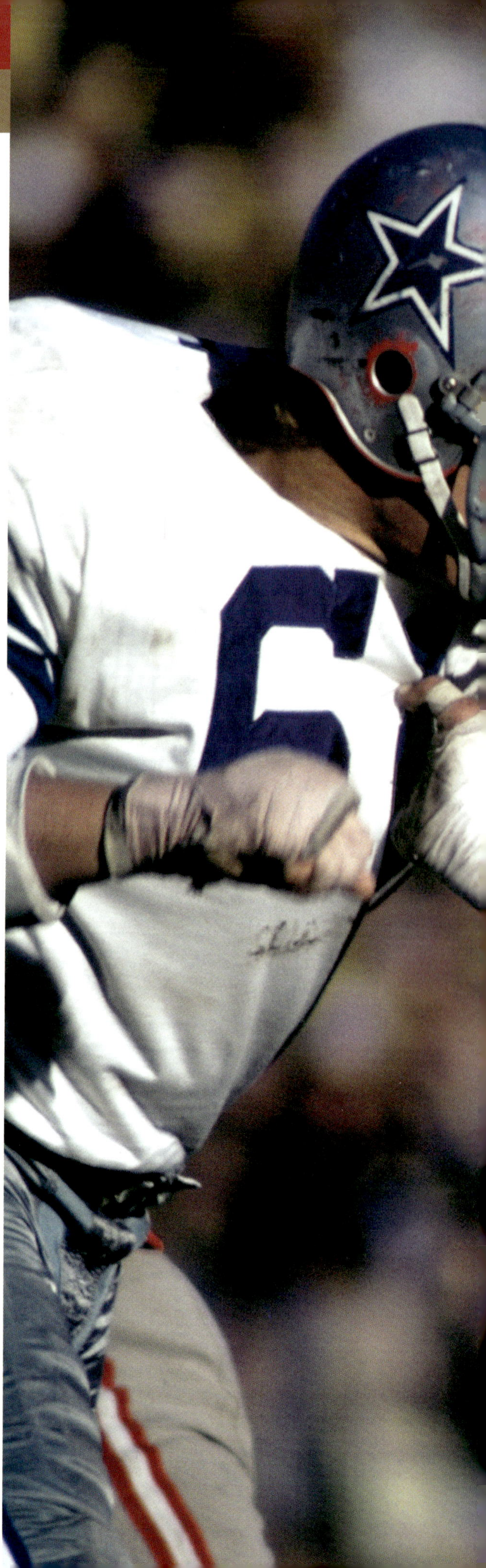

Krueger and the Niners battled the Cowboys and Blaine Nye in the NFC Championship Game in 1971.

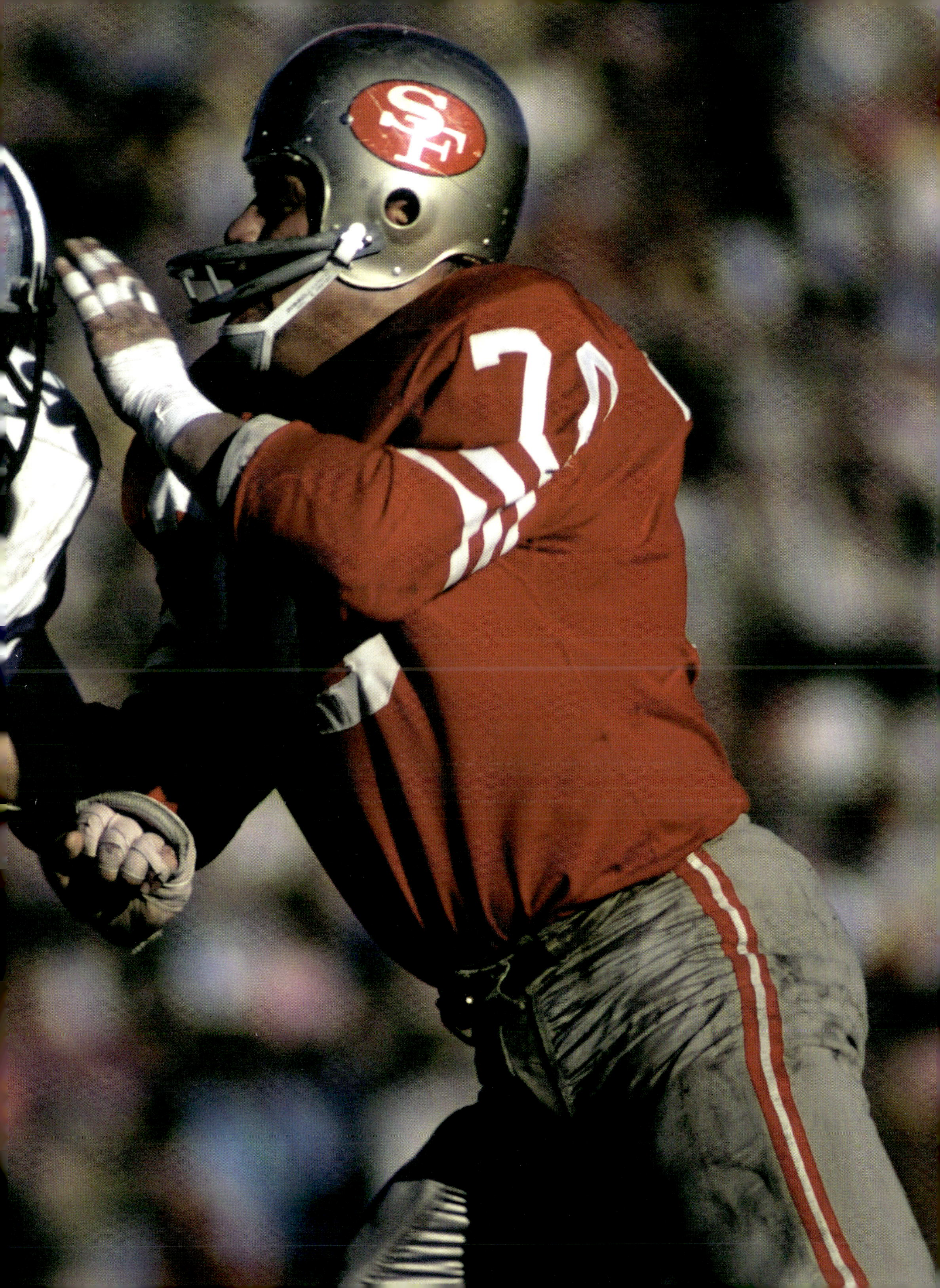
SF

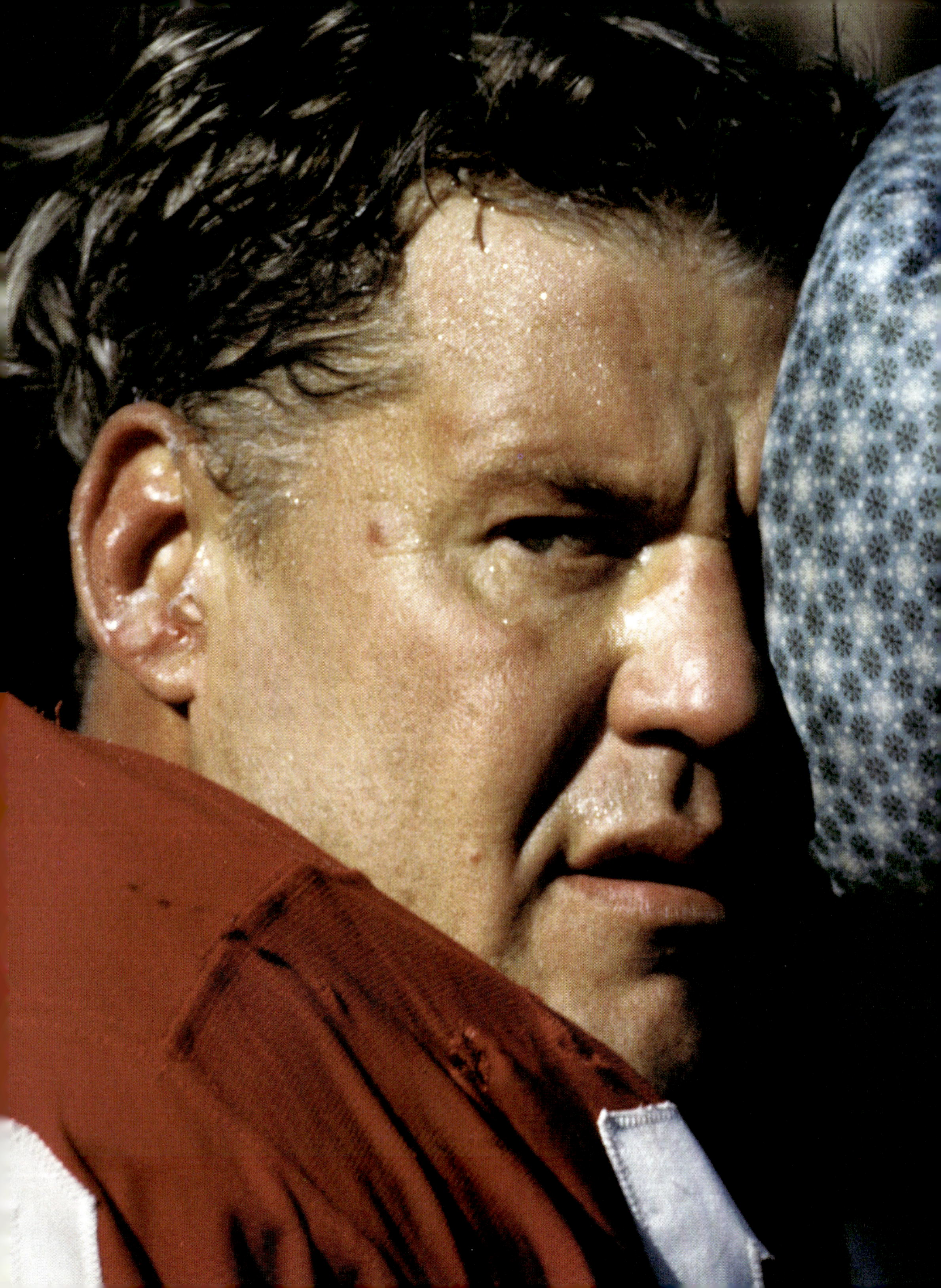

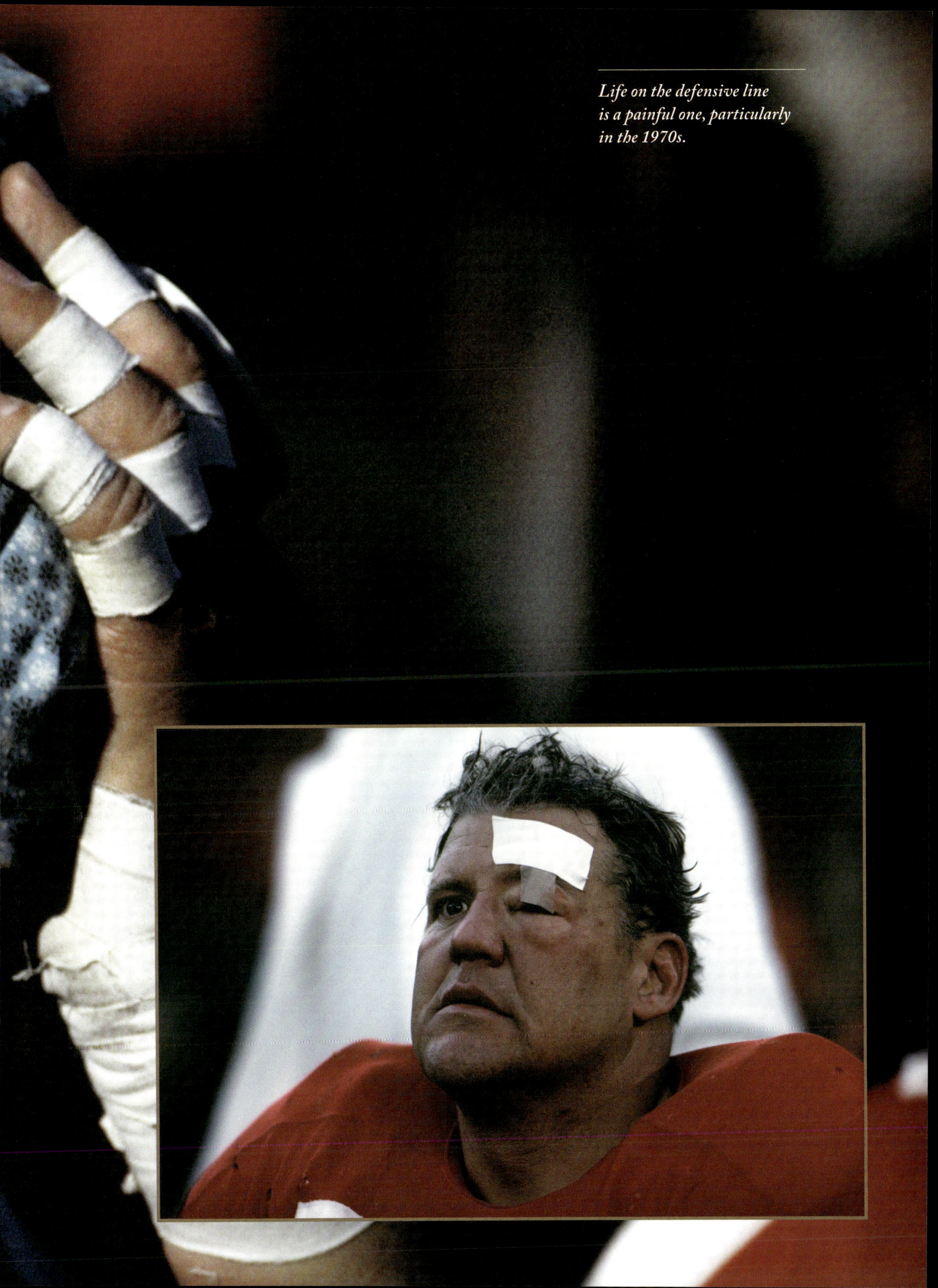

Life on the defensive line is a painful one, particularly in the 1970s.

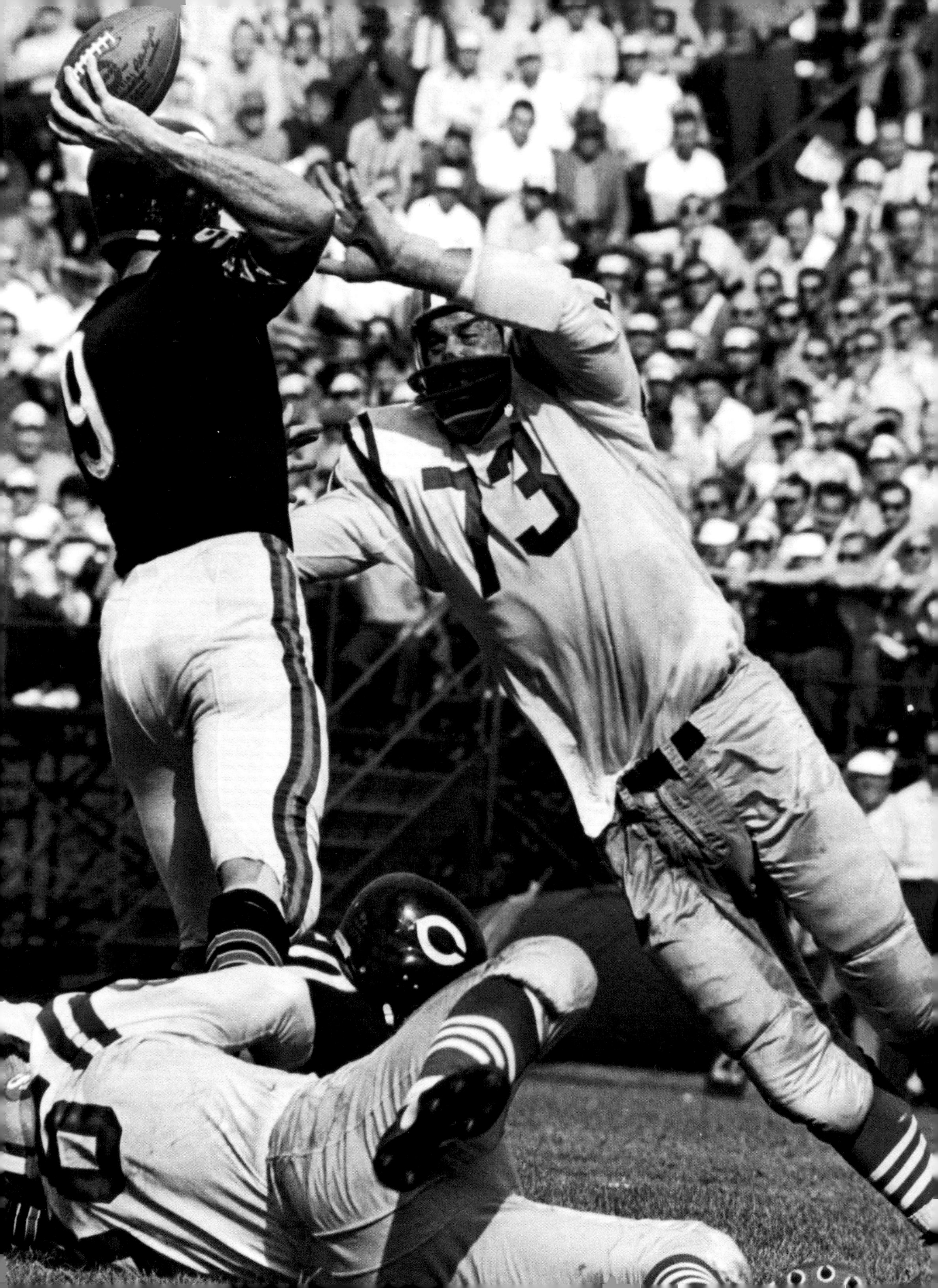

LEO NOMELLINI

- » **Defensive Tackle/Offensive Tackle 1950–1963**
- » **Nine-time All-Pro**
- » **10-time Pro Bowl selection**
- » **Pro Football Hall of Fame 1969**
- » **San Francisco jersey #73 retired 1971**

Leo Nomellini was a double-threat both on and off the field. Born in Italy, Nomellini didn't play the game of football until joining the Marines after high school. He was drafted by the Niners in 1950, the team's first in the NFL, and proceeded to excel on both offense and defense for the next 15 seasons. When he wasn't wreaking havoc at the line of scrimmage, he was doing so in a wrestling ring, moonlighting as Leo "The Lion" Nomellini. When asked in the pages of *Sports Illustrated* which vocation was tougher, he responded, "Oh, wrestling is much tougher. Every night you have to drive a lot of miles to another arena."

Nomellini played in every game for the 49ers from 1950 to 1963.

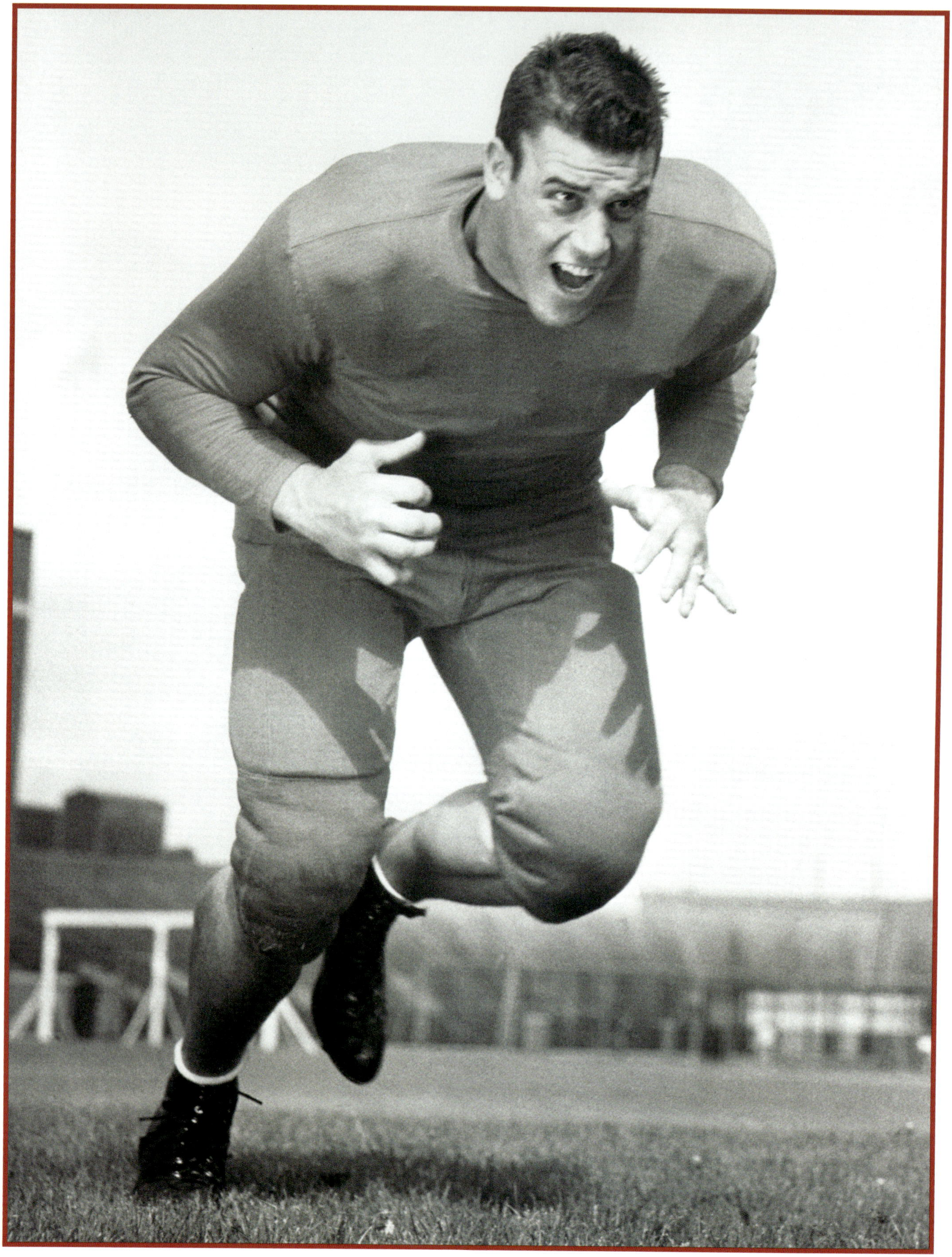

Nomellini charged at quarterbacks on Sundays (above) and professional wrestlers at night (right).

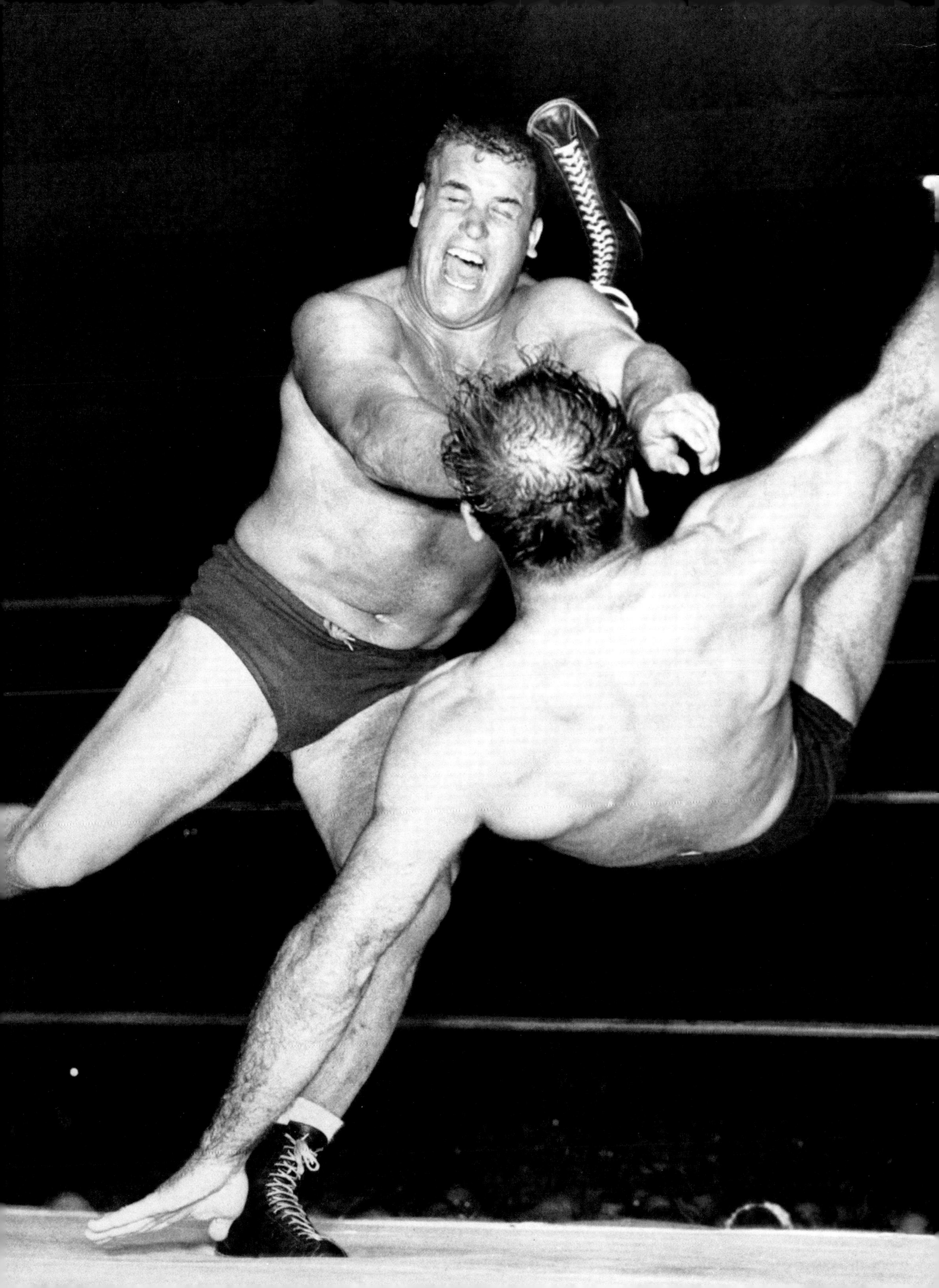

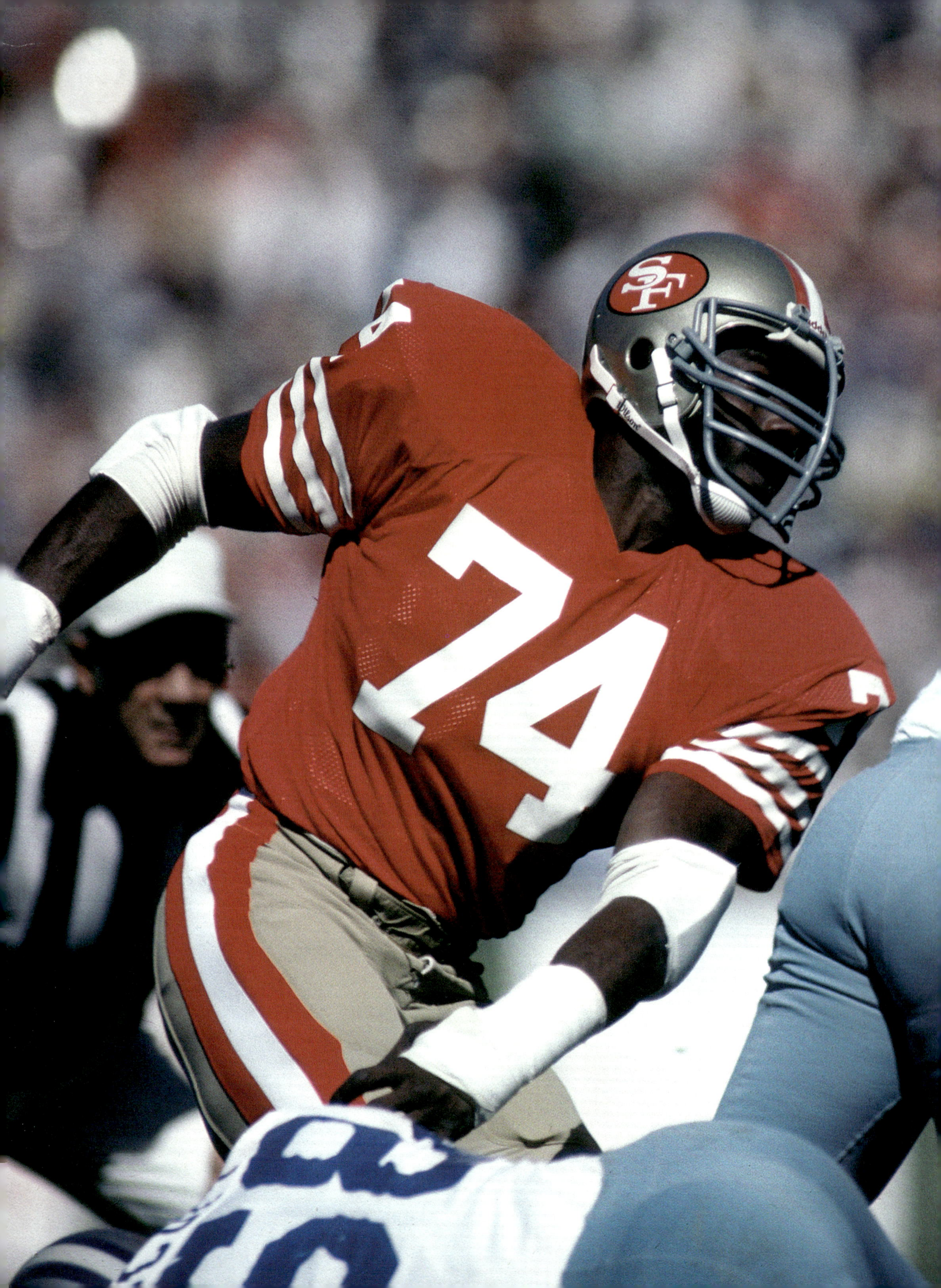

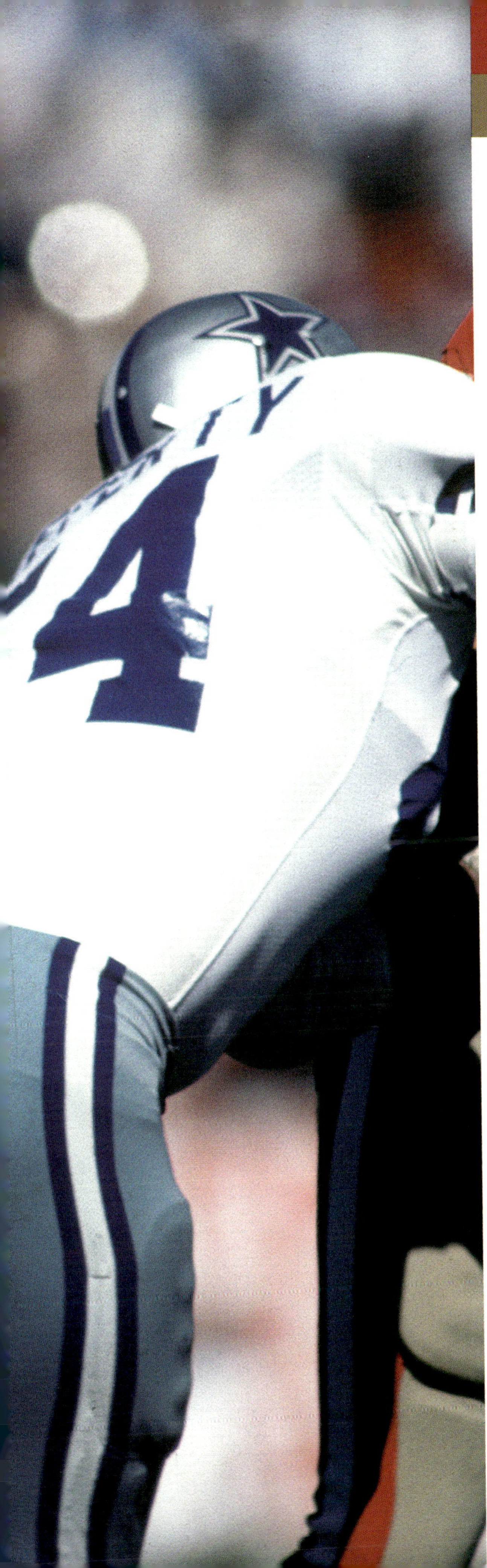

FRED DEAN

» **Defensive End 1981–1985**

» **Two-time Super Bowl champion**

» **Two-time All-Pro**

» **Four-time Pro Bowl selection**

» **Pro Football Hall of Fame 2008**

In an era before sacks were an official statistic, Fred Dean terrorized quarterbacks and pioneered the role of the situational pass rusher. He was traded to the Niners after a contract dispute with the San Diego Chargers; as reported by Paul Zimmerman in Sports Illustrated, "San Francisco signed Dean for roughly double what he was making and told him to start collecting sacks." After a 6–10 season in 1980, the Niners were 3-2 when they traded for Dean; they went on to win 13 of their last 14 games, including the Super Bowl.

Dean was a charter member of the 49ers Hall of Fame.

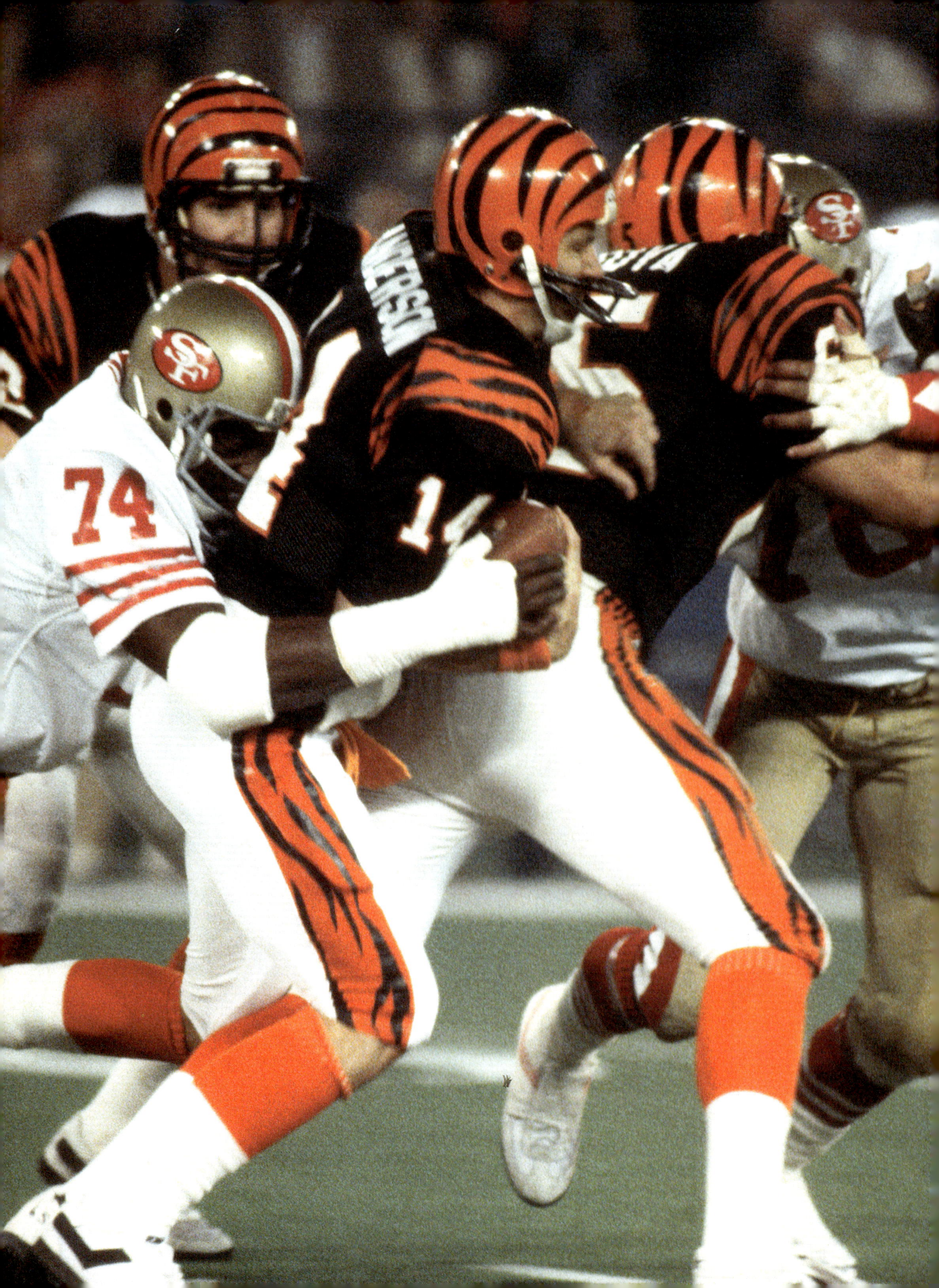
74

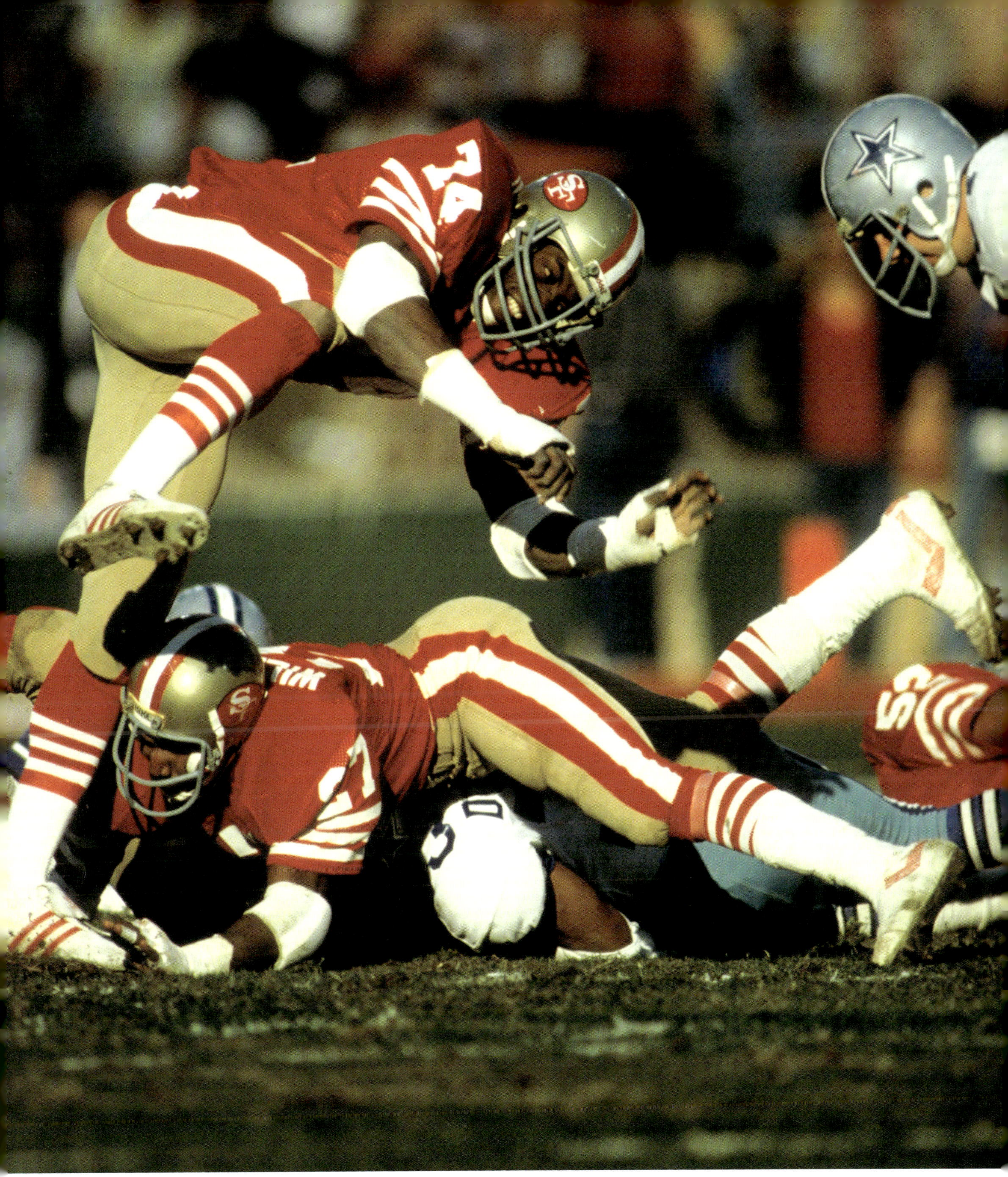

Dean brought down quarterback Ken Anderson in Super Bowl XVI (left) and finished a tackle against Dallas in 1982 (above).

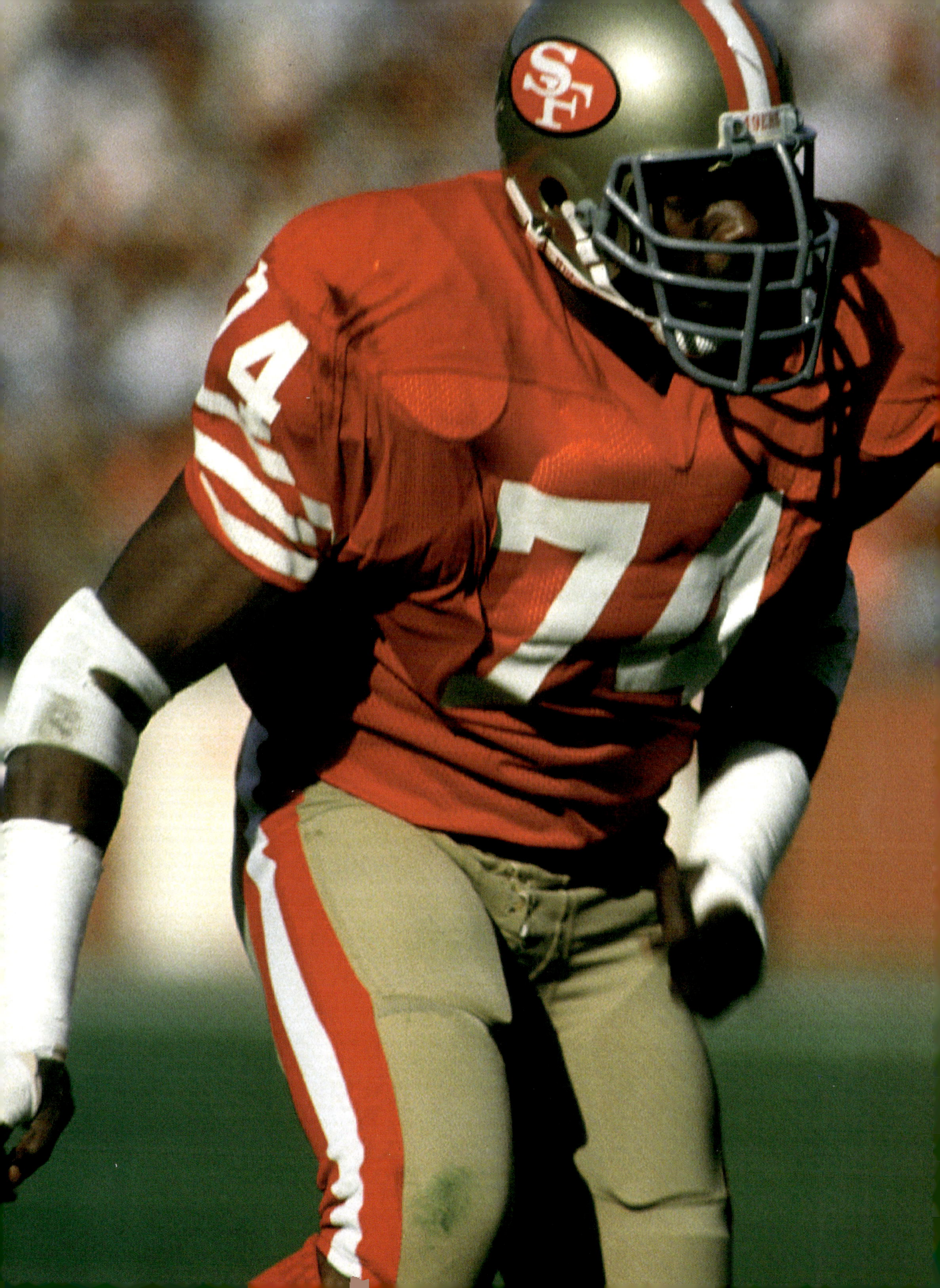
74

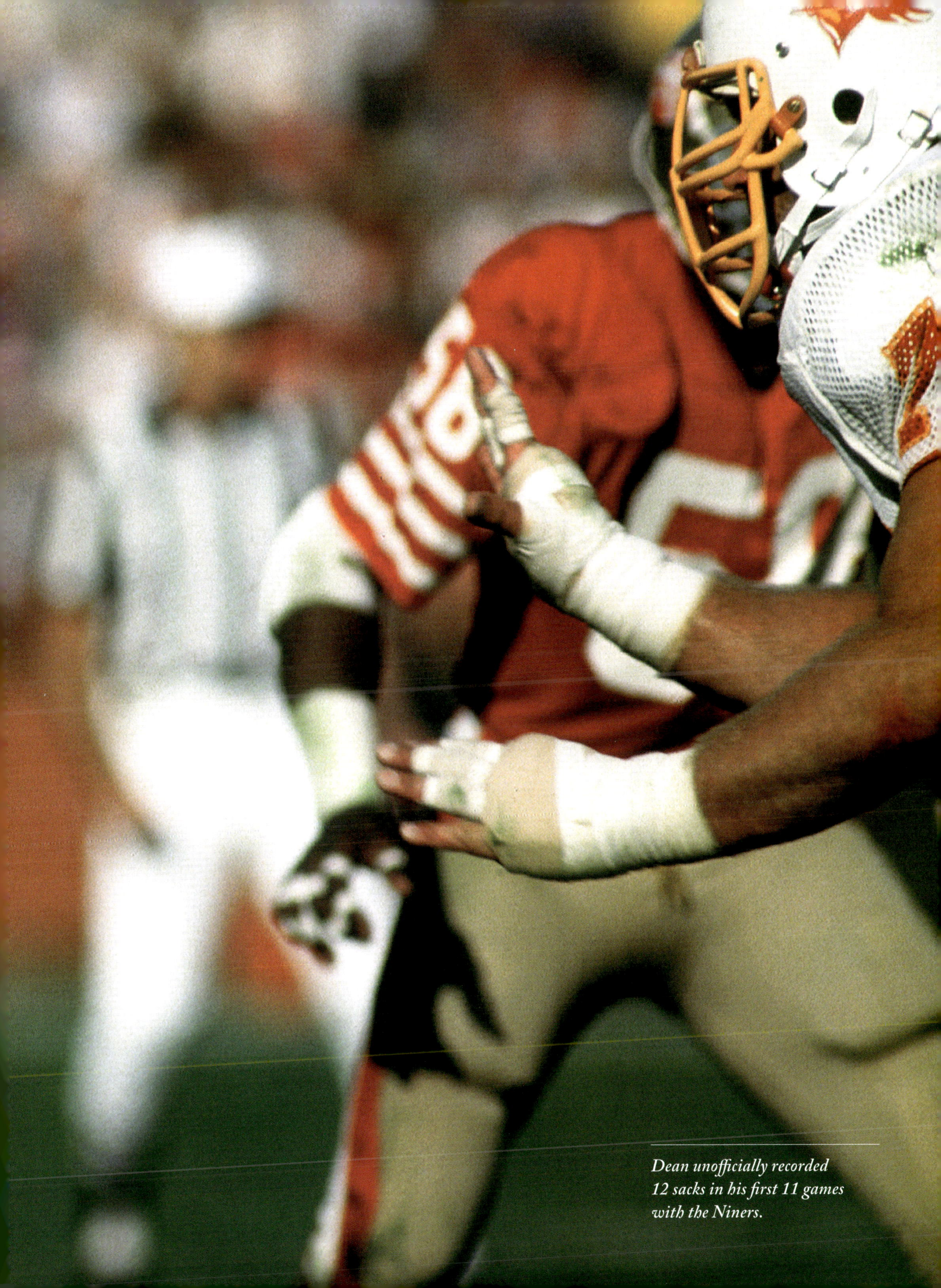

Dean unofficially recorded 12 sacks in his first 11 games with the Niners.

BOB ST. CLAIR

- » **Offensive Tackle 1953–1963**
- » **Nine-time All-Pro**
- » **Five-time Pro Bowl selection**
- » **Pro Football Hall of Fame 1990**
- » **San Francisco jersey #79 retired 2001**

If ever a player was born to be a 49er, it was Bob St. Clair. A San Francisco native, he attended Polytechnic High School, located across the street from Kezar Stadium, then went to college at the University of San Francisco. St. Clair was drafted by the 49ers in 1953 and spent his entire 11-season career with the team. To honor the total of 17 seasons and 189 home games he played there, the city renamed Kezar Stadium's field after him.

At 6'8", St. Clair is one of the tallest players in the Pro Football Hall of Fame.

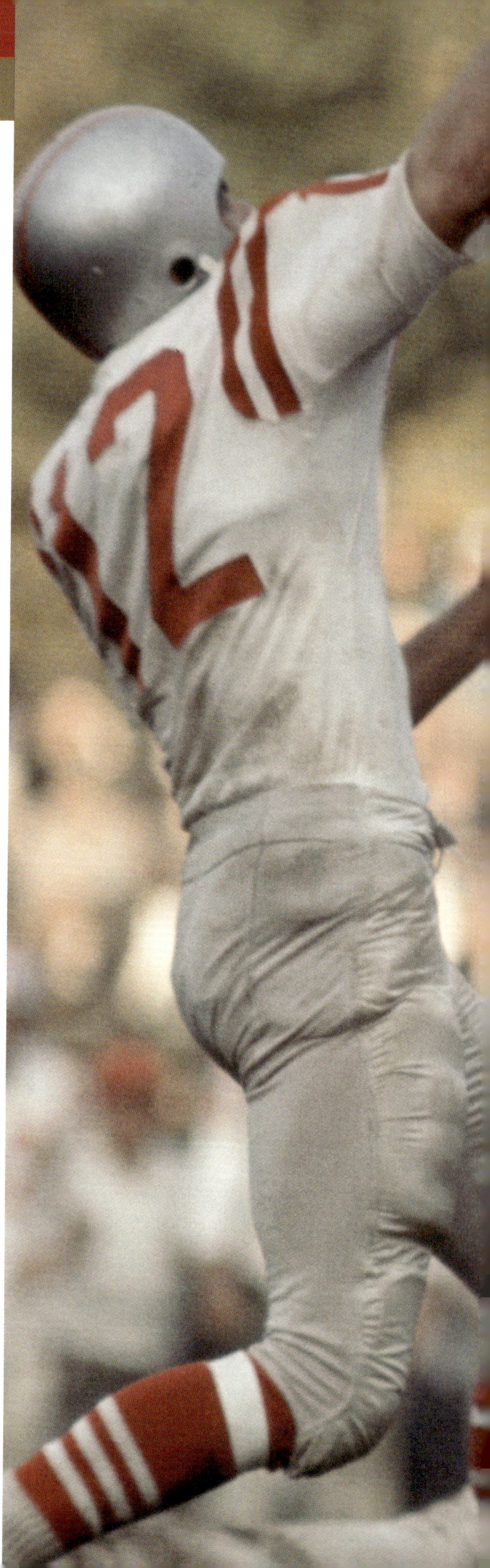

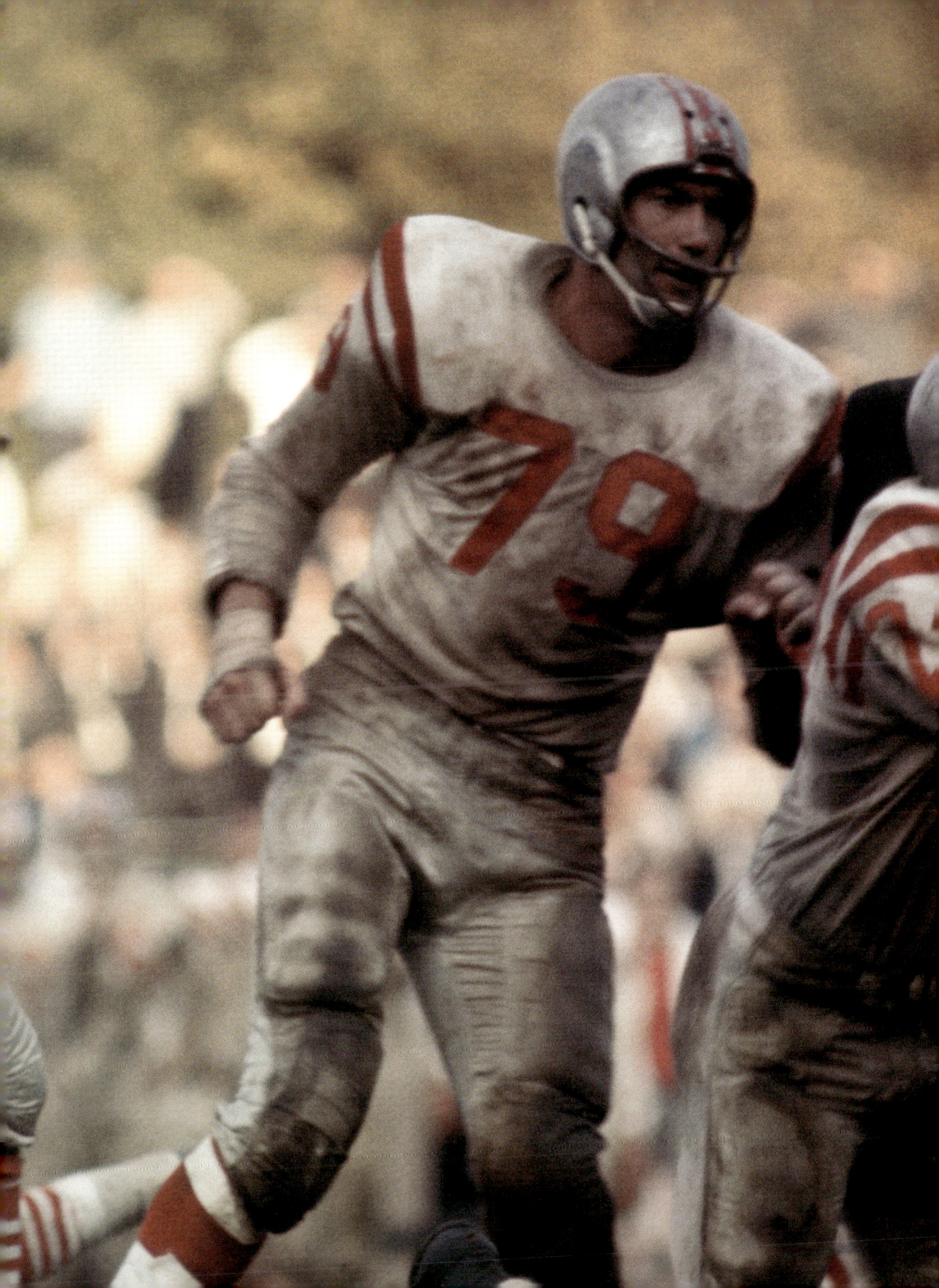

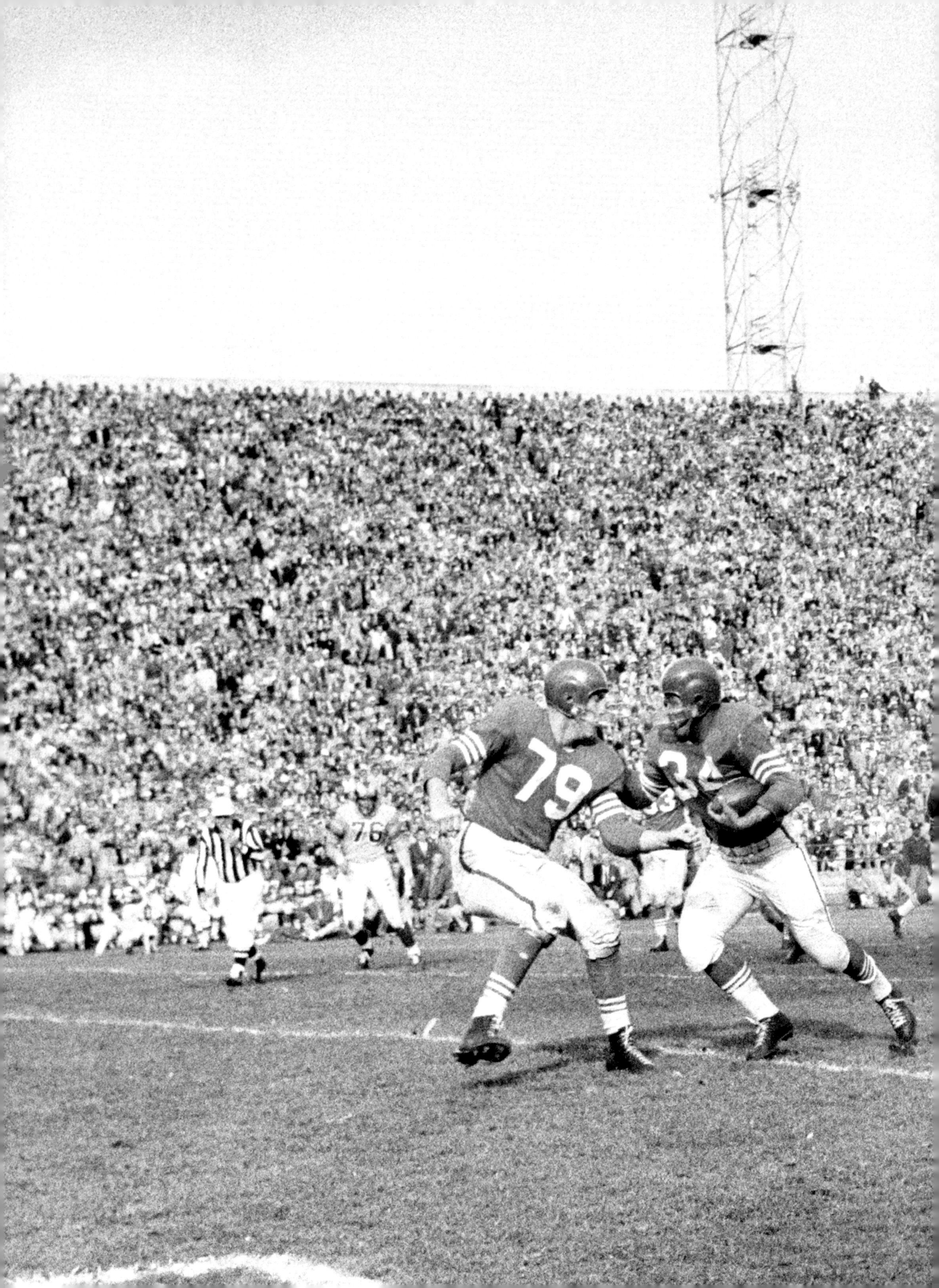

St. Clair (79) blocked for Joe Perry (34) and the rest of the Niners' Million Dollar Backfield.

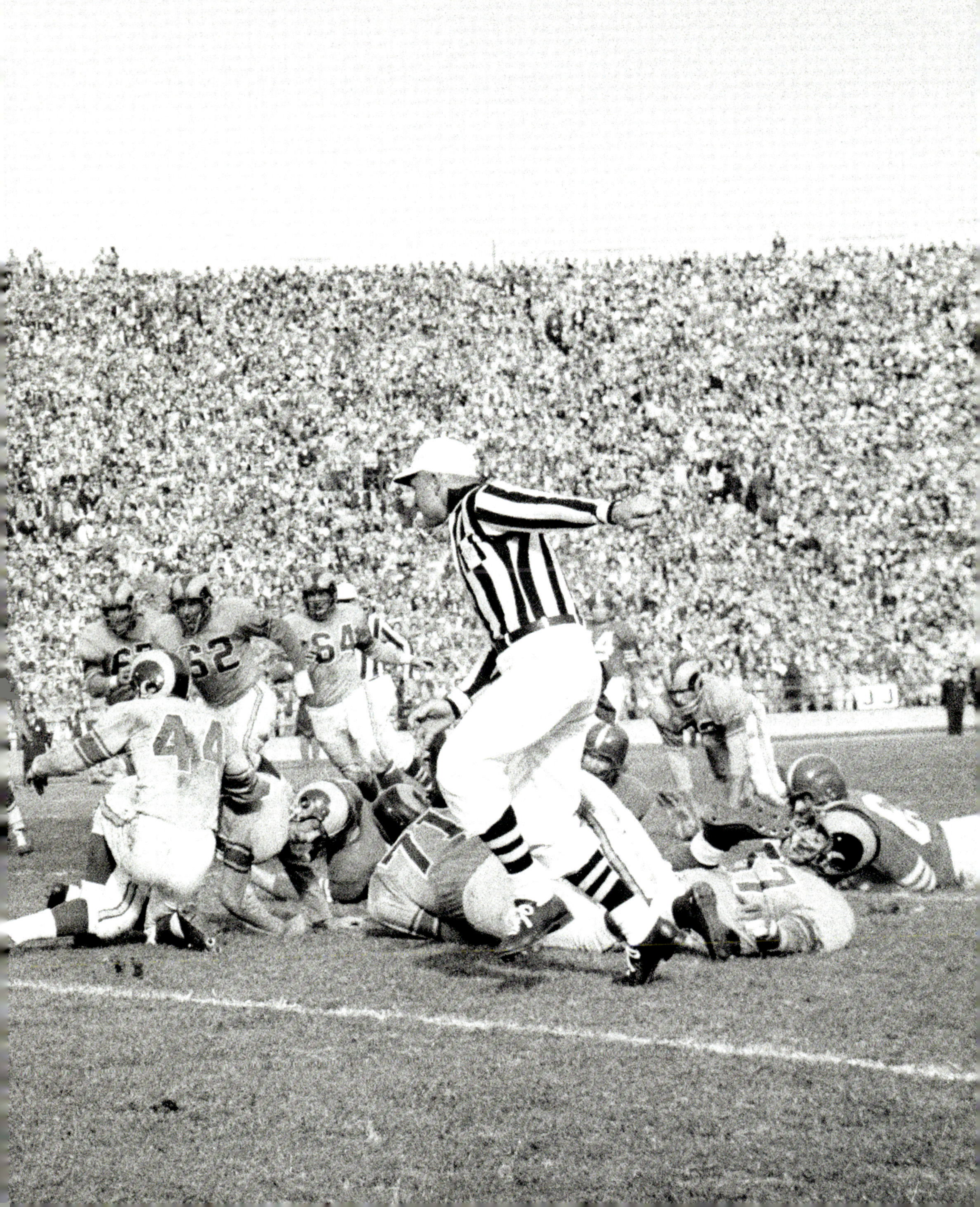

DWIGHT CLARK

- » **Wide Receiver 1979–1987**
- » **Two-time Super Bowl champion**
- » **All-Pro 1982**
- » **Two-time Pro Bowl selection**
- » **San Francisco jersey #87 retired 1988**

Dwight Clark retired with 554 career receptions, but he is remembered for one of them above all others. An unheralded prospect, Clark was chosen by the Niners in the 10th round of the 1979 draft, seven rounds after the team selected Joe Montana. The duo soon developed a connection on the field, never more evident than in the 1981 NFC Championship Game against the Dallas Cowboys. Trailing by six points with 58 seconds to play, Clark leaped in the air to secure Montana's pass in the back of the end zone, and the ensuing extra point sent the Niners to Super Bowl XVI. The reception is known simply as "The Catch."

Any Niners fan will confirm that Clark made the most memorable catch in NFL history.

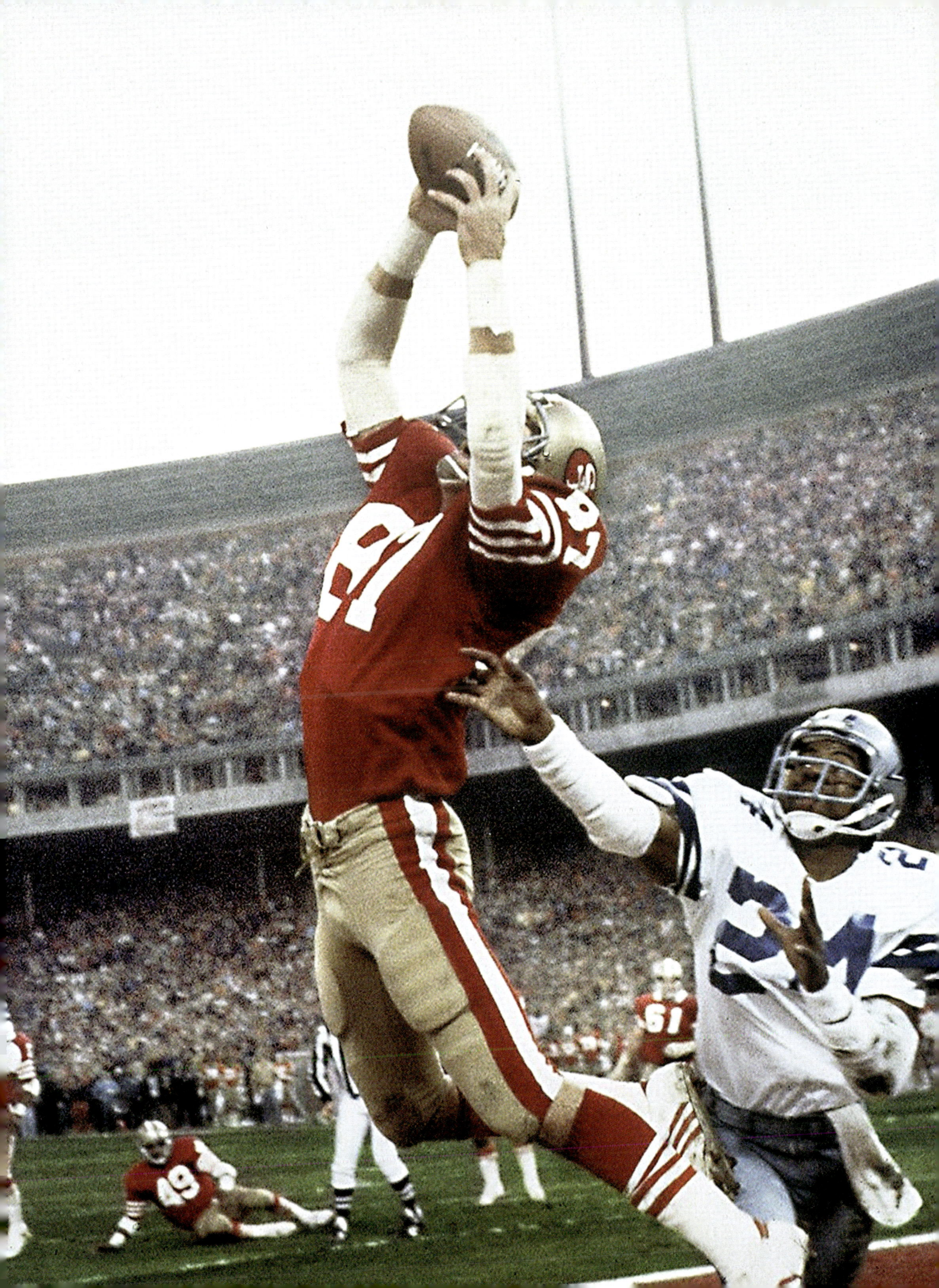

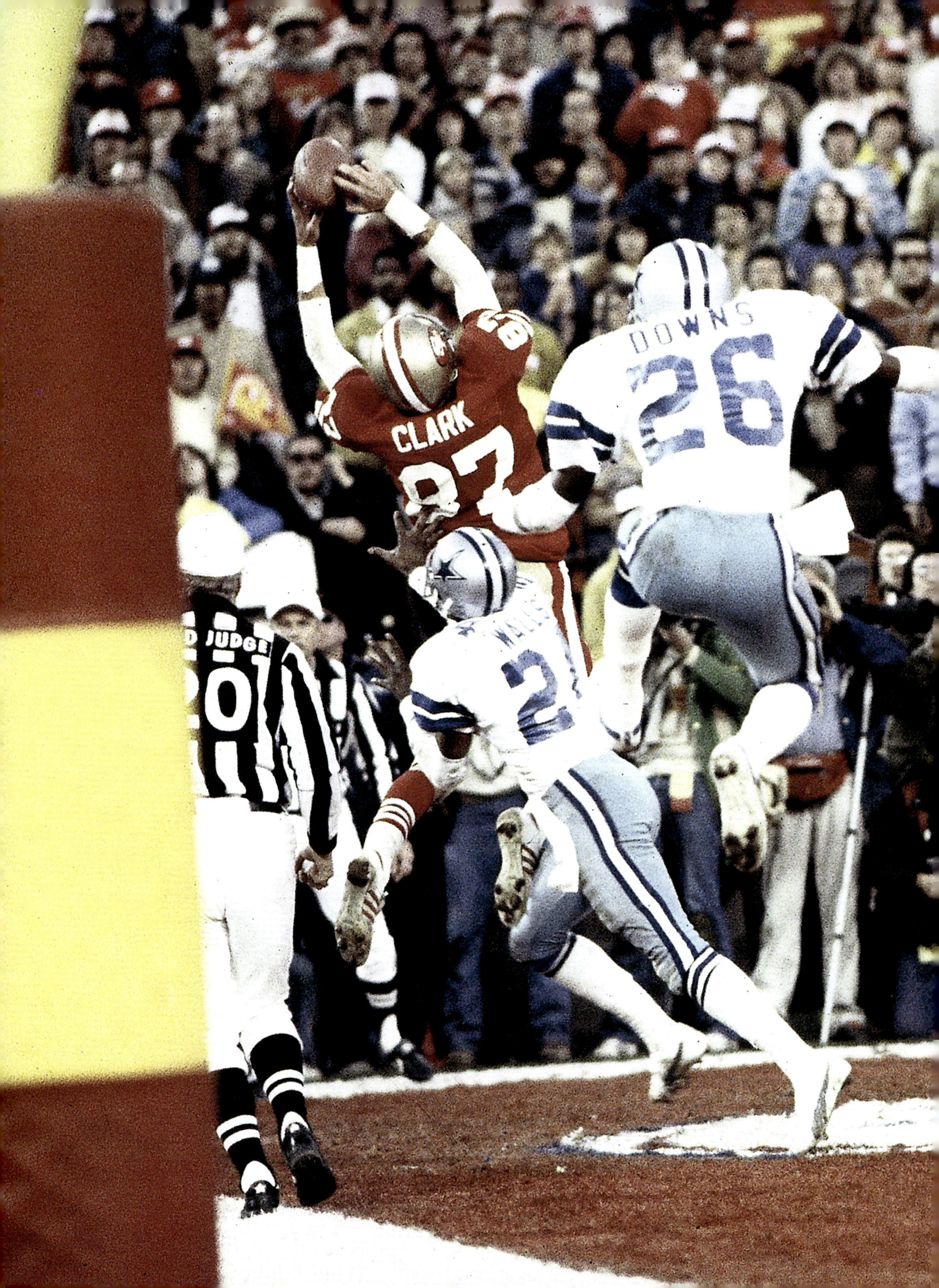
CLARK
87
DOWNS
26

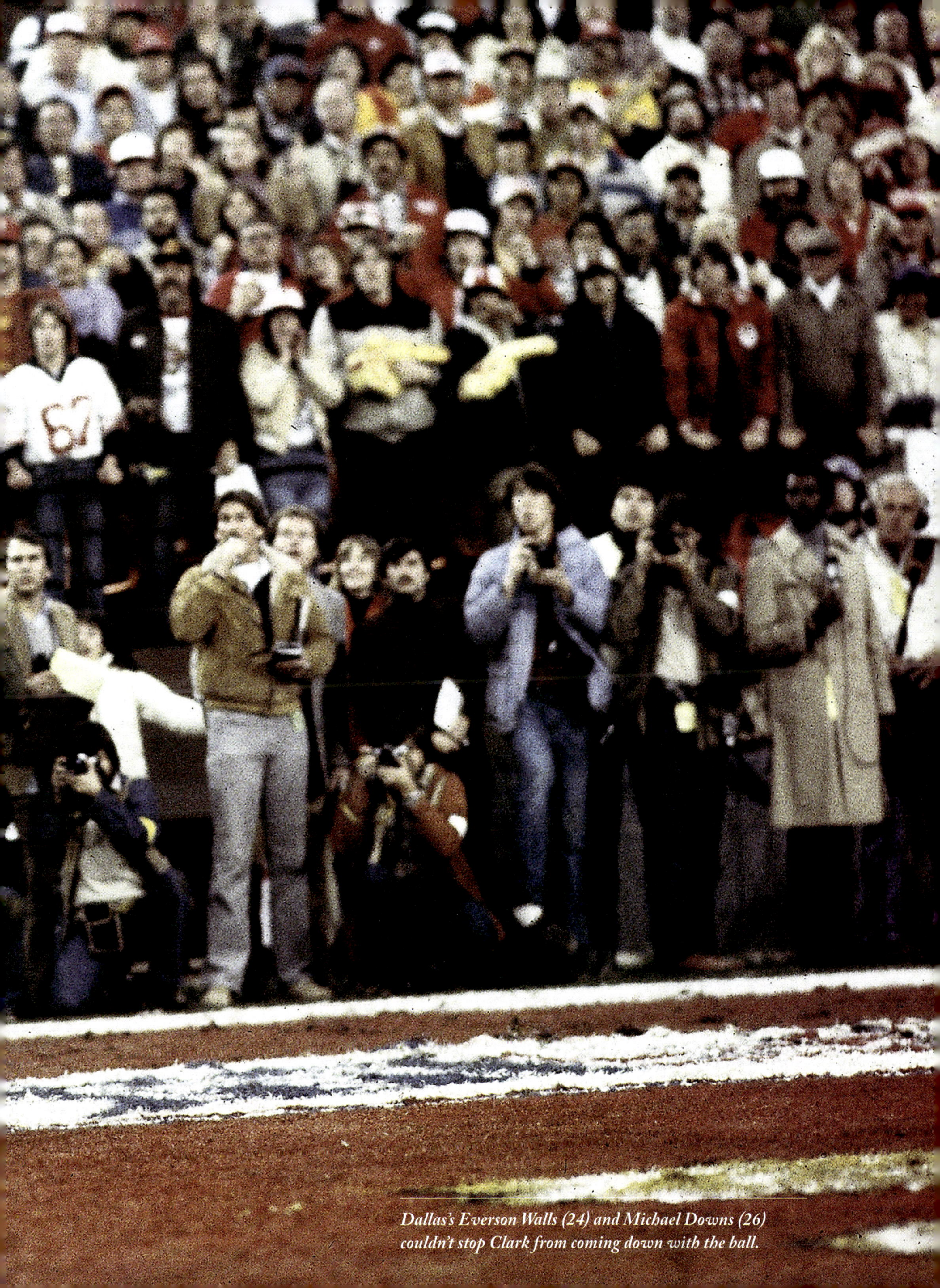

Dallas's Everson Walls (24) and Michael Downs (26) couldn't stop Clark from coming down with the ball.

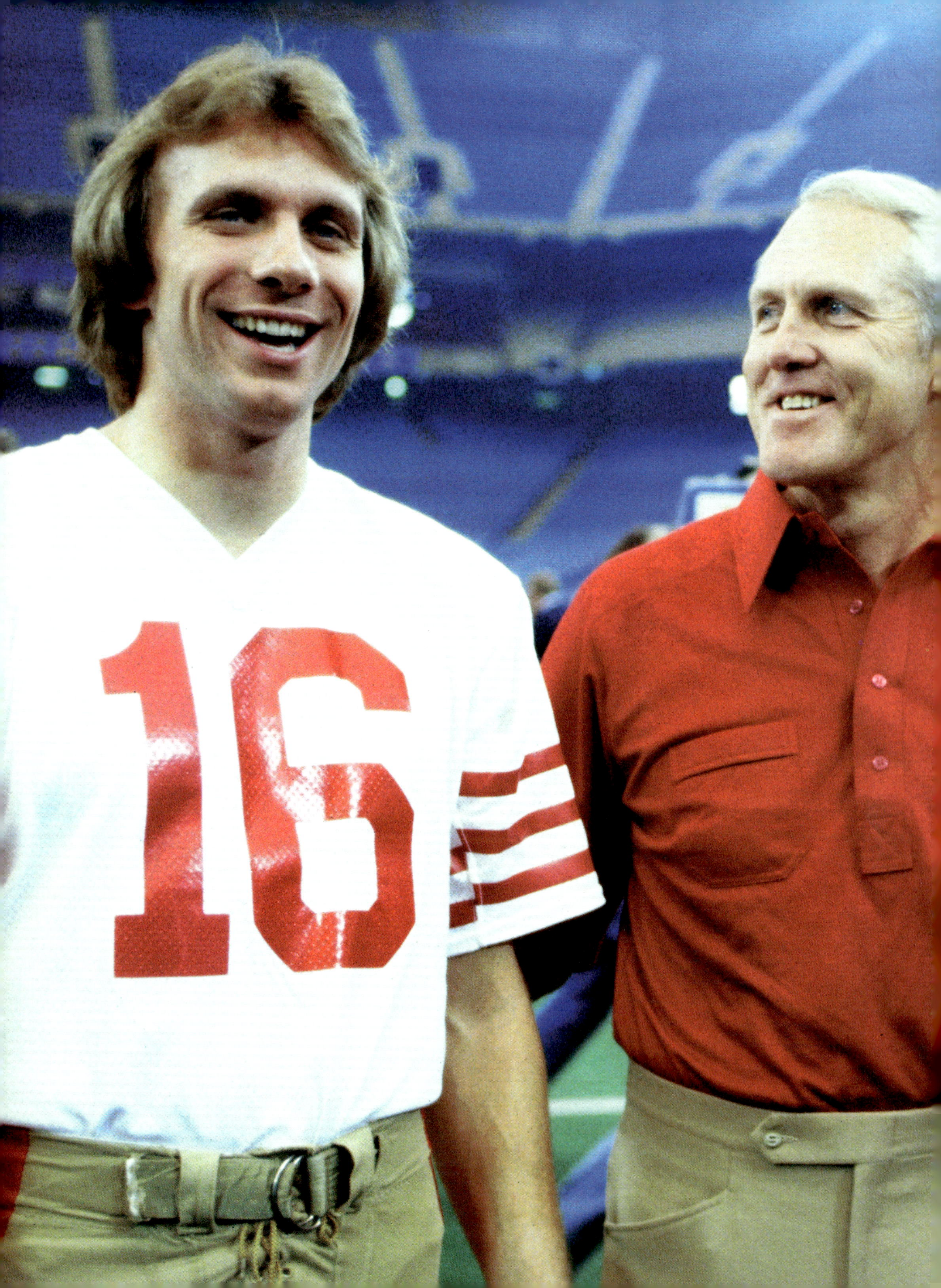
16

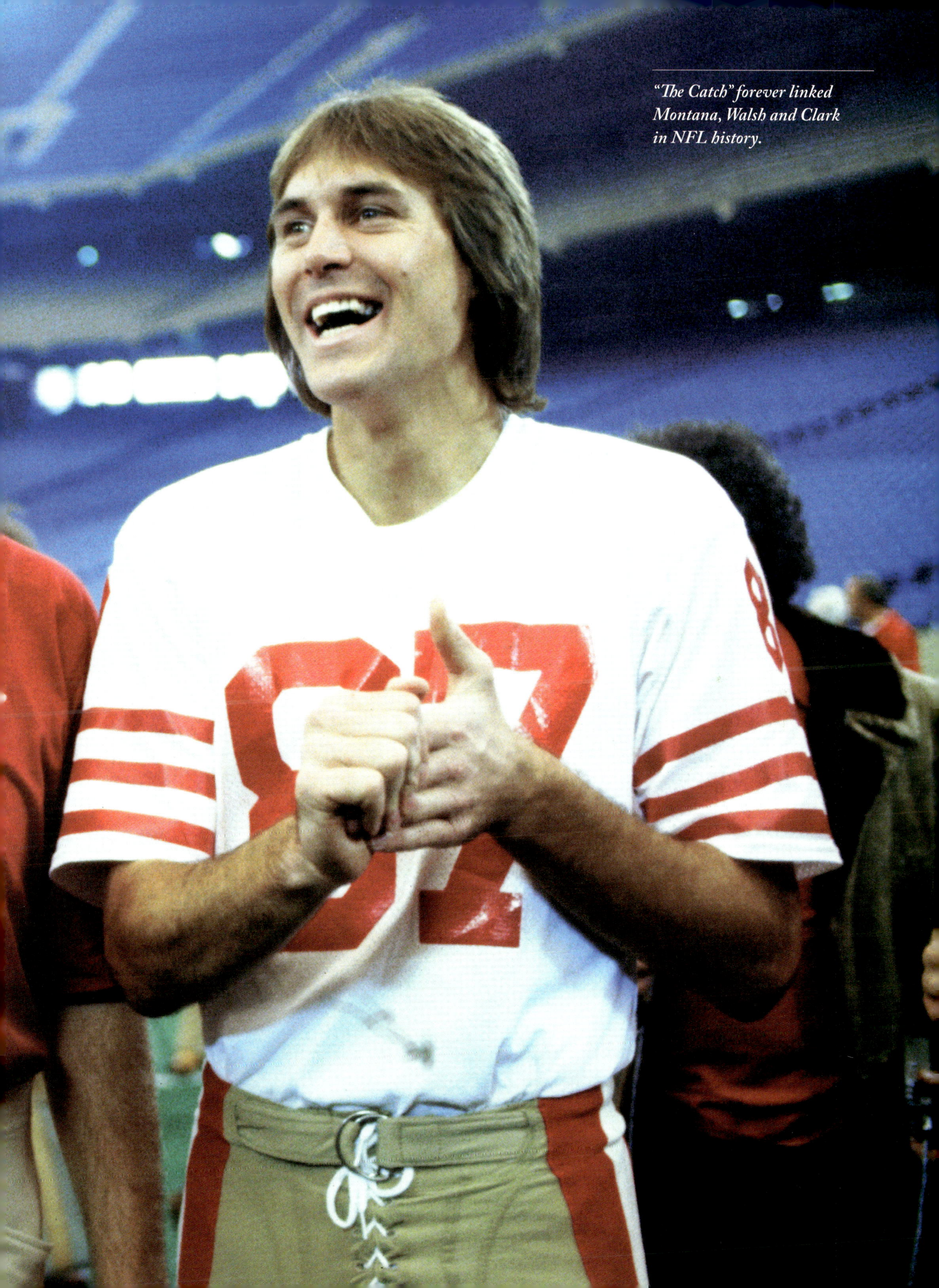

"The Catch" forever linked Montana, Walsh and Clark in NFL history.

JERRY RICE

- » Wide Receiver 1985–2000
- » Three-time Super Bowl champion
- » Super Bowl XXIII MVP
- » NFL MVP 1987
- » 11-time All-Pro
- » 13-time Pro Bowl selection
- » Pro Football Hall of Fame 2010
- » San Francisco jersey #80 retired 2010

Jerry Rice is rightfully regarded by most observers to be the greatest wide receiver in the history of football. Over his 20-year career, 16 seasons of which were in San Francisco, Rice rewrote the record books. Among the more than 100 NFL records he holds are most career receptions, receiving yards, touchdown receptions and total touchdowns.

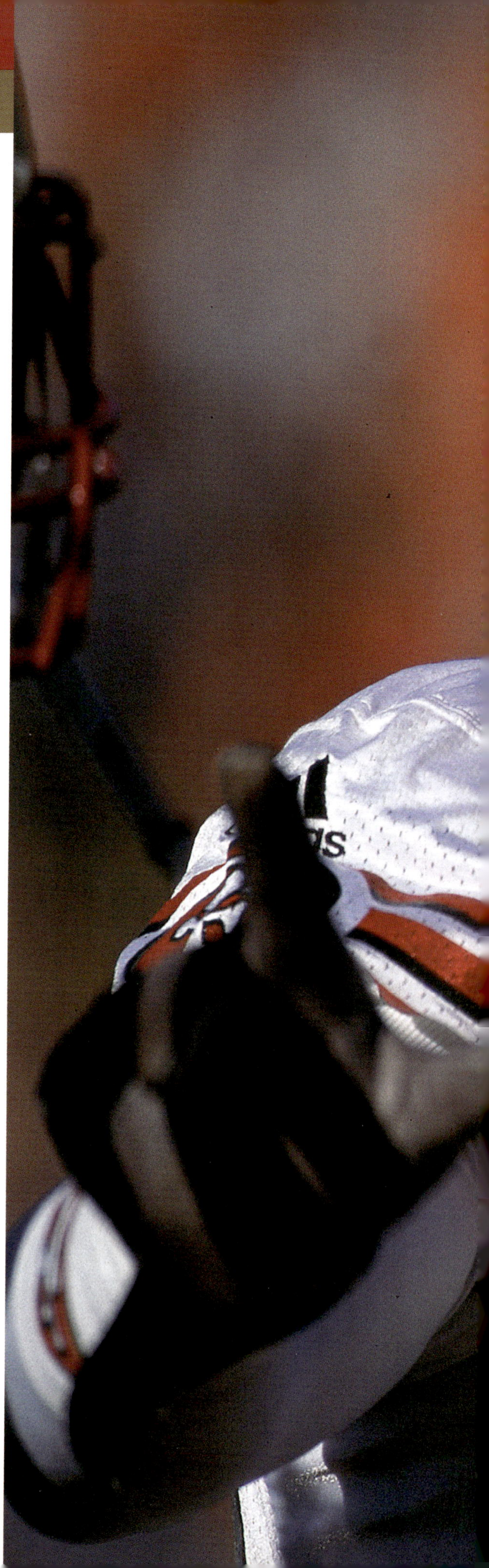

Rice was a favorite target of both Joe Montana and Steve Young.

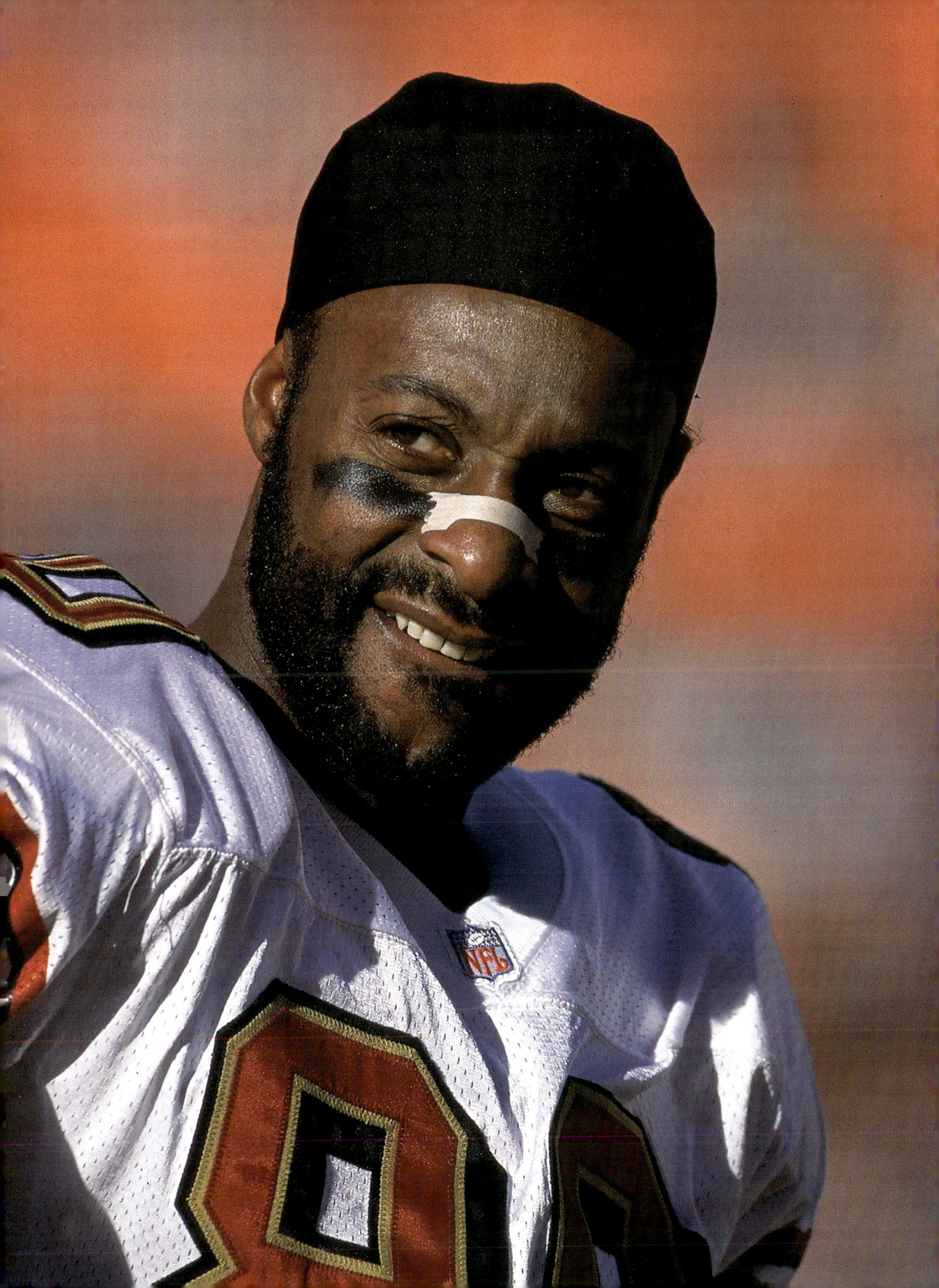

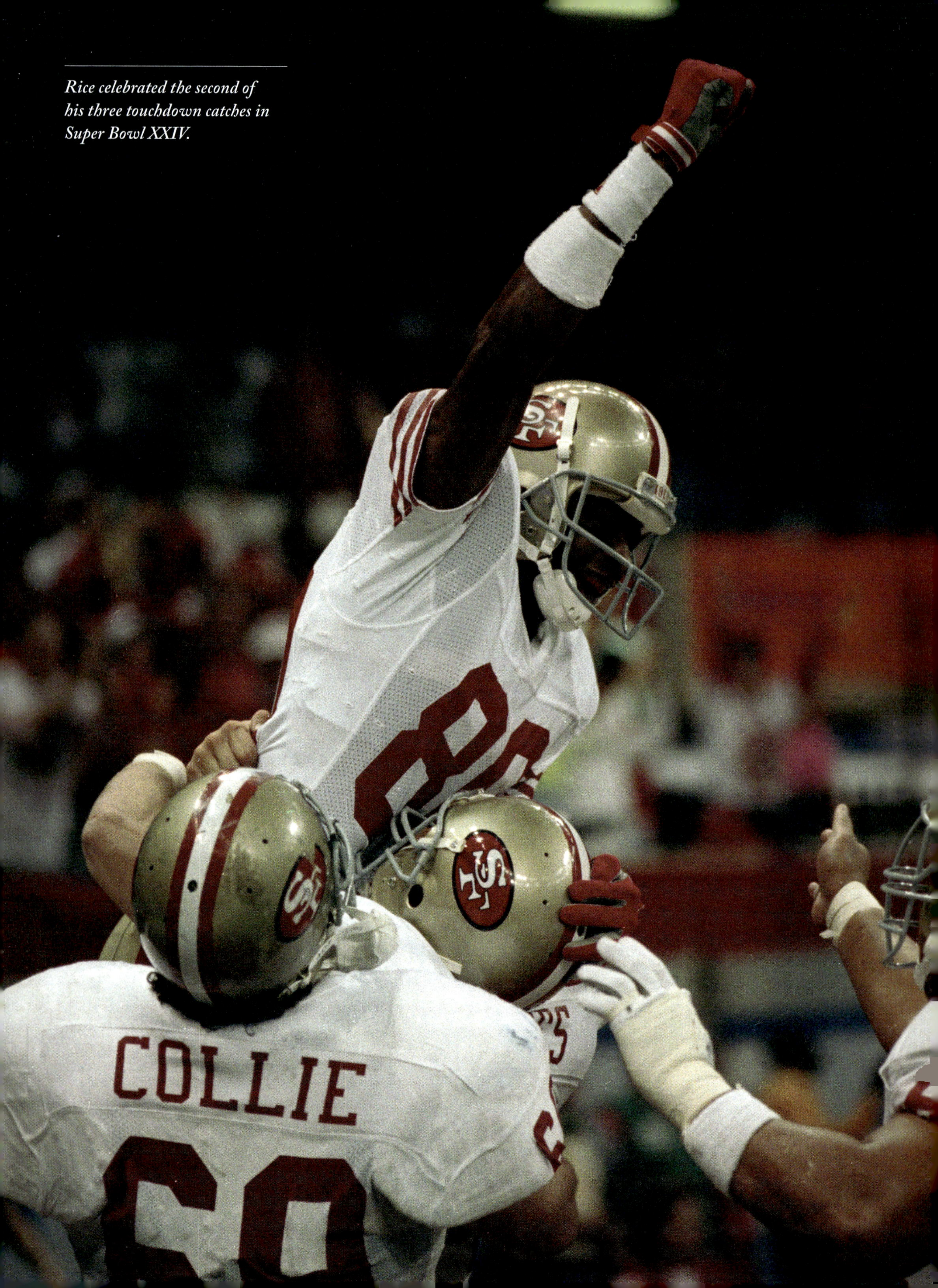

Rice celebrated the second of his three touchdown catches in Super Bowl XXIV.

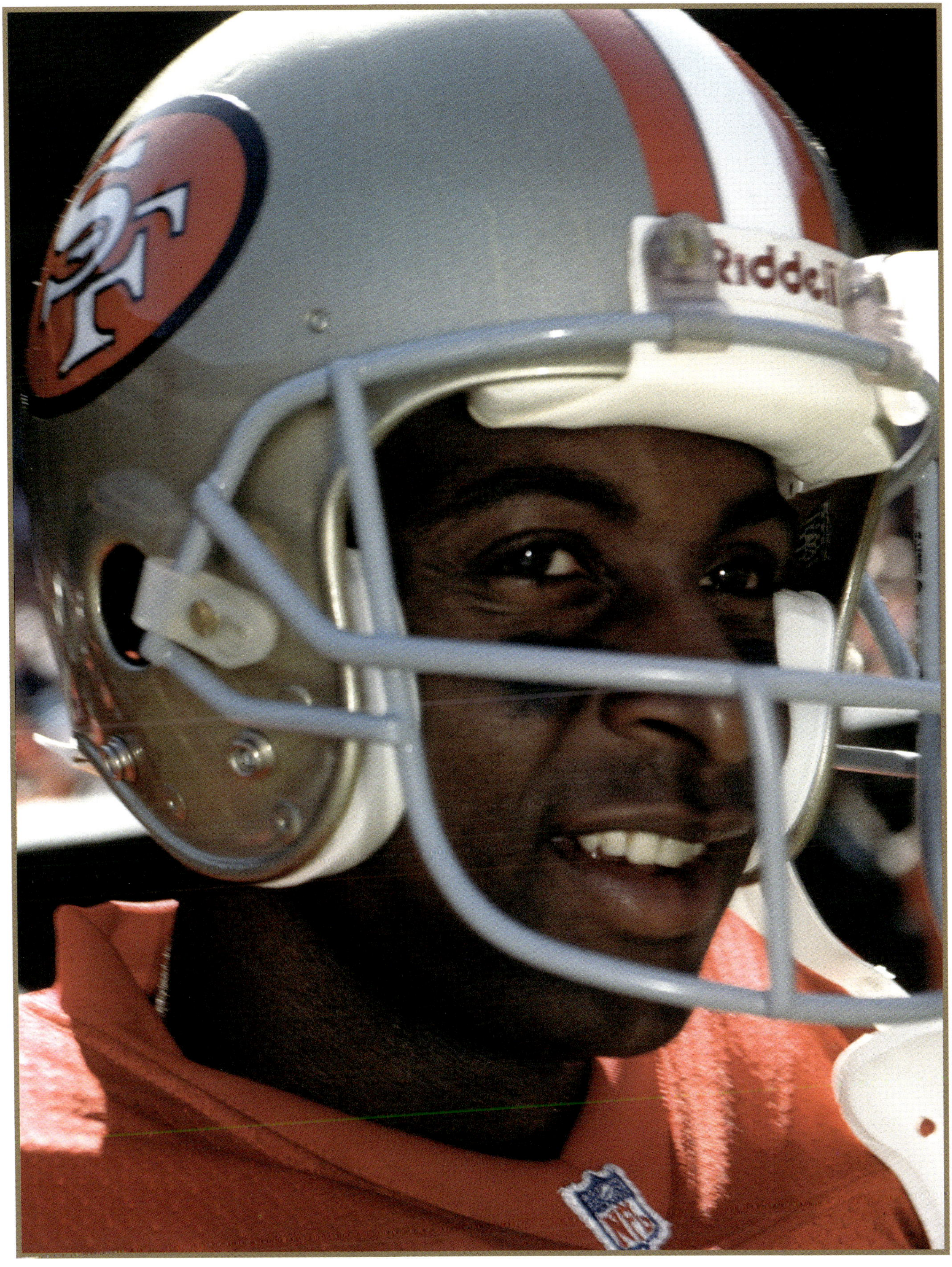

Rice is the highest scoring non-kicker in NFL history.

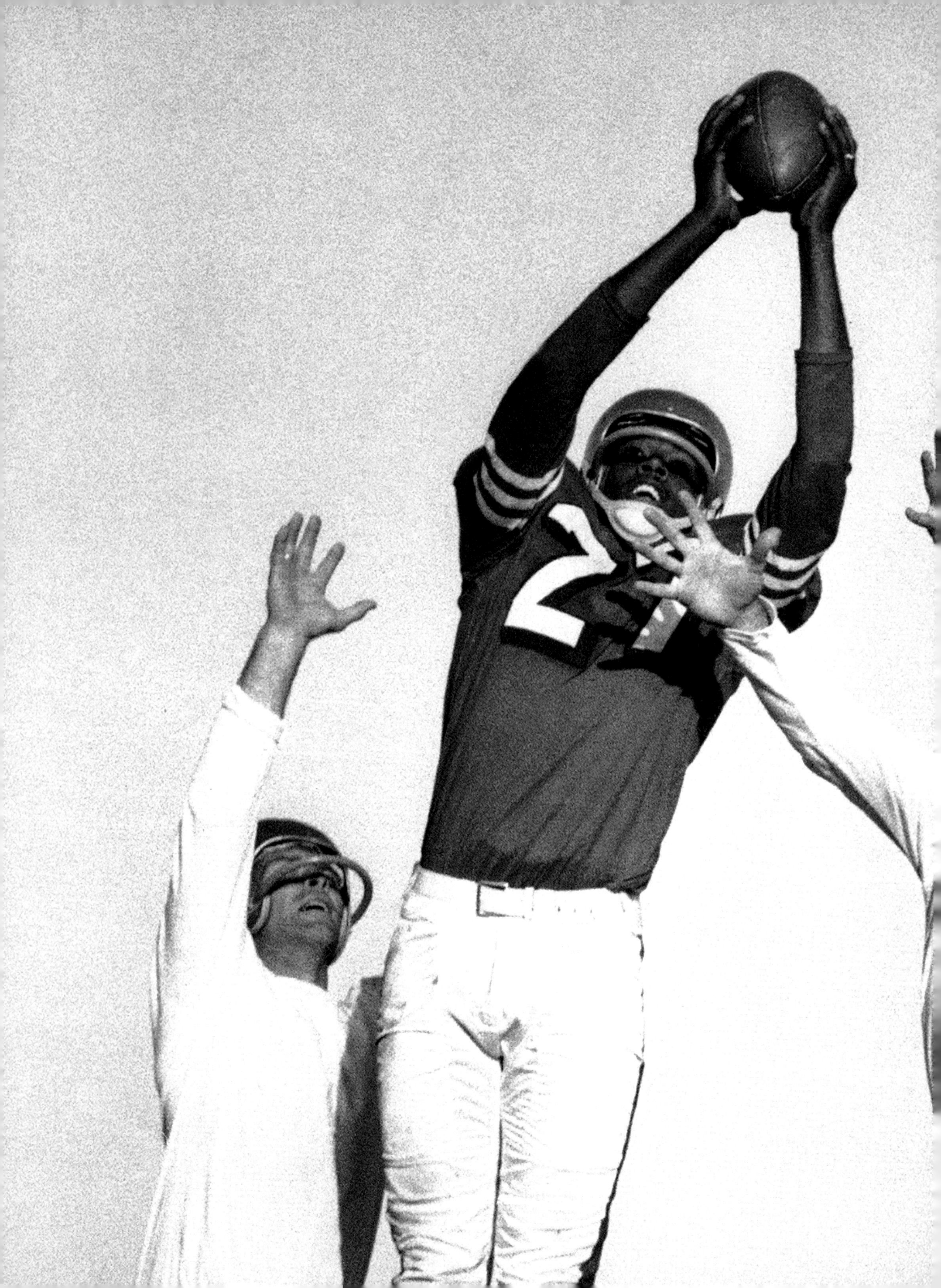

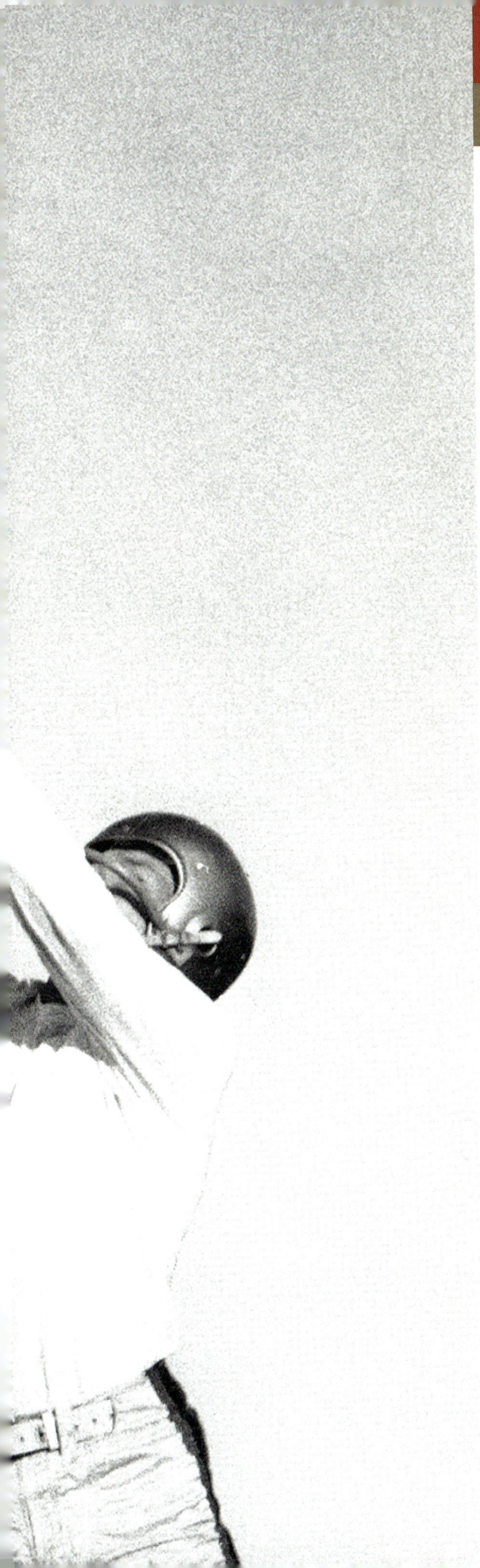

R.C. OWENS

» **Wide Receiver 1957–1961**

» **All-Pro 1960**

Raleigh Climon Owens was born in Louisiana but grew up in Southern California. The 160th overall pick in the 1956 draft, he paid immediate dividends for the Niners in 1957, catching 27 passes, including five touchdowns. In 1961, he became the first 1,000-yard receiver in franchise history. But Owens is best remembered for developing the "alley-oop" pass play, along with Niners quarterback Y.A. Tittle. Thanks to his 6'3" frame and leaping ability, Owens was uniquely suited to catching passes thrown high above any would-be defenders. Though the phrase is more commonly used in basketball, according to the *Oxford English Dictionary*, the Owens-Tittle version predates it by two years.

Owens's leaping ability made him difficult for defenders to cover.

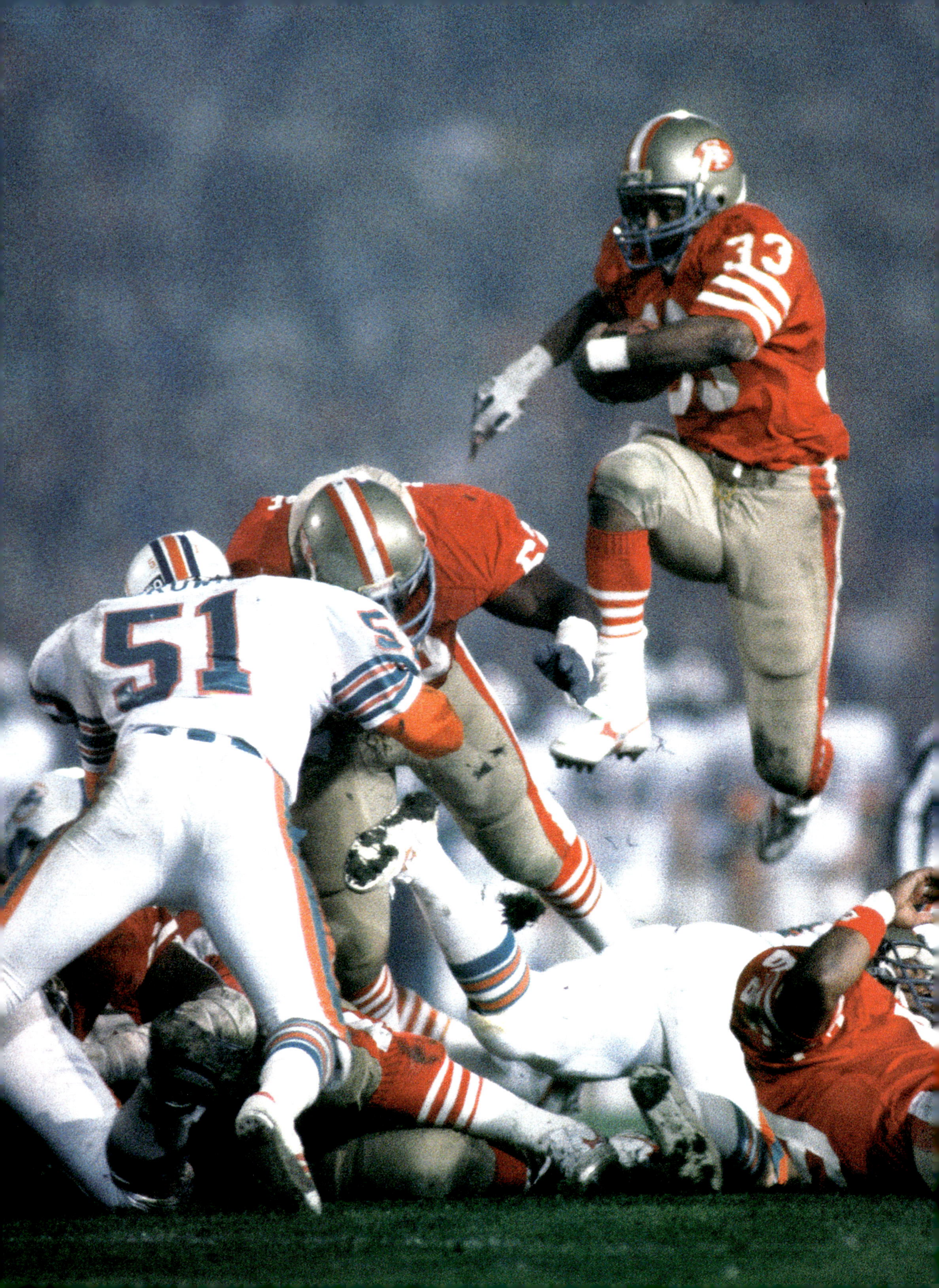

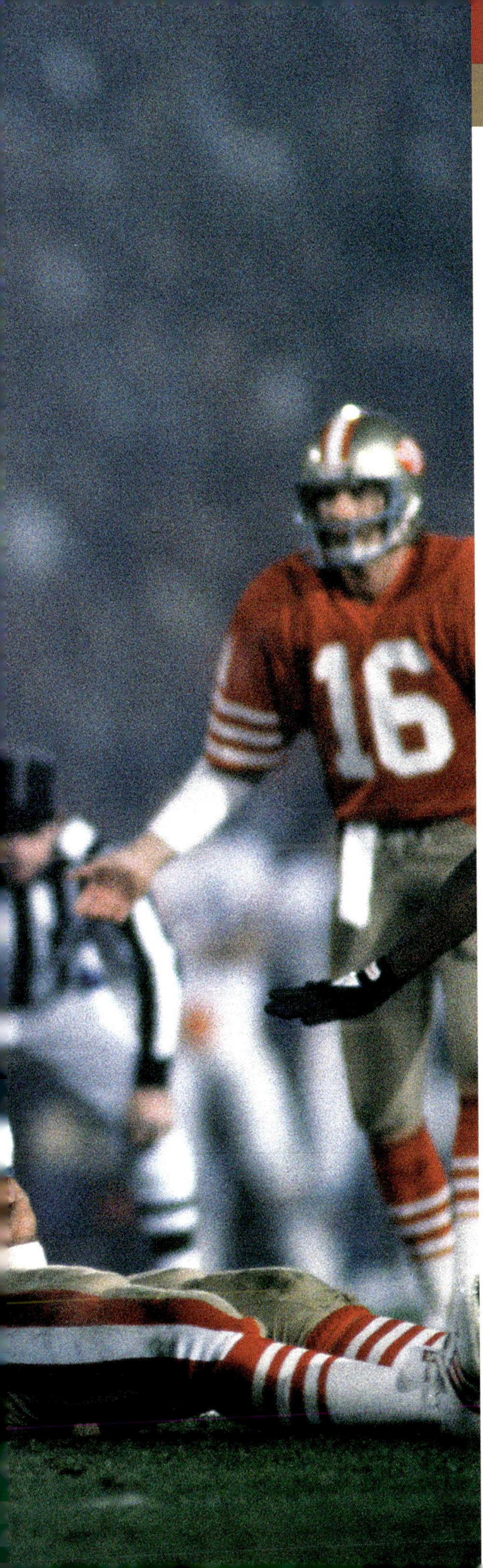

ROGER CRAIG

- » **Running Back 1983–1990**
- » **Three-time Super Bowl champion**
- » **Two-time All-Pro**
- » **Four-time Pro Bowl selection**

Once running back Roger Craig learned he'd be playing for the San Francisco 49ers in 1983, he immediately set about improving his skills as...a receiver. Within coach Bill Walsh's West Coast offense, Craig proved to be a revolutionary weapon, catching Joe Montana's passes out of the backfield and setting the template for the modern NFL running back. In Super Bowl XIX, he became the first player to ever score three touchdowns in a Super Bowl. The following year, he was the first NFL player to gain 1,000 yards rushing and 1,000 yards receiving in the same season, and even led the entire league in receptions.

Craig and the Niners hurdled over the Dolphins in Super Bowl XIX.

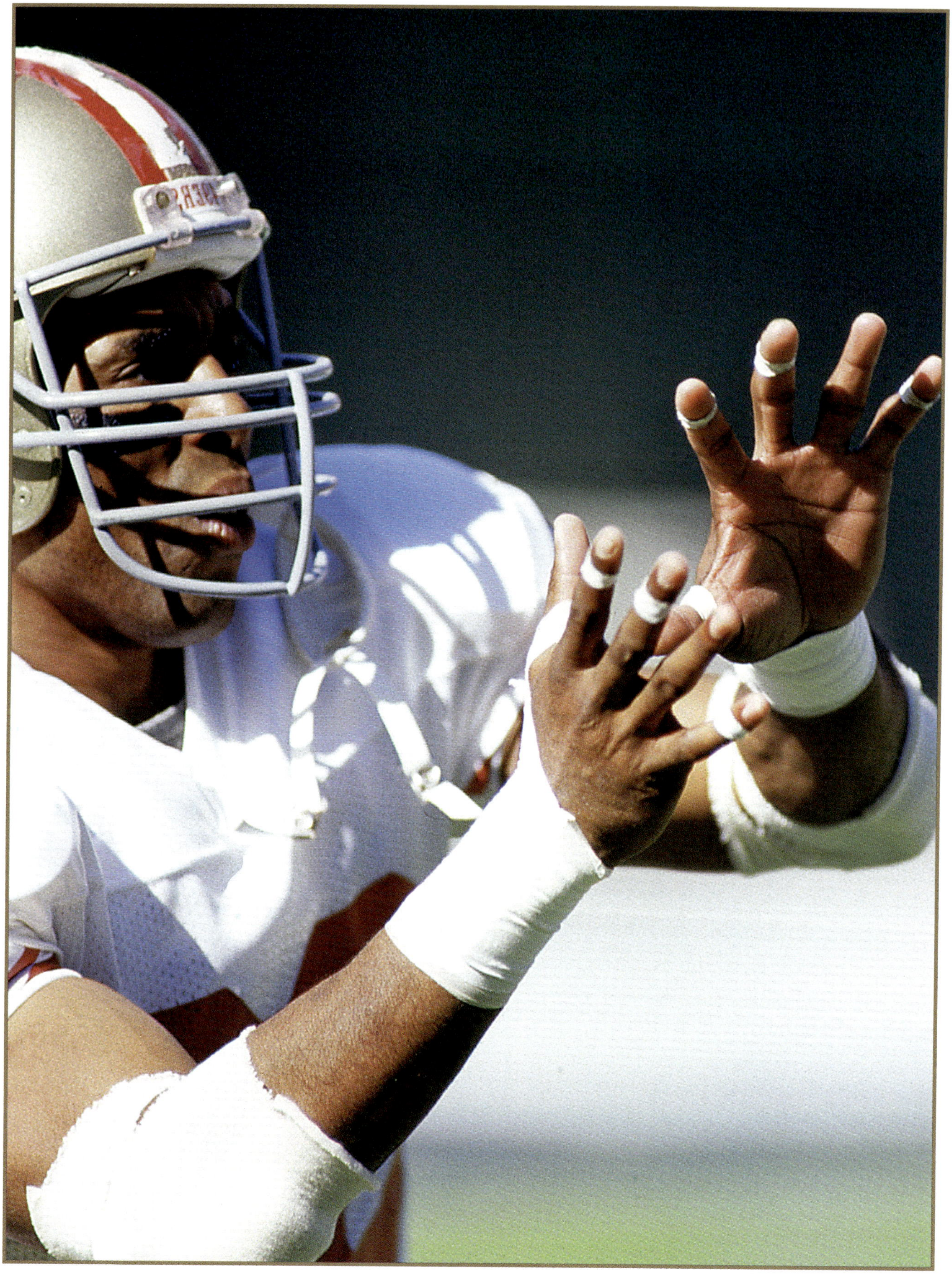

Craig's abilities as a receiver (above) and blocker (right) made him an unsung hero of San Francisco's offense.

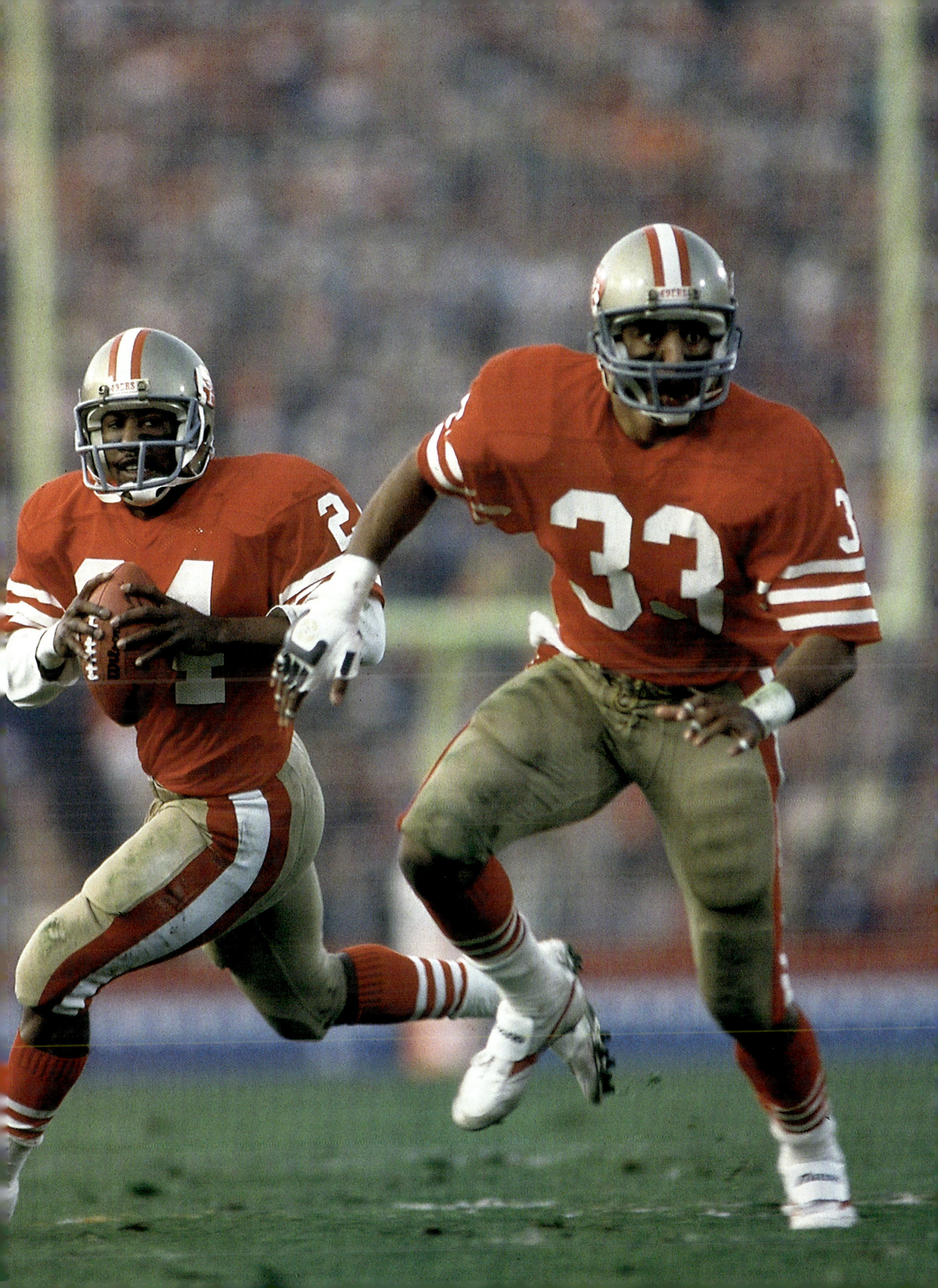

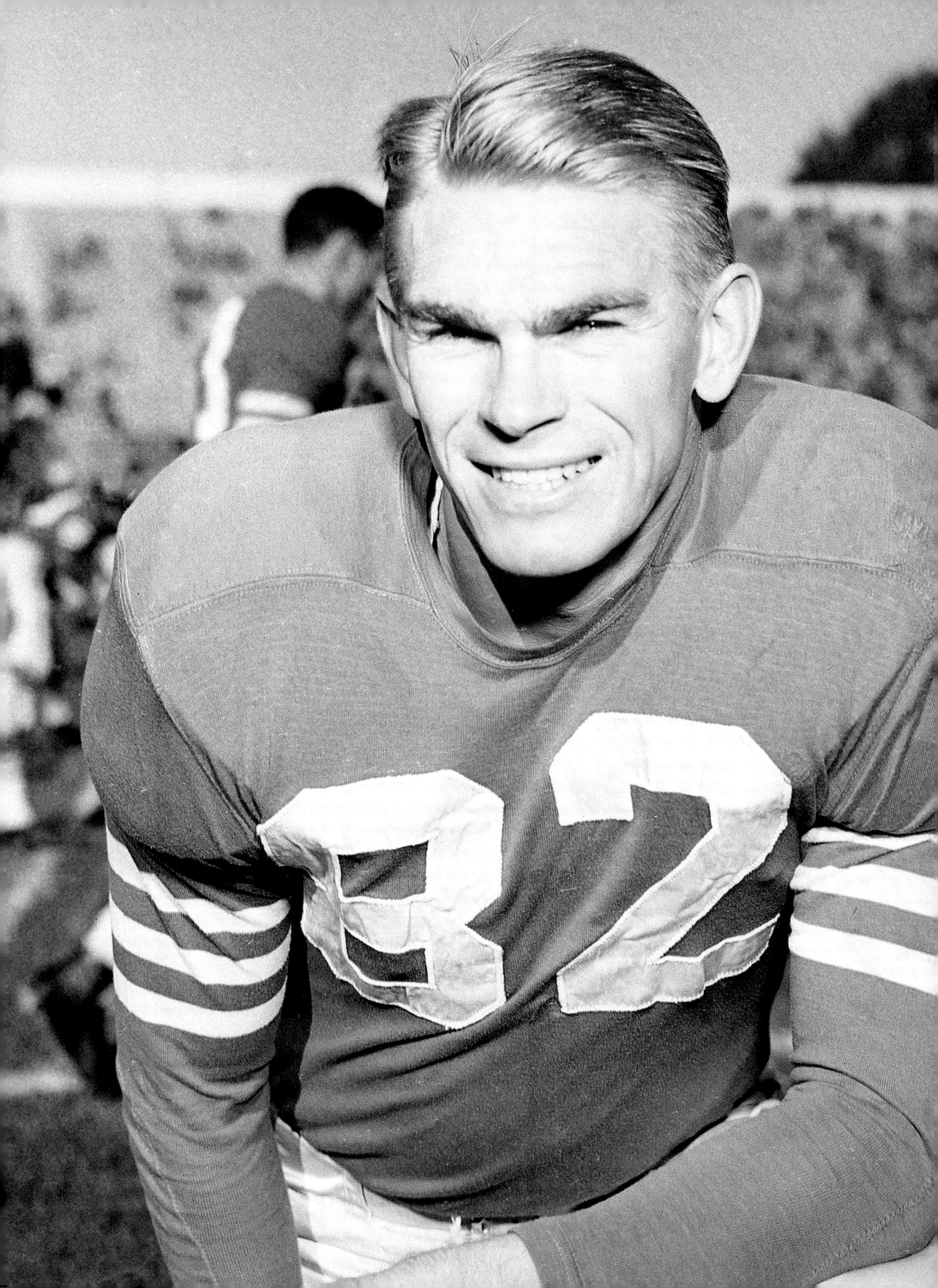

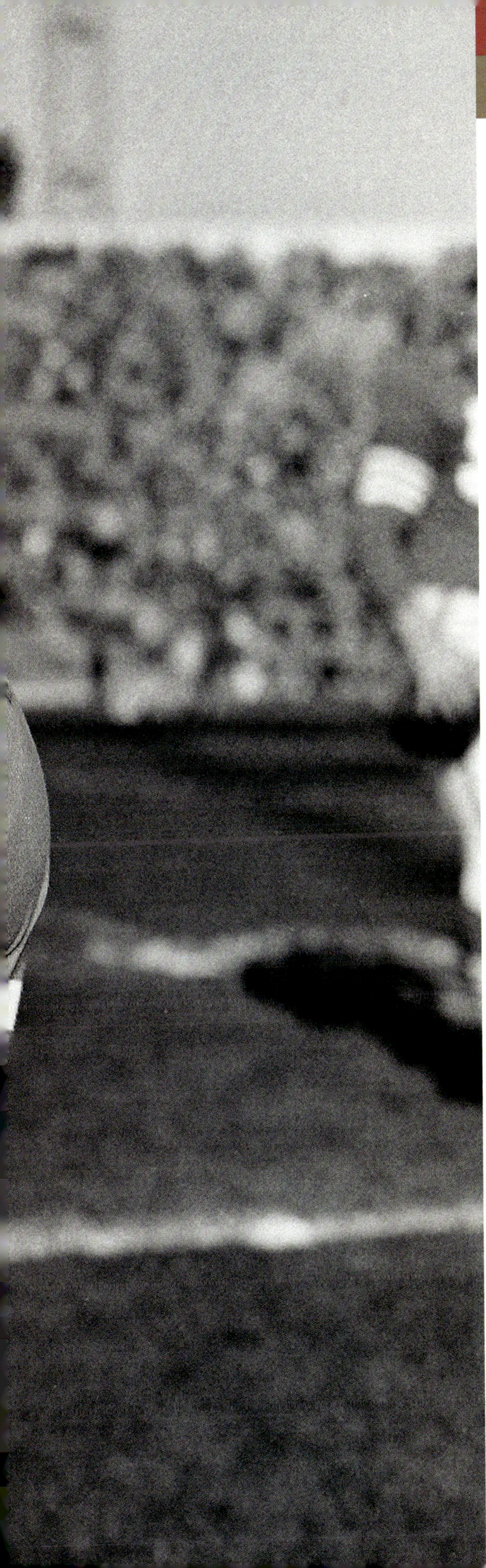

GORDON SOLTAU

- » **Wide Receiver/Kicker 1950–1958**
- » **Three-time All-Pro**
- » **Three-time Pro Bowl selection**

Gordon Soltau was one of the most versatile players in San Francisco 49ers history. After serving in the Navy during World War II, the Minnesota-born Soltau joined the Niners in 1950, their first season in the NFL. In the era of two-way players, Soltau racked up points at both wide receiver and kicker. Against the Los Angeles Rams in 1951, he caught three touchdown passes, kicked a field goal and converted five extra-point attempts. He led the NFL in scoring in 1952 and 1953. One of the game's original iron men, Soltau missed only two games during his entire nine-year career in San Francisco, and was the first Niner to reach 100 games played.

Soltau led the Niners in scoring in eight of his nine seasons.

CHARLES HALEY

- » **Defensive End/Linebacker 1986–1991, 1998–1999**
- » **Five-time Super Bowl champion**
- » **Two-time All-Pro**
- » **Five-time Pro Bowl selection**
- » **Pro Football Hall of Fame 2015**

Charles Haley was a destructive force on the field and a complicated figure off of it. Diagnosed with bipolar disorder only after his playing career was over, Haley was often at odds with teammates and opponents alike at a time when mental illness was less widely acknowledged. Beyond question was his ability to win at the highest level: only quarterback Tom Brady has won more Super Bowls than Haley's five, the first two of which came with the Niners. He racked up 12 sacks as a rookie in 1986, then 11.5 and 10.5 in 1989 and 1990, respectively, as San Francisco won back-to-back Super Bowls.

Haley became a prototype for the modern pass rusher after being drafted by the Niners in 1986.

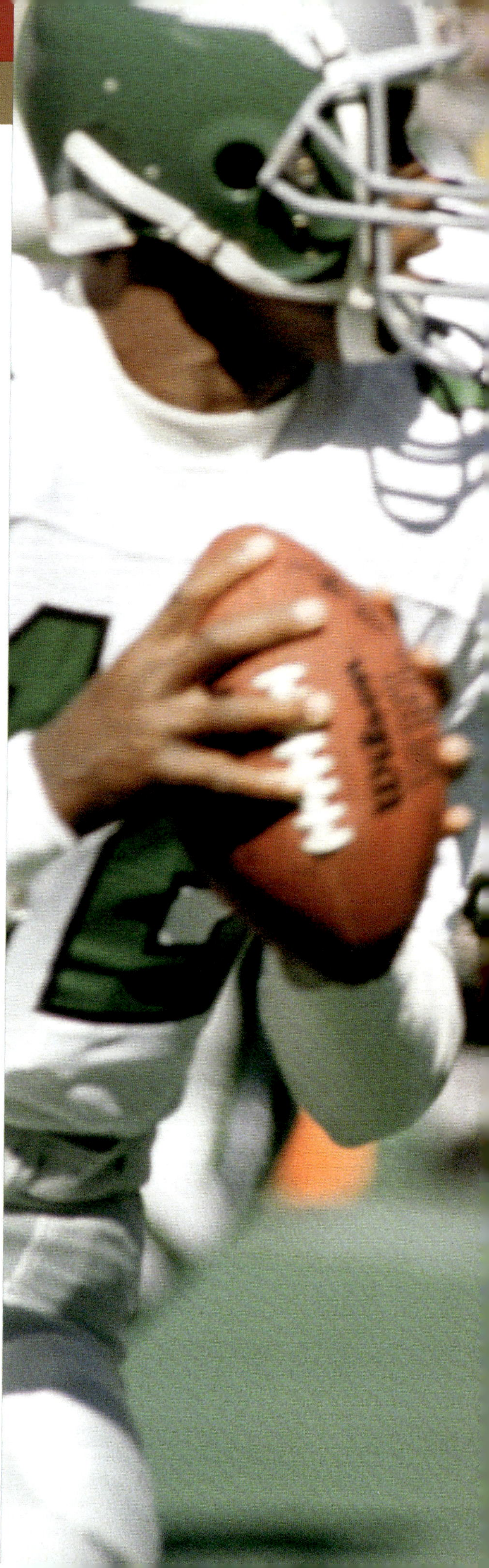

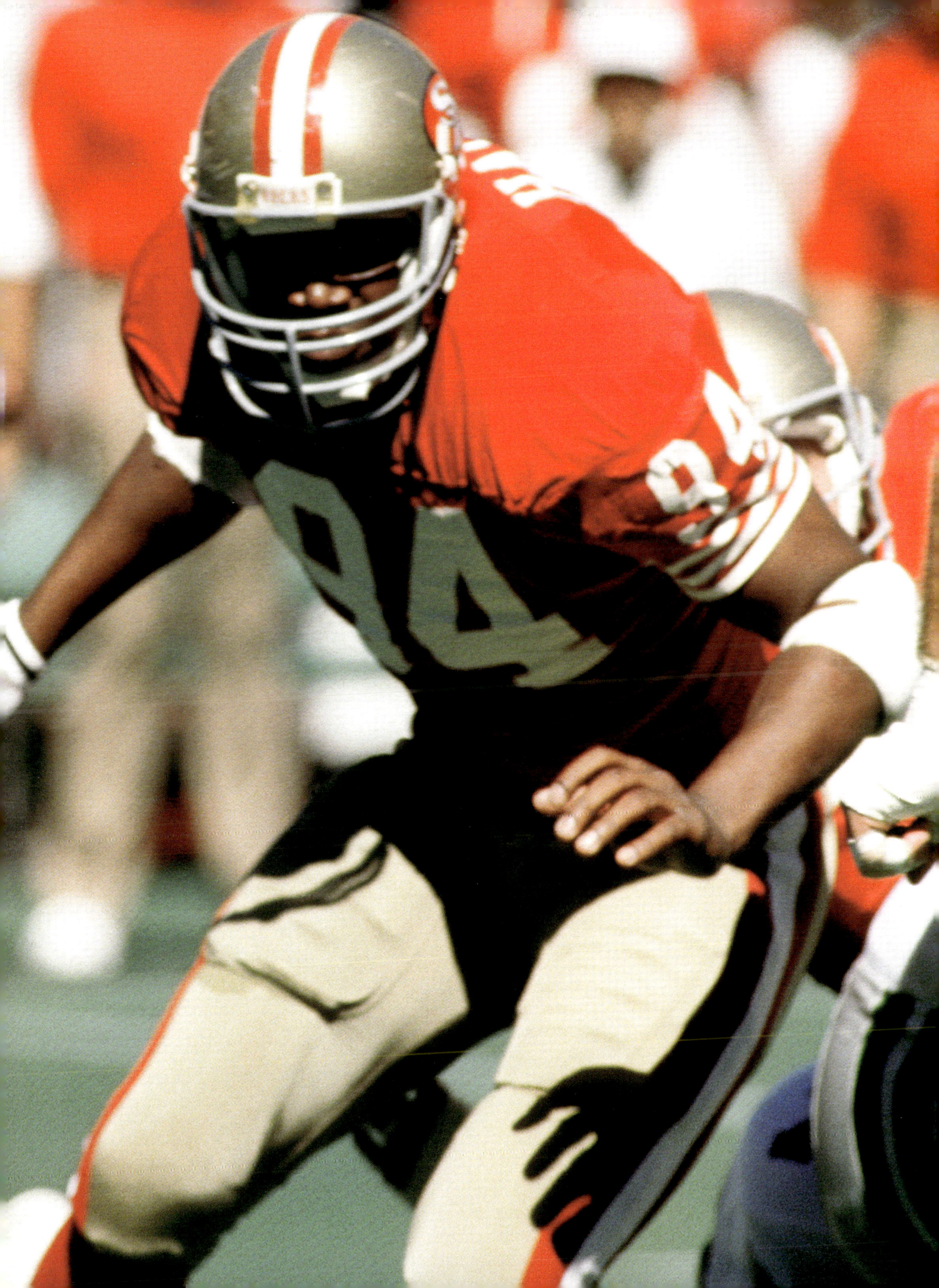

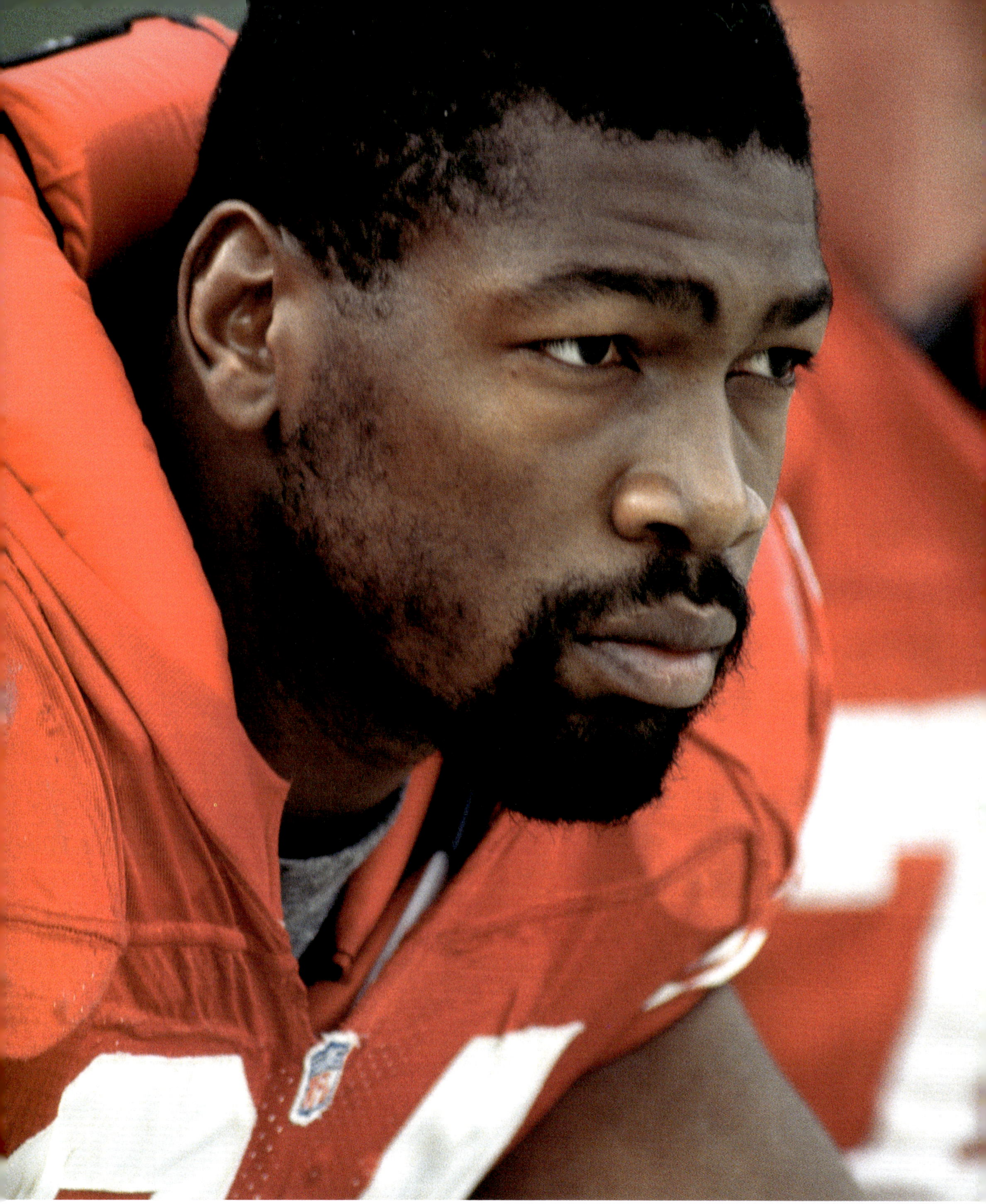

Though often misunderstood by those around him, there was no doubt Haley was too much for most blockers to handle (right).

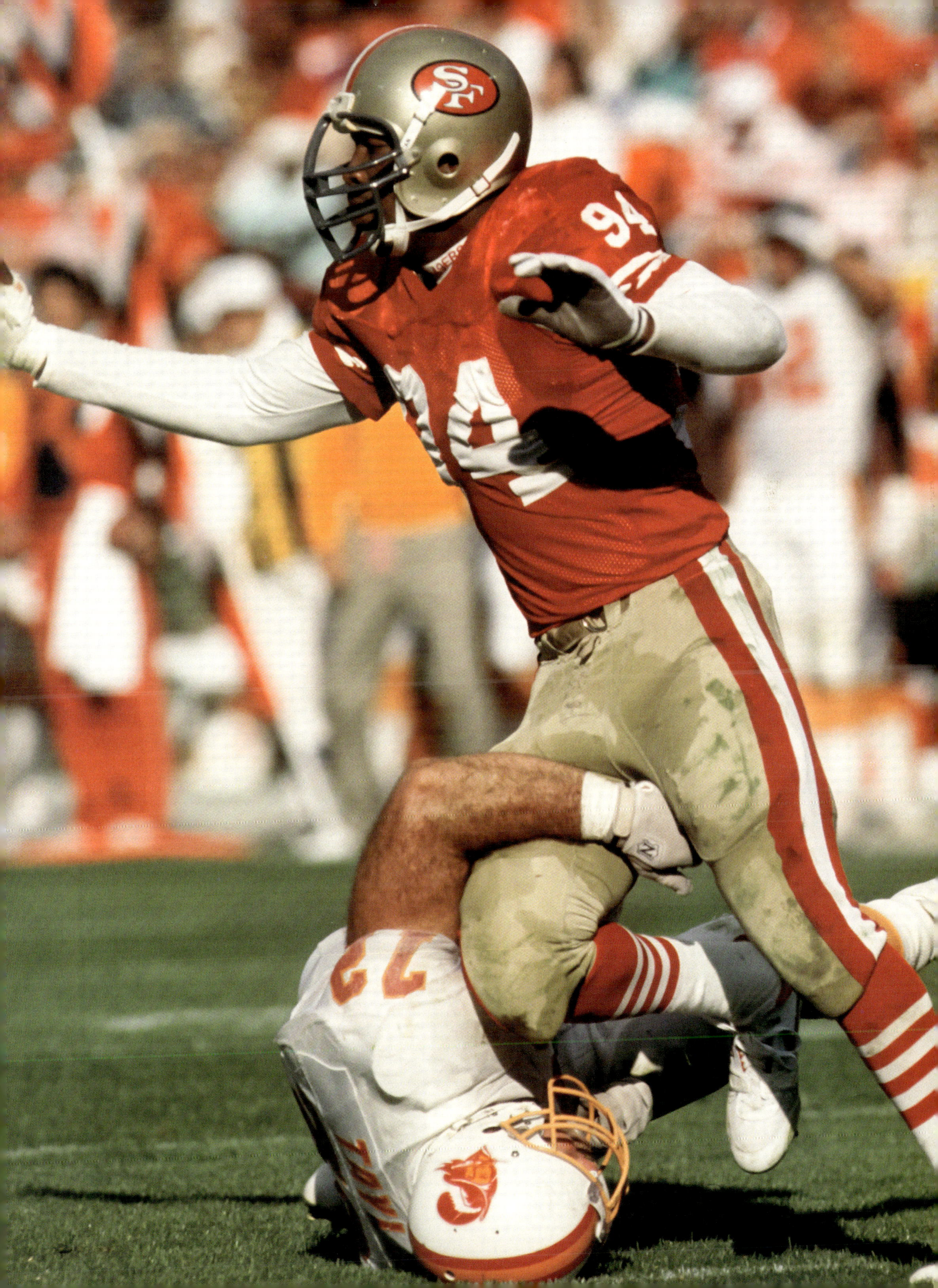

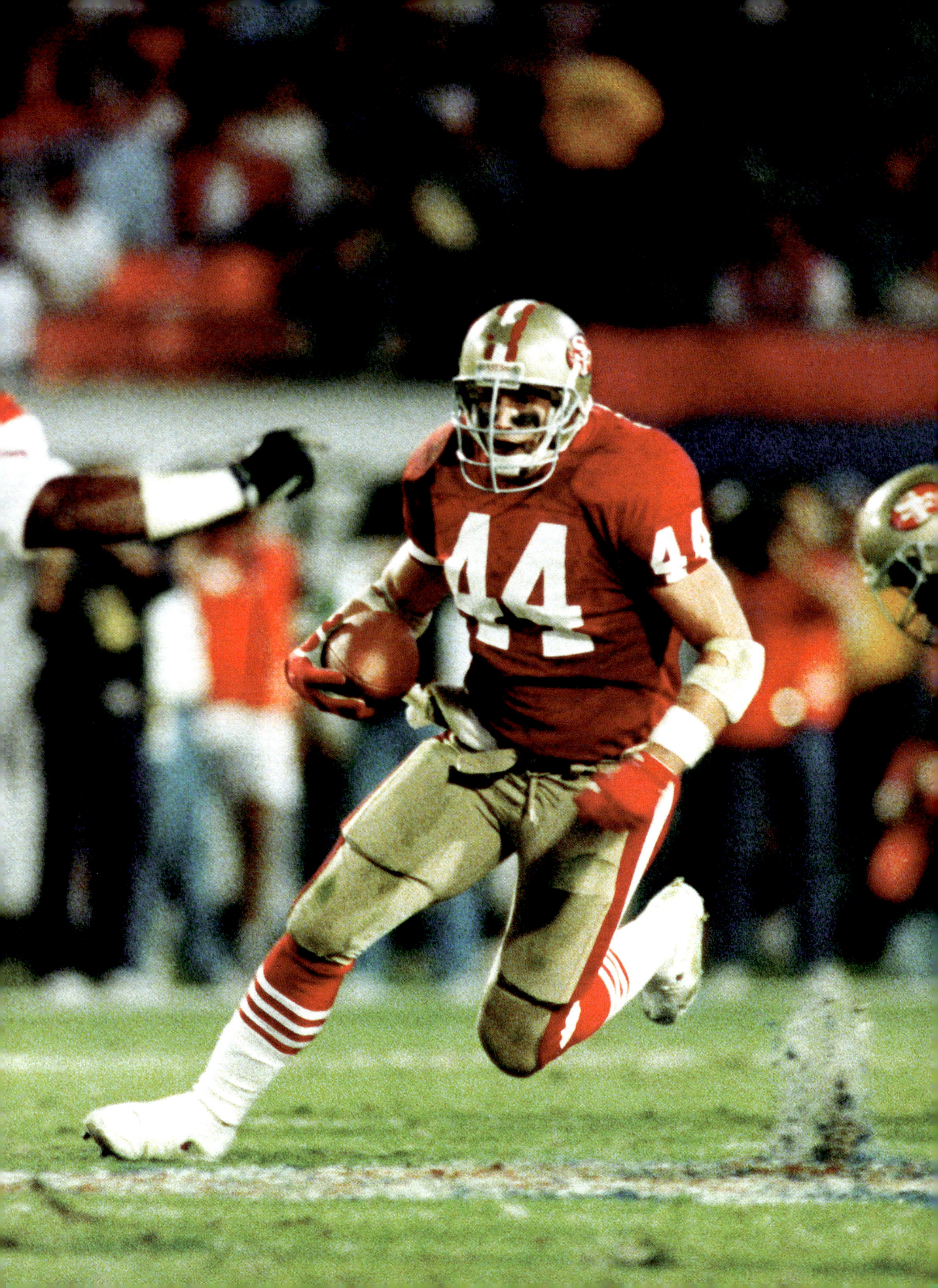
44
44

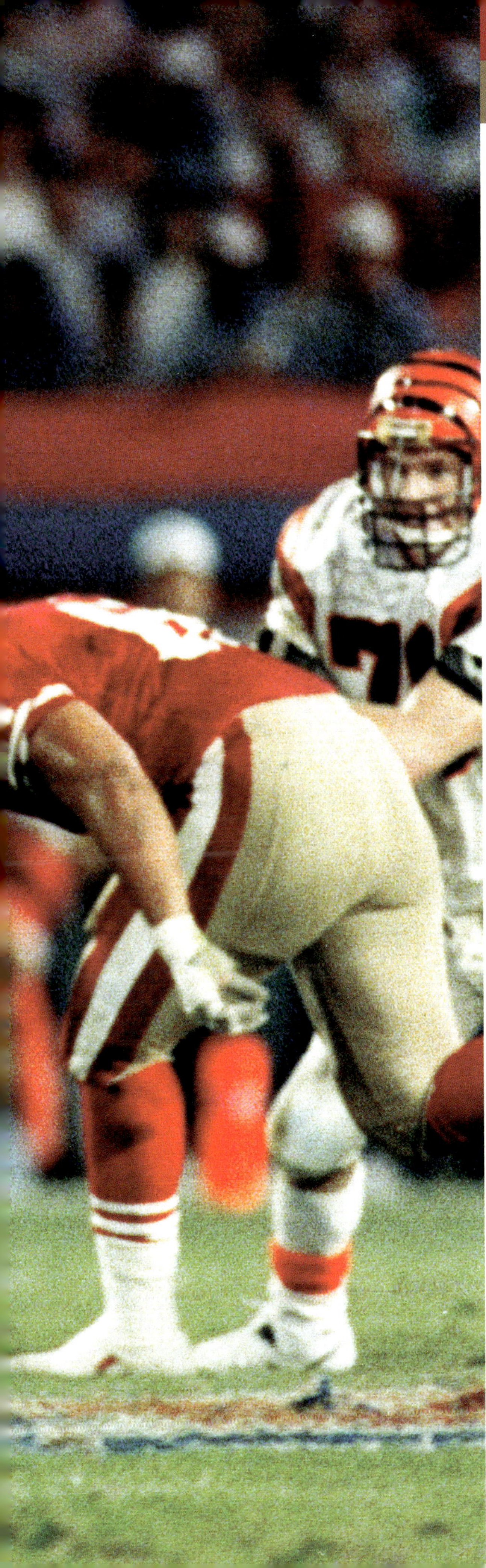

TOM RATHMAN

» **Fullback 1986–1993**

» **Two-time Super Bowl champion**

Though less heralded than teammates such as Joe Montana and Jerry Rice, fullback Tom Rathman played a critical role in Bill Walsh's West Coast offense of the 1980s. A bruising blocker drafted out of the University of Nebraska in 1986, Rathman opened up holes for fellow Husker alumnus Roger Craig and gained yards on his own as both a runner and receiver. In Super Bowl XXIV, he rushed for 38 yards, caught four passes for 43 more and scored two touchdowns. He retired after racking up 4,704 total yards and 34 touchdowns. After his playing days were over, he served two separate stints as San Francisco's running backs coach.

Rathman was a productive runner when he wasn't blocking for Roger Craig or protecting Joe Montana.

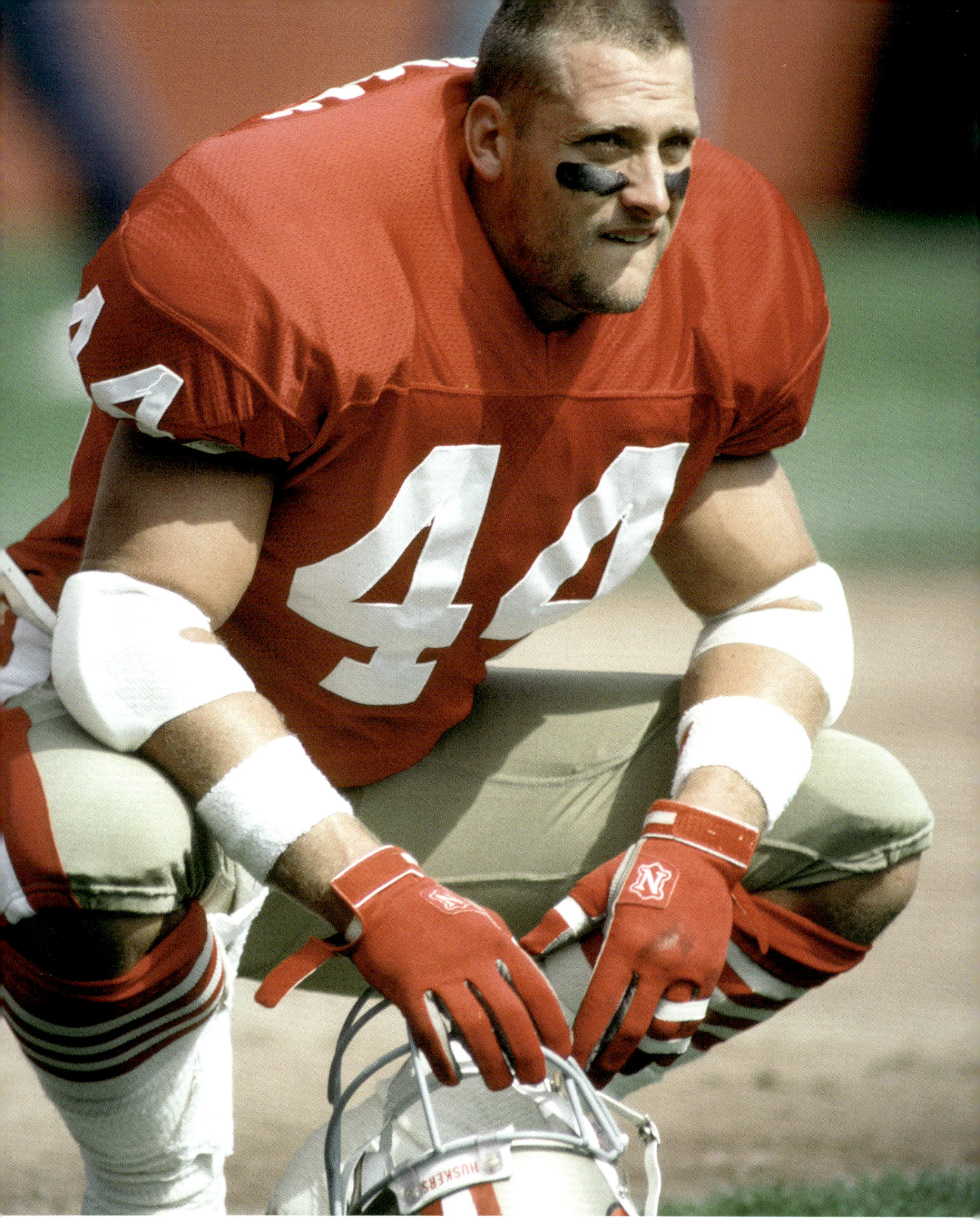

After the best regular season of his career, Rathman carried the ball 11 times and scored twice against Denver in Super Bowl XXIV.

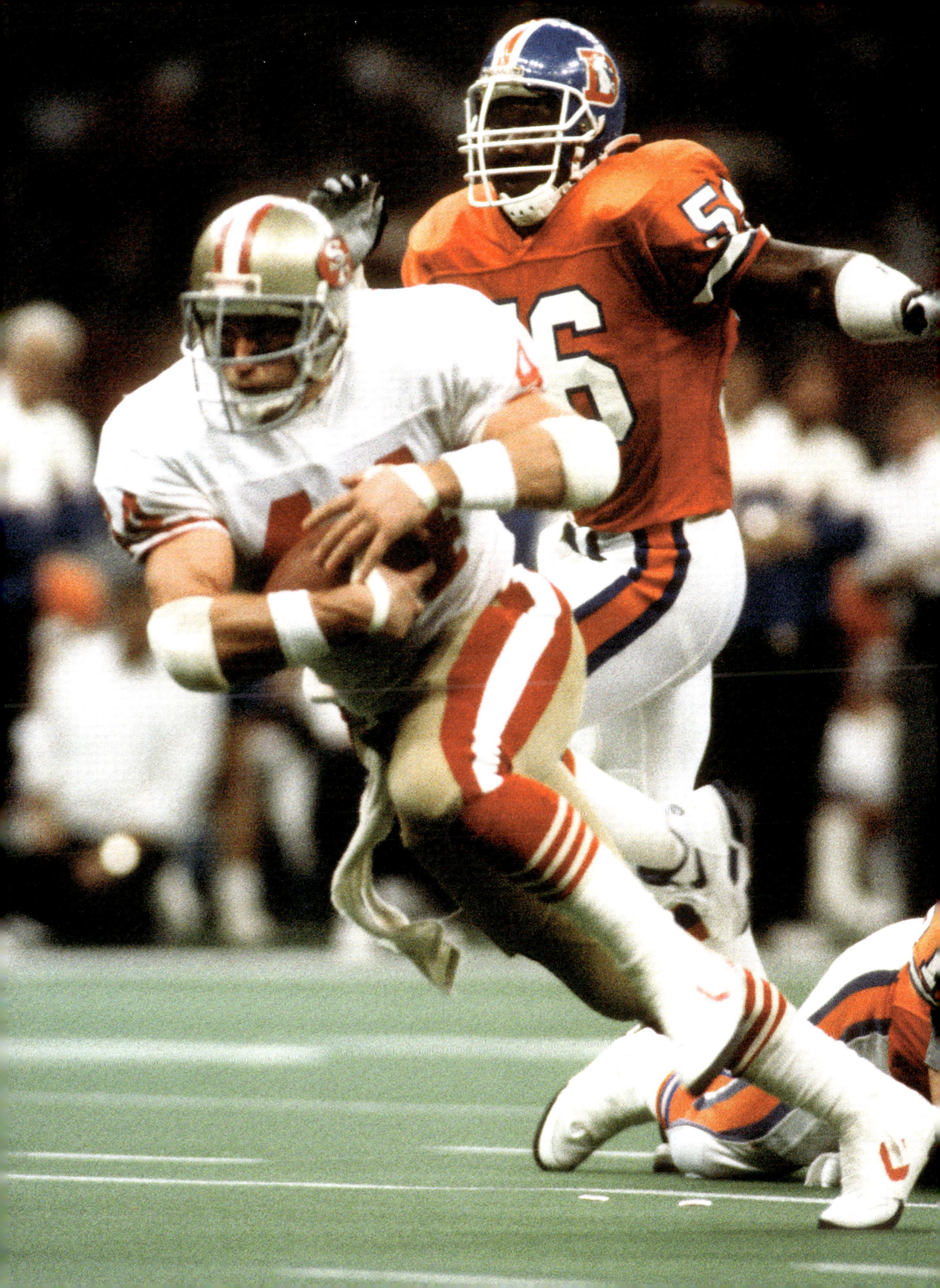

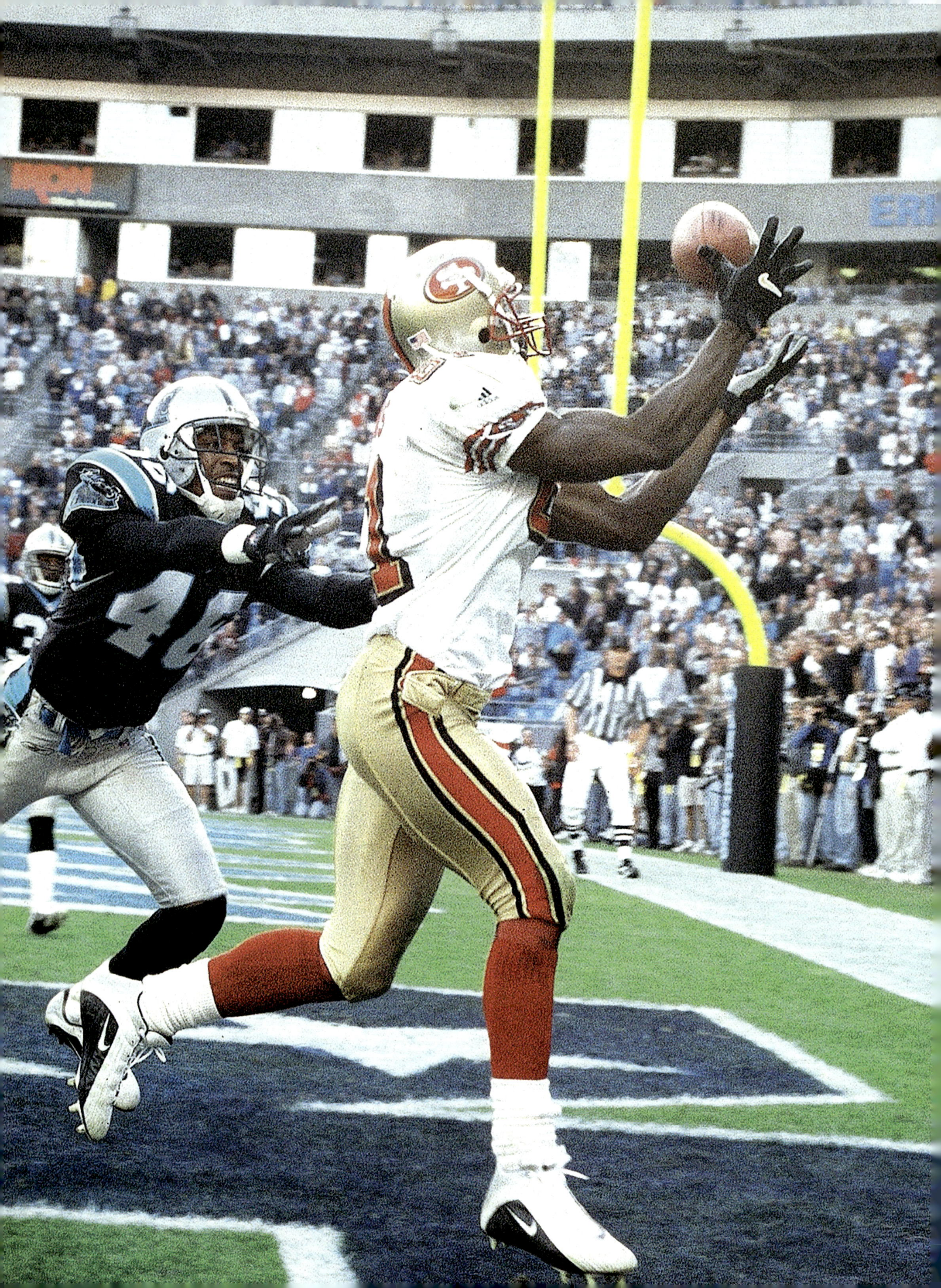
46

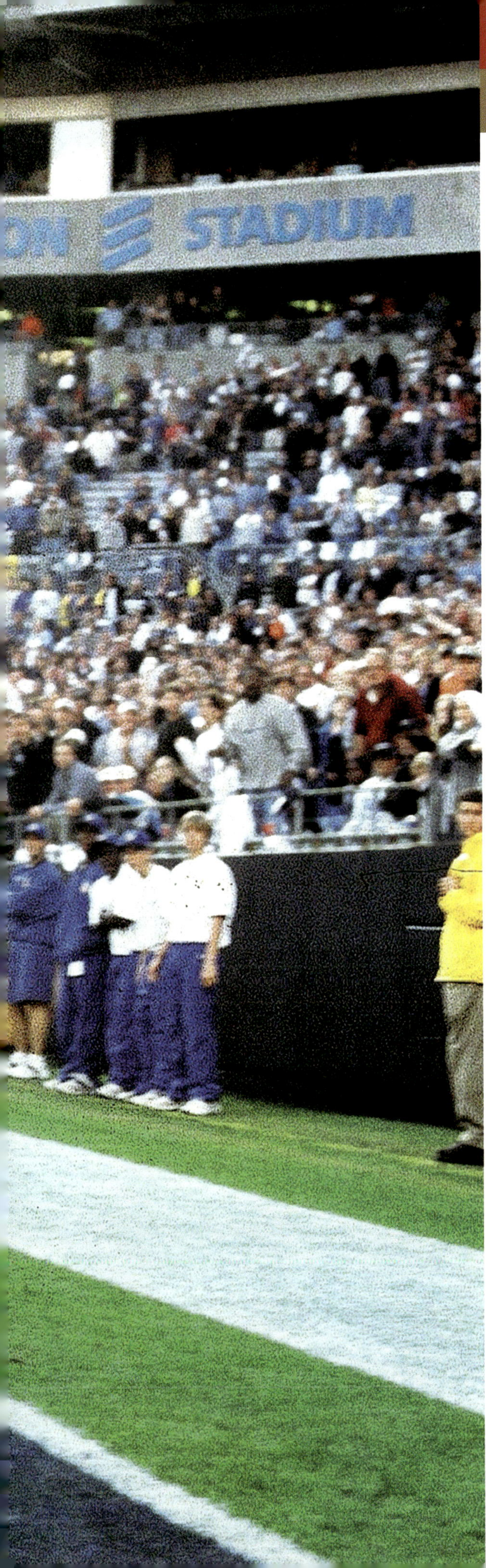

TERRELL OWENS

- » **Wide Receiver 1996–2003**
- » **Five-time All-Pro**
- » **Six-time Pro Bowl selection**
- » **Pro Football Hall of Fame 2018**

While Jerry Rice may be the most accomplished wide receiver in Niners history, Terrell Owens may be the most colorful. Selected in the third round of the 1996 NFL draft, Owens stepped in for an injured Rice in 1987 and recorded 936 receiving yards and eight touchdowns. The following year, Owens gained 1,097 yards, the first of his nine career 1,000-yard seasons. In 1999, he made one of the most memorable receptions in team history, hauling in a game-winning touchdown pass from Steve Young with eight seconds left to beat the Green Bay Packers in a playoff game. He ranks third in NFL history in both receiving yards and touchdown catches, and is second to only Rice in Niners history in yards, catches and touchdowns.

Though mercurial in private, there was no denying Terrell Owens's ability on the field.

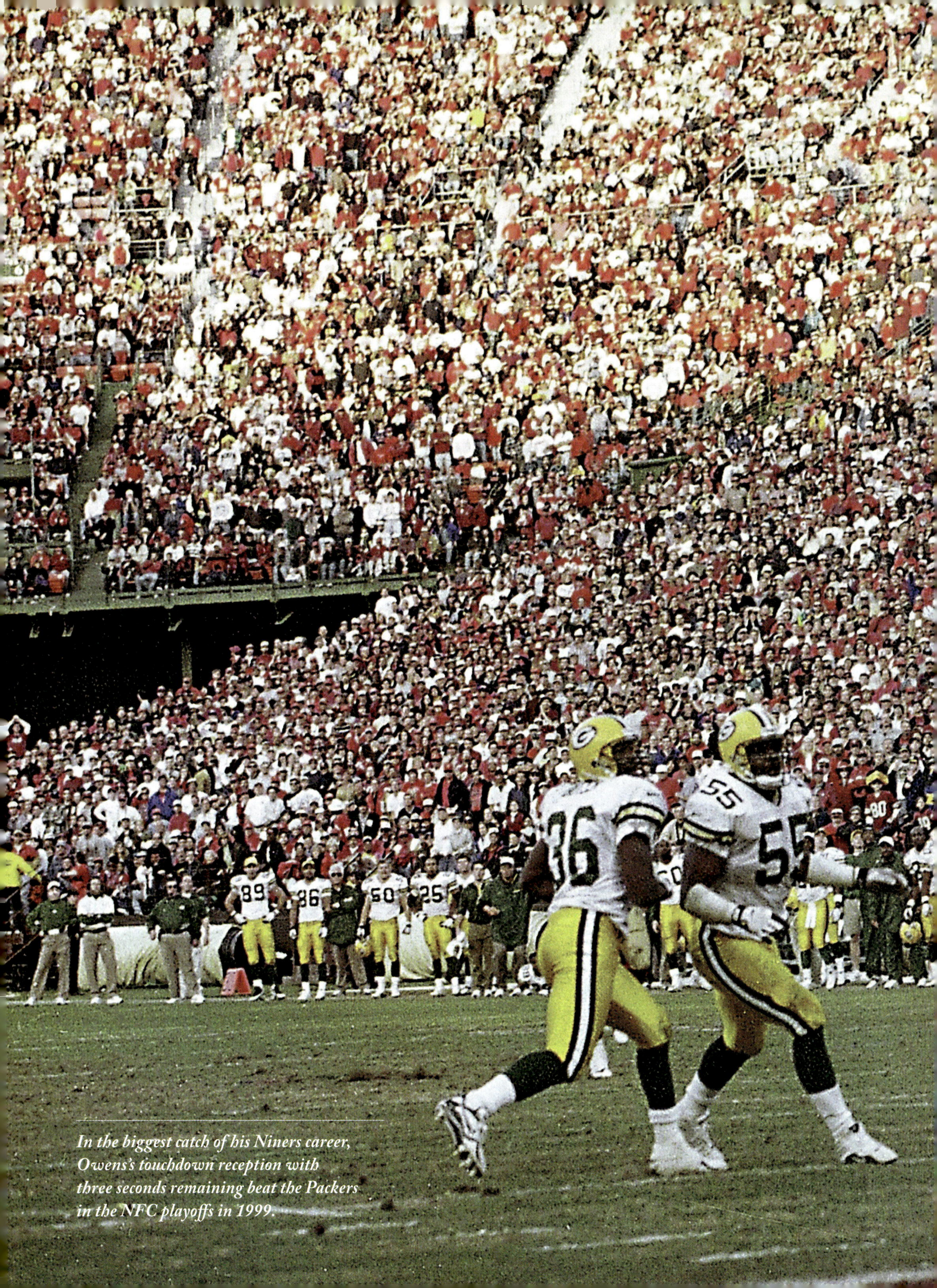

In the biggest catch of his Niners career, Owens's touchdown reception with three seconds remaining beat the Packers in the NFC playoffs in 1999.

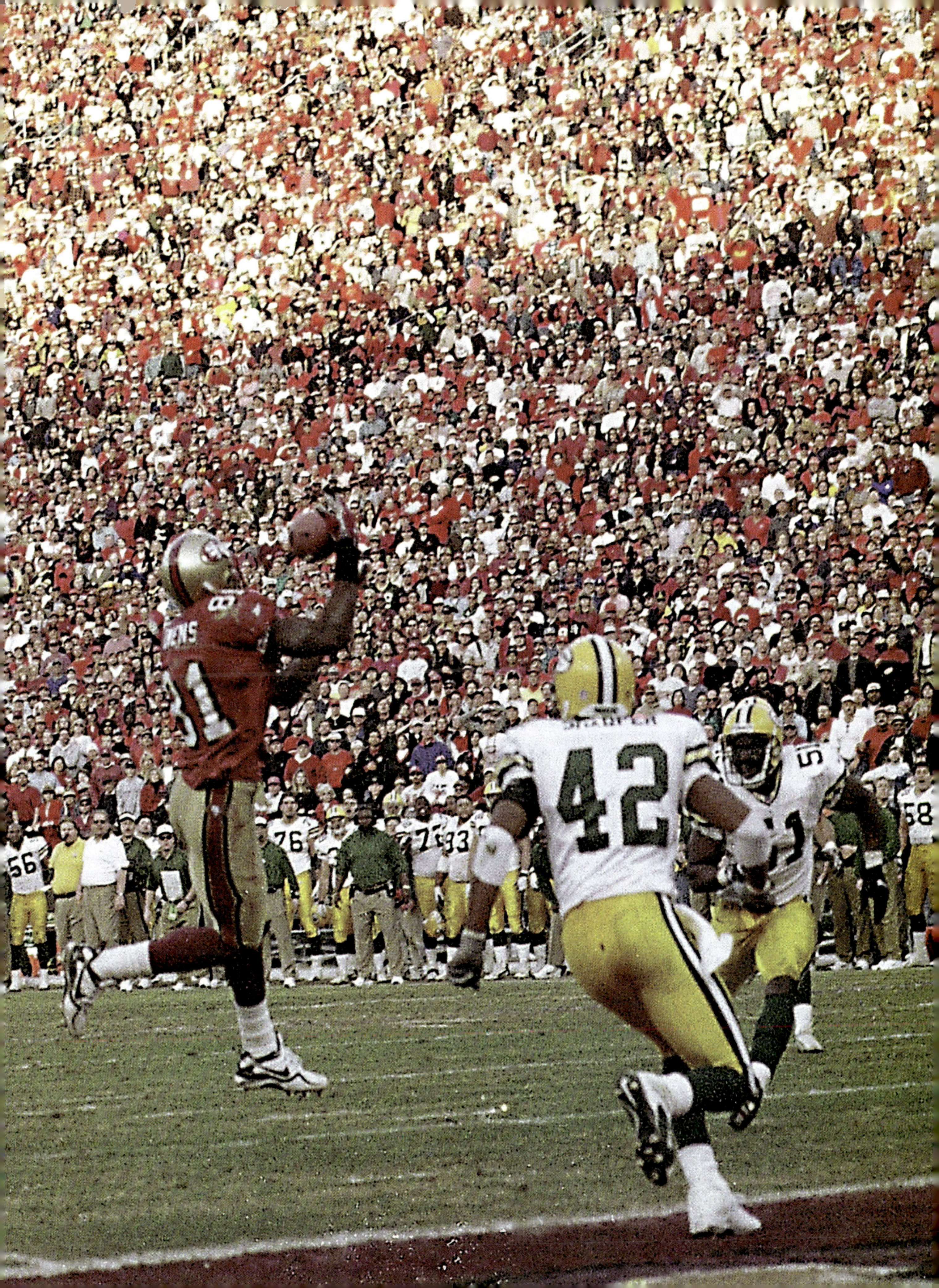

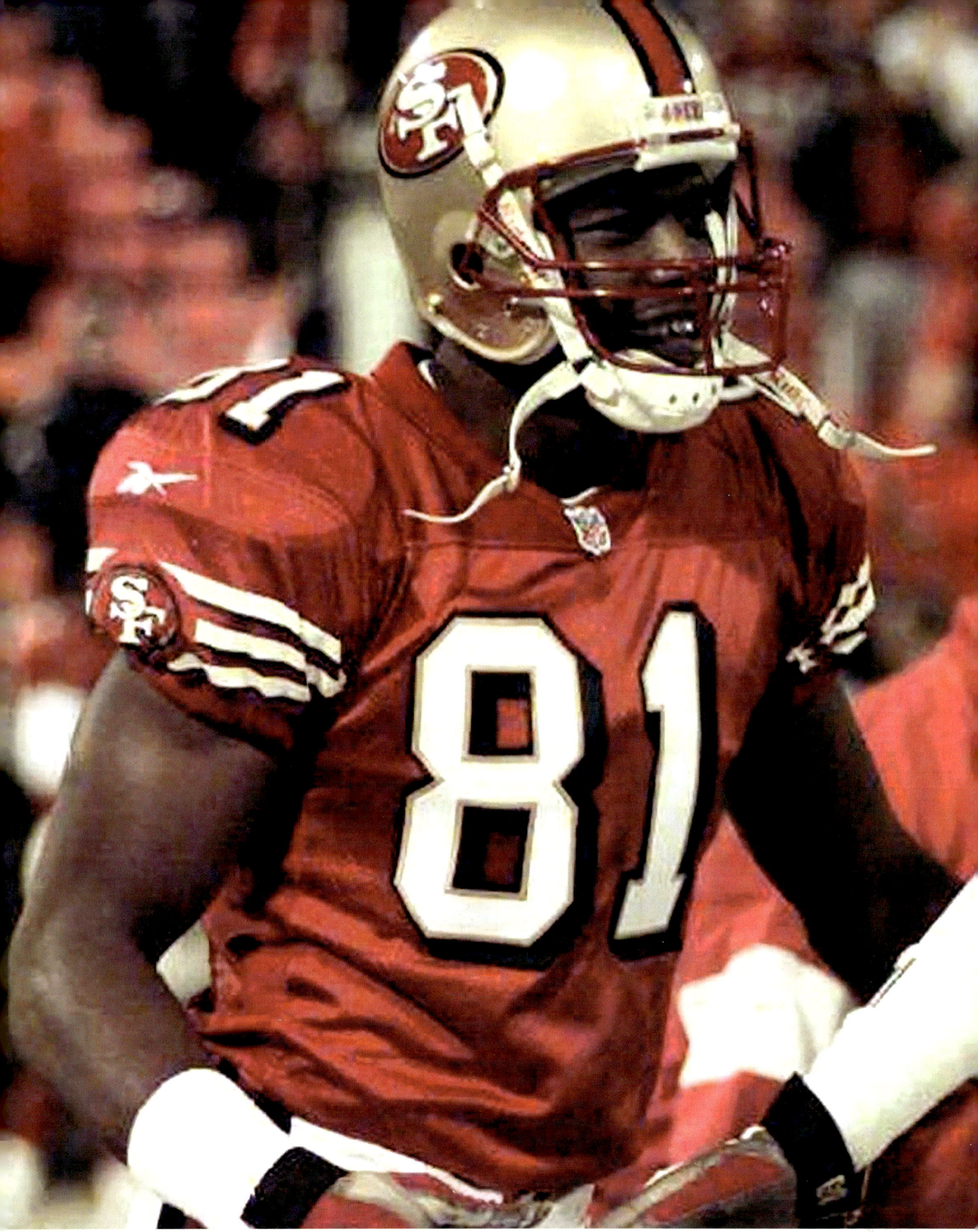

Owens's physical stature made him difficult to cover for most cornerbacks.

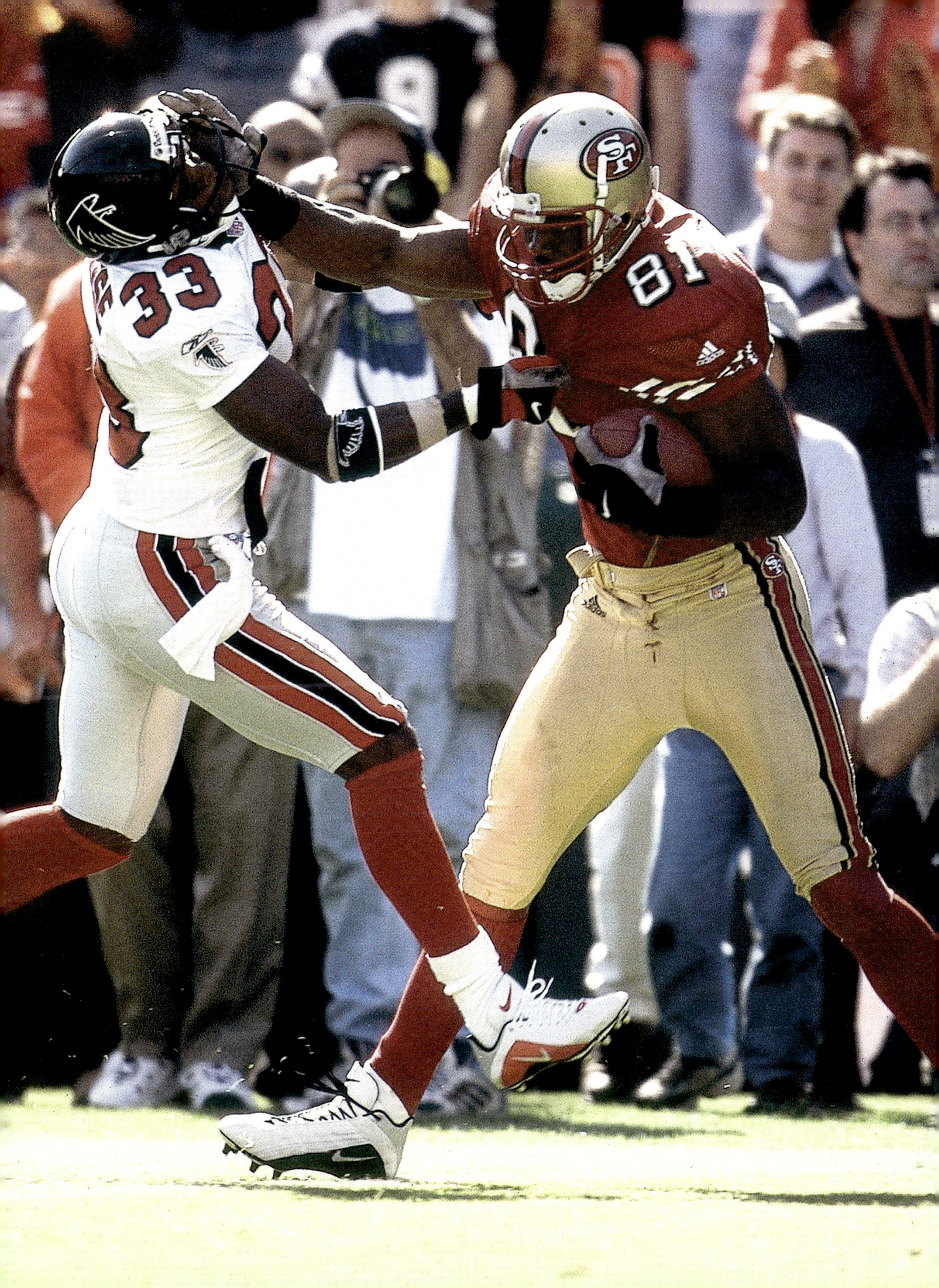
33
81

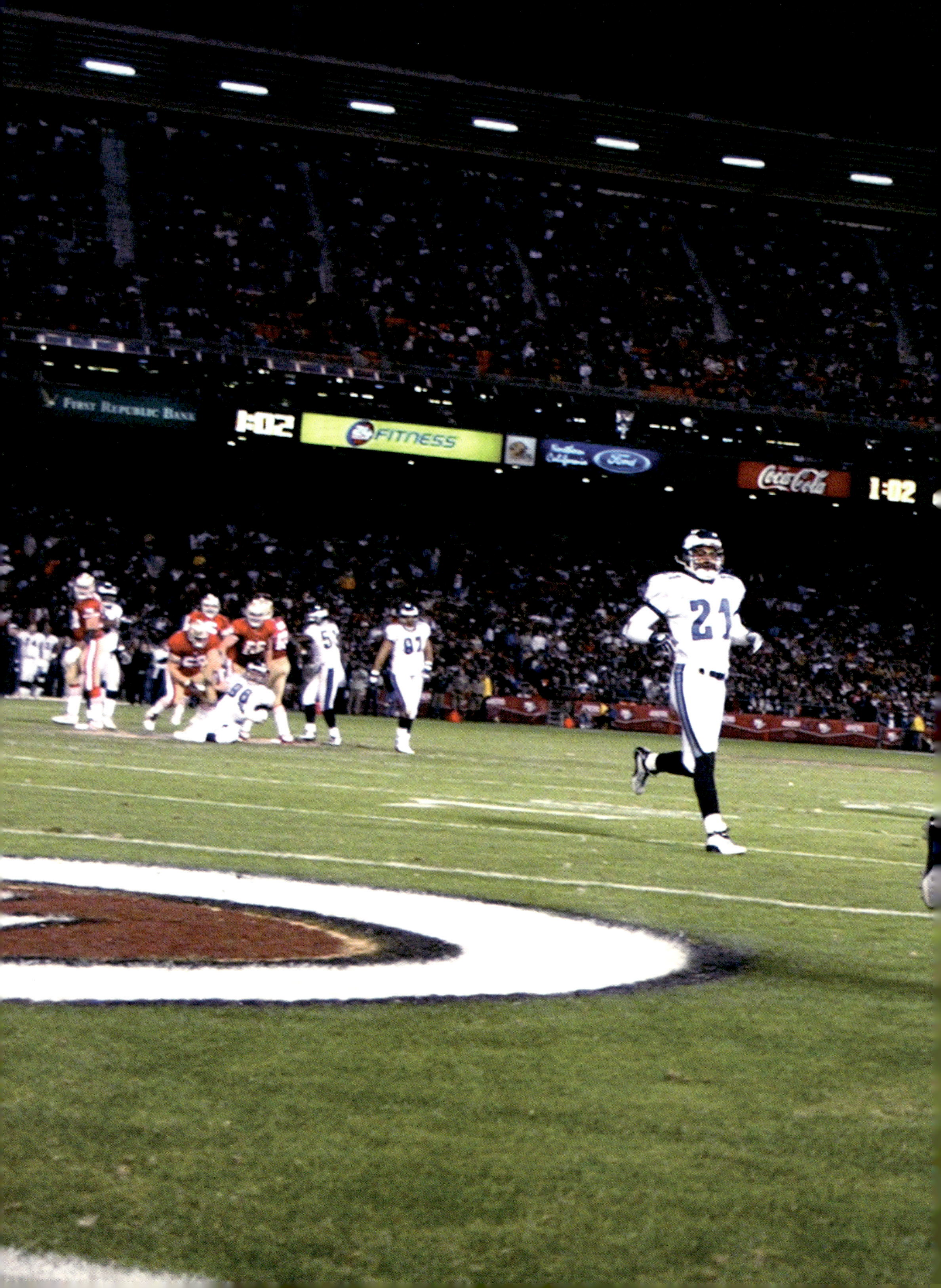
First Republic Bank
1:02
FITNESS
Ford
Coca-Cola
1:02

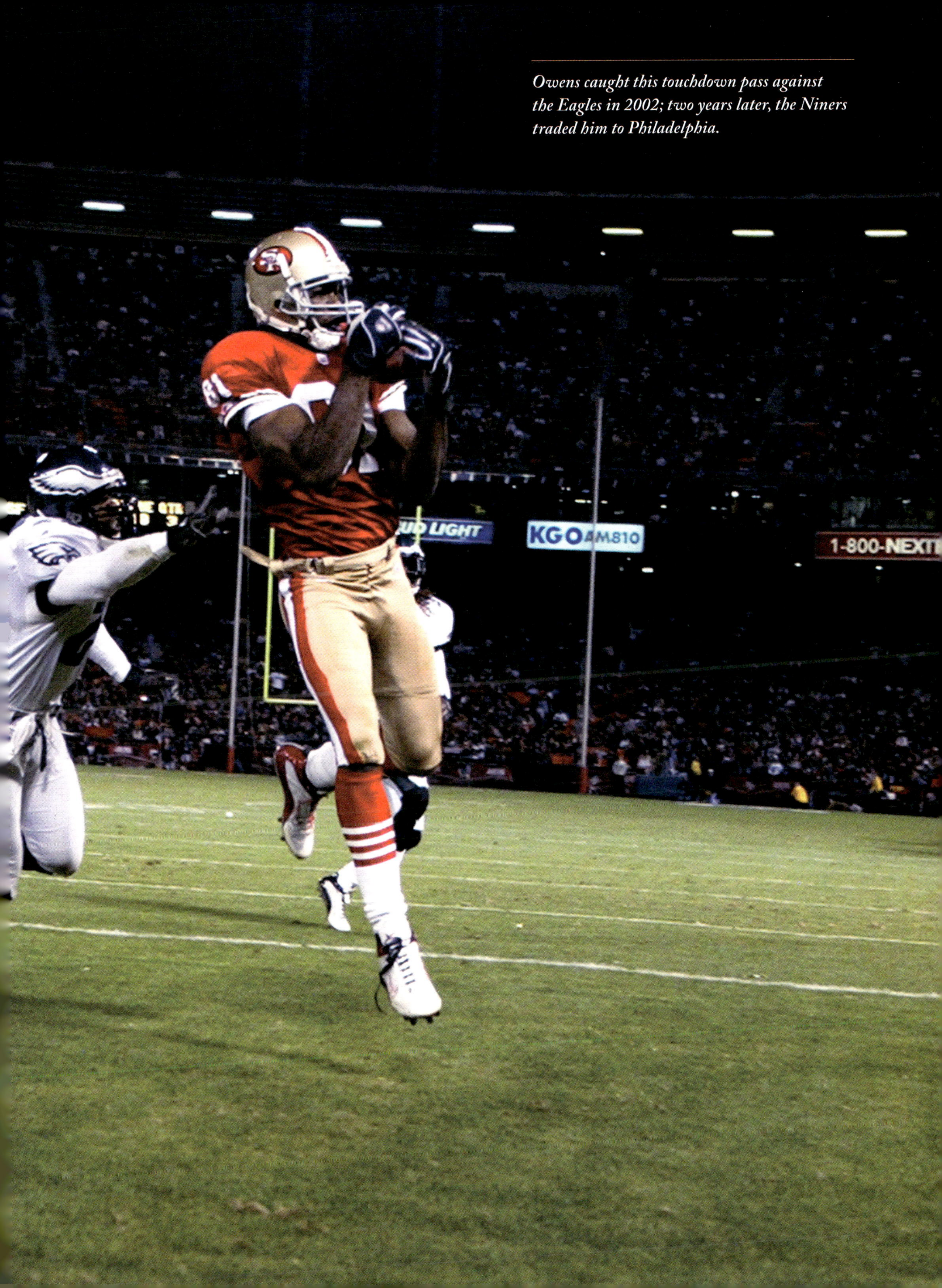

Owens caught this touchdown pass against the Eagles in 2002; two years later, the Niners traded him to Philadelphia.

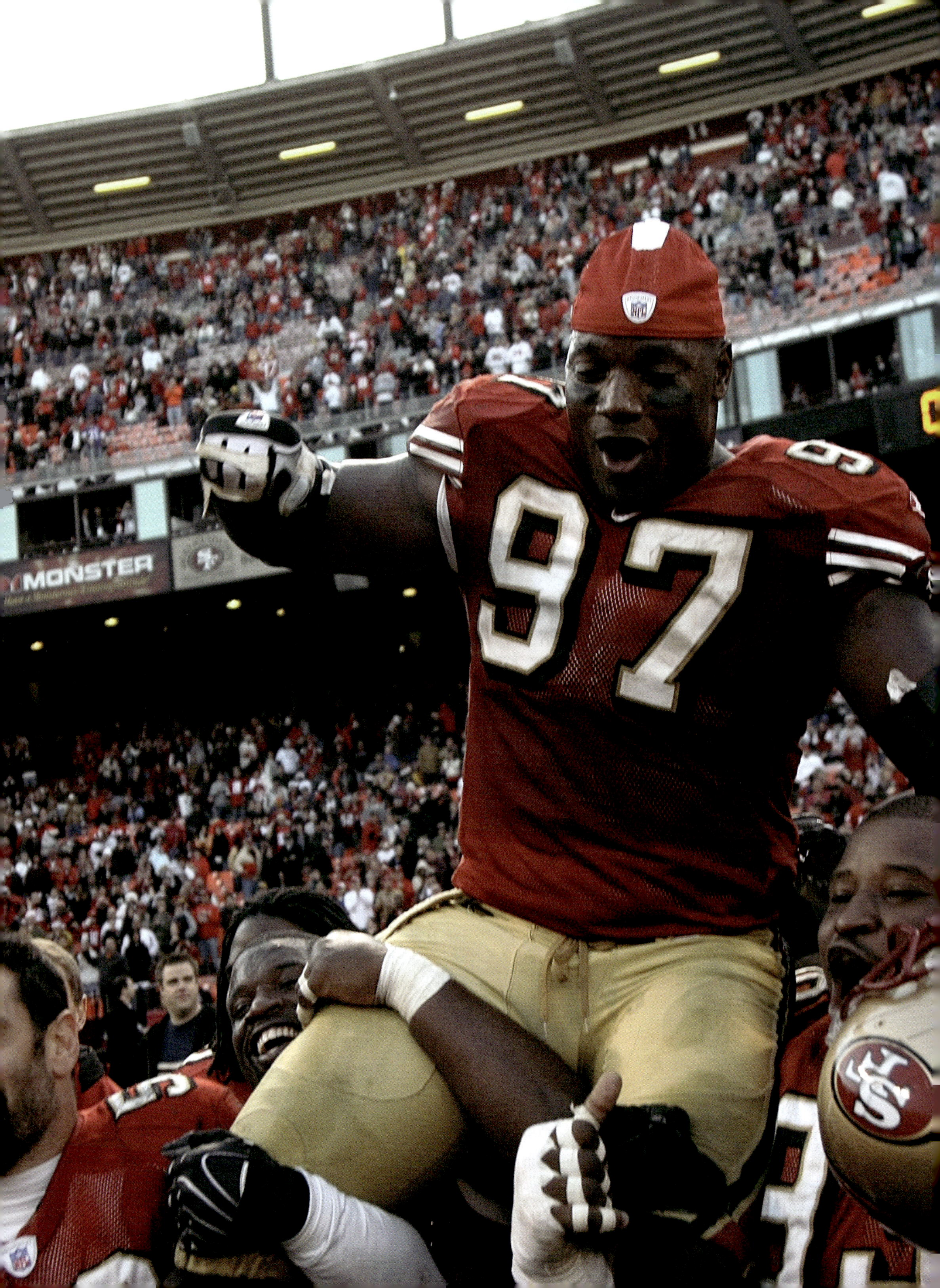
MONSTER
97

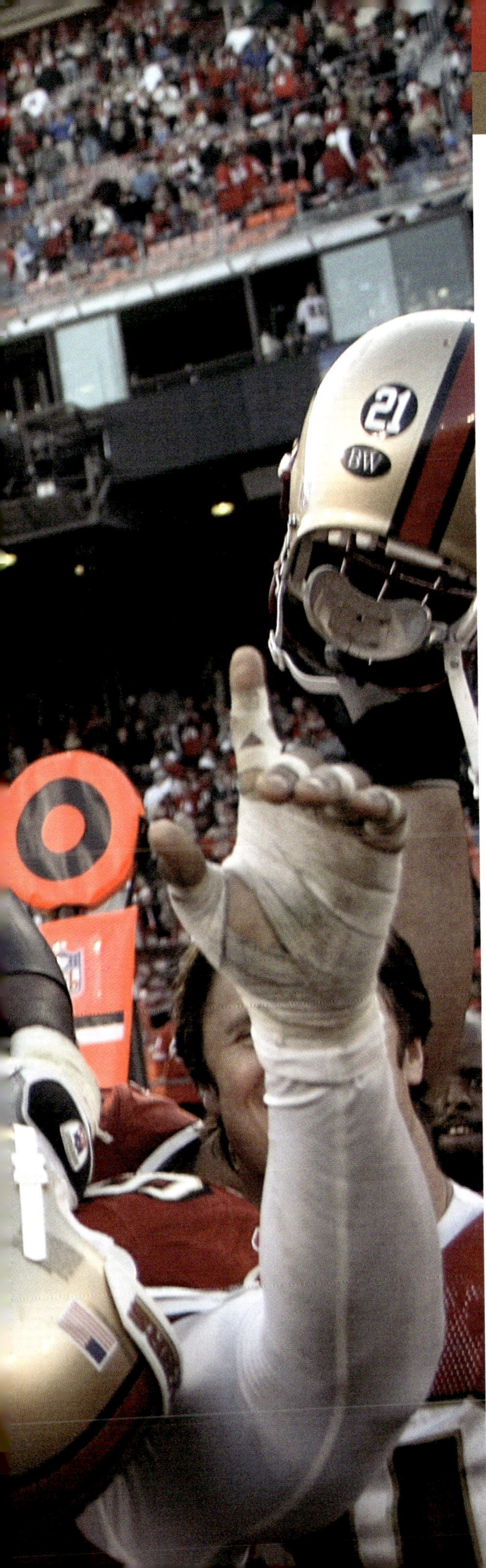

BRYANT YOUNG

- » **Defensive Tackle 1994–2007**
- » **Super Bowl champion**
- » **Four-time All-Pro**
- » **Four-time Pro Bowl selection**

As a rookie in 1994, Bryant Young joined an excellent Niners team that would win Super Bowl XXIX at the end of that season. It turned out to be the only championship of Bryant's 14-year career in San Francisco, but he remains a beloved figure in team history for his steadying influence and leadership skills. Young played in 208 games during his career, all of them starts. The Len Eshmont Award, which the team awards to the player who "best exemplifies the inspirational and courageous play" of its namesake, was given to Bryant an unprecedented eight times.

Beloved by teammates, Young was carried off the field on their shoulders following his final home game in San Francisco.

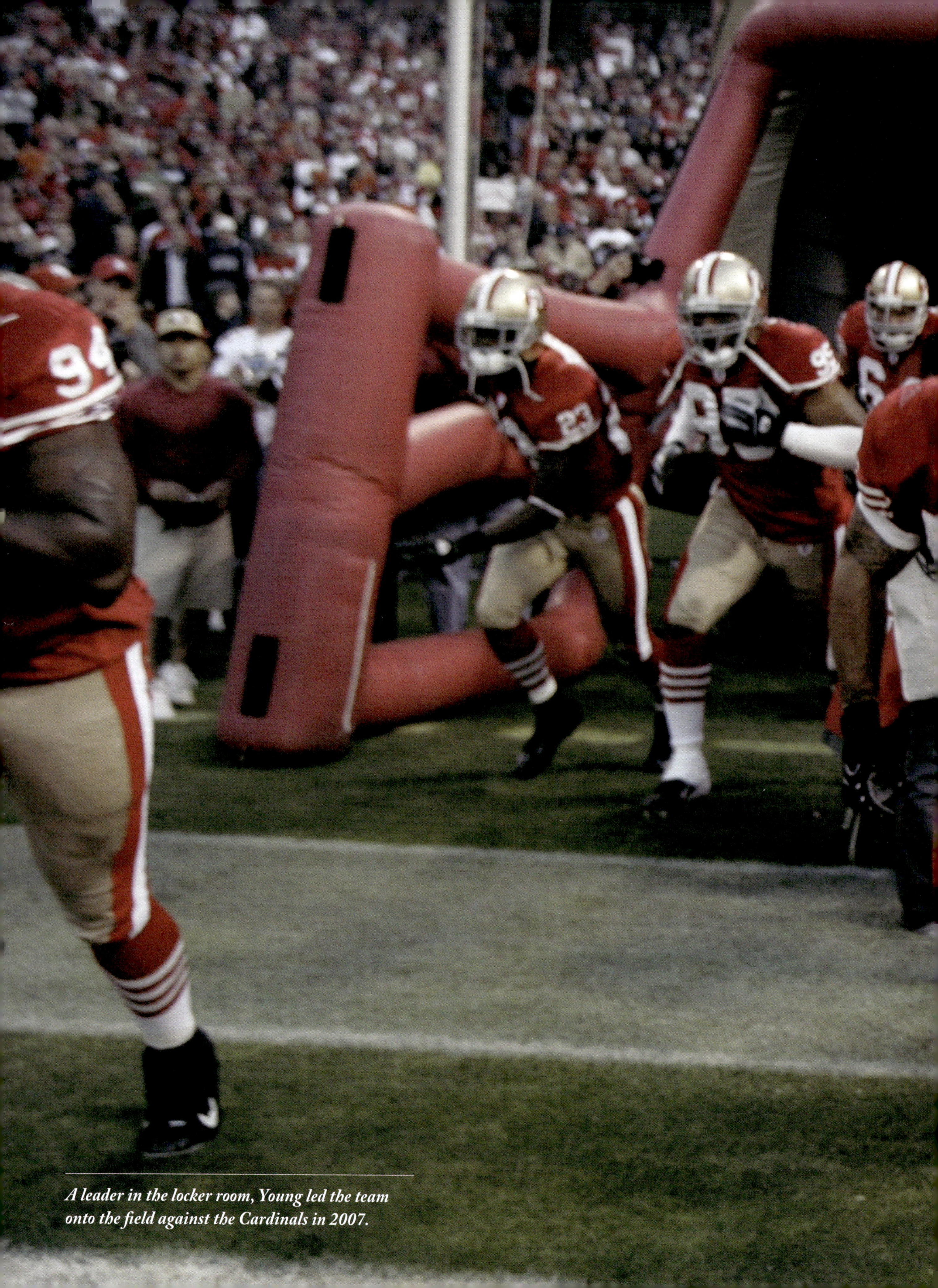

A leader in the locker room, Young led the team onto the field against the Cardinals in 2007.

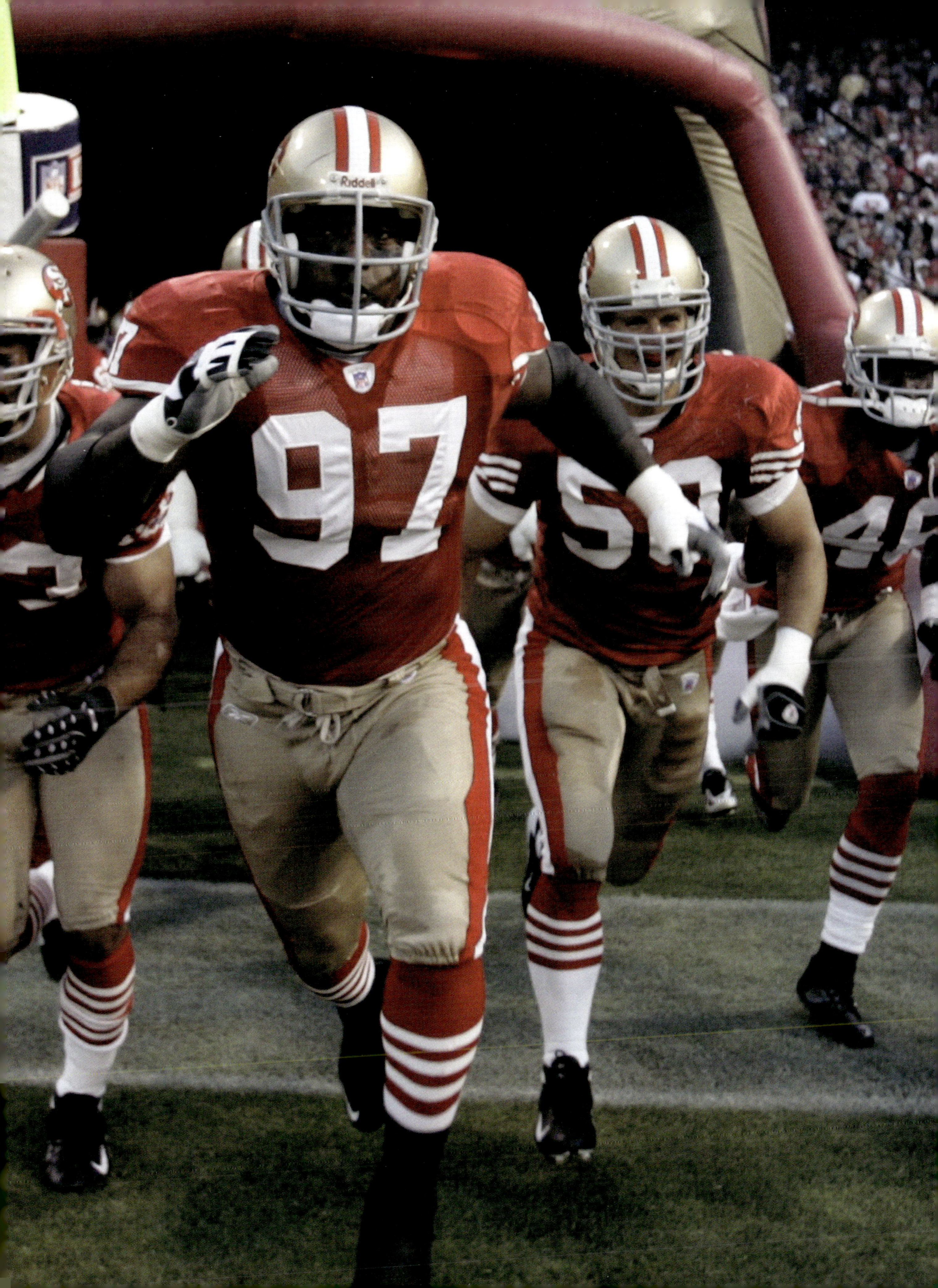
97

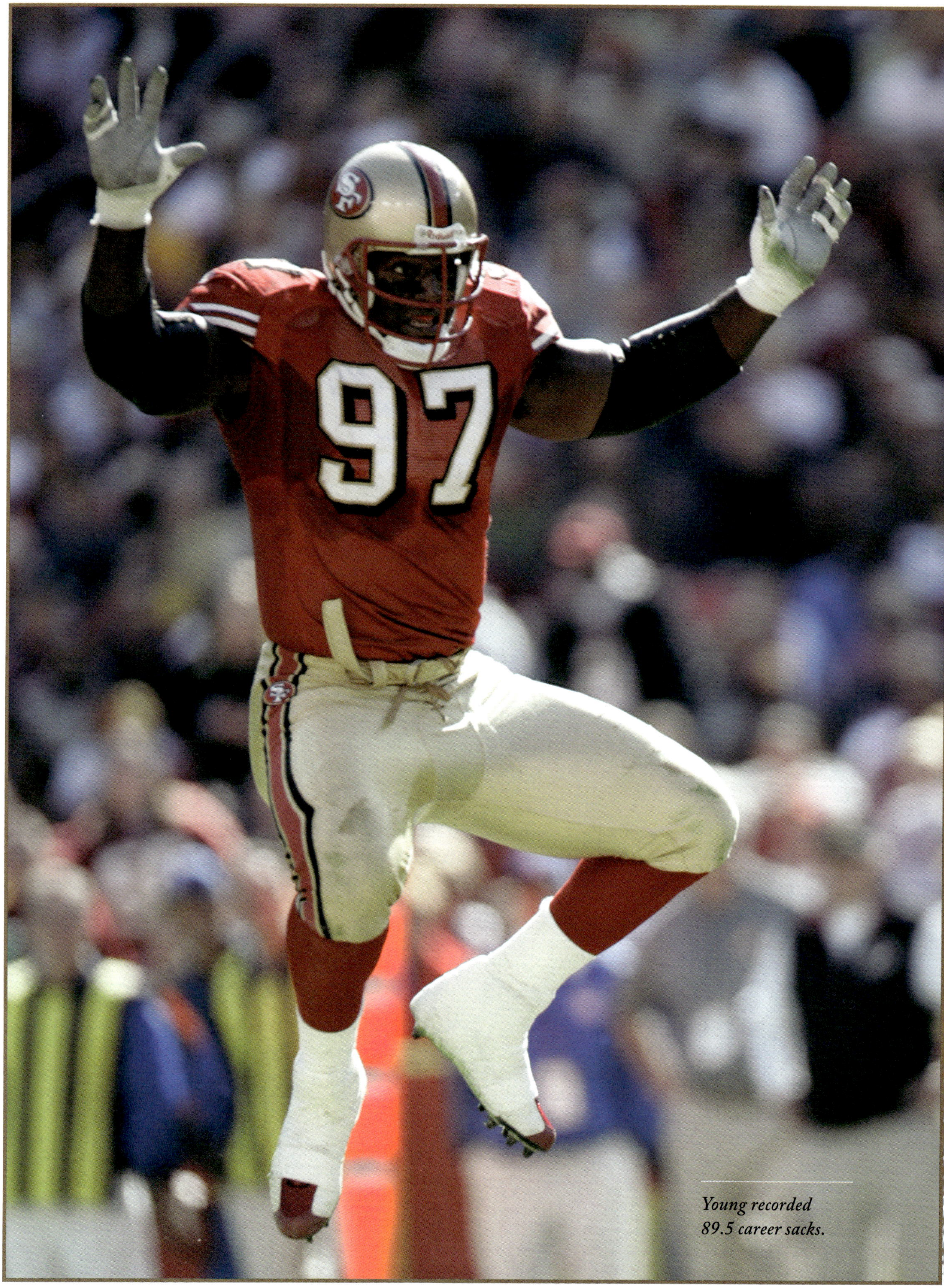

Young recorded 89.5 career sacks.

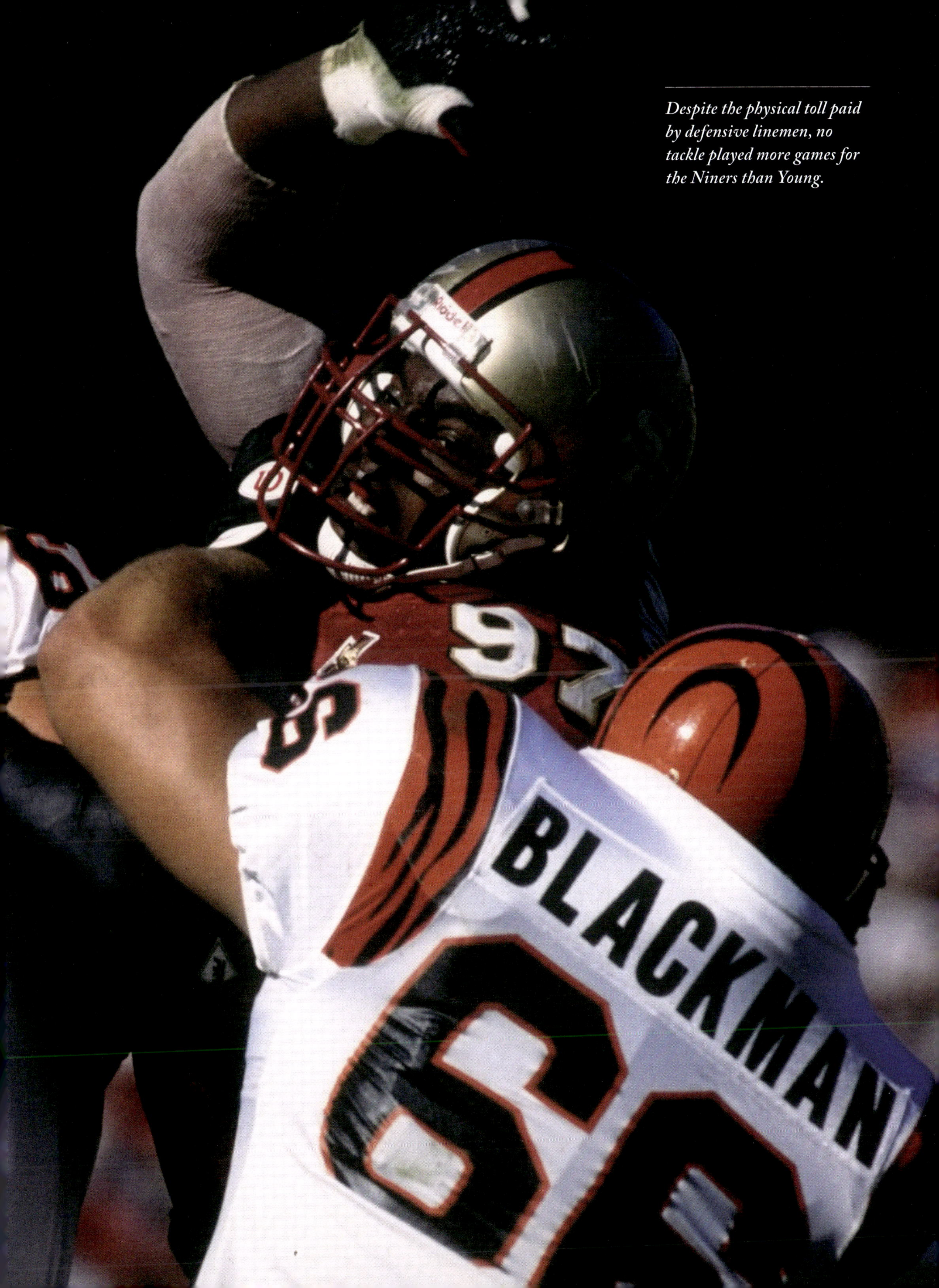

Despite the physical toll paid by defensive linemen, no tackle played more games for the Niners than Young.

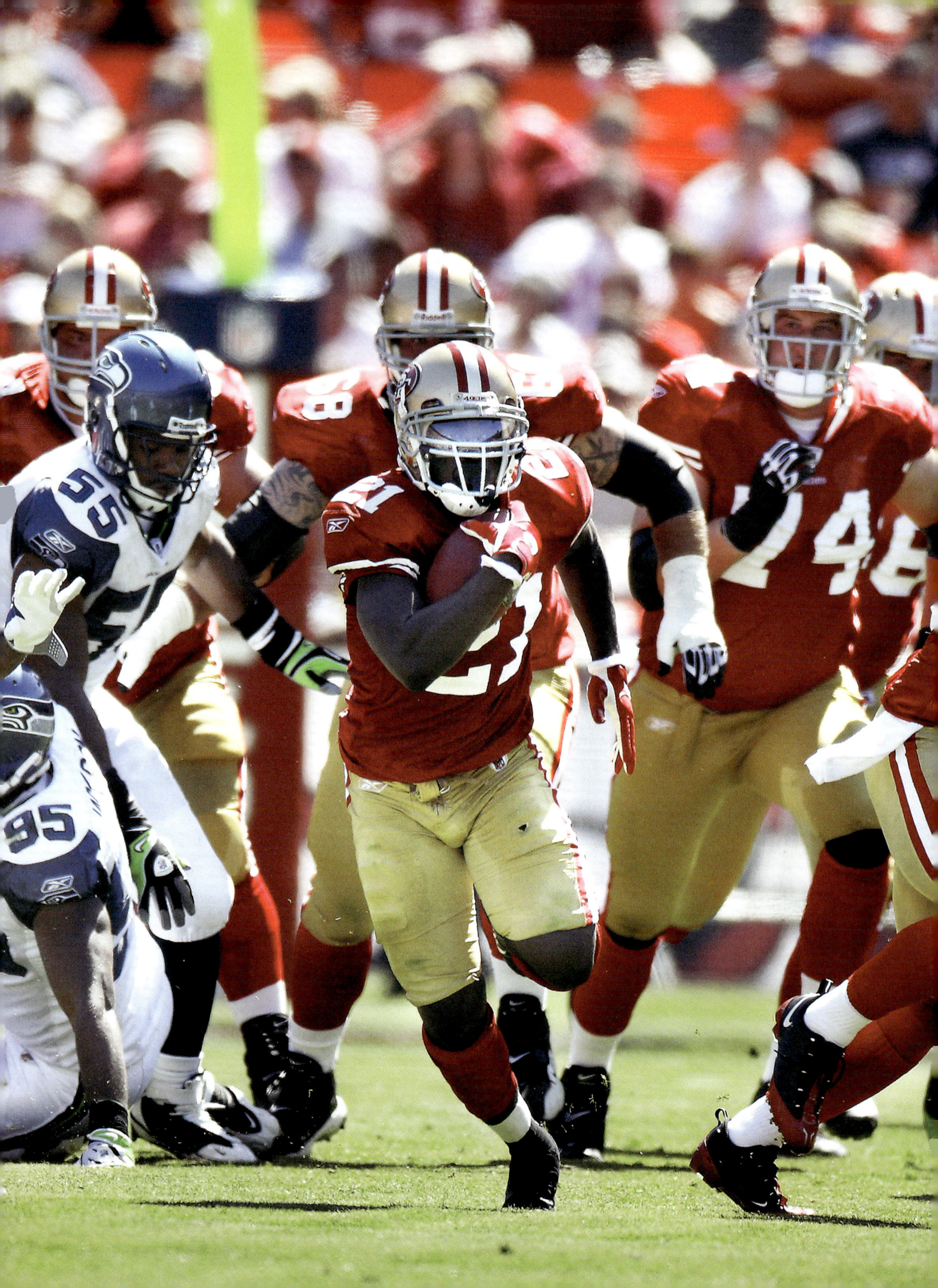

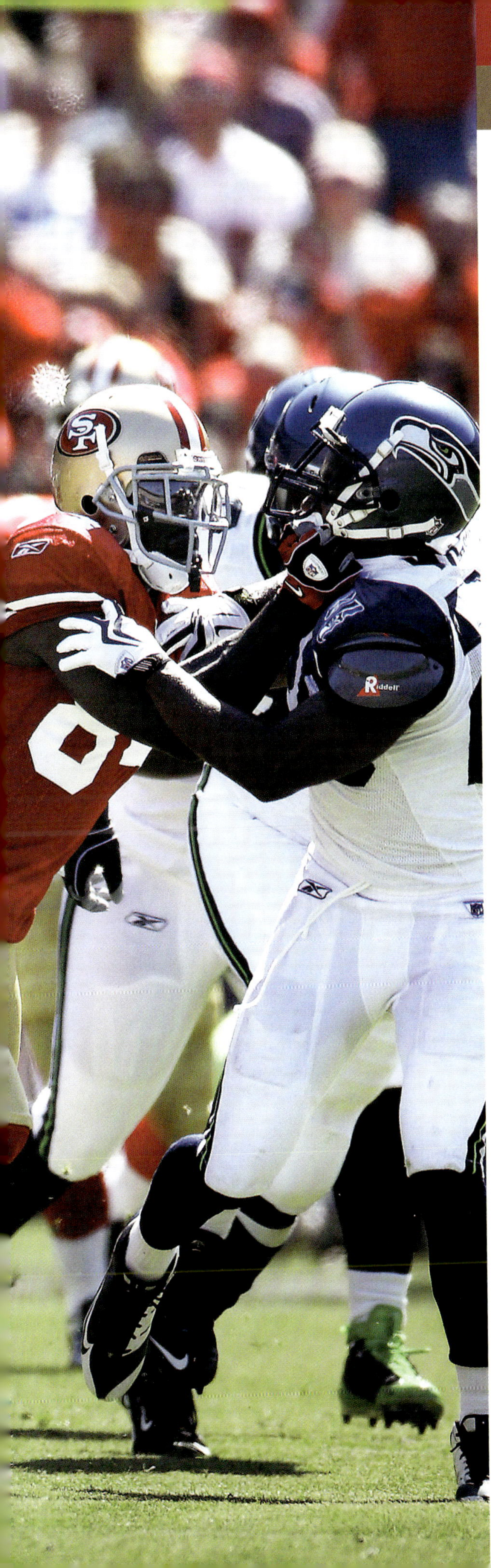

FRANK GORE

- » **Running Back 2005–2014**
- » **All-Pro 2006**
- » **Five-time Pro Bowl selection**

Frank Gore is the Niners' all-time leader in career rushing yards, with 11,073. Drafted out of the University of Miami in 2005, Gore was a model of consistency in San Francisco; after his rookie season, he gained at least 1,200 total yards from scrimmage every year. He holds a slew of other team records, including most rushing yards in one game (212), most rushing yards in a season (1,695) and most 100-yard rushing games in a season (9). He is currently third on the NFL's all-time rushing list and is one of only three players to run for at least 16,000 yards.

The sixth running back selected in the 2005 draft, Frank Gore has outgained every player chosen before him.

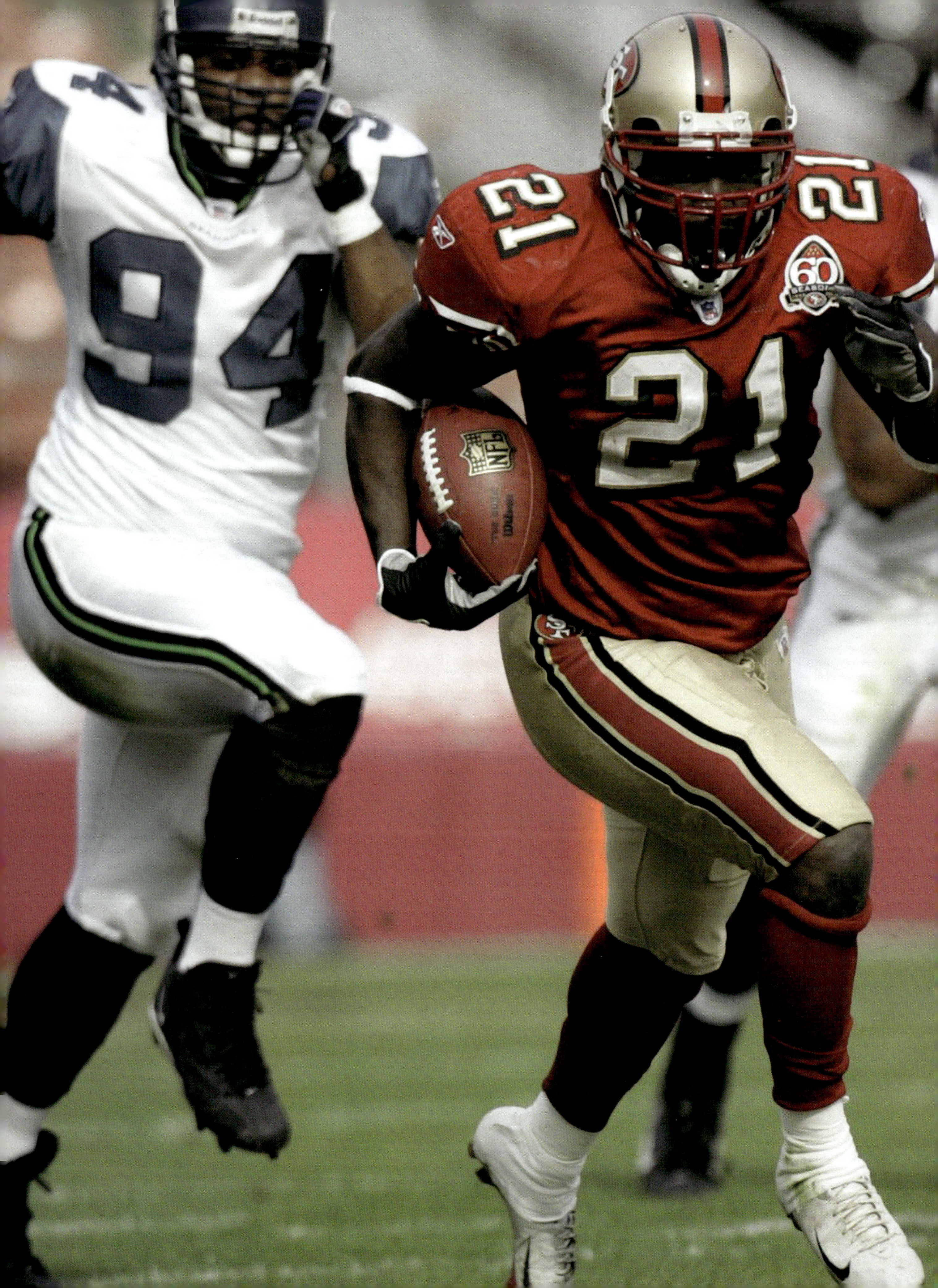

Gore's career rushing yards total as a Niner is 2,384 more than Joe Perry's and 4,009 more than Roger Craig's.

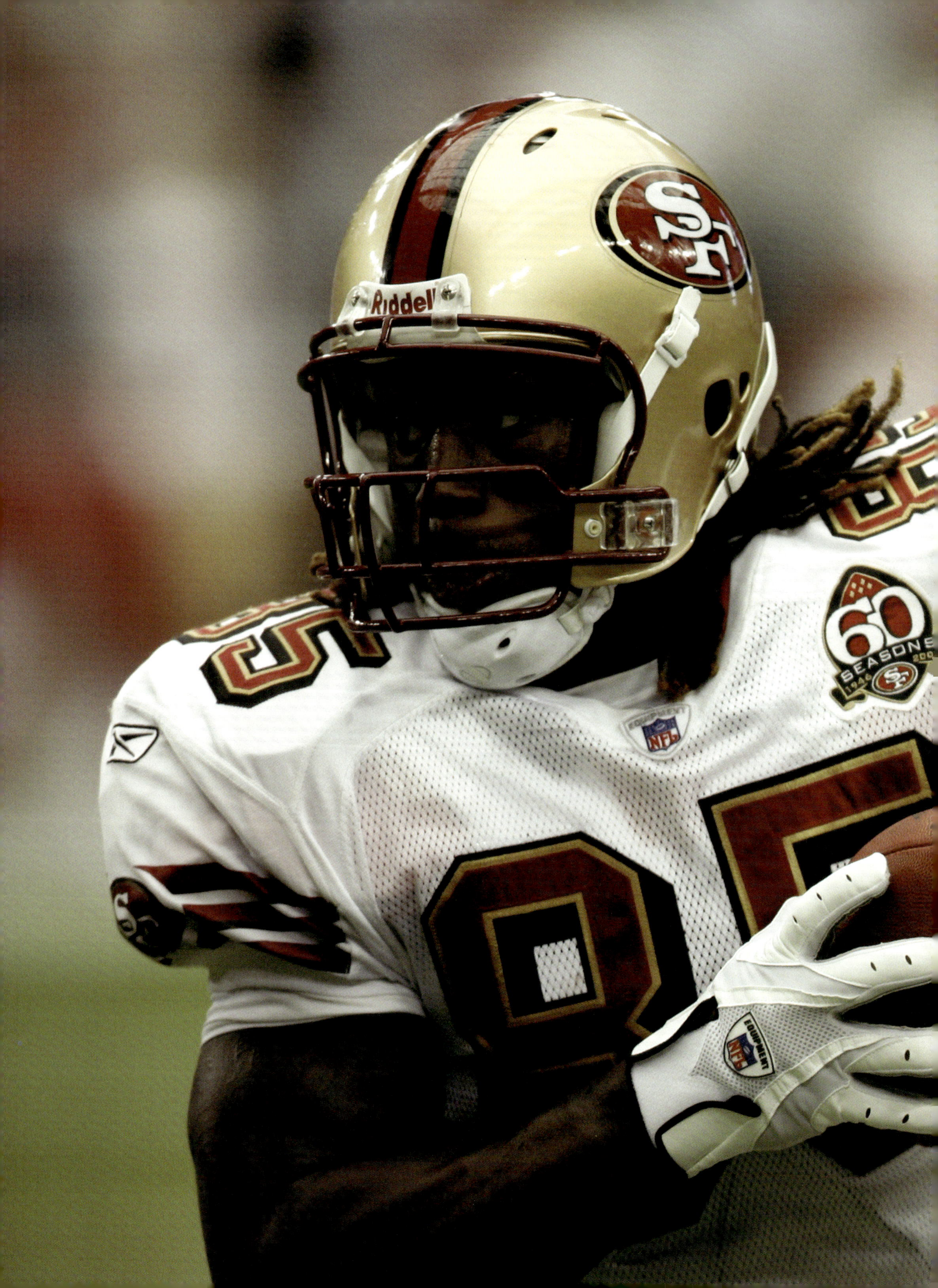
Riddell
60
SEASONS

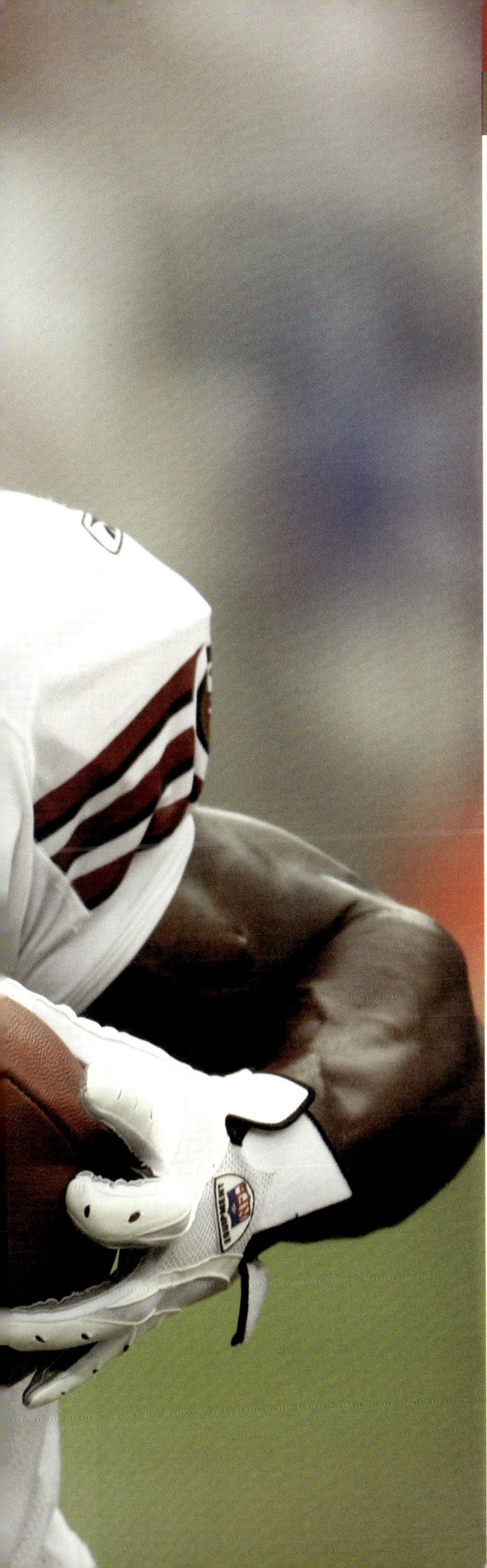

VERNON DAVIS

- » **Tight End 2006–2015**
- » **All-Pro 2013**
- » **Two-time Pro Bowl selection**

Vernon Davis is the most accomplished tight end in Niners history, leading his position in career receptions (441), receiving yards (5,640) and touchdown catches (55). His most memorable game came during the 2011 playoffs against the New Orleans Saints. Davis broke the NFL postseason record with 180 yards on seven receptions, including two touchdowns. On the Niners' game-winning drive, he caught one pass from quarterback Alex Smith that put the team in scoring position, then caught the winning pass with nine seconds remaining, a reception referred to by San Francisco fans as "The Catch III."

An amazing athlete, Davis set multiple weightlifting records while playing in college at Maryland.

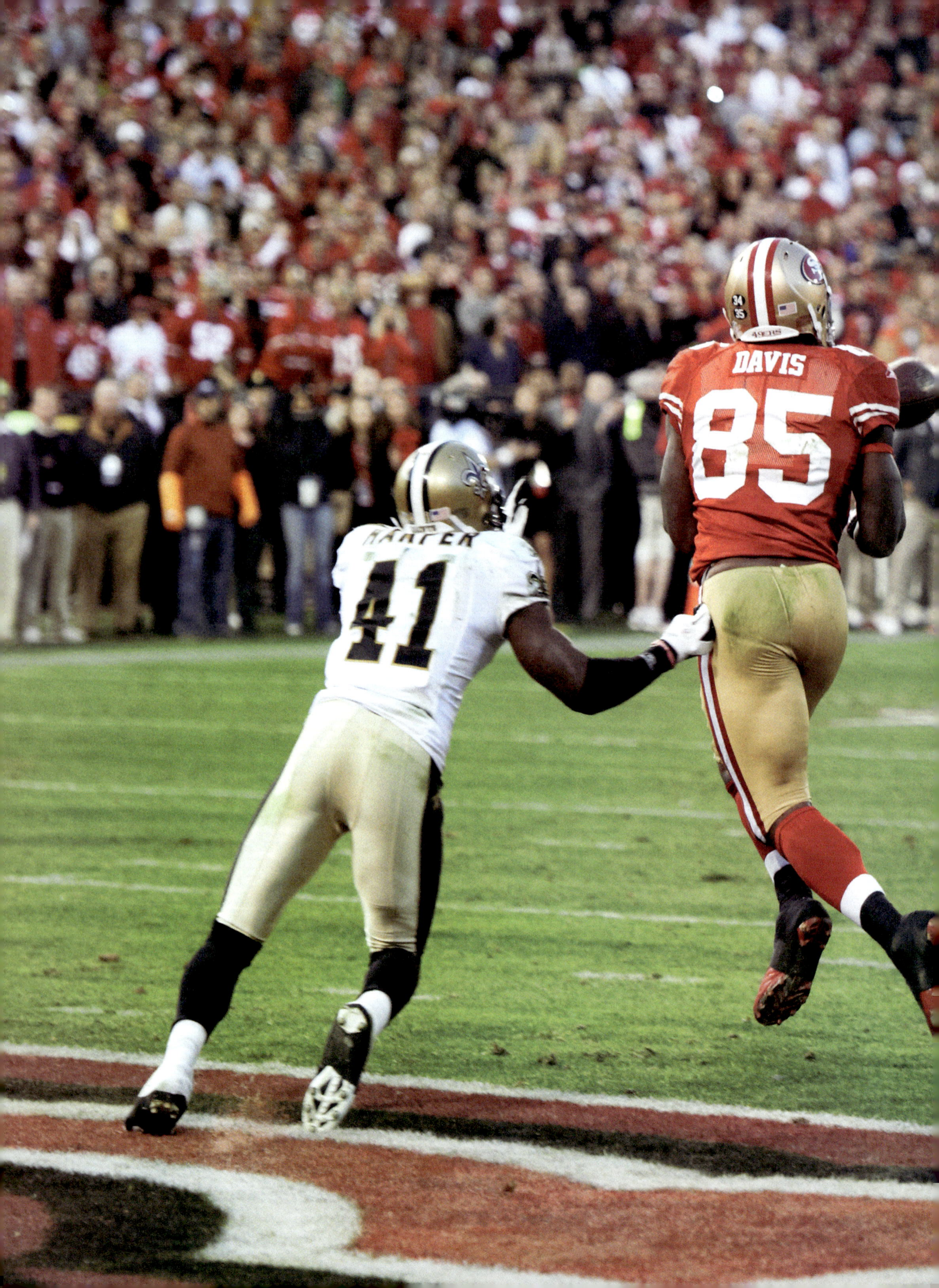
DAVIS
85
41

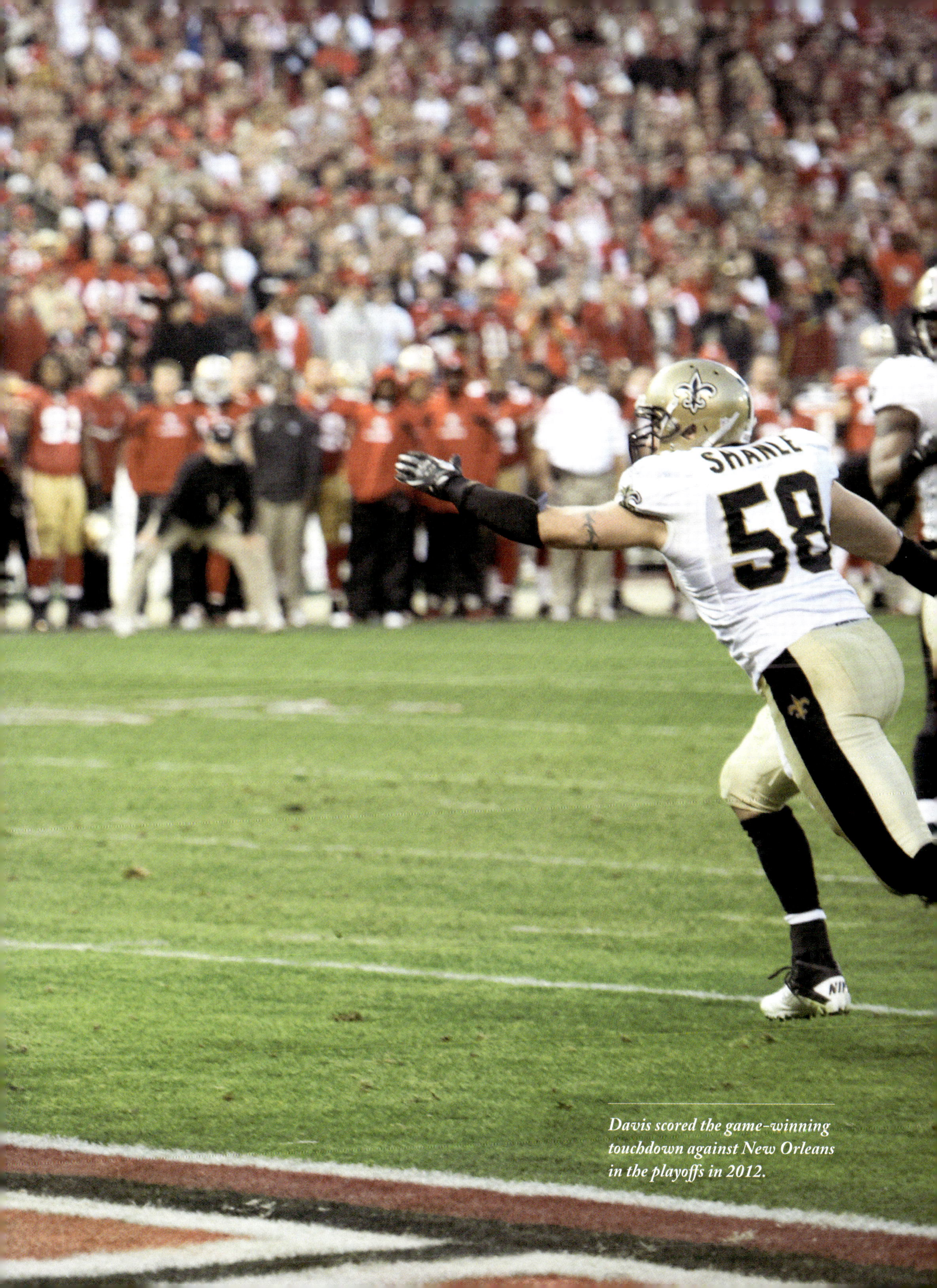

Davis scored the game-winning touchdown against New Orleans in the playoffs in 2012.

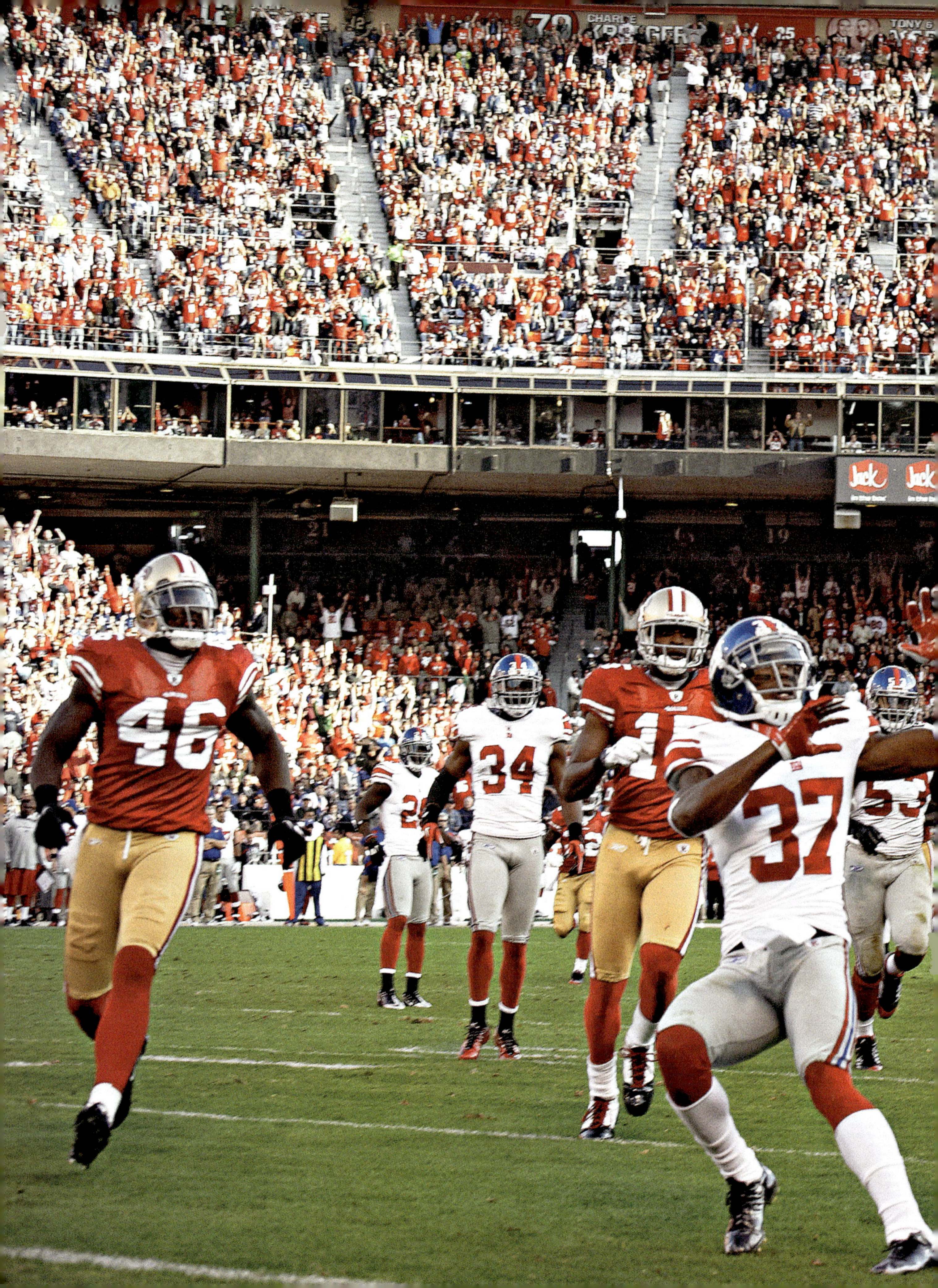
70
CHARLIE
25
Jack
Jack
46
34
37

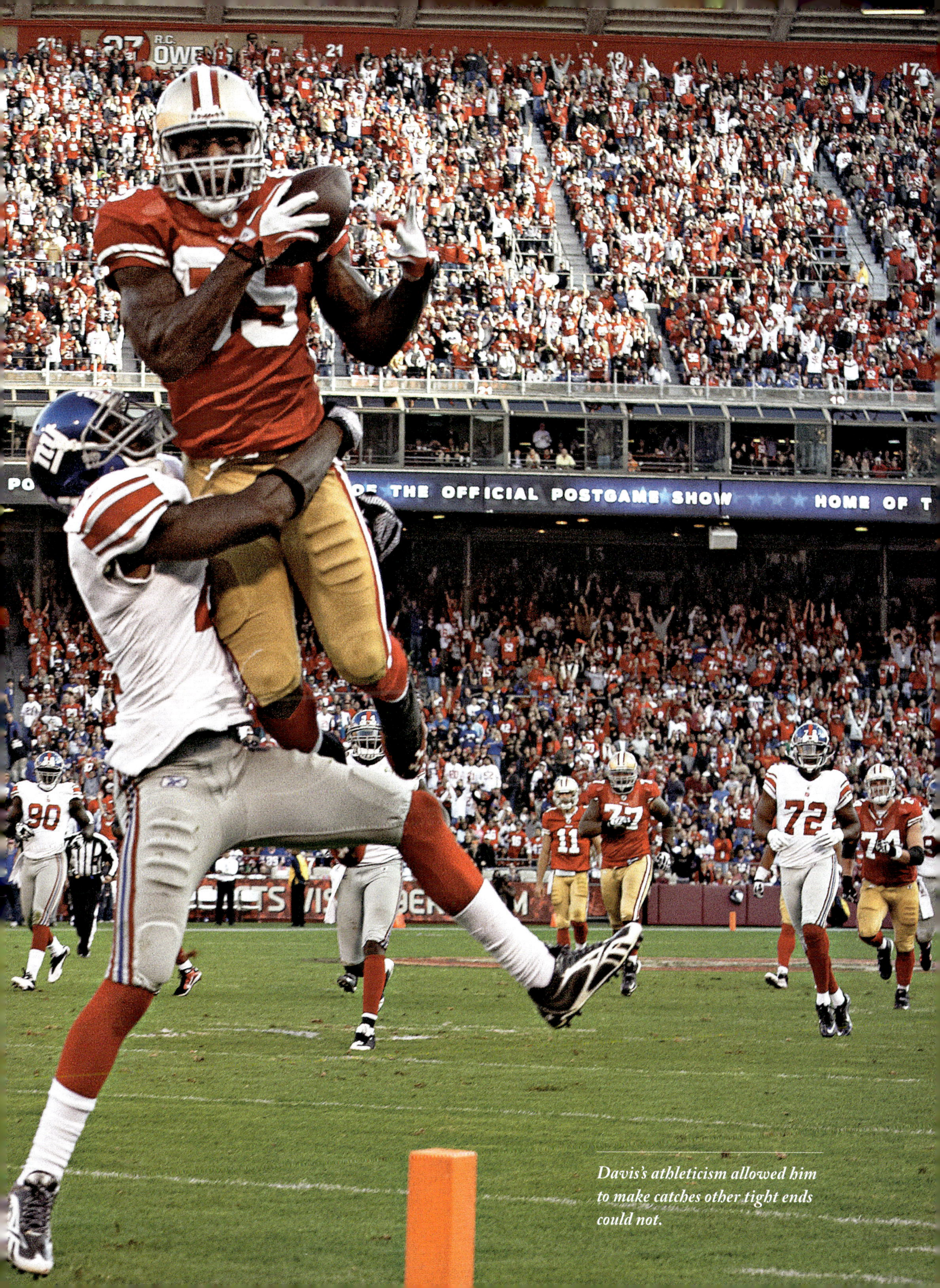

Davis's athleticism allowed him to make catches other tight ends could not.

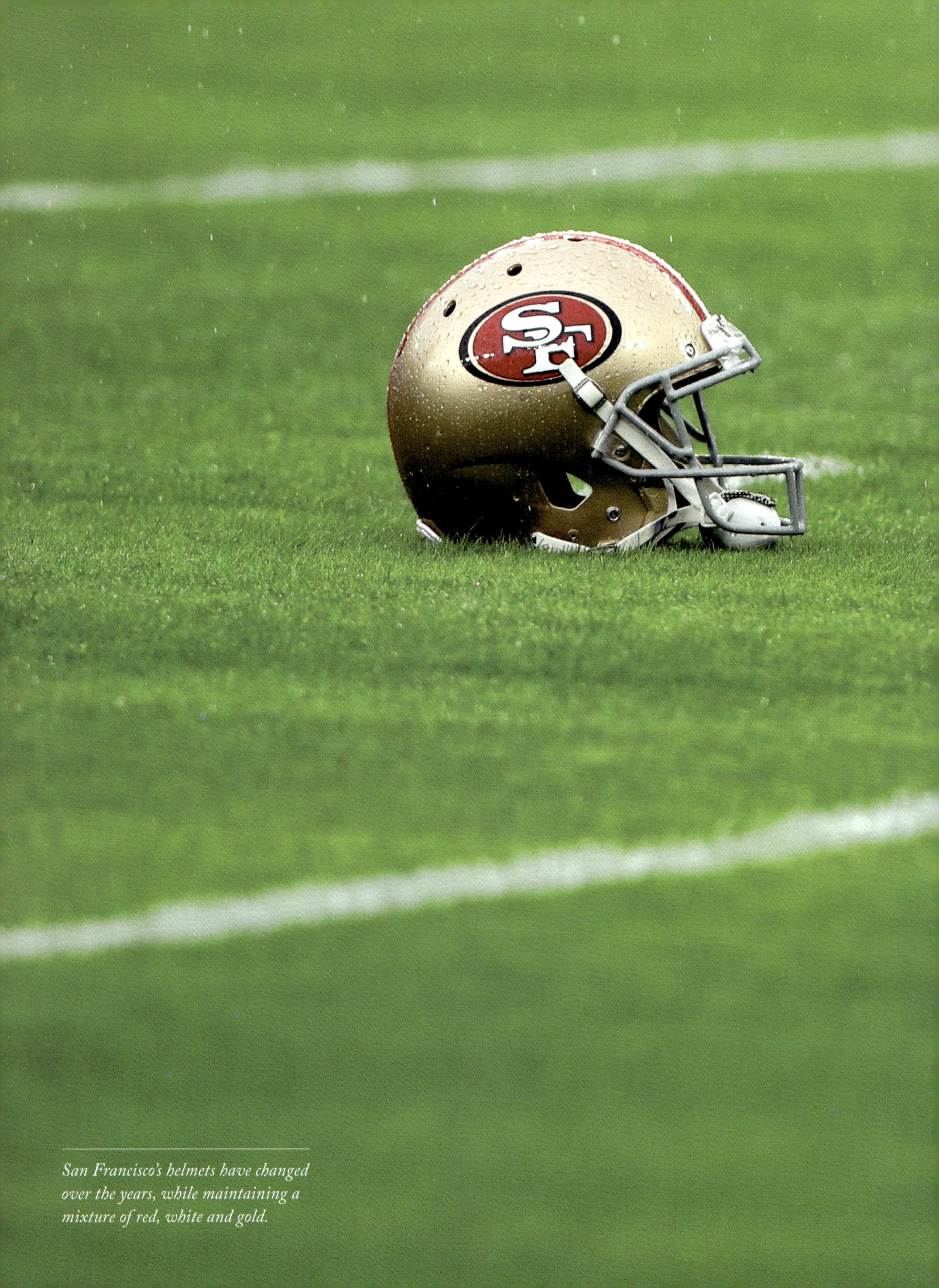

San Francisco's helmets have changed over the years, while maintaining a mixture of red, white and gold.

THE STORIES

The 49ers' history is a rich one, filled with great characters and memorable games. SPORTS ILLUSTRATED has written about it extensively over the years

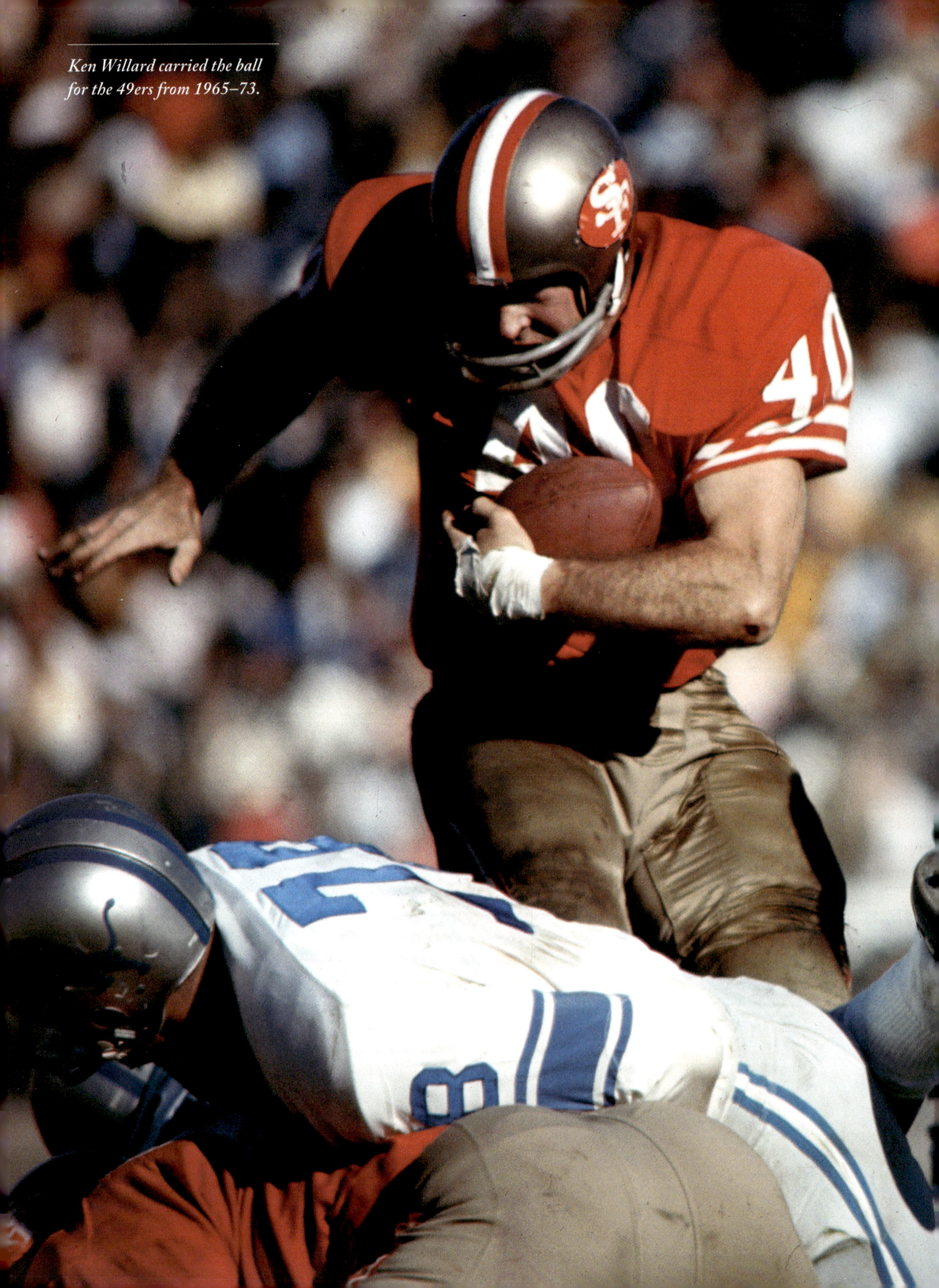

Ken Willard carried the ball for the 49ers from 1965–73.

EXCERPTED FROM SPORTS ILLUSTRATED | OCTOBER 11, 1965

THE 49ERS LOSE THEIR COOL AND GET HOT

In mannerly San Francisco the pros are sitting down to rah-rah dinners, and the city's sedate fans are applauding politely again BY TEX MAULE

AFTER THE SAN FRANCISCO 49ERS WON THEIR SECOND STRAIGHT GAME OF THE SEASON AT KEZAR STADIUM, the team repaired to a dining room atop a nearby brewery for a postgame dinner. This kind of togetherness is not unusual elsewhere in the league, but in genteel San Francisco, where the fraternal roar of Lions is greeted with pained shudders, it is practically unheard of. Remarkably, it was the players themselves who arranged the party. In earlier times they finished their game and went their separate ways. The dinner marked a first for the 49ers and was evidence of a new and burgeoning spirit.

"We were never together as a team," says John Brodie, the quarterback. "At practice the offensive and defensive units are separate. After practice everyone went off in different directions—across the Golden Gate Bridge to Marin County, over the Bay Bridge to Oakland, out the Bayshore Freeway to Redwood City or Atherton or Palo Alto. We never had a kind of team feeling, so some of us thought that a dinner like this would help."

He paused for a moment.

"Of course," he said cautiously, "we don't want to overdo it. I think three or four times a year will be enough."

This sophisticated attitude toward team spirit is as much a reflection of San Francisco as it is of the players. The 49er fan is probably the best mannered, least excitable in pro football. In most NFL parks you will see banners flying with fulsome phrases such as "We Love Our Colts" (with the O's in the form of a heart), or you will be deafened by the blast of air horns celebrating a home-team touchdown, but in Kezar Stadium a crayoned bed sheet is frowned upon, and a man who dares tootle a raucous horn is promptly escorted from the premises to the polite applause of his neighbors.

The press box in Kezar Stadium has the air of a country club; it is the only one in pro football where women are not only allowed, but welcomed. It is populated in large part by civic officials and their wives, with working sports-writers spotted here and there like raisins in a poundcake.

In recent years, as the 49er fortunes ebbed, there have been times when there were as many people in the press box as in the stands. Their combined total often was exceeded by the squadrons of gulls which appear about the middle of the fourth period looking for rare bits of popcorn and creating an understandable nervousness in punt receivers, who must look up for the ball.

Unfortunately the sophistication that makes San Francisco a delightful city has made the 49ers, over the years, a less than frightening football team. One coach, quitting after a couple of years of despairing effort, explained that too many of the players owned convertibles and that there were too many distractions in the Bay area.

Red Hickey, a tough coach of the blood-and-guts school, tried to whip the 49ers into an appropriate frenzy by the free application of an abrasive tongue, but he succeeded only in creating a mood of sullen rebellion. Under Hickey, the 49ers subsided after one lone year near the top—they tied Detroit for the Western Conference lead in 1957 but lost the title in a playoff game—to the bottom of the Western Division and stayed there two more years under his successor, Jack Christiansen. But Christiansen, a tough, aggressive player on a reckless Detroit team in the 1950s, now seems to have discovered how to get the most out of his team. The 49ers are on the move, as they proved in a rip-roaring second half in Sunday's 27–24 loss to the powerful Colts, and the fans are becoming enthusiastic.

"No one thing started us back," says Lou Spadia, the general manager. "A lot of small things started us down, and a lot of small things have contributed to our comeback, too."

Spadia is only partially correct. The 49ers' rise can be traced, as Spadia says, to a number of things, but none of them is very small. The most important is Christiansen. Another is Brodie, a handsome whilom golf pro, who has suddenly learned to control his approach shots. Then there is Ken Willard, a powerfully built outfielder who turned down $80,000 from the Boston Red Sox—and probably more than that from the American Football League—to play in the NFL. And finally there is John David Crow, the injury-ridden halfback who is one of the best runners in football when a) he is allowed to play, and b) he remembers to take the ball with him on his runs.

Put them all together and add a good, experienced offensive line, exceptional receivers and a quick and opportunistic defense and you get the most improved football team in the league.

It may also be the NFL's happiest and most relaxed team, an excellent state of affairs brought about by Christiansen, who came to the 49ers in 1959 as an assistant coach after eight years with the Lions. There he was the leader of Chris's Crew which, for four or five years, was the best secondary defense in football, and he still holds the league record for scoring on punt returns. He started working on the rudiments of this achievement as a rookie, when he shared safety on punts with Doak Walker. In a game against the Los Angeles Rams, Joe Stydahar, the Ram head coach, told Norman Van Brocklin, "Punt away from Walker. Punt it to that skinny rookie." The spindly-legged Christiansen ran the ensuing punt back 69 yards for a touchdown. Later in the game Stydahar, believing the run to have been an accident, again instructed Van Brocklin to punt to the skinny rookie. This time Christiansen ran the punt back 47 yards for another touchdown.

As the leader of Chris's Crew, Christiansen created a feeling of insouciant daring and an immense pride on the Detroit defensive team, and he did this without the bravura that generally accompanies such deeds. Just as quietly he has instilled the same qualities this season in the entire San Francisco team; if, as some claim, a team reflects the personality of its coach, this is nowhere more true than with the 49ers.

"He's the easiest coach I ever played for," says Crow, who has played for many and who came to San Francisco from the St. Louis Cardinals in the off season in a trade for Defensive Back Abe Woodson. "Oh, he may get mad and chew you out if you need it, but he's been a player recently and he knows how to treat players. He doesn't humiliate you, and he doesn't talk it up too much. This is a game for professionals and we don't need pep talks, and here we don't get them."

Crow, who has been one of the best running backs in the league for seven years, helps the 49ers not only as a ballcarrier but as a stabilizing influence on the rest of the San Francisco backfield, which is composed of rookies and second-year men.

"I'm the old head with a bunch of kids," he says, "but I learn a lot from them, too. Of course, I don't help them so much that one of them will take my job away. That's too much."

Crow fitted easily into the 49er offense.

"It's simpler than the Cardinal offense," he says. "We have fewer plays, but we hit every hole and we hit them all in several different ways. Only trouble I had was getting used to the offensive line. You'd be surprised how different it looks to a running back behind a new line. I had to get my timing worked out with the guards and tackles; I played behind Ken Gray at St. Louis for seven years and I knew what he was thinking, and then Charley Johnson and I used to talk things over a lot; he was a young quarterback and I could talk to him. Brodie is a veteran, and he knows his own mind and what he is going to do. We don't have to talk so much."

It has been only recently that Brodie, despite his eight years in the league, has known his own mind. The former Stanford star started the season by completing an extraordinary 75% of his passes in the first two 49er games against Chicago and Pittsburgh. On at least one occasion last year (against the Baltimore Colts in a 14–3 loss) he was so far off target that he sat in the dressing room and wept after the game.

The 49ers' rise can be traced, as Spadia says, to a number of things, but none of them is very small. The most important is Christiansen.

"I was confused," he said the other day, "and because of that I didn't throw well. Now everything has been simplified. Our line blocking has been standardized. Our pass patterns are simpler, and the receivers run them exactly. Dave Parks, for instance, has made the biggest improvement of any player I have ever seen, primarily because he runs his patterns exactly this year. A lot of that is due to Christiansen, but a lot comes from Y.A. Tittle, too. You have to have a quarterback coach who used to be a quarterback. If you've never played the position, you can't think like a quarterback. You watch what happens with Charley Johnson, now that the Cardinals have Bobby Layne working with him. He's bound to improve. What did he throw against the Browns? Six touchdowns? And Layne had been working with him for only a week!"

Although Brodie is reluctant to talk about it, his improvement as a quarterback stems from the departure of Red Hickey, who quit as head coach of the 49ers after the third game of the 1963 season. Hickey's scarifying tongue had wounded but did not inspire Brodie.

"We used to learn a new offense every week," Brodie said. "We had the shotgun for a long time, with me at tailback if we were going to throw and Kilmer at tailback if we were going to run. We were telegraphing our punches. Then in one game against the Rams, we tried to fool them. I was going to do the running, and Kilmer would pass. We got clobbered, and I nearly got both ankles broken trying to run. I'm not valuable to the team running; I'm valuable throwing the ball. Tittle knows that and so does Jack."

Unfortunately, in 1964, Christiansen's first full season as the San Francisco head coach, Brodie was about as good a runner as the 49ers had. J.D. Smith and Don Lisbon were injured, and by the end of the season the top ballcarrier on the club was a rookie free agent named Dave Kopay. He gained an anemic 271 yards in 75 carries. Kopay is improved this year, but he has the club to thank for this as much as his own hard work. The 49ers went after the best running back available in this year's draft—the 230-pound Ken Willard, an All-America at North Carolina—and they signed him. Willard's pro debut was spectacular. After his first two games he was second only to Jim Brown in rushing.

"It feels good," Brodie says. "It's comforting to look back and see those good runners and know that the defense isn't stacking against your passes."

Willard is a thickly built, crew-cut blond with the heavy thighs and strong buttocks of a power runner. He also has surprising speed and he is intelligent, which does not hurt his running either. He averaged B as an undergraduate at North Carolina and is now studying law at Santa Clara.

"I could have quit high school when I was 17 and signed with Boston to play baseball," he said the other day. "I was just about as big then as I am now and I could hit the long ball often enough. They sent Ted Williams down to Richmond to talk to me and they offered me a lot of money. I thought about it, but I wasn't sure I would be dedicated enough to my education to go back winters to get my degree. Then I had read somewhere that only about 7% of all baseball rookies ever make it in the major leagues, and I thought about traveling around in buses in the minors and I hate buses. So I went to North Carolina on a football scholarship."

Willard, who became a strong NFL supporter through watching Washington Redskin telecasts during his high school and college years, never considered the AFL, although Buffalo wanted him. "I was picked by Buffalo in a secret draft a week before the 49ers drafted me, but I wasn't interested in the AFL and I didn't like the secret draft. I guess maybe if I had come up to the pros five or 10 years from now, when the AFL is better established, I might have been interested."

Willard did not report immediately to the 49ers this summer. Instead he played with the College All-Stars against the Cleveland Browns, a preparation for pro ball that he would recommend to any aspiring rookie. "It is a gradual indoctrination," he says. "I started with the All-Star Game in Buffalo, where you play against the best college players. Then I went to the All-Star camp at Northwestern. We scrimmaged the Chicago Bears, and I got my first taste of the pros. Then we played the best of the pros—the Cleveland Browns—in the All-Star Game. So the transition from college to professional football was gradual."

Ken and Bonnie, his young, lovely wife from Richmond, live a two-minute drive from the 49er in-season camp at Redwood City with Scott, a three-month-old son who looks like a future tackle.

"I learned a lot from watching John David," Willard said the other day, while Bonnie gave Scott a bottle. "He's a finesse runner. He runs with a low, shuffling stride, like Jim Taylor or Jim Brown. They don't pick their feet up, and they are always on balance. In college I hit the hole as fast as I could. But I noticed Taylor takes his first couple of steps very quickly, then hesitates and looks for an opening. I tried that against the Steelers and it worked out pretty well, I think."

"One thing I like about pro football," Willard said, echoing Crow, "is that the coach doesn't spend any time trying to key you up. These guys are pretty easy about a game. You'll see someone, just before the start, sitting reading a book. This is an intangible, but it is important. I don't like to be pumped up before a game. I'll get myself up and I don't need outside help."

Of his noninspirational technique, Christiansen says: "It's all over by Saturday. Nothing I can say just before a game is going to change it. If you are properly prepared, you'll play well. If you're not, Sunday before a game is too late."

Christiansen, tall but no longer spindly, is open and honest about himself. He was surprised when he was named head coach of the 49ers, because there were other coaches on the staff who had more experience. He was selected during a two-hour conference between Spadia and Vic Morabito, the president of the 49ers, who has since died. Spadia today cannot remember exactly why they settled on Christiansen.

"I liked him because the players liked him, and he always had something to offer in meetings," Spadia says. "Logically, we should have picked a guy like Moose Myers, who had coached College of the Pacific, but we picked Jack. We're happy about it. It was a complete change from Hickey, who did a good job for us and wasn't fired. Coaches get praised too much for winning and blamed too much for losing."

Basically, the difference between Christiansen and Hickey was in their first approach. While Hickey was critical and demanding, Christiansen was critical and tolerant.

"You get a lot of young ball players in camp, but always they seem to break down to two kinds," Christiansen says. "There are a few who need to be kicked in the butt to produce; there are a lot more you have to handle gently and to praise. Our idea is to handle everyone gently at first, not hurting the sensitive ones. Later we can use the needle on the ones who need it."

Christiansen believes in delegating responsibility, a factor that many think has helped the team.

"A head coach doesn't have time to coach anymore," Christiansen says. "He has to take care of public relations and organization. All I do on the practice field is supervise. Last year I tried to work with the backs, but I didn't have the time. So now Tittle works with them. When we're concentrating on defense, he's over at the side working with Brodie and George Mira and the receivers. It helps."

The 49ers work even after practice, a fact that has impressed Hugh McElhenney, San Francisco's marvelous halfback of some years ago. "This is the first time in a long while I've seen this kind of a 49er club," he said. "I watched them practice the other day. Used to be when practice was over everyone went in. Now they stay out and run pass patterns or plays. They work extra. They think they can win it." •

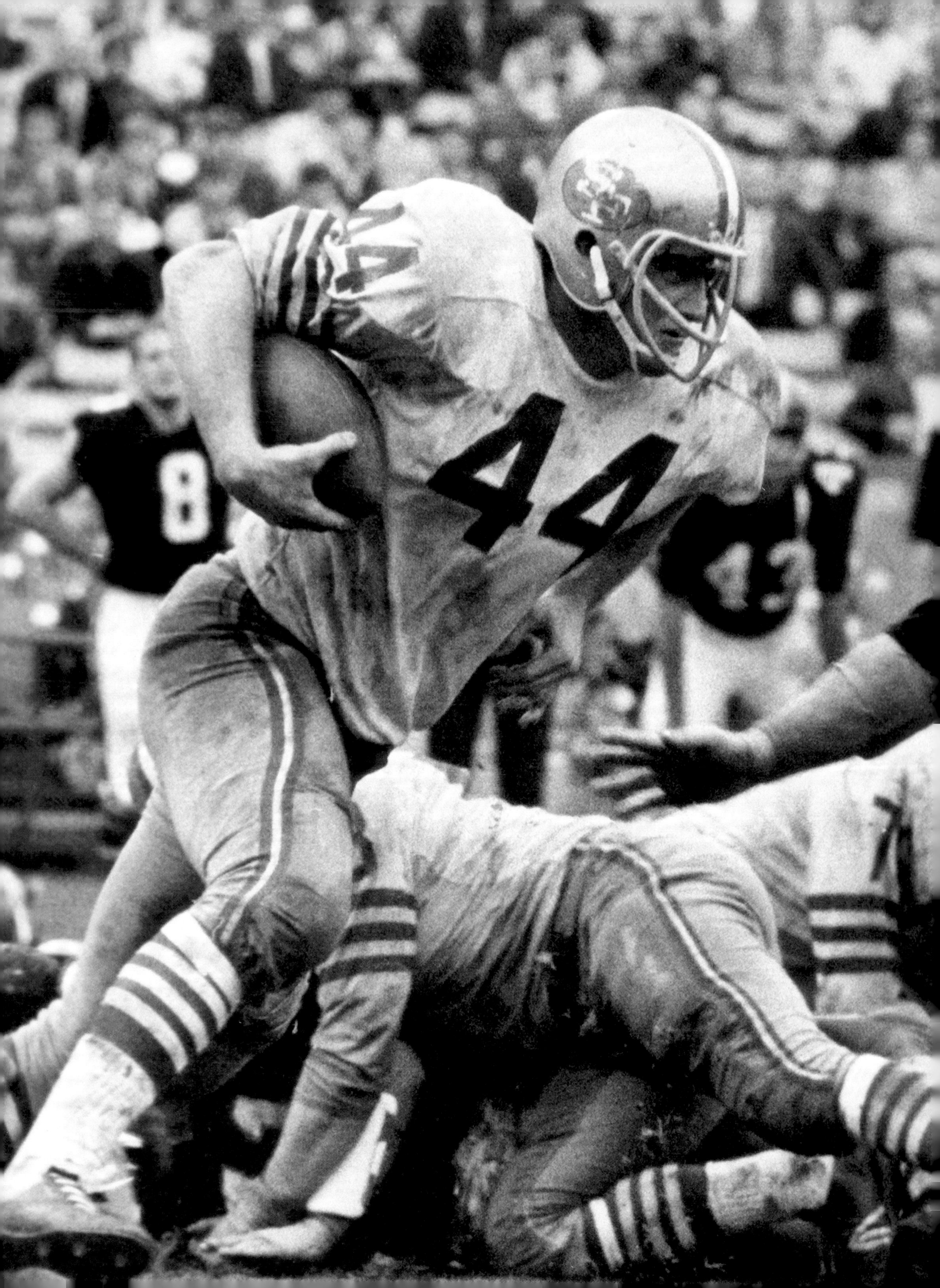

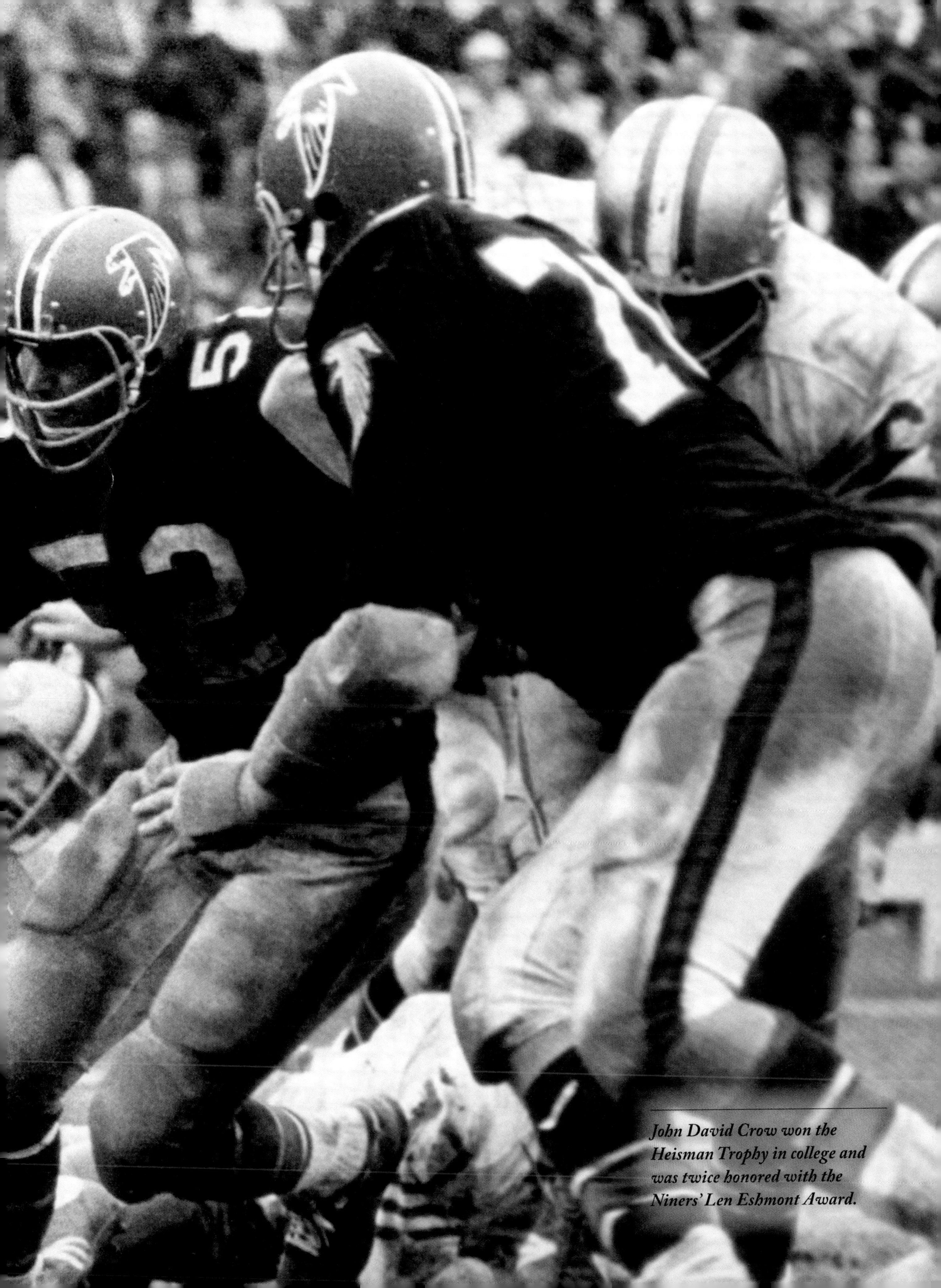

John David Crow won the Heisman Trophy in college and was twice honored with the Niners' Len Eshmont Award.

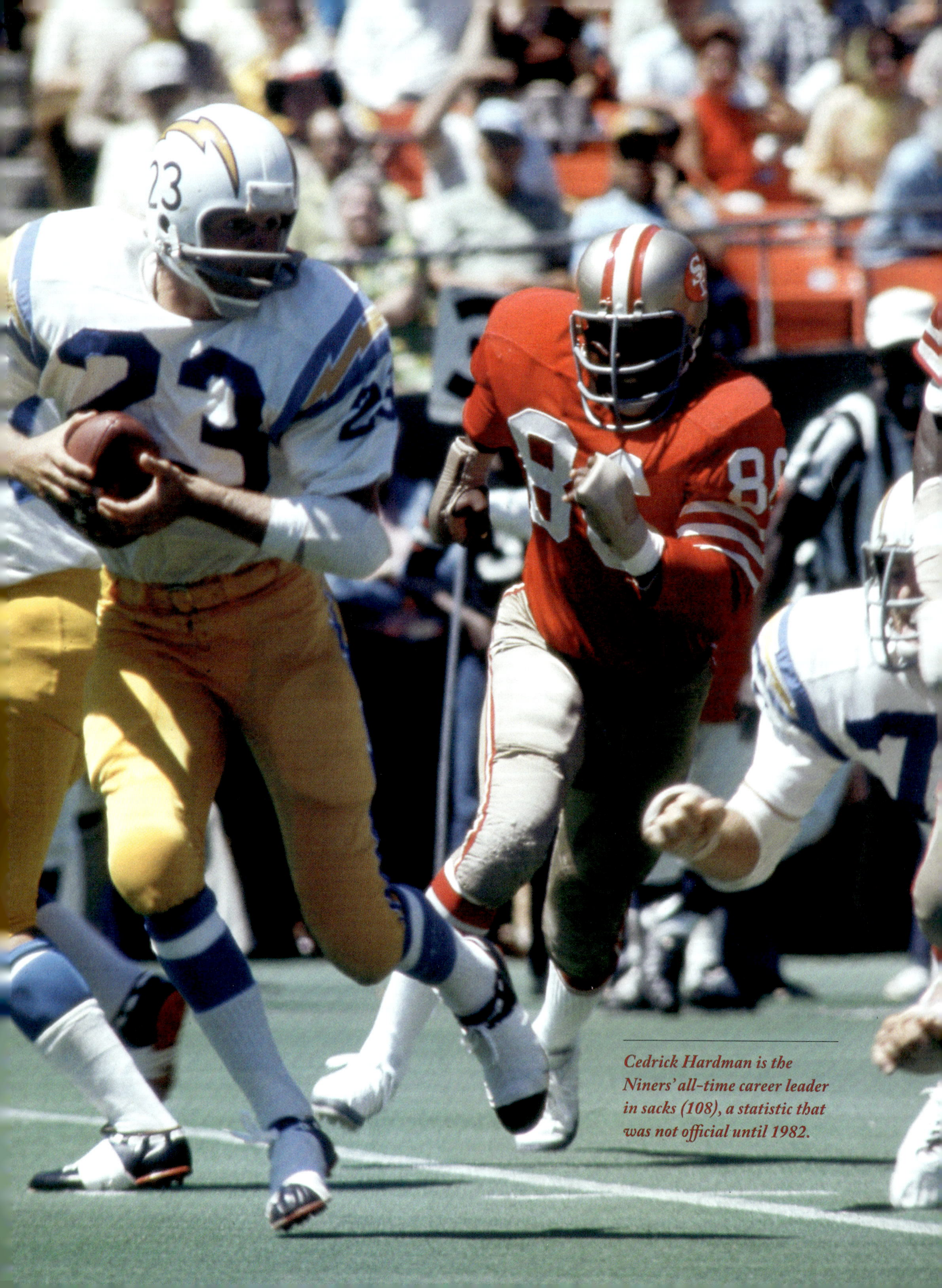

Cedrick Hardman is the Niners' all-time career leader in sacks (108), a statistic that was not official until 1982.

EXCERPTED FROM SPORTS ILLUSTRATED | OCTOBER 26, 1970

THERE'S GOLD IN THEM THAR SPILLS

In years past, the San Francisco 49ers have been almost defenseless, but now they've got the hitting to go with John Brodie's passing and are making a run at the NFC West title BY TEX MAULE

THE SAN FRANCISCO 49ERS, IN 25 YEARS OF PRO FOOTBALL SELDOM A BRIDESMAID AND NEVER A BRIDE, looked last Sunday as if they were determined to follow their familiar pattern: early success followed by sudden collapse. After having played superbly the week before in beating Los Angeles 20–6, they were tied by lowly New Orleans 20–20.

But, in this case, the wedding hasn't been called off just yet. This isn't a typical San Francisco club bursting with nonchalance, going for broke on offense and breaking down on defense.

Under head coach Dick Nolan, the 49ers are all fired up, and the tie with the Saints still leaves them only half a game behind the Rams in their division, with another game against L.A. in Kezar Stadium coming up at the end of November.

"We have a real good shot at it this year," says running back Ken Willard. "I'm tired of hearing about how we have all the personnel and still can't win. That's never been true. We didn't have the kind of people we have now and we've never been as deep as we are."

But the biggest improvements in the 49ers are the kicking game and the defense. "In 1969 we lost three or four games because we didn't have a capable kicker," Nolan said last week at the team's training grounds in Redwood City. "That's why we traded for Bruce Gossett. And it wasn't just placekicking. Our special teams cost us games, too. That's not happening this year."

Special teams are usually manned by youngsters waiting to move up to either the offensive or defensive units and by veterans who aren't quite good enough to do anything else. But, as Nolan points out, no team can win a championship with ordinary specials. To improve his, Nolan hired Doug Scovil, who was head coach at the University of Pacific, and he named Ed Beard, a San Francisco middle linebacker until injured and supplanted by Frank Nunley, captain of the special teams.

Beard has made it an honor to be picked for the specials. "When he comes to you and asks you to play on one of the special teams, he makes you feel like he's doing you a favor," one player says. "You don't feel like you're in there as cannon fodder. You feel like you're making a real contribution."

Ironically, in the 49ers' one-point loss to Atlanta three weeks ago—their only defeat of the season—it was a special team that failed. Gossett, who rarely misses from inside the 40 on field goals, blew one from the 19.

It is a mark of the new spirit of the 49ers that on the plane from Atlanta to San Francisco every player on the squad went up to Gossett and consoled him. Lou Spadia, the president of the club, called Gossett when he got home. "Don't get your dauber down," Spadia said. "That happens to everyone. You're the best placekicker we have had here in 25 years, just remember that." The following week Gossett kicked two field goals to help beat the Rams.

Spadia has been with San Francisco since 1946, when the team originated as a member of the old All-America Conference, and he is keenly aware of the difference between this team and those of the past. "You think back on all the All-Pro players we've had," he said last week. "Joe Perry, John Henry Johnson, Hugh McElhenny, Y.A. Tittle, Gordy Soltau, Billy Wilson. I could go on for a long time, but the significant thing is that they were all offensive players. We had a fine team in 1952 and I'll bet you can't remember any defensive player with the exception of Leo Nomellini. We've always been offense oriented and I finally figured that no club ever wins a title without a great defense."

Nolan came to the 49ers from Dallas, where he was defensive coach under Tom Landry, who was himself once a defensive coach. Nolan has almost completely rebuilt the San Francisco defense, only four starters being left from the club he took over two seasons ago.

One of the key members of the revitalized unit is Nunley, who is 6'2", 230 and looks about as hard as a softboiled egg, but he hits like Dick Butkus and roams as widely as Tommy Nobis. His teammates call him "Fudge Hammer." "Because he's so sweet and hits so hard," says Willard.

Nunley is also known for his gung-ho attitude. "He is the most positive man I've ever met," says John Brodie, the 35-year-old quarterback who is having the best season of his life in his 14th year as a pro. "The big difference between this club and the other 49er teams I have played with is the terrific morale, and Nunley has had a lot to do with that, I think."

"He'll call any defense in the book and he's a gambler," says Nolan. "My only problem with him is holding him down. And he has one great quality. If he makes a mistake—and he makes some—he forgets it immediately. He doesn't brood or sulk about it."

Nunley himself has another explanation for the club's new zest. "When I came here four years ago, there was a real sharp division on the team. There was a nucleus of oldtimers and then there were the young players, and the two groups just didn't get along. Now most of the old ones have gone and the young guys are really keyed up."

He looked across the dressing room at a big, powerful man who had thrown his head back to laugh at something another player had said. "Now we got guys like him," Nunley said.

He was speaking of rookie defensive end Cedrick Hardman. In the Ram game Hardman sacked Los Angeles quarterback Roman Gabriel twice; Brodie wasn't dumped once by the Fearsome Foursome. Deacon Jones, who is considered the best defensive end in the game, was often double-teamed, and when he wasn't, Casimir Banaszek, a tight end Nolan made into an offensive tackle, fended Jones off.

After the game, Hardman, attired in a white double-breasted suit and a flowered ascot, went to the Ram dressing room to talk to Jones. In a story in a Los Angeles paper earlier in the week, Jones was quoted as saying that while Hardman showed some potential, he was still just a kid and no threat to Jones's eminence at their position.

At 6'3" and 250, Hardman is a bit smaller than Jones, but he braced the Ram veteran coolly. He asked Jones if the quotes were accurate. "I might have said something like that," Jones allowed. "Maybe not just exactly that, but something near it."

"You may be the best now, Deacon," Hardman said, "but you better be ready to retire in a couple more years."

In the dressing room at Redwood City, Hardman laughed, thinking of the confrontation. "He's the best now, I guess," he said. "But I can be just as good as I want to be and I'm going to be the best."

Now he was all duded up in a black cowboy outfit that has earned him the nickname "Fontana." It has no special meaning, but Willard, who conferred it, figured Hardman deserved a name and a horse as much as any other Western hero. He called Hardman's imaginary horse "Sugar." Two days before the 49ers played the Saints, Hardman was 20 minutes late to a meeting, and when he came in Willard had written "Poor old Sugar" on the blackboard and Nolan pointed a finger at Hardman and said, "That'll cost you a hundred."

After practice, walking out to his red Lincoln Continental with Texas plates reading NASTY, Hardman laughed. "If I'd known it wasn't going to cost no more than that, I'd have missed the whole meeting," he said.

He patted the flank of the big car fondly, then grew serious. "I meant it about being the best. I only played as a starting defensive end for one year at North Texas State—my senior year. I went there as a 180-pound running back and then got too big. My first two years, all I played was sideline. So I still have a lot to learn, but I'm learning every day."

"He learns very fast," Nolan says. "He still makes the mistakes you expect from rookies, but he's so quick he outruns most of them. I remember in an exhibition with Cleveland, Bo Scott got outside of him and into the clear and Hardman ran him down from behind. There aren't many men as big as he is who can run down backs in the open field."

And there aren't many coaches like Nolan. "He's a listener," Brodie says. "If you come to him with a suggestion, he thinks it over and he's not afraid to use ideas from the players."

The players might have had any number of suggestions after the tie, but they were almost inarticulate with rage. "We used to lose big on our bad days," one veteran muttered. "We should have won on this one. We won't have any more. Bet on that." •

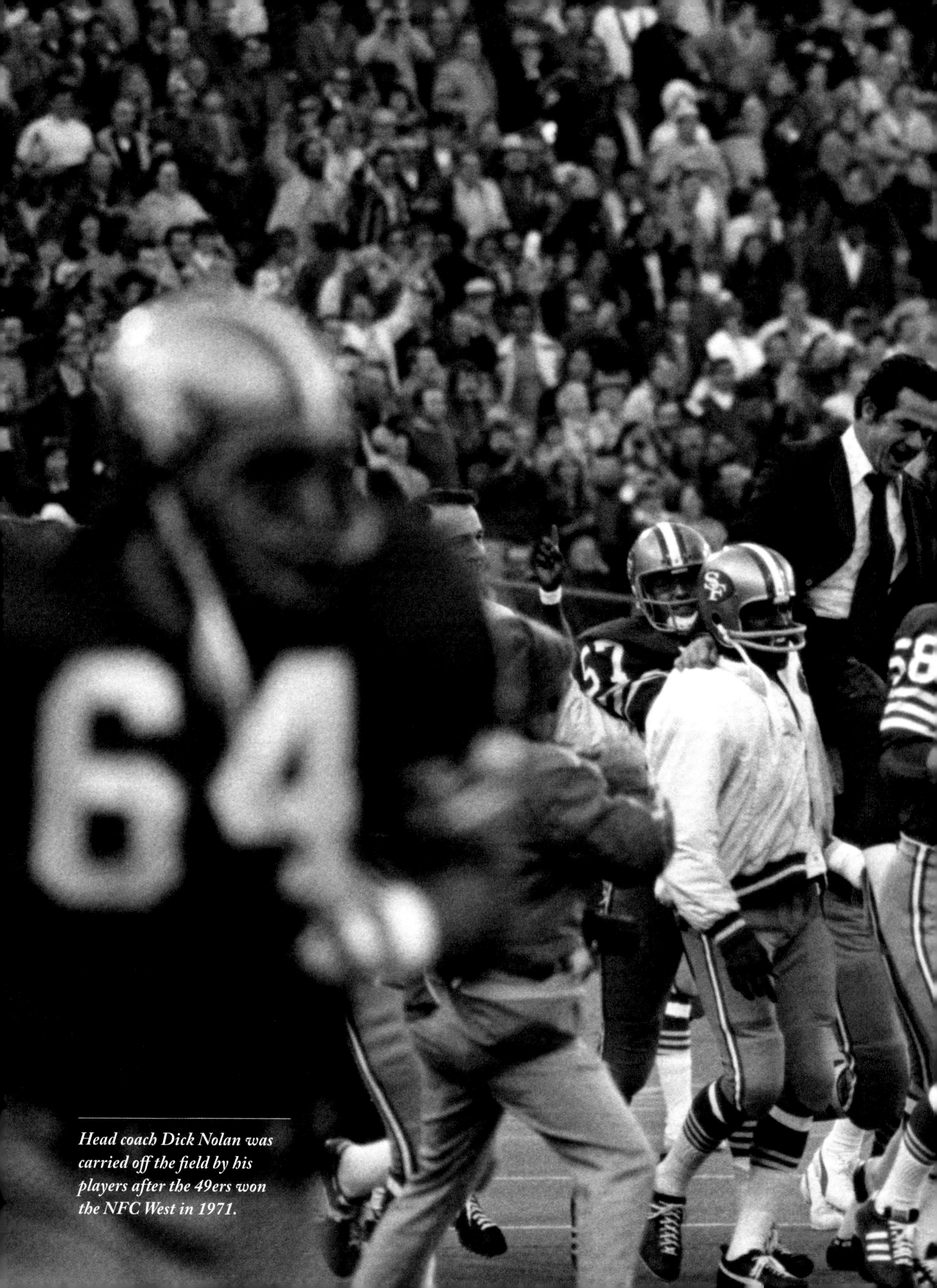

Head coach Dick Nolan was carried off the field by his players after the 49ers won the NFC West in 1971.

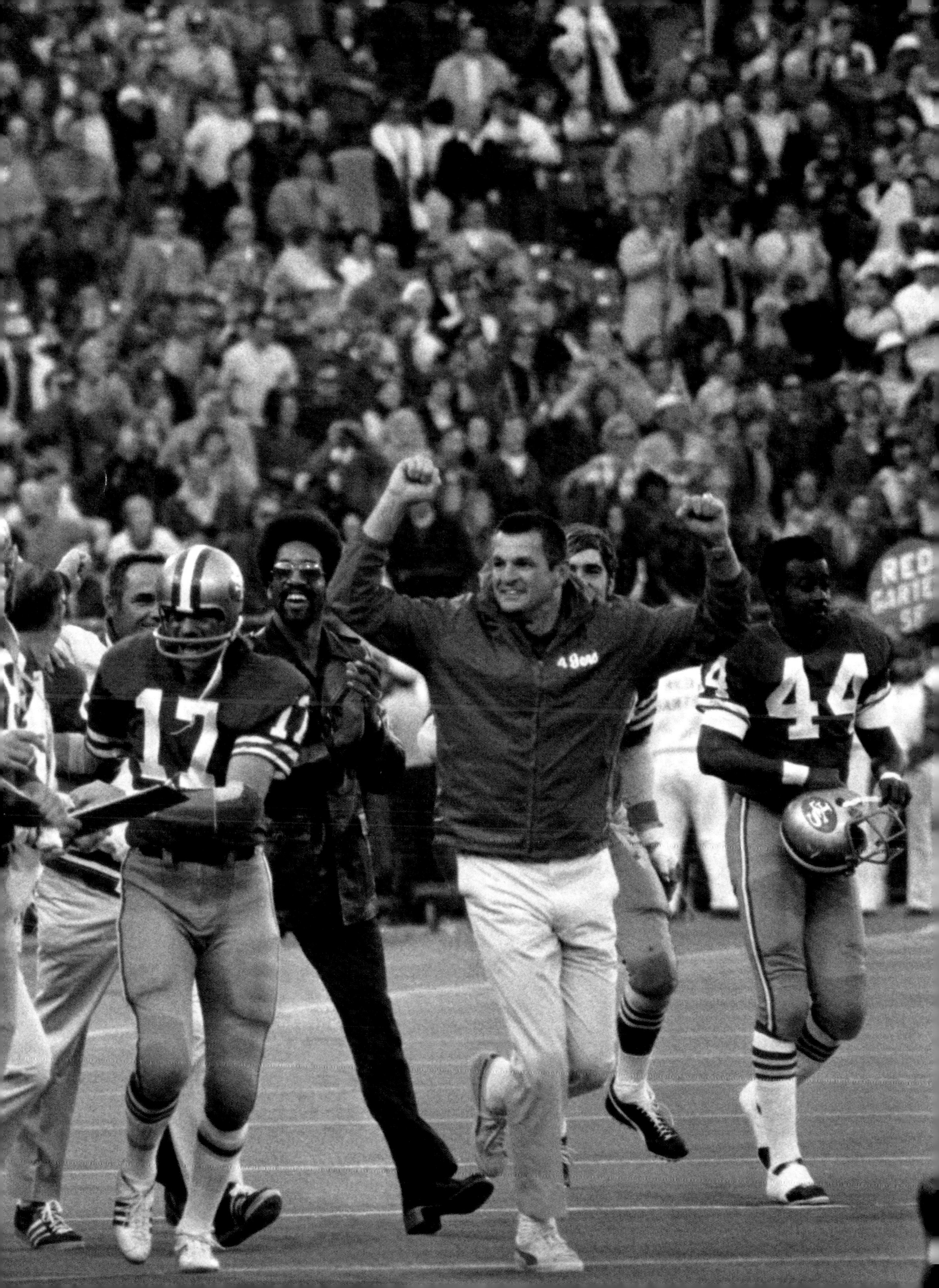
17
49ers
44

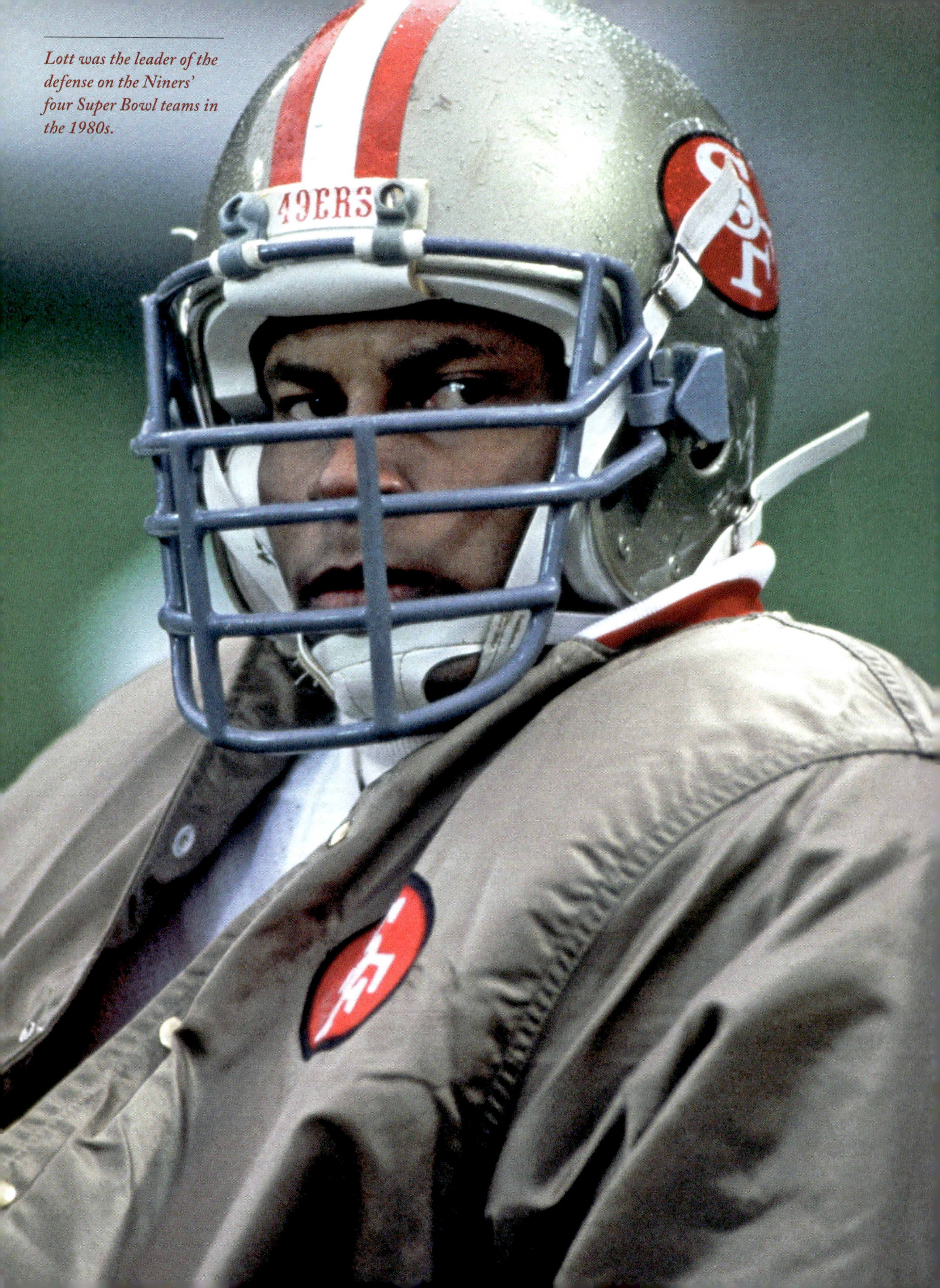

Lott was the leader of the defense on the Niners' four Super Bowl teams in the 1980s.

EXCERPTED FROM SPORTS ILLUSTRATED | JANUARY 23, 1989

HITTER WITH HEART

San Francisco's All-Pro safety, Ronnie Lott, is as generous with his time as he is with his tackles BY JILL LIEBER

BOB AND MARIA BURCINA. A VIVACIOUS MIDDLE-AGED COUPLE, WERE TWO OF THE FRIENDLIEST PEOPLE ON Cadiz Drive in San Jose, Calif. They organized neighborhood ice cream socials, opened their kitchen for breakfast get-togethers and set up a hot dog stand in their driveway for the street's annual June garage sale. When their neighbor Toni Scurti had a baby, Bob welcomed her home from the hospital with a large banner that read IT'S A BOY.

So when Bob was diagnosed as having lung cancer, Scurti surprised him with a real-life get-well card—a visit from her friend All-Pro safety Ronnie Lott of the San Francisco 49ers.

"We walked in, and Bob was hunched over in a chair, his arm in a sling," recalls Scurti. "The radiation treatments had taken a lot out of him, but when he saw Ronnie, he sprang up and said, 'I'm going to walk across the room to shake this man's hand.'"

For two hours Lott shared stories about his teammates and life in the NFL. Bob reminisced about old-time 49ers and critiqued the current team's losses to the Phoenix Cardinals and the Los Angeles Raiders earlier in the season. After Lott's visit, Marie couldn't get Bob to wear anything but his red-and-gold 49er sweatpants and cap. On Sundays he watched the Niners' games from his bed, often with tears in his eyes. When he died two days before Christmas, at 57, he was surrounded by the people and things he loved most—his family and his 49er mementos.

"Ronnie gave him energy," says Marie. "The cancer was wearing on him at all times, but for those few hours Ronnie gave my husband peace of mind. That was something no one else was able to give."

Lott, 29, is forever comforting those in need. To them he's more than just the best free safety in the NFL—he's a patron saint in blue jeans and a baseball cap. A few months ago a woman Lott had never met knocked on his door and asked him to visit a friend who had recently broken his neck. No problem, said Lott, and while he was at the hospital, he also consoled a man with a crushed hip. One morning a friend of Lott's phoned to request an autographed football for a sick colleague. By early afternoon the ball was on his friend's desk. Lott also donates money to two San Francisco churches to help feed the homeless, and he is planning to organize food drives at several 49er games next season.

"It's easy to help others, to give them some hope, some belief that they can make it," says Lott. "You've got to share yourself. You can't forget where you came from and that you should help people. The rewards you get from that are better than any others."

Lott gives as much of himself on the field, but in a much different way. He plays the game with passion, throwing his six-foot, 200-pound body at running backs, wide receivers and tight ends with abandon. He is not only one of the hardest hitters in the NFL but also one of its most respected players. "Ronnie slams into guys full force, straight up," says Jack Tatum, the former Oakland Raider All-Pro defensive back. "But he has to refine his style. He does as much damage to himself as he does to the other guy."

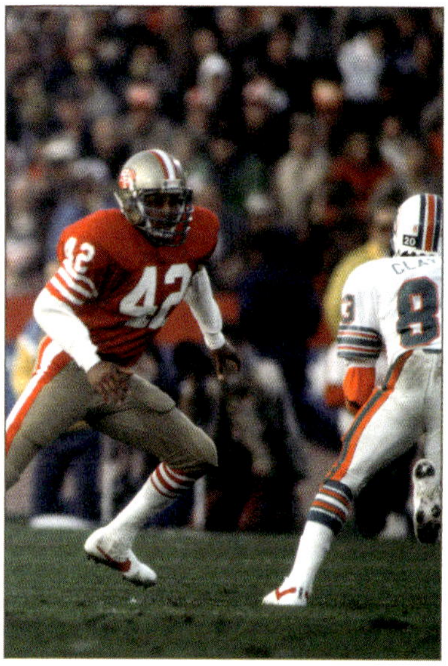

Lott struck fear into runners.

Lott estimates that he has been knocked unconscious at least six times making tackles. "I'm dinged and dazed, like a boxer who's trying to wake up," he says. "On the sidelines, I'm always trying to trick the doctors into believing I'm all right. When they say, 'You're out of the game,' I say, 'The hell I am.'"

Lott has separated or dislocated his right shoulder twice and separated the left one once. He has pinched a nerve in his neck and broken or sprained three of his fingers. In 1985 he got his left pinkie caught between his shoulder pads and the helmet of Dallas running back Timmy Newsome. The bone at the tip of the finger was shattered, and when the bone failed to heal, Lott had the tip amputated. He has also played with torn cartilage in his right knee and with a cracked tibia in his right leg.

Lott is such an intimidating force that scouts contend some wide receivers cringe at the thought of running routes into his territory. They sometimes fail to reach up for passes, opting instead to stay low and protect their bodies from Lott's devastating blows. Ray Rhodes, San Francisco's defensive-backfield coach, likes to call these hard hits "woo licks" because they make stadium crowds—and opponents studying game films—let out cries of wonder at every crunch. Wooooooo!

"When you see Ronnie taking out guys on film, it puts thoughts in the back of your mind," says Dallas Cowboys tight end Doug Cosbie. "You know he's going to hit you, and it's not going to be a whole lot of fun. It's like a prizefighter who has to face Mike Tyson; he can't flinch every time Tyson throws a punch."

At the moment of contact, Lott says he can gauge how-hard his hit is but not how effective it will be. The world around him goes silent, and he claims he never hears his victim grunt, groan or squeal. "That's because he knocks the wind out of each one of them," says Dennis Thurman, who coaches the Cardinals' defensive backs.

Lott laughs when asked about his hardest hit, a head-on-collision with Atlanta Falcons running back William Andrews in 1982. "I ran 10 yards straight at him, as hard as I could," he recalls. "He didn't see me. The whole time I was saying to myself, This is it! Then, boom. I slid off of him like butter. I hit the ground, and he didn't go down. I was thinking, What?"

"People are always asking where I'll be 10 years from now, if I'll be able to walk," continues Lott. "I'm just thankful to be here today. It's not important to be known as someone who hits hard. It's important to be thought of as a guy who gives his all. Sure, I'm taking a risk of getting injured or being burned. But one thing you don't do is sell out on your heart."

Lott started learning that lesson very early in life. The oldest of Roy and Mary Lott's three children, Ronnie was born in Albuquerque, then moved to Washington, D.C., five years later when his father, who was in the Air Force, was given the job of chauffeuring generals between Boiling Air Force Base and the Pentagon. Growing up in the inner city toughened Ronnie. "You learned how to compete," he recalls. "Either you were good or you didn't play." But city life also squelched the freedom and spontaneity he had enjoyed in Albuquerque. The schoolyard was far from home, so Lott played baseball in an abandoned parking lot and football in the street with his brother, Roy Jr., and their friends, Richard and Stanley Walker. "I pretended I was Charley Taylor," says Lott. "Richard called himself Daryle Lamonica. Stanley was Larry Brown, and Roy thought he was Billy Kilmer."

At Christmas the Lott brothers and their playmates begged their parents for Washington Redskins helmets and uniforms. Ronnie also pleaded for a pair of P.F. Flyers, insisting that those particular shoes would make him run faster and jump higher than the rest of the kids. "To demonstrate how good the sneakers were, he jumped from our second-floor apartment window to the first-floor landing," says Roy Sr. with a laugh. "That landing was only four feet square. He hit it perfectly and didn't even hurt himself. That really shocked me."

When Ronnie was nine, the Lotts moved to San Bernardino, Calif., 50 miles east of Los Angeles, and a year later settled in nearby Rialto. Ronnie had difficulty channeling the aggressiveness he had developed playing games on pavement. During one recess Lott clobbered a fifth-grade teacher with a kickball while making a tag and was ordered to write and illustrate a booklet on sportsmanship, which his mother still has.

Ronnie convinced his parents to let him try out for Little League baseball by promising to wash and iron his own uniform. And when he and Roy Jr. started playing Pop Warner football, everybody in the family got involved. Roy Sr. was a league administrator, sister Suzie was a cheerleader and Mary provided sandwiches and sodas after games.

Crisscrossing the country as a military family, Mary believes, brought the Lotts closer together. "We were the only family we had," she says. "It was just the five of us. We made sure everybody shared, everybody gave. And we kept our focus humble."

Says Lott, "I never really had a best friend until my freshman year at Southern Cal. I couldn't get close to anybody because we were always leaving town. My parents were like my friends."

At USC, Lott was a consensus All-America at safety in both his junior and senior seasons. As a junior he also played reserve point guard on the basketball team.

Since being selected by San Francisco in the first round of the 1981 draft, he has led the Niners in interceptions four times (twice sharing the lead with others) and has been selected for the Pro Bowl in seven of his eight seasons—four times at cornerback, which he played until 1985, and three at safety. Only two other players, Mel Renfro and Dave Grayson, have ever been named All-Pro at both positions.

Despite an annual salary of $842,500, which makes him one of the highest paid defensive backs in the league, Lott remains remarkably down-to-earth. He has owned a couple of Mercedes, but he now drives a Volkswagen Rabbit. He lives in a modest two-bedroom condominium in Santa Clara, Calif. On the tables in his den are his college diploma (he graduated in four years from USC with a degree in public administration), Suzie's wedding picture and some handmade cards from young 49er fans. The walls of his breakfast nook are covered with inspirational poems and prayers collected by his mother. And his high school diploma is on the nightstand in the guest room.

During the season Lott writes a weekly column for the *San Jose Mercury News* and does a weekly sports show for KNTV in San Jose. Part of his reimbursement for the show is free commercial time for his restaurant, Sports City Cafe, which he created, and owns with several others, including teammates Roger Craig, Keena Turner and Eric Wright. Lott also has become a devotee of Asian art and culture. "I'm intrigued by the peacefulness," he says. Since 1986, taekwondo has been part of his off-season conditioning program. Three times a week he performs a routine that includes 700 sit-ups, 400 push-ups and hundreds of kicks and punches.

Lott collects photographs of children who have written fan letters to him. Two of his buddies are Tony and Matt Kelly, who are students at Santa Clara High. He met the boys seven years ago at a local park. Lott plays pickup basketball with them and takes them shopping at the mall and out to dinner. For Christmas, the Kellys gave Lott a new basketball.

Lott has recently received letters from Bob Burcina's 15 grandchildren. Each thanked him for having visited their grandpa. Just before he died, Bob also sent Lott a note. Too weak to write, he dictated it to Marie. Along with the letter he included a poem he had written for the 49ers in 1982 that was read on the radio before they faced the Cincinnati Bengals in Super Bowl XVI. Marie says Bob sensed that he might not make it to this year's Super Bowl, but he wanted to cheer on his new friend. Bob ended the poem this way:

God goes with you on your trip to the bowl,
and if for some reason you don't reach your goal;
Come back to us with heads held high,
for we surely know you gave it one hell of a try.
But on a sad note let's not linger.
You're coming home WITH THAT RING ON YOUR FINGER. •

Lott, 29, is forever comforting those in need. To them he's more than just the best free safety in the NFL—he's a patron saint in blue jeans and a baseball cap.

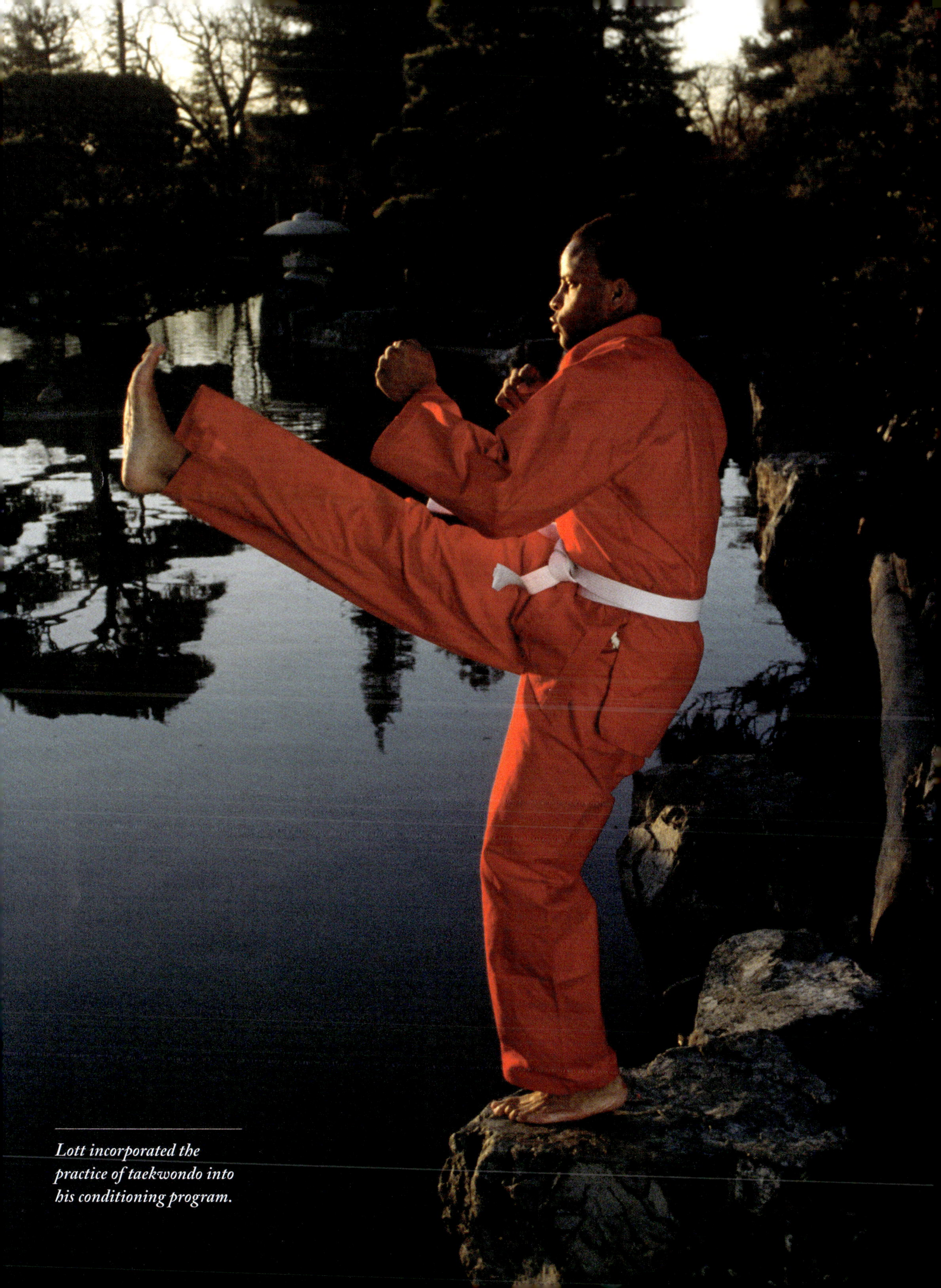

Lott incorporated the practice of taekwondo into his conditioning program.

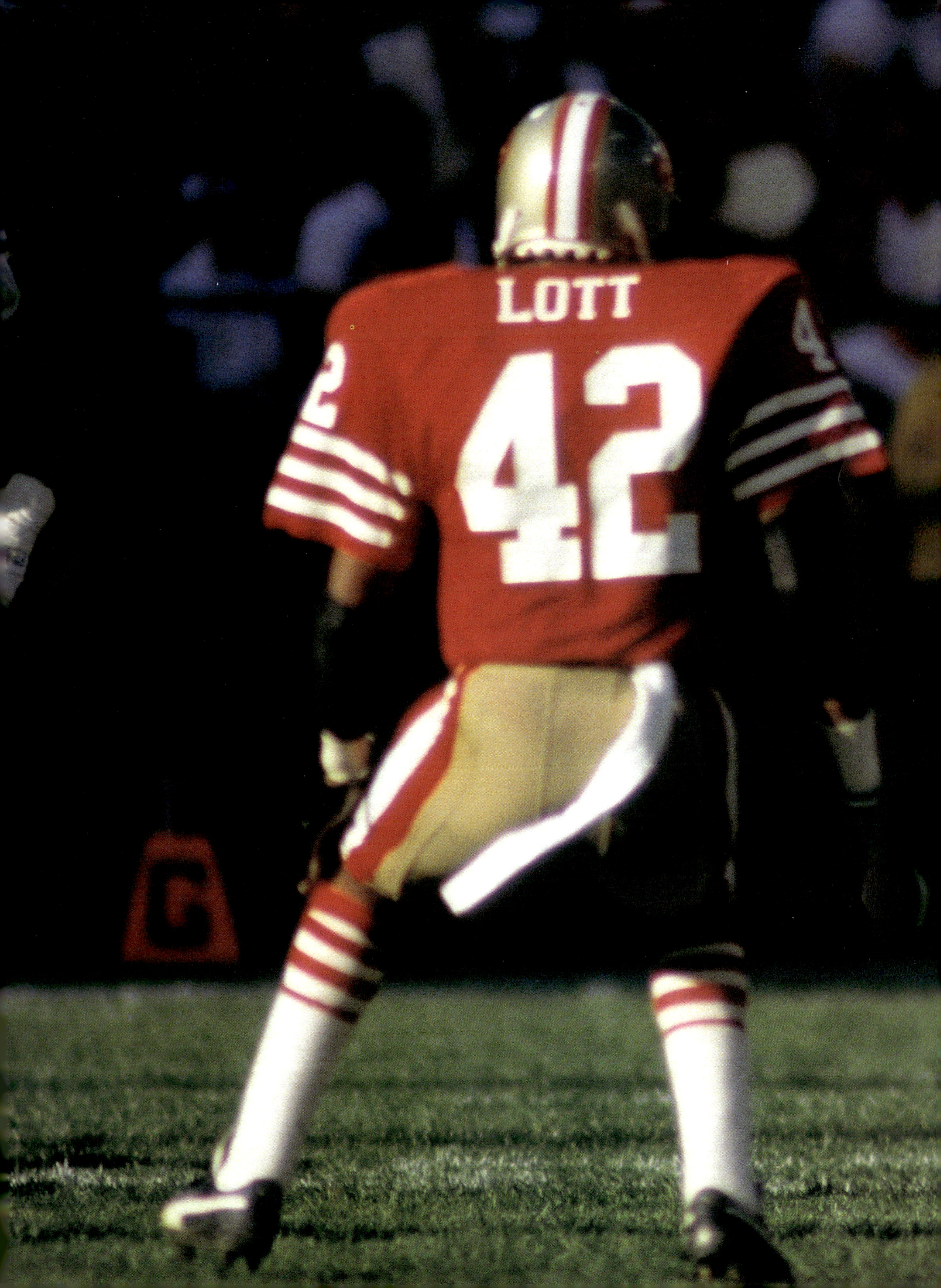
LOTT
42

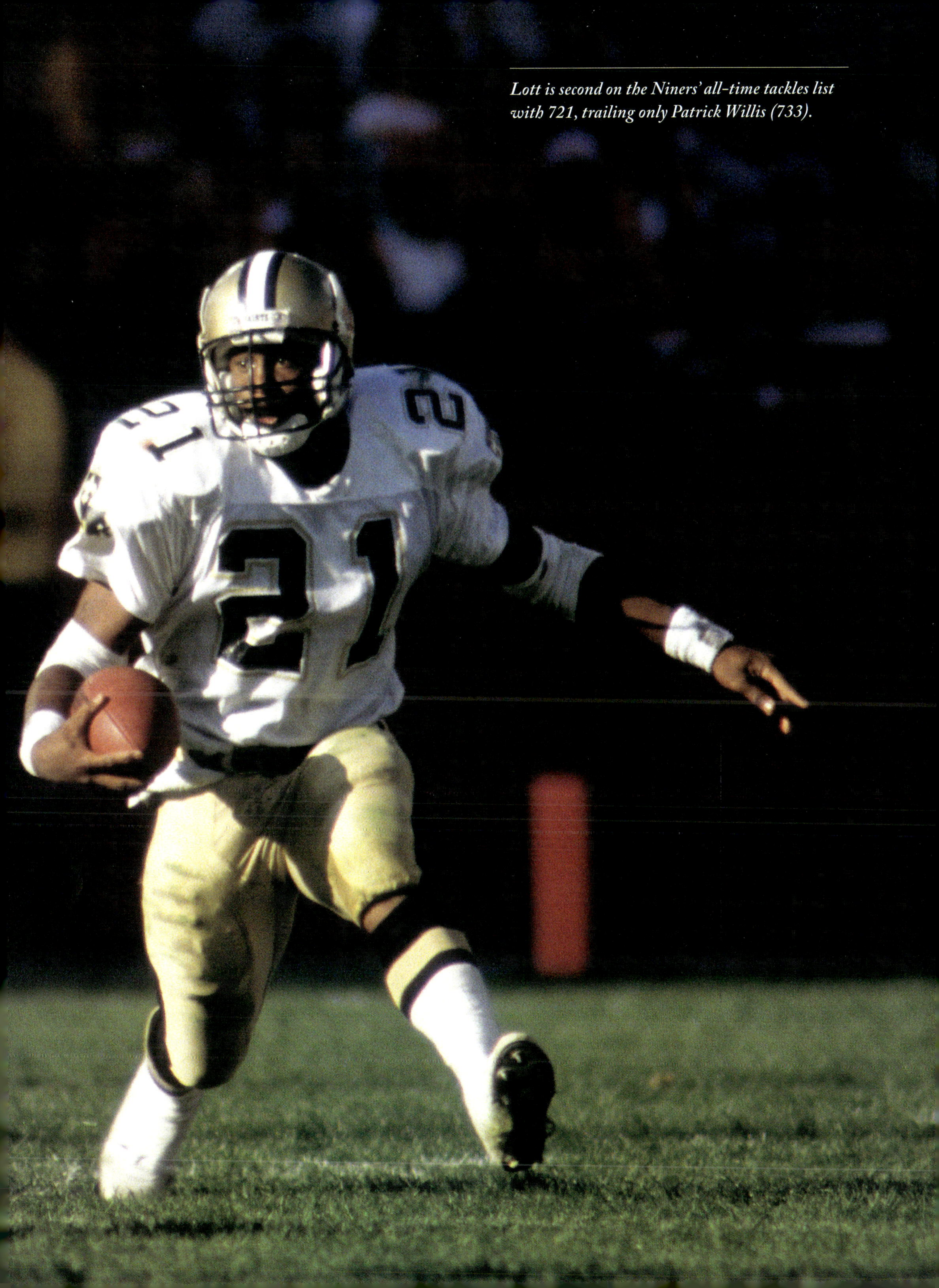

Lott is second on the Niners' all-time tackles list with 721, trailing only Patrick Willis (733).

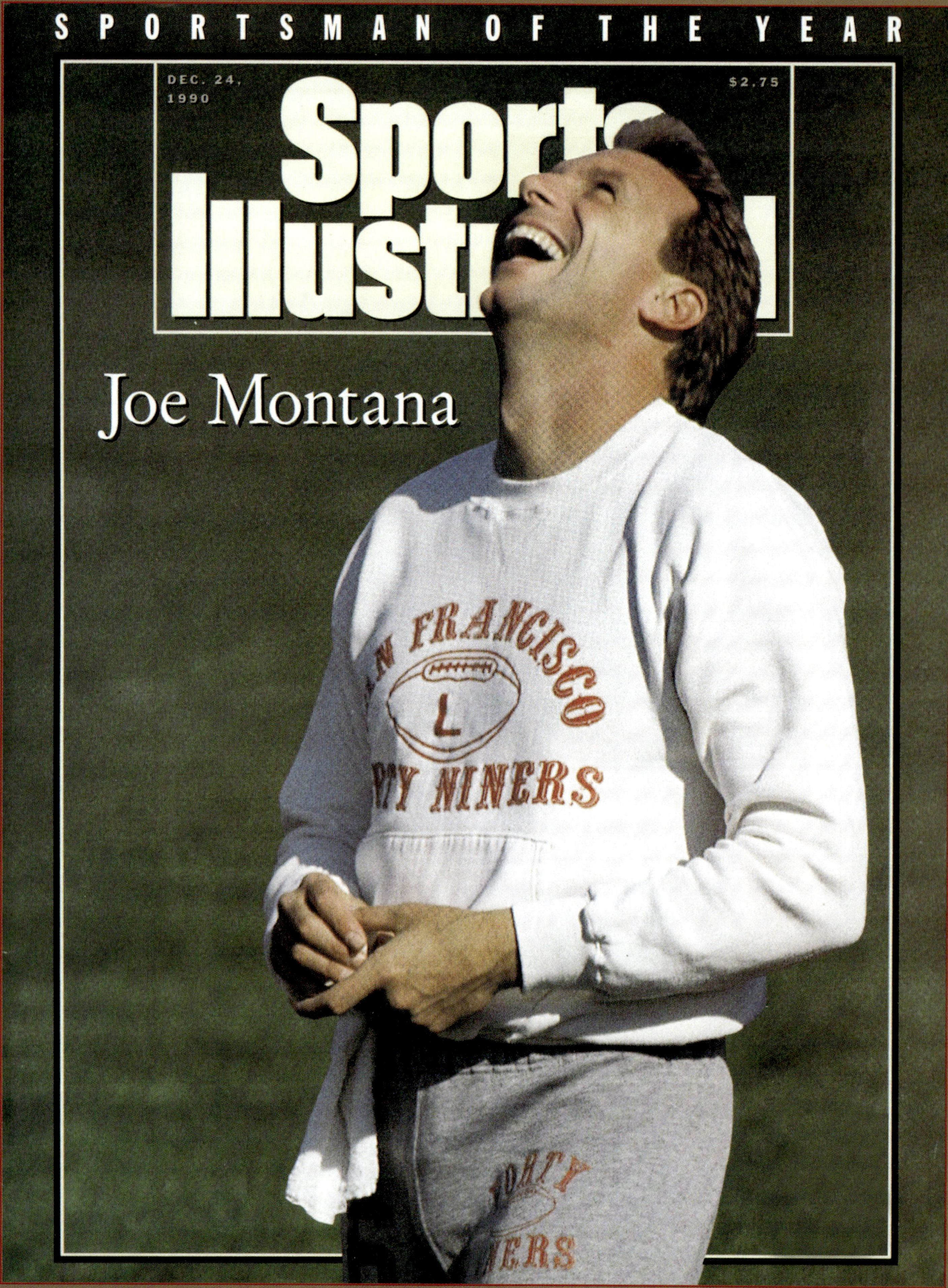
SPORTSMAN OF THE YEAR
DEC. 24, 1990
$2.75
Joe Montana

EXCERPTED FROM SPORTS ILLUSTRATED | DECEMBER 24, 1990

AN AMERICAN DREAM

What kid doesn't want to grow up to be quarterback Joe Montana? BY LEIGH MONTVILLE

YOU LOOK AT THE POSTER ON THE BEDROOM WALL. YOU COULD BE JOE MONTANA. YES, YOU COULD. YOU THROW your official NFL ball into the air, narrowly missing the model airplanes hanging from the ceiling by strings. You catch the ball and dive onto the bed. Montana to Rice! Touchdown! You could do that. You could hear the same noises Joe Montana hears. You could do the same things he does. Yes, you could.

"What's your name, son?"

"Joe Montana. Like the state. Montana."

The possibility is not out of reach. You would not have to be exceptionally fast. You would not have to grow exceedingly tall. You would not have to develop unbelievable strength. Your game would be wits and grace and style and reactions. These are gifts you could have. Cool. You could have cool. The Neanderthals from the defensive line would charge at your face and you would step to the right, step to the left, let them pass with their misguided fury. Cool. The disguises of the defensive backfield would fall away before your eyes. Who is open? How far do I throw? There never would be doubt. You simply would deliver the mail.

Quarterback. That is your position. Has to be. Your father spent a lot of time in this same room thinking he could be Johnny Unitas. His father thought he could be Sid Luckman. Isn't that the American boyhood dream? You could be Joe. Those pennants, held down against the floral wallpaper by thumbtacks now, could be waving in the brisk autumn air. Those street noises outside could be 60,000 people, mad for a moment. You could be holding your hands out for quiet. You could be changing the play at the line of scrimmage, the rest of your San Francisco 49er teammates crouched and ready to go. You could be picking the perfect play for the perfect moment, then running it perfectly.

Nothing would be different. You would have that same boyish humility, amazing everyone and then telling the reporters that it was "no big deal." You would drive the red Ferrari and be married to the television personality and have three pretty children for the Christmas card. The contract would be for multimillions for multiyears. The adulation would grow daily. You would be the star of the best team of a decade, winning four Super Bowls and heading for a possible fifth. The experts would say you were "the best ever," or at least a candidate. The success would not go to your head. You would be All-Pro, a starter in the Pro Bowl, a salesman for the latest wicked-awesome fluorescent sneakers. You would be named SPORTS ILLUSTRATED's Sportsman of the Year for 1990, the first pro football player to win the award outright in its 37 years.

How would that feel?

You could handle it. You could be Joe Montana.

The poster costs five bucks. Send the five bucks to a mail-order house in Fenton, Mo., and you can receive a poster of Bo Jackson or Michael Jordan or Magic Johnson. Or the 2-by 3-foot picture can show Joe Montana throwing a football. He is wearing his white jersey with the red No. 16 on the front. White wristbands. A white towel hanging from his belt. The ball coming from behind his gold 49er helmet.

An 11-year-old kid named Justin Rozen from Branford, Conn., bought the poster because he "just likes Joe and his talent." A man named Ken Hall from Clinton, Ind., bought one for his nine-year-old son, Kenny, because "Kenny had all these pictures of Joe, cut out from sports magazines, on his wall already." A 12-year-old named Azriel Chelst from Southfield, Mich., bought one because "Joe can pass, and I love his two-minute drill, and I want to be a quarterback.

"My friend and I are pretty good. I'm always Joe Montana and he's always Jerry Rice. We have a deep pass that always works. Well, mostly always. If my friend catches the ball. Then I say the words at the end of the Super Bowl."

The words?

"I'm going to Disney World."

You like to watch him on television. Especially during the hard times. The hard times are best. You know all about him during the hard times. You have read all the stories, read the books, listened to all the commentators. He is at his best when the chips are down. Isn't that what they say? You love to watch him when the chips are down.

He somehow seems to breathe slower when everyone else breathes fast, seems to have a different metabolism. Remember that final drive in the 1989 Super Bowl? You fell off the chair. You rolled on the floor with excitement. Was there ever any doubt that he simply was going to move those Niners 92 yards down the field in the final 3:20 to beat the Cincinnati Bengals? Of course not. He completed one pass, and then another, and another. Eight of nine passes during the drive. Was there ever any better high-pressure bit of football business? Didn't you read what he said at the start of the drive?

"Hey, check it out," he said to tackle Harris Barton.

"Check out what?" Barton asked.

"There, in the stands, standing near the exit ramp," Joe said. "There's John Candy."

Wasn't that the greatest? There are lists of the comebacks he has quarterbacked in 12 seasons with the Niners and four college seasons at Notre Dame. The lists are so long that they look like the itinerary for a breakout tour by a heavy-metal band. Your father remembers reading about someone named Chip Hilton who did the same things Joe does. Your grandfather mentions someone named Frank Merriwell. You don't know any of that. Weren't those characters from fiction? Joe is real. A real Joe.

One of your favorite comebacks was at the Cotton Bowl in 1979, when he directed the Fighting Irish to 23 points in the final

7:37. They won 35–34 over the University of Houston. The day was cold…and Joe was fighting hypothermia, was filled with bullion to get his temperature back near normal…and he went into the ice and wind and did the job. Did the job? Twenty-three points in 7:37?

You look at his record, and he has led the Niners to a comeback win every year since he has been a starter. He had four on the way to last season's Super Bowl win. This year, through Dec. 16, he had three. It seemed for a while that he was doing magic tricks every week, two minutes to play, pushing the 49ers down the field. His total now is 26 fourth-quarter comeback wins as a pro. Doesn't that have to be some kind of a record?

"Let me take a chance at this," Joe says when times are hard.

"Is that good enough?" he says when he turns the score upside down.

You look at his life and it has been a series of challenges that he has met and mastered. He wasn't one of those one-sport robot athletes in high school, needing summer camp and year-round practice to get a handle on one particular game. He was a kid. He played football and basketball and baseball in Monongahela, Pa., each sport in its season. The football coach benched him as a junior, and he came back the same season and was the best. He went to Notre Dame. He was listed seventh on the depth chart, and he rose to the top. He was the best. The pros neglected him, the Niners drafting him in the third round, and he met the challenge again. He was the best. He even had back surgery—the doctors doubted he would play again—and he overcame that, too. He is the best.

His story is the traditional athletic parable. Forget any frayed edges that are mentioned in the tabloids. The core of the story is good and true. You can't do it! Yes, I can! Isn't that the heartbeat of sport? Isn't that the best sight to see? This 34-year-old guy has delivered more often than anyone else who's around now, maybe more often than anyone ever. He proves detractors wrong. He makes them shut up.

"Here's how Joe's luck goes," says Jerry Walker, the 49ers' director of public relations. "I help him with his mail. My wife also helps. One day, I was cleaning out the car, and I found a letter to Joe that had somehow fallen behind a seat. The letter was about 10 months old, a request from a girl for an autograph. We sent out a picture, and about a week later I notice another envelope arrive with the same name and handwriting. I somehow remembered. I opened the envelope, and the girl had written a thank-you note. She said she was amazed at how thoughtful Joe had been, waiting 10 months to time the arrival of his picture to the exact date of her birthday. Anyone else.... That's just Joe. Things somehow work out."

Remember that final drive in the 1989 Super Bowl?

You fell off the chair. You rolled on the floor with excitement.

The mail arrives in bunches. A nationally televised game brings bigger bunches. A record brings even bigger bunches. A Super Bowl win? There are 10 U.S. Postal Service bins filled with mail, almost a year's worth, still awaiting replies in Walker's office. The bunches form an avalanche that no human can handle. Included in the avalanche are special T-shirts and Christmas ornaments and knitted key chains and just about any personalized gift imaginable. Birthday cards are a separate avalanche.

"It's an amazing phenomenon," Walker says. "My daughter broke her arm two years ago. She came to practice, and Joe saw her and signed her cast: 'To Kelly, my one and only girl. Joe Montana.' At school the next day she received various offers for the cast. One kid offered his entire baseball and football card collection. She didn't make the deal. At the same school, I attended a Halloween parade of costumes. A little grammar school in Palo Alto. I counted 17 kids dressed as Joe Montana in the parade. The number was probably high because this is California, but 17 Joe Montanas?"

You see him up close. Just once. The game is in Dallas on a warm Sunday night this season. The Niners are unbeaten at the time, flying. Joe is flying. You watch him shred the poor Cowboys, 24–6. The game is never a contest. By halftime Joe has completed 15 of 18 passes for 188 yards. The Niners have a 17–6 lead. At each end of Texas Stadium, giant replay screens seem to show Joe's face after every play. A 30-foot face. A 6'2" man. How would that be, looking at your own 30-foot face all the time? Joe does not seem to notice.

At the end of the game, you have special credentials to go into the locker room. Don't say how you got them. You go to Joe's locker and wait for him to appear, but a man comes in and says Joe will talk to the press in another room. You go to that room, and there he is. He is standing on a bench. Ten microphones are held in front of his face. Four cameras are rolling. He is wearing gray gym shorts and his white-and-red game socks and a T-shirt. The T-shirt presumably once was white, but it has become almost pink because of red dye bleeding from the perspiration-soaked red jersey that he wore during the game. His arms are crossed, and there is a touch of real blood on his right elbow.

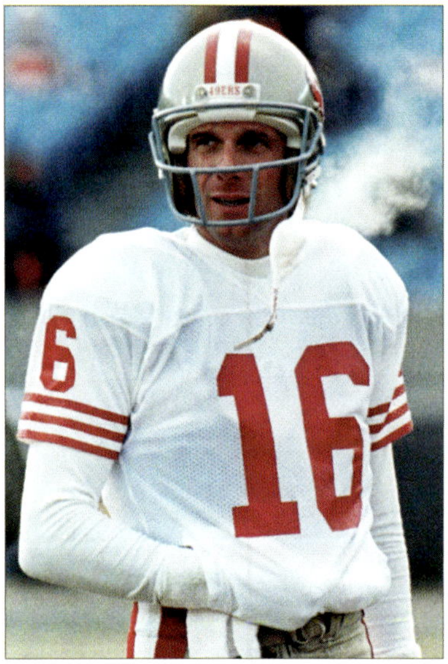

Despite appearances, Montana was anything but average.

"We didn't do some things.... We got away with it this time," he says. "The next time, we might not. I think we played just average. I played just average."

Just average? He scored a touchdown. He threw for a touchdown. He completed 27 of 37 passes for 290 yards. He was touched by the Dallas defense no more than four times. Just average. You study his face. He looks a little like the singer Barry Manilow. He smiles and seems easy with words, but he does not say much. He is not a nightclub comedian or a politician or an evangelist. He is a football player.

The press conference—lasting no longer than seven minutes—is finished when a heavy-set man named Jim Warren tells Joe that he has to get rolling. Warren carries a walkie-talkie and also has a little audio plug in one ear. He's one of the Niners' private security guards on game days, and most of the time he watches out for Joe. On the way out the door, Joe is asked to do an interview with a television crew that has arrived late. Joe says, "It wouldn't be fair to all of those other guys." He smiles. He is off to the trainer's room.

"I've been guarding him since 1981," Warren says. "Everywhere we go, I figure ways to get him out of the stadium. There always are so many people waiting. You have to find different routes. In L.A., I take him right up through the stands and out a side door. In Atlanta, we go way through the back, through this concessions area. Dallas here isn't bad. For the most part, the people are kept away from the buses."

The buses wait in a fenced-off runway on the side of the stadium. There are three of them, all in a row. There also are two equipment trucks and a four-man motorcycle escort. All engines are running, everyone is waiting, when Joe finally emerges from the locker room. He comes out on the run, behind Warren, as people yell his name and try to hand slips of paper to him. Warren directs him to the second bus in the line, and he gets on and walks to the last seat and sits next to safety Ronnie Lott. You can see Lott hand him a beer before the lights go out on the bus. The motorcycles start rolling. The buses and trucks start rolling.

You somehow notice the number on the back of Joe's bus. It's 711. Somehow you think that is perfect.

An 11-year-old named Matthew Hart, from Red Bluff, Calif., had a brain tumor. He was at the University of California at San Francisco Hospital. This was in July. The doctors told his parents he had 48 hours to live. During his radiation treatments, the kid had worn a 49er jersey. His favorite player was Joe Montana.

"We got a call from Matt's mother, Sally, asking if it were possible for Joe to visit Matt," says Ronie Saake of the Sacramento Make-A-Wish Foundation. "We were able to get through to one of Joe's representatives, and she was able to get through to him. Ironically, he was on his way to sign his new contract extension for this season. He said, 'Well, I could be late for the contract' and came to the hospital. He was beautiful. He wasn't some guy who was saying, 'I'm a superstar here to help.' He said he was honored and humbled that Matt had asked for him."

The meeting lasted 45 minutes. Matt was on a morphine drip and would drift in and out of consciousness. He would grab Joe's hand every time he awoke, just to make sure he was seeing real life instead of a dream. Joe left. Matt's crisis passed. Three weeks later, he was strong enough to walk out of the hospital. He is still sick, undergoing treatments, but in September he went to a 49er game. He was Joe's guest.

The attitude never changes. You always are a kid when you see Joe Montana or read about him or simply hear his name and the latest things he has done. You are 11 years old, maybe 12 or 13. The other years do not count, no matter how many have been piled onto the total, no matter what else you might have done. You are wrapped in the blind faith of childhood. Dinner is on the table at the appointed time. Clean clothes always are in the dresser drawers. The afternoon bell at school always signals freedom. A grass field and a game await—a pure time of physical pleasure and active imagination.

What could be better than to be the best quarterback of all, to be in charge, to be famous, to be a picture on everyone else's wall? You could be anything you want to be, but you want most to be this one man. He stands alone on his 100-yard field. He has answered all the questions on all the physical tests, finished where everyone else wanted to finish, the one guy to complete the American boyhood dream.

You could have been…would have been… who knows? You still might be. •

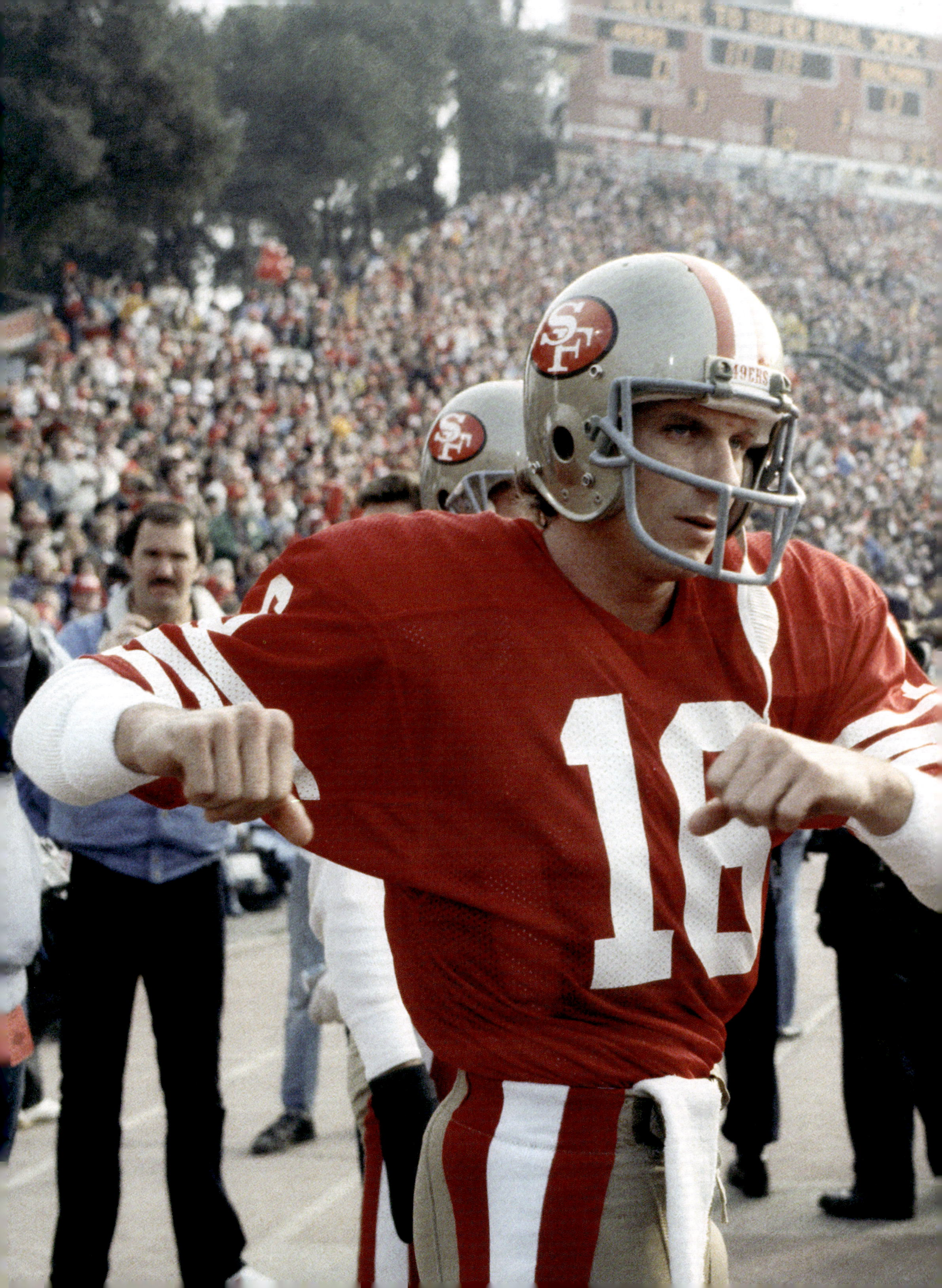
49ERS
16

Montana was never flustered, even moments before Super Bowl XIX.

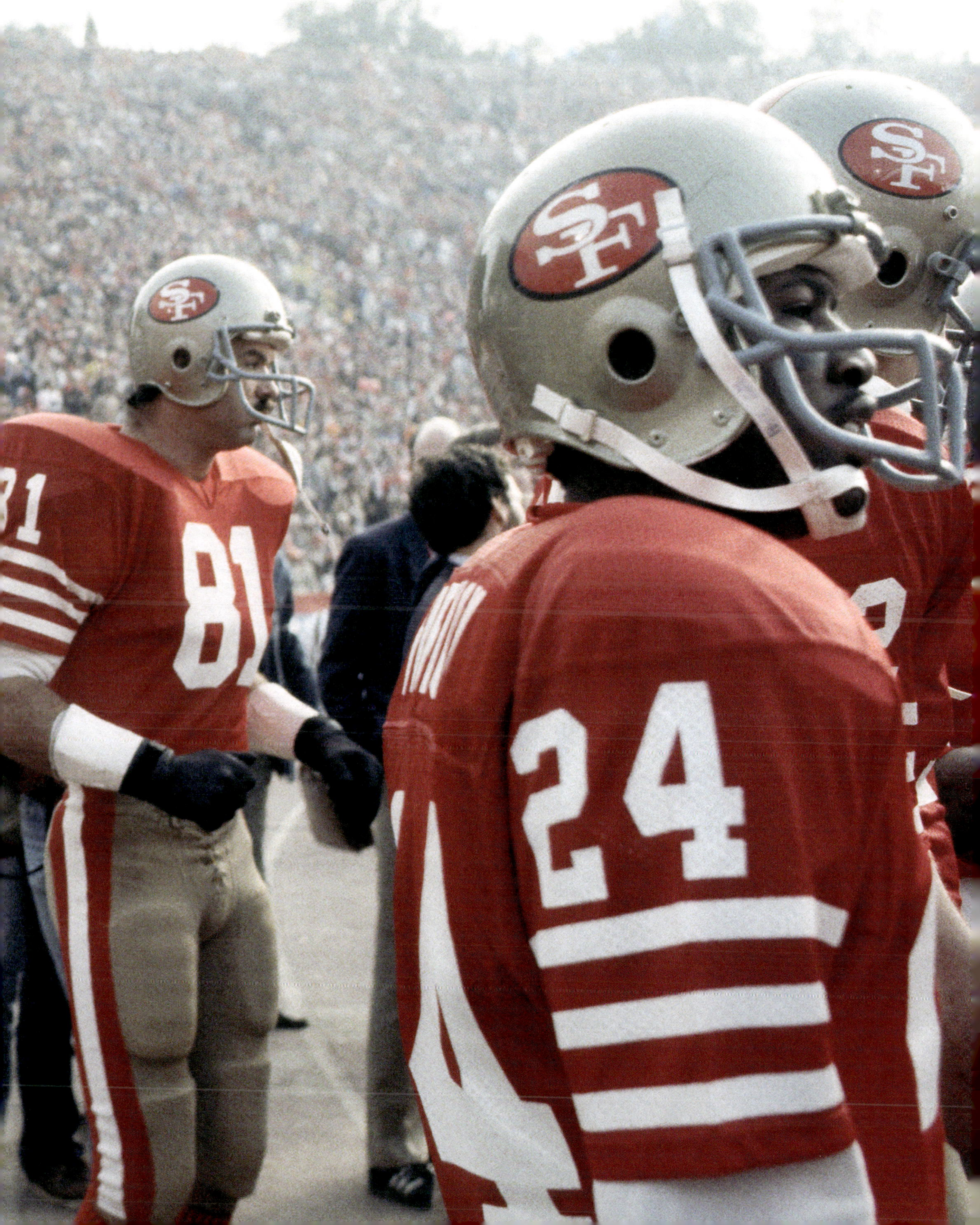

Montana was named the MVP of Super Bowl XIX after completing 24 of 35 passes for a record 331 yards against the Dolphins.

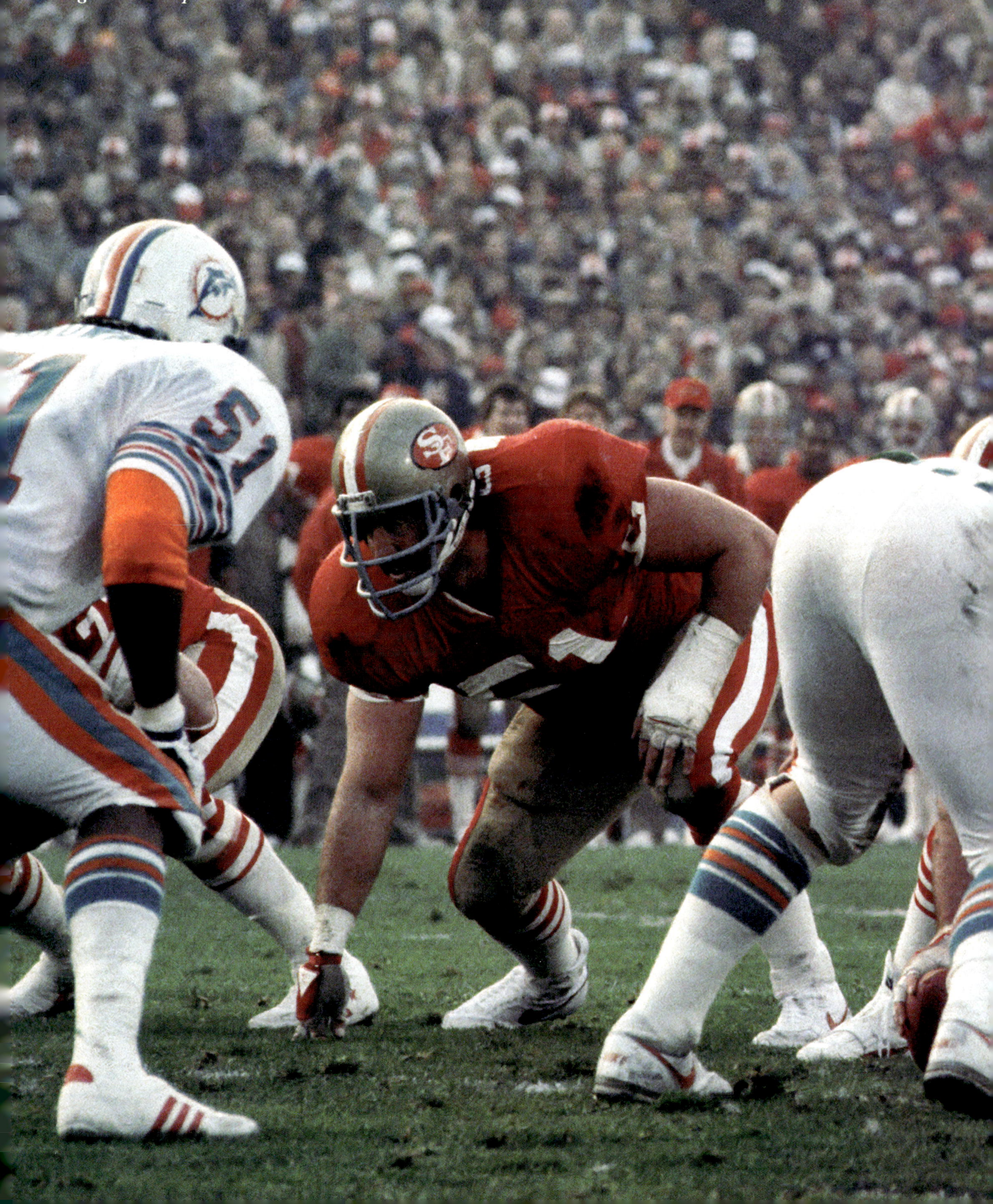

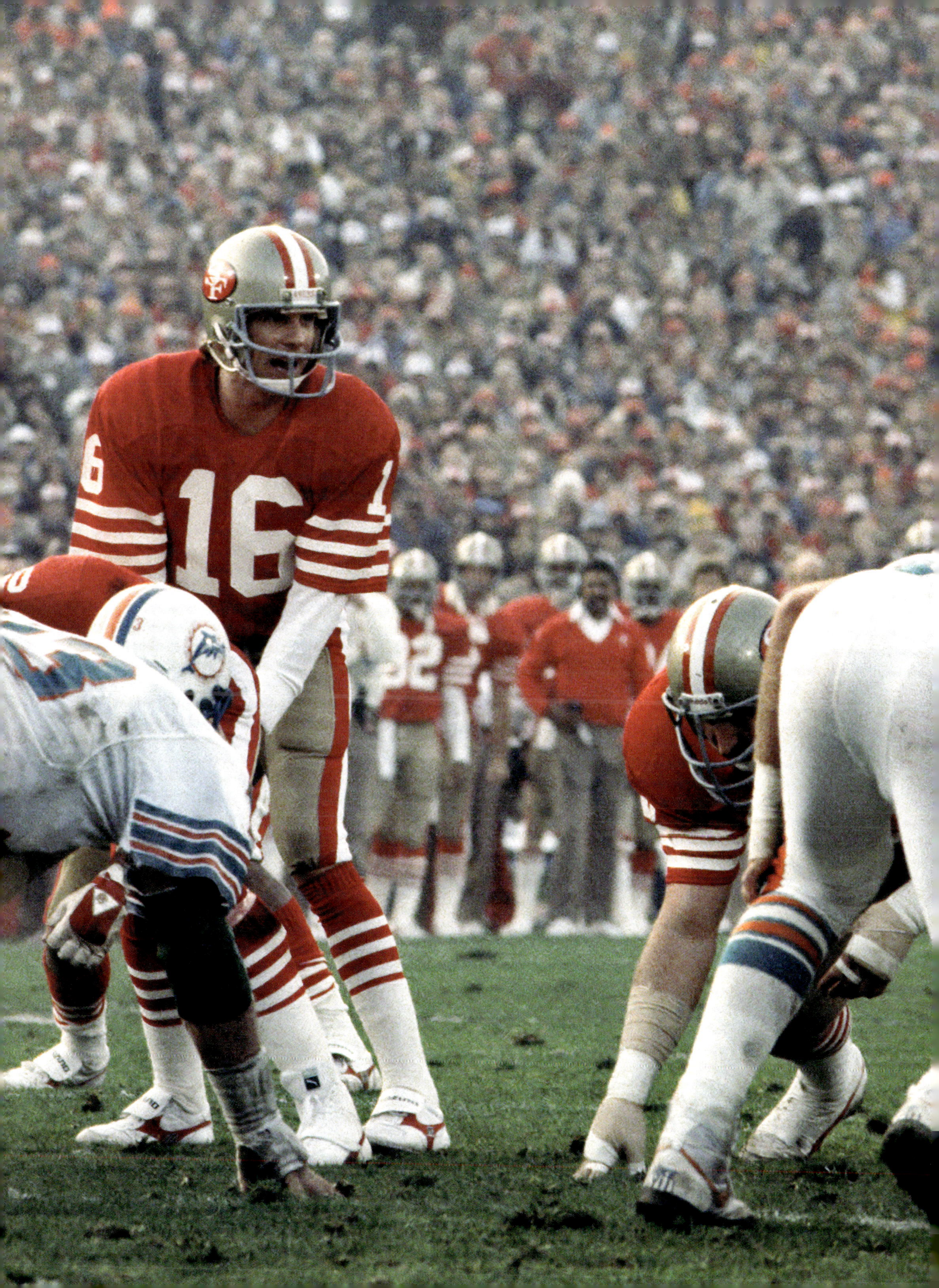

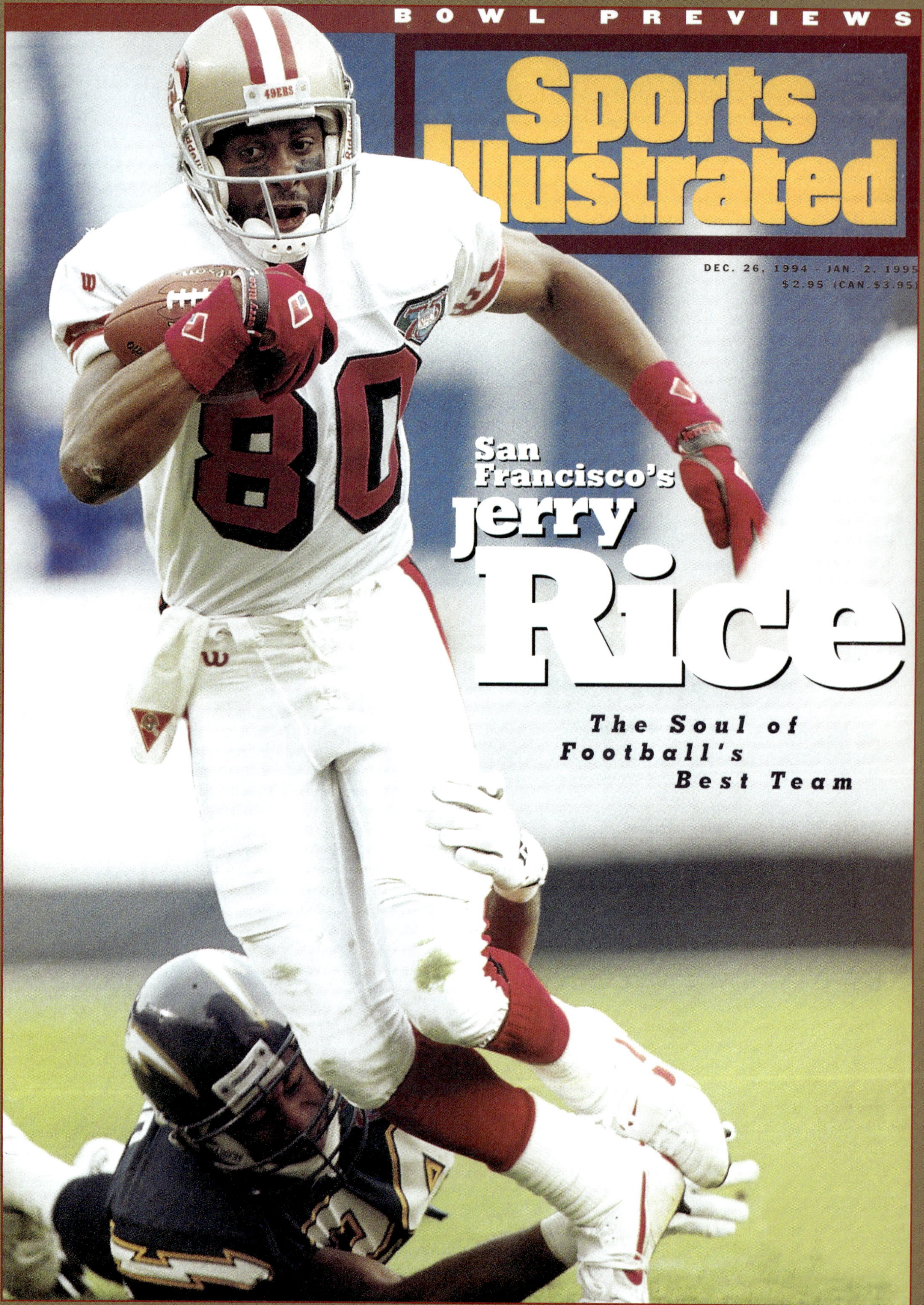
BOWL PREVIEWS
Sports Illustrated
DEC. 26, 1994 - JAN. 2, 1995
$2.95 (CAN. $3.95)
San Francisco's
Jerry
Rice
The Soul of
Football's
Best Team

EXCERPTED FROM SPORTS ILLUSTRATED | DECEMBER 26, 1994

NOTHING SHORT OF PERFECTION

Jerry Rice has proved to everyone—including himself—that he is the finest receiver ever BY RICK TELANDER

THE BEST?

He's here, in blue tights and a red windbreaker, as bitchy as a diva with a headache.

The best ever?

He's right here, sitting at his locker, taking off his rain gear after practice, edgy as a cat in a sawmill.

Around him swirls the clamor of big men winding down, messing around. Two bare-chested linemen start to grapple, rasslin' each other and snorting like trash-talking sumo wrestlers. Other players laugh, but not the best ever.

"Guys," he says irritably. "Hey, guys!" Someone could get hurt.

The two wrestlers slowly come apart, his voice bringing them to their senses. They've heard the voice before; it's their fourth-grade teacher scolding them for rolling spitballs. It's the voice of San Francisco 49er Jerry Rice, the best wide receiver ever to play football.

The 6'2", tightly braided coil of nerves, fast-twitch fibers, delicate grasping skills and unadulterated want-to is setting such high standards for the position that they will probably never be approached again, and he can't stand distractions while he works.

Rice does not fool around. Ever. He works so hard at his conditioning that during the off-season, he virtually exits his body and studies his physical package the way a potter studies clay. "I mess with it," he says. "I like to do different things to motivate myself. I set goals and go after them."

As a rookie in 1985 he came to the 49ers at a muscular 208 pounds, but now he weighs 196. He is so lean that you wonder if he's sick. He likes to mess with his body fat, wants it to know that he is its master. For Rice, fat is a cornerback in man coverage with no safety in sight, a minor and ultimately irrelevant nuisance. Eschewing dietary fat, he got down to 189 a year or so ago, but the weight loss was too much. His starved body was literally eating up his muscles. His trainer ordered him to start eating things like ice cream.

"Under four percent body fat and I don't feel good," Rice says. "I'm a health-food fanatic, but getting that low hurt my performance. I'm at 4.8 percent now, and I feel good."

Well, not really good. Not the way you or I might feel good if we knew that not only were we certifiably the best receiver in the history of football but also, perhaps, the greatest offensive player ever. That argument can be made. Rice already has more receiving touchdowns (131) and more total touchdowns (139) than anyone else in NFL history. He has more 1,000-yard seasons (nine) than any other receiver and more consecutive games with a touchdown reception (13) than anyone.

Was he this good in college? Imagine, for a moment, that it's September 1984, and you are in sweltering Itta Bena, Miss., watching Mississippi Valley State coach Archie (Gunslinger) Cooley direct his Satellite Express offense, with quarterback Willie Totten flinging passes to a senior wideout named Rice, who races out of a stacked receiver formation that looks something like a Motown chorus line. In the first four games of that season, Rice caught 64 passes for 917 yards and 12 touchdowns. As a junior, he caught 24 passes in one game, an all-division record. He left school with 18 NCAA I-AA records. Yes, he was good.

Rice never missed a game in college, nor has he missed one as a pro. Since he joined the 49ers, the team has gone 130–46–1 (the best record in the NFL during that period) and won three Super Bowls. And at the seemingly advanced age of 32, he is still in his prime. On Nov. 20, in a 31–27 win over the Los Angeles Rams, Rice snagged 16 passes for 165 yards and three touchdowns. Three weeks later, he caught 12 passes for 144 yards in a 38–15 win against the San Diego Chargers. Rice finished the regular season with 112 catches for 1,499 yards and 13 touchdowns.

In a typical week, Rice remains civil until Thursday. But on the Wednesday before the Niners' game against the Denver Broncos on Dec. 17, Rice was already badly game-faced. The game was on a Saturday. Rice's schedule had been moved ahead 24 hours. A gold earring sparkled in his left ear; a gold-flecked tattoo of a 49er helmet on his right deltoid flashed. Rice was miserable. "I'm so grouchy," he said with a tight grin, "my wife is going to move out."

He showered. Earlier in the season, he had talked about his compulsion to prove himself, to never let up even for an instant out of fear that everything might come apart. He had started at the bottom, and he could be back there in a heartbeat; people would forget him, and if that happened…would he even exist?

"There's always doubt about me," he said. "I was disappointed coming out of college that Al Toon and Eddie Brown were drafted ahead of me, but they went to major colleges. You would think that in my 10th season there wouldn't be any doubt, but it's still out there."

It is? Both Toon, who played with the New York Jets, and Brown, who played with the Cincinnati Bengals, are long gone.

There was an article last year in a magazine, he explained, that ranked him as the third-best receiver in the league at the time, behind Michael Irvin of the Dallas Cowboys and Sterling Sharpe of the Green Bay Packers. "I read that," he said.

"You have to have confidence, and guys like that, they're prolonging my career."

Rodney Knox, the 49er publicist, remembered the article too.

"After that," Knox said, "Jerry just exploded."

Afield, as in life, Rice is evasive. He almost never takes a direct, crushing blow after catching a pass. He controls his body like a master puppeteer working a marionette. A one-handed grab here, a tiptoe up the sideline there, an unscathed sprint through two closing safeties when it seems decapitation is imminent.

"I don't think I've ever seen him all stretched out," says 49er quarterback Steve Young of Rice's ability to avoid big hits. Rice jumps only when he has to, and unlike almost all other receivers, he catches passes in mid-stride and effortlessly continues running, the ball like a sprinter's baton in his hand. It's almost certain that no one has run for more yardage after catching the ball than Rice.

Though he's not particularly fast, he has a fluid stride and a sudden burst that, as Young says, "is a speed you can't clock."

And the hands. Clad in gloves, the hands are so supple and sure that last year they snared a touchdown pass by latching onto the tail end of a fading ball. "That was not giving up on the ball," explained Rice. Sounds simple. In reality it's like grabbing the back end of a greased pig.

Rice's hands and agility allow him to catch the ball comfortably no matter where it's thrown. "He makes a lot of catches around his ankles," says Young. At a practice before the 1992 Pro Bowl, Cowboy quarterback Troy Aikman saw from a different perspective

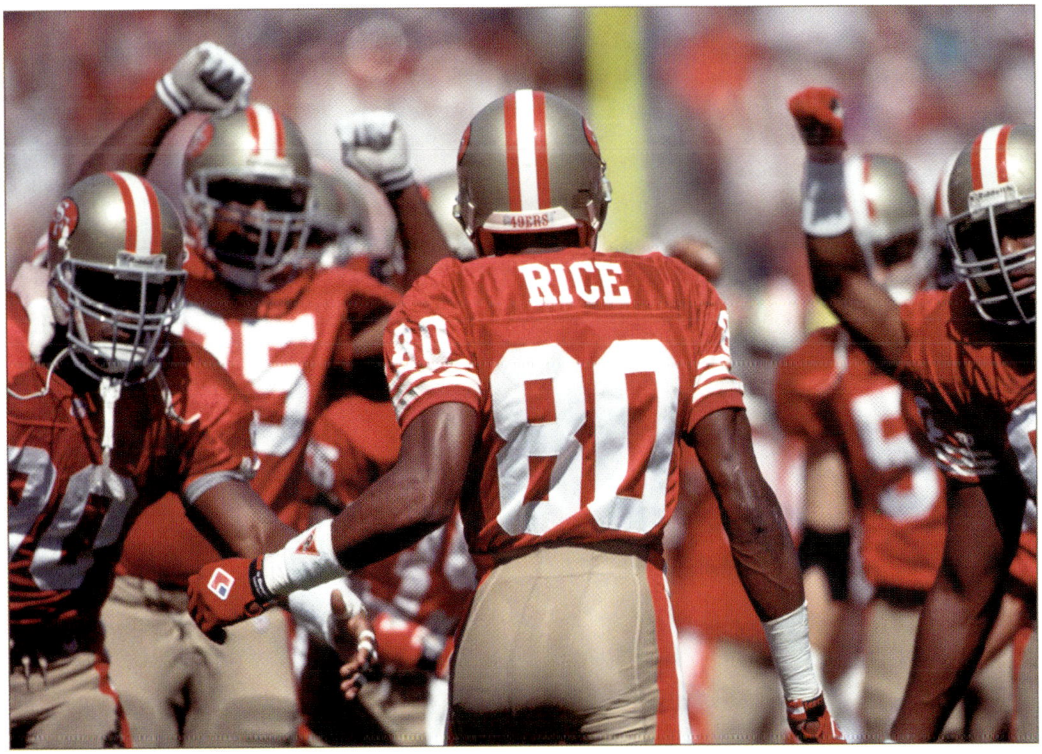

Few players took game days more seriously than Rice.

just what he and his teammates are up against when they play the 49ers. "We were running a quick out," recalled Aikman, "and I guess at San Francisco they run it different than we do, which is I drop back five steps and fire it. My arm was strong because I hadn't thrown in a while, and the ball was in the air, and I was sure I was going to kill him. He was still making moves, and the ball was almost at his head, and it wasn't so much that he just reached up and caught it. It was that he didn't even flinch."

Rice's dad, Joe Nathan, was a bricklayer, and much has been made of the fact that as a teenager, Jerry worked eight-hour shifts with his dad and his brothers on scorching summer days back in Starkville, Miss., hoisting mortar and catching the bricks tossed up to him on the scaffold. This repetitive action, it has been written, is what forged Rice into the greatest pass catcher ever. The story is nice but probably not true—at least not in the way people would believe. After all, catching bricks is to catching footballs as sawing logs is to slicing sushi. "Catching bricks," said Rice, "taught me the meaning of hard work."

His dad was "very strict and demanding," Rice explained in a way that leaves one with the sense that his father was considerably more than that. Still, after work Rice would jog to the high school football field and exercise for two hours, then jog home—in his work clothes.

After he got to the NFL, Rice had difficulty turning down his competitive flame when it wasn't needed. "My first five years, I had a hard time turning it off," he said. "If things didn't go right for me in football, I'd find myself not turning it off at home." His wife, Jackie, is a strong woman, but even she'd had enough of his intensity. Rice forced himself to let up. "You hear about stereotypes, about football players being very abusive off the field," he said. "I'd seen things when I was growing up, and I decided I wouldn't be like that."

What had he seen?

"I really don't want to go into that."

In the early winter, the rainy season in San Francisco, Rice has limited opportunity to hit golf balls or ride his Harley—the two things he does to keep from coming apart at the seams. On the Wednesday before the Bronco game, he watched TV and played with his two children, seven-year-old Jaqui and three-year-old Jerry Jr., but he was not at ease.

"People come up to me and say, 'I'd love to be in your shoes,'" he said with a sigh. "I say, 'No, you wouldn't.' They don't know what it's like. The pressure. Before games, I can't sleep. I can't relax. I should be able to enjoy it, but I can't. The table can turn."

Someday Rice will probably score his 200th touchdown, which will be 74 more than his closest competitor, Jim Brown, had. It's a figure so high, it's crazy. But it may not be enough for this most graceful and obsessive of men.

"It's a lot of wear and tear on me," he said of his intensity down the stretch. "I might not survive."

Constant vigilance is required. The table must not move. •

And the hands. Clad in gloves, the hands are so supple and sure that last year they snared a touchdown pass by latching onto the tail end of a fading ball.

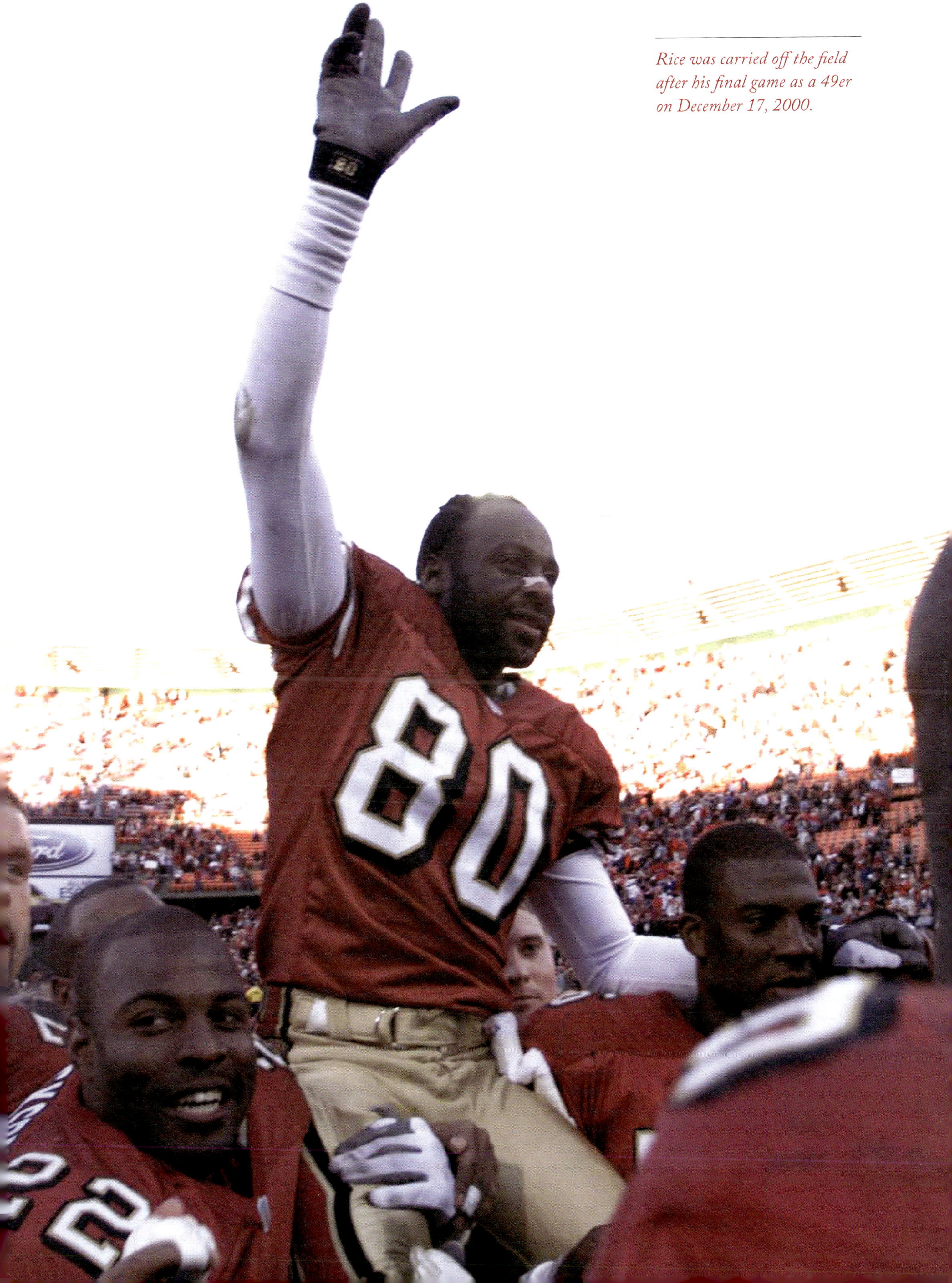

Rice was carried off the field after his final game as a 49er on December 17, 2000.

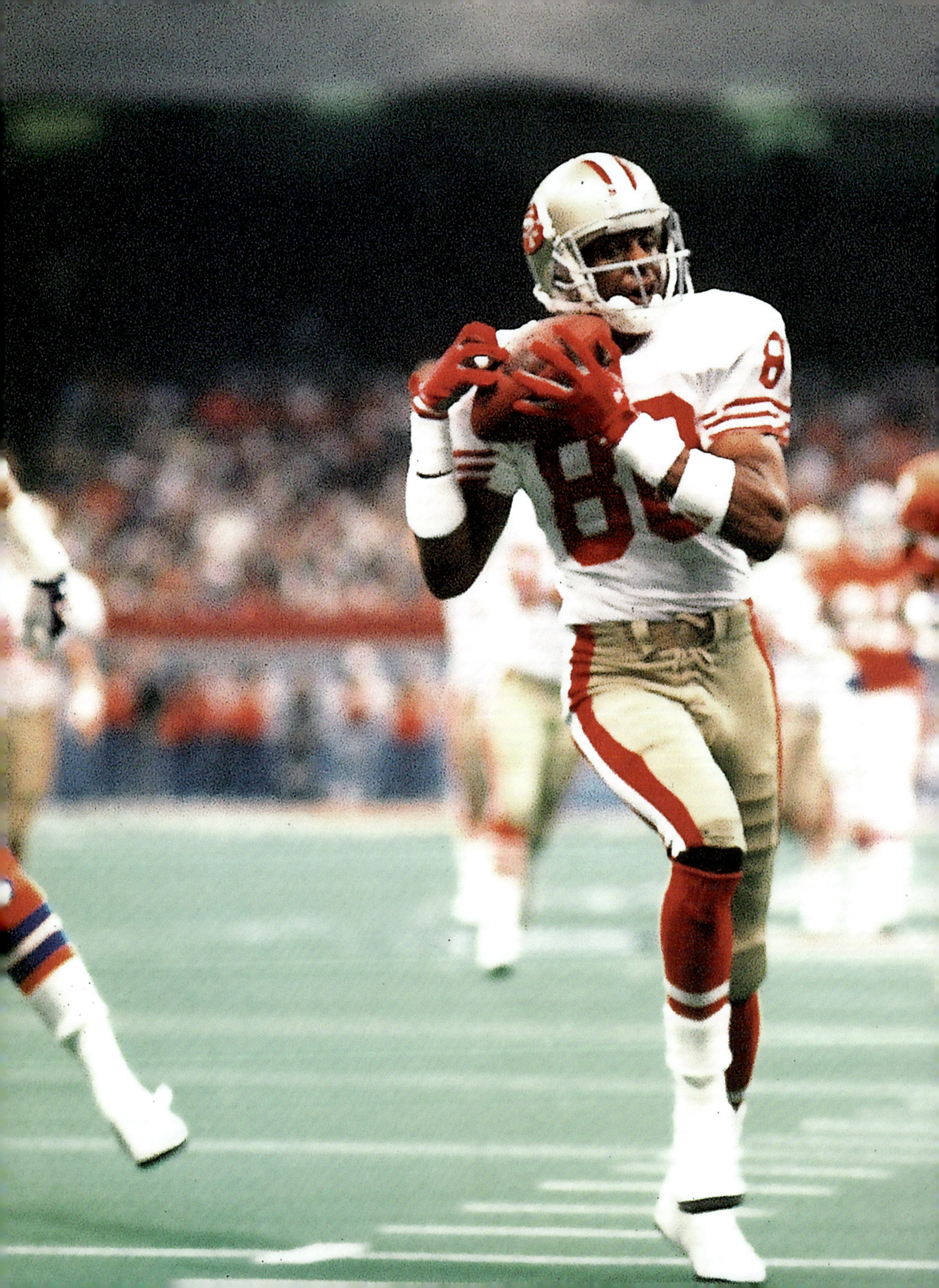

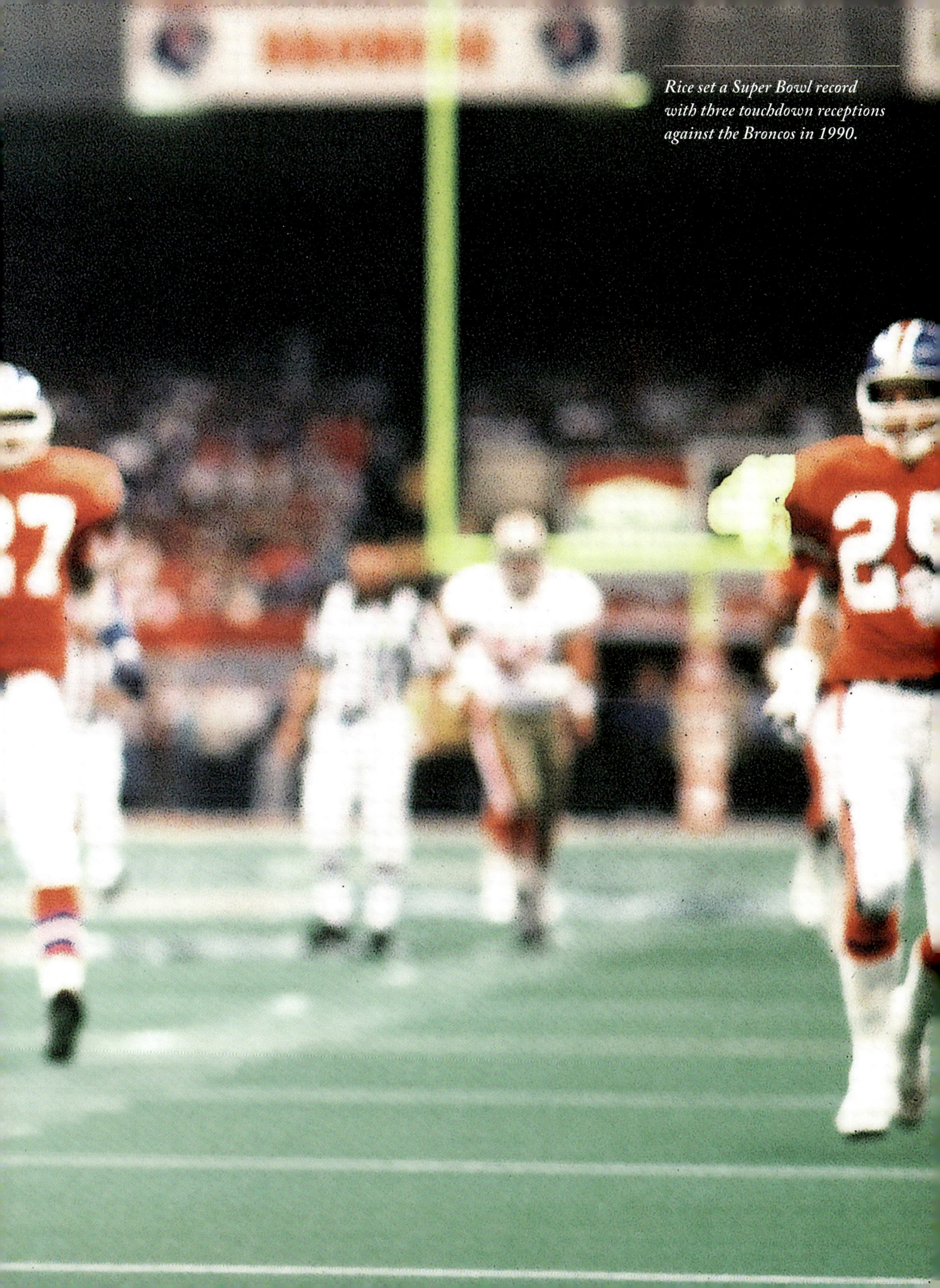

Rice set a Super Bowl record with three touchdown receptions against the Broncos in 1990.

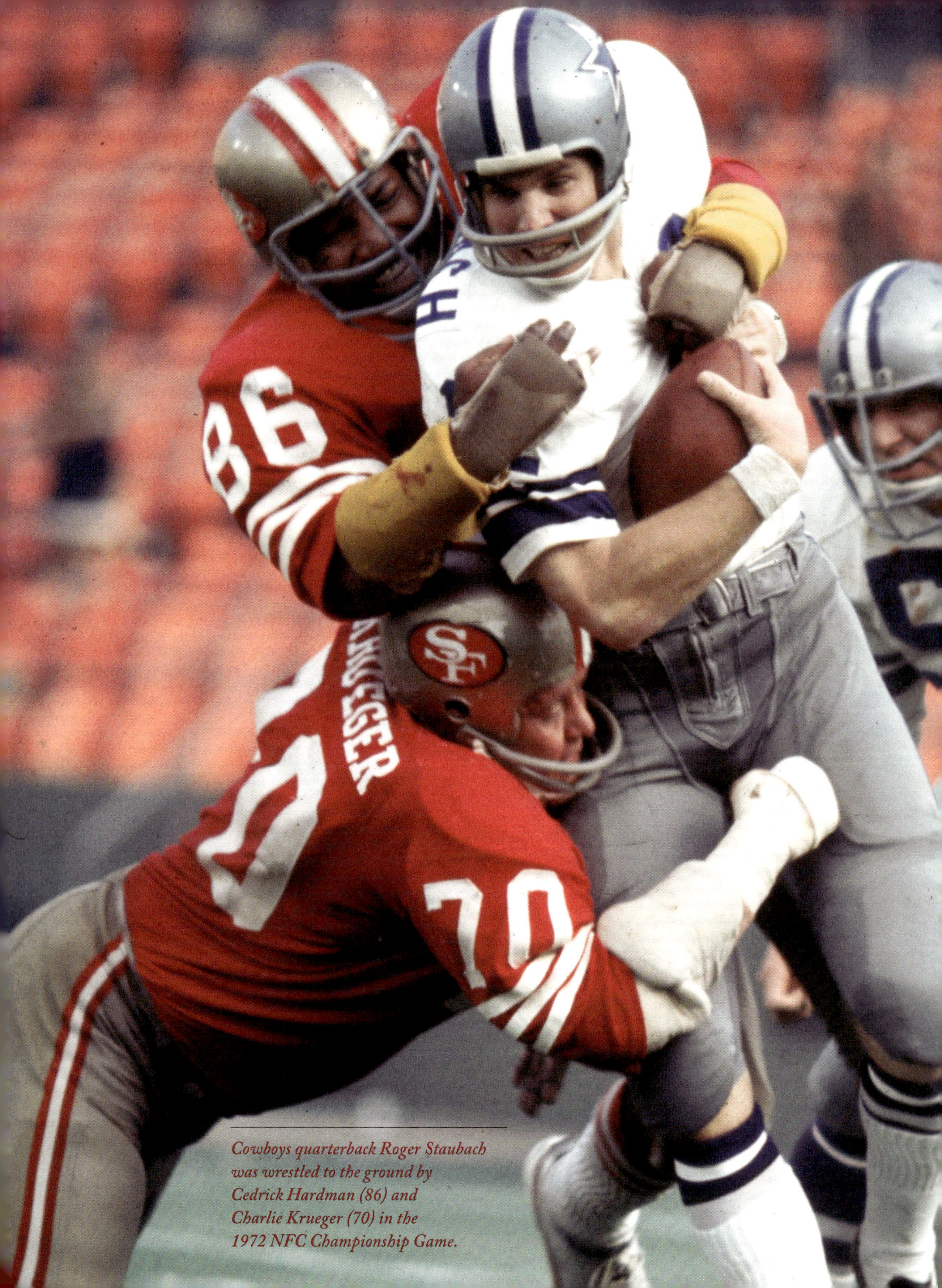

Cowboys quarterback Roger Staubach was wrestled to the ground by Cedrick Hardman (86) and Charlie Krueger (70) in the 1972 NFC Championship Game.

EXCERPTED FROM SPORTS ILLUSTRATED | FEBRUARY 16, 1995

THE GREATEST OF RIVALS

The 49ers and the Cowboys have dogged one another for the last 25 years BY AUSTIN MURPHY

FOR A QUARTER CENTURY THEY HAVE BEEN EACH OTHER'S GREATEST OBSTACLE AND SPUR. BETWEEN THEM, THE Dallas Cowboys and the San Francisco 49ers have won five of the last seven Super Bowls, seven of the last 14. The Niners' 38–28 win over Dallas on a sodden Candlestick field last month was but a natural phase in the waxing and waning of power in the NFL's most sublime rivalry. This time it was Dallas's turn to get waxed.

Disregard the internationally televised, Roman-numeraled anticlimax that occurred a fortnight later in Miami: For the third time in as many years, the NFC Championship Game served as the de facto Super Bowl. Considering the Super futility experienced by the AFC over the previous decade, one could hardly blame 49er president Carmen Policy for saying, on the eve of the NFC title game, "In our minds, if we get to the Super Bowl, we win."

Once there, in other words, the hard part of their season is over: They've gotten past Dallas. And the converse applies—did apply the previous two seasons, as the Cowboys beat the Niners in two conference title games and, as an afterthought, twice crushed the Buffalo Bills for the Lombardi Trophy.

Considering the up-and-down pattern of this rivalry (the rise of one has nearly always come at the expense of the other), it seems appropriate that the seeds of San Francisco's return to the Super Bowl were planted in an elevator. Down-and-out after watching their team get manhandled by the Cowboys in the January '94 conference championship game, Policy and team owner Eddie DeBartolo Jr. boarded the elevator to the locker room in Texas Stadium and vowed during their descent that the 49ers—having just lost to the Cowboys for the third time in a row and having been expelled from the playoffs by Dallas for the second straight year—would fall no further. They began to plot the housecleaning and the binge signing of defensive free agents that would lead to their return to the Super Bowl. Why the urgency to retool?

"(The Cowboys) are the enemy incarnate," Policy recently told *The Dallas Morning News*. "They are the force that has to be overcome for us to achieve what we are duty- and honor-bound to achieve."

So transcendent is this rivalry that its defining moment has a two-word title that, 13 years after the fact, still resonates throughout the land: Video clips of The Catch are trotted out every time the Niners face the 'Boys. Fewer people, however, remember The Drop.

Preston Riley remembers. The 49ers had lost consecutive NFC title games to the Cowboys when the two teams hooked up in the '72 divisional playoffs. The Niners led by 12 points with 90 seconds to play when things went very wrong at the Stick. First, Cowboy quarterback Roger Staubach threw a 20-yard touchdown pass. Then Riley, a 49er wideout, fumbled Toni Fritsch's onside kick: The Drop. Staubach's second TD pass in under two minutes sank San Francisco. "With five minutes to go, I don't think any of us felt we had a chance to win," admitted Blaine Nye, a Cowboy guard. One game account described dispirited 49er Vic Washington, his 97-yard kickoff return squandered, sitting in his cubicle throwing up and Riley smoking a cigarette as tears streamed down his face. It would be nine more years before the 49ers made it to their first Super Bowl. The Cowboys played in five of them—winning two—in the '70s, a decade that saw them go 6–1 against the Niners, knocking them out of the playoffs three times. By the conclusion of that decade, however, the luck of America's Team had begun to change. After suffering the fifth concussion of his career, in a 1979 playoff loss to the Los Angeles Rams, Staubach retired, leaving the controls of the Cowboy offense to a succession of less effective field generals such as Danny White, Gary Hogeboom, Steve Pelleur and Babe Laufenberg.

In the 1981 draft, the Cowboy brain trust decided that Baylor linebacker Mike Singletary was too small to make it in the NFL and used the club's first-round pick on…tackle Howard Richards. Doesn't really ring a bell, does it? This would be the first in a series of poor drafts that plagued the Cowboys until Jimmy Johnson was hired in 1989. In contrast, the 49ers were making quantum leaps due to the inspired, often brilliant selections of Bill Walsh, who'd taken over as 49er coach before the '79 season. After going 2–14 that year, the Niners improved to 6–10 the following season and…what's this? A bit of backsliding? So it appeared when the Niners dropped two of their first three games in '81. They then won 13 of their next 14. But in the NFC title game against Dallas, which had eliminated the Niners from their last three playoffs, San Francisco was dreadful, turning the ball over six times and committing numerous dumb penalties. Two interference calls on their rookie cornerback, a kid by the name of Lott, led to 10 Dallas points. Even so, as the 49ers took possession on their own 11-yard line with 4:54 left, they trailed only 27–21.

"Almost five minutes left, and (we had) all our timeouts," Walsh would say. "I liked our chances." Why not? This Montana guy, a third-year man out of Notre Dame, had engineered some nifty comebacks for the Fighting Irish. Maybe he had some magic up his sleeve.

Montana commenced whittling away at the Cowboy defense. Twelve plays got San Francisco to the Cowboy six-yard line with :58 to play. Walsh's call: sprint right option. Lining up right, wide receiver Dwight Clark had a lot to think about. He was to clear out for primary receiver Freddie Solomon, setting a sort of semipick; cut across the end zone right to left; then, if he still wasn't open, pull a U-turn and break back to the right. He was completing this last part of his route with Cowboy cornerback Everson Walls breathing down the nape of his neck when Montana, forced up against the sideline by "Too Tall" Jones and Larry Bethea, let 'er rip. Recalls Clark, "I thought, Uh-oh, I can't jump that high."

Because Clark was wrong—he skied for the game-winning catch, or Catch—the 49ers went on to the first of the four Super Bowls they would win in nine years.

Walsh had taken Clark in the 10th round of the '79 draft—the same class that yielded Montana, a third-rounder. Though through '84 Walsh and his staff also chose Keena Turner, Ronnie Lott, Jesse Sapolu, Roger Craig and Todd Shell, it was Walsh's first-round pick on April 30, 1985, that would go down as one of the shrewdest draft-day maneuvers ever, a turn of events that confounded the Cowboys then and haunts them to this day.

The top four wide receivers coming out of college that year were Eddie Brown of Miami, Wisconsin's Al Toon, Jessie Hester of Florida State and Mississippi Valley State's Jerry Rice. We intend no slight to Walsh (the Genius) by pointing out that he wanted Brown—a lot of people did—and phoned Cincinnati Bengal general manager Paul Brown, who held the 13th pick, offering San Francisco's first-round pick (28th) plus second- and third-round choices for Cincinnati's first and third. Brown never returned the call and on draft day snatched Eddie Brown for himself.

Walsh phoned the New England Patriots, who had the 16th spot, and offered them the deal he'd offered Cincinnati. The Pats jumped, and Walsh snatched Rice out from under the noses of the Cowboys, who also coveted him. In addition to his 139 career touchdowns, Rice—widely deemed the best wide receiver in the history of the game—has caught 17 touchdowns in the playoffs, among the more recent of which was a 28-yard reception that ultimately proved to be the winning score in San Francisco's latest victory over Dallas.

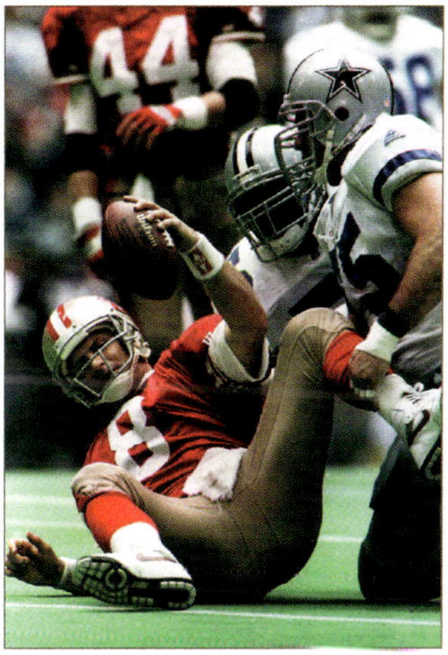

The Niners have taken their share of lumps from Dallas over the years.

It doesn't seem all that long ago that the Cowboys were at rock bottom. In 1989, new owner Jerry Jones replaced coach Tom Landry with Johnson, who lost 15 of his first 16 games. The 49ers, meanwhile, were winning their second consecutive Super Bowl. Unbowed, Johnson built a frightfully fast team around a frighteningly good quarterback. While the 49ers, now under George Seifert, failed to make the playoffs after the '91 season, the Cowboys reached the division final. Once again, the teams were headed in opposite directions.

One could not help but be impressed by the talent assembled by Johnson, which by '94 included Charles Haley, who had worn out his welcome in San Francisco. A third straight Super Bowl seemed a very reasonable ambition.

But what the 49ers had not been able to do to the Cowboys, the Cowboys did to themselves. The momentum of the Dallas juggernaut was slowed by something every bit as colossal and formidable as the team itself: the ego of Jerry Jones. Displeased with how little credit he was receiving for the Cowboys' success and how much of it Johnson was getting, Jerry served Jimmy his walking papers and brought on the bootlegger's boy, former Oklahoma coach Barry Switzer.

Switzer went to the Cowboys with high expectations, and his arrival was embraced by almost everyone in Dallas. However, only one coach in NFL history—Seifert of the '89 Niners—had ever led a defending Super Bowl champion to another title in his first year. Meanwhile, in San Francisco, Seifert's Super Bowl win had long been forgotten, and rumors of his dismissal swirled until the 49ers ousted the Cowboys in the NFC title game. After that contest, the finger-pointing began in Dallas.

Surprisingly, Switzer's predecessor is not throwing stones, at least not from his bully pulpit as a Fox network analyst. Johnson's Miami Beach restaurant features a Jerry and Barry sandwich—"a lot of tongue and baloney," says the ex (for now) coach, who recently implied that Switzer had screwed up, then absolved him of responsibility for screwing up when he told *USA Today*, "It isn't Switzer's fault. Jerry's the one who put him in that situation." Sure, the departure of Johnson may have hastened the Cowboys' decline. But as any student of this rich rivalry can tell you, that fall was inevitable. Dallas quarterback Troy Aikman demonstrated both his class and his grasp of this verity when he caught up with Steve Young after their last game.

"This is your year," said Aikman. "It's your turn." •

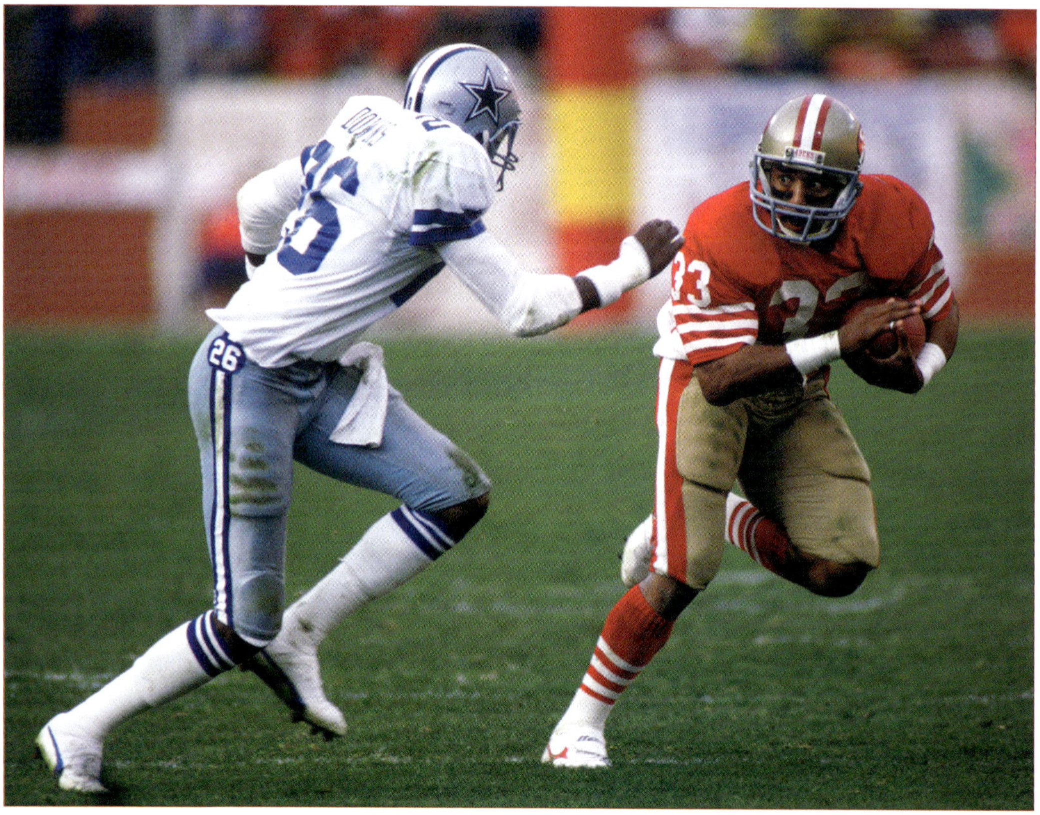

Roger Craig gained 72 yards in a 49ers victory against Dallas in 1985.

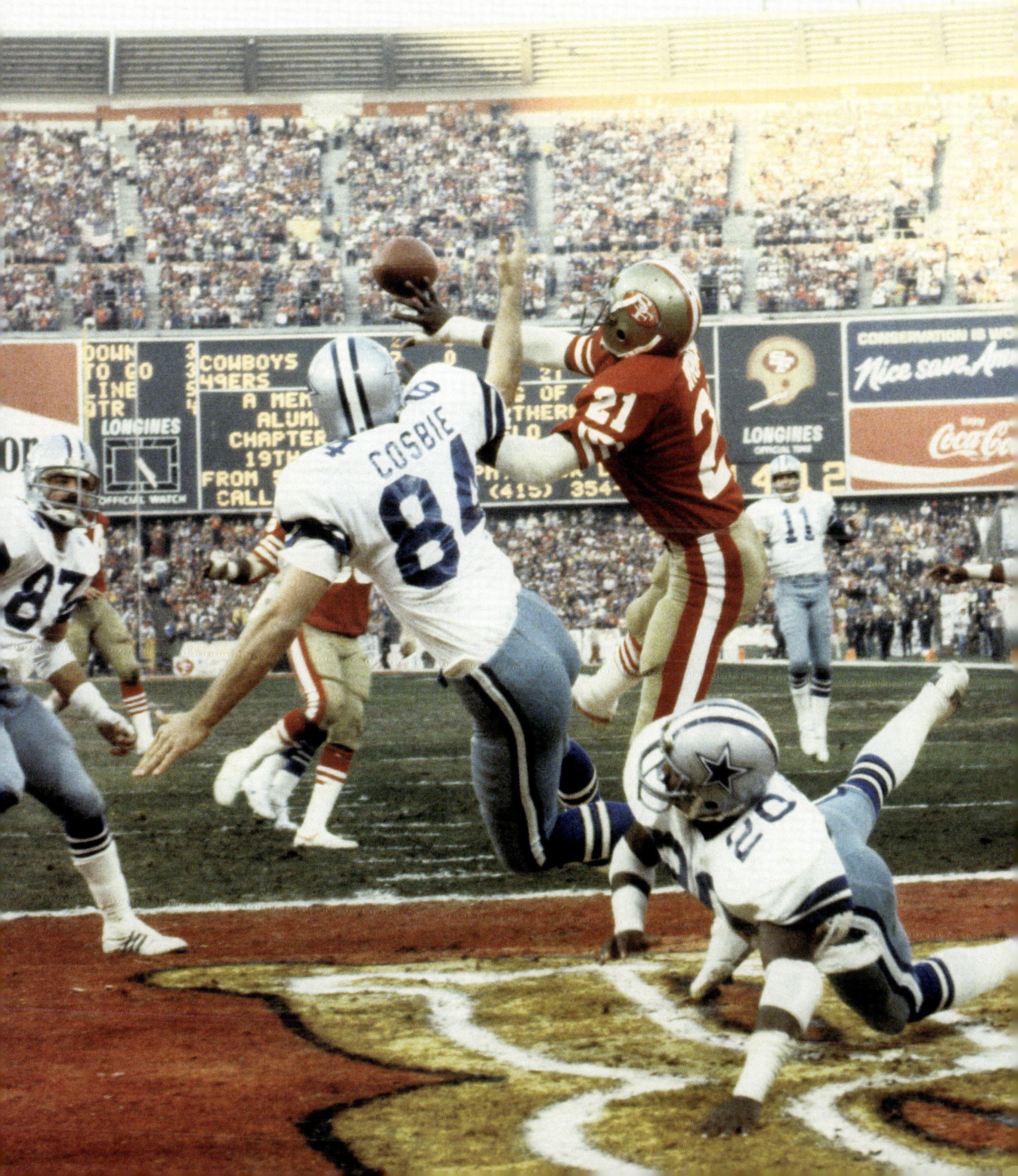

San Francisco's Eric Wright broke up a pass to Dallas's Doug Cosbie during the NFC Championship Game in 1982.

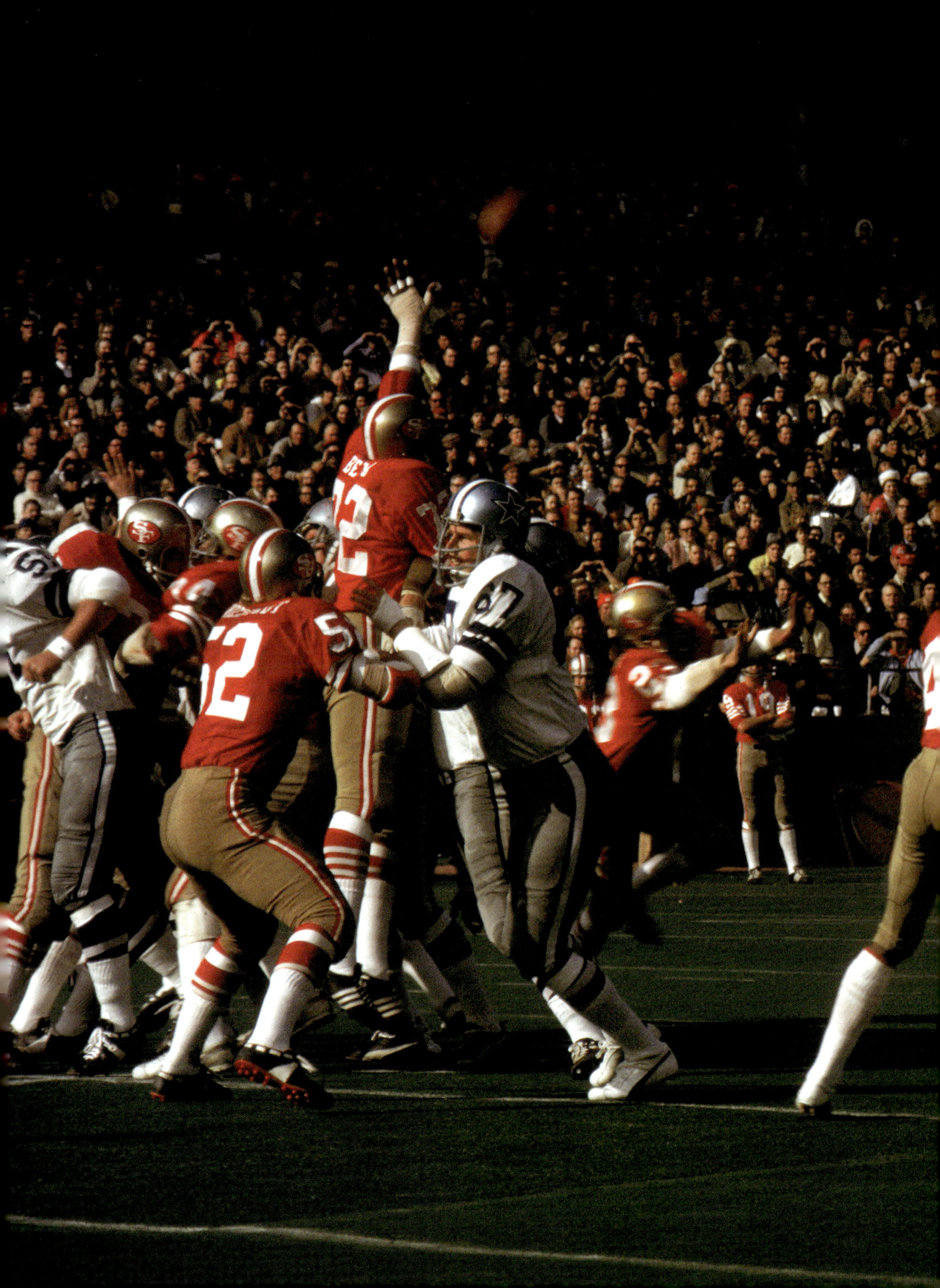

Dallas's Toni Fritsch kicked a field goal against the 49ers during the Cowboys' NFC Championship Game victory in 1972.

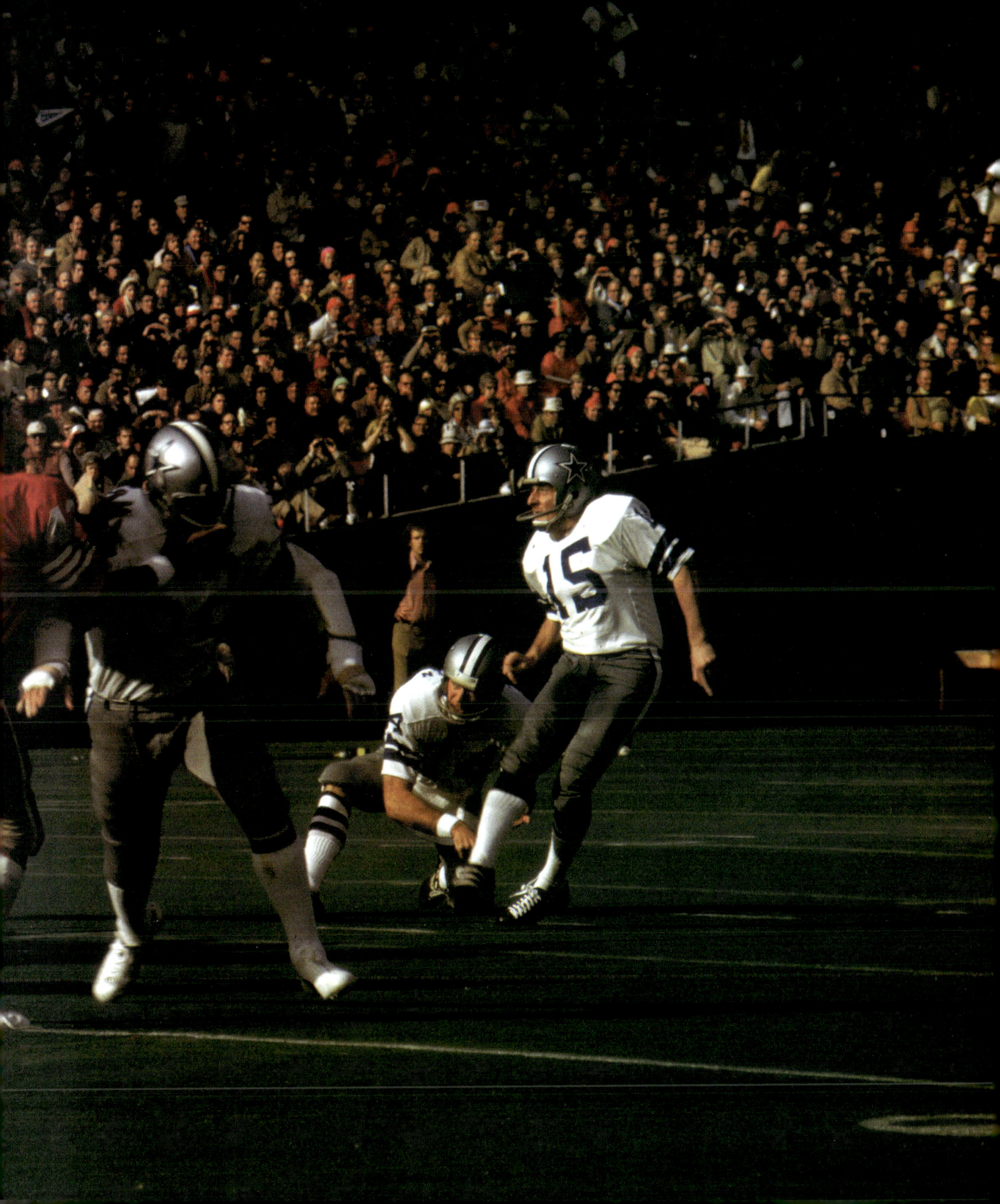

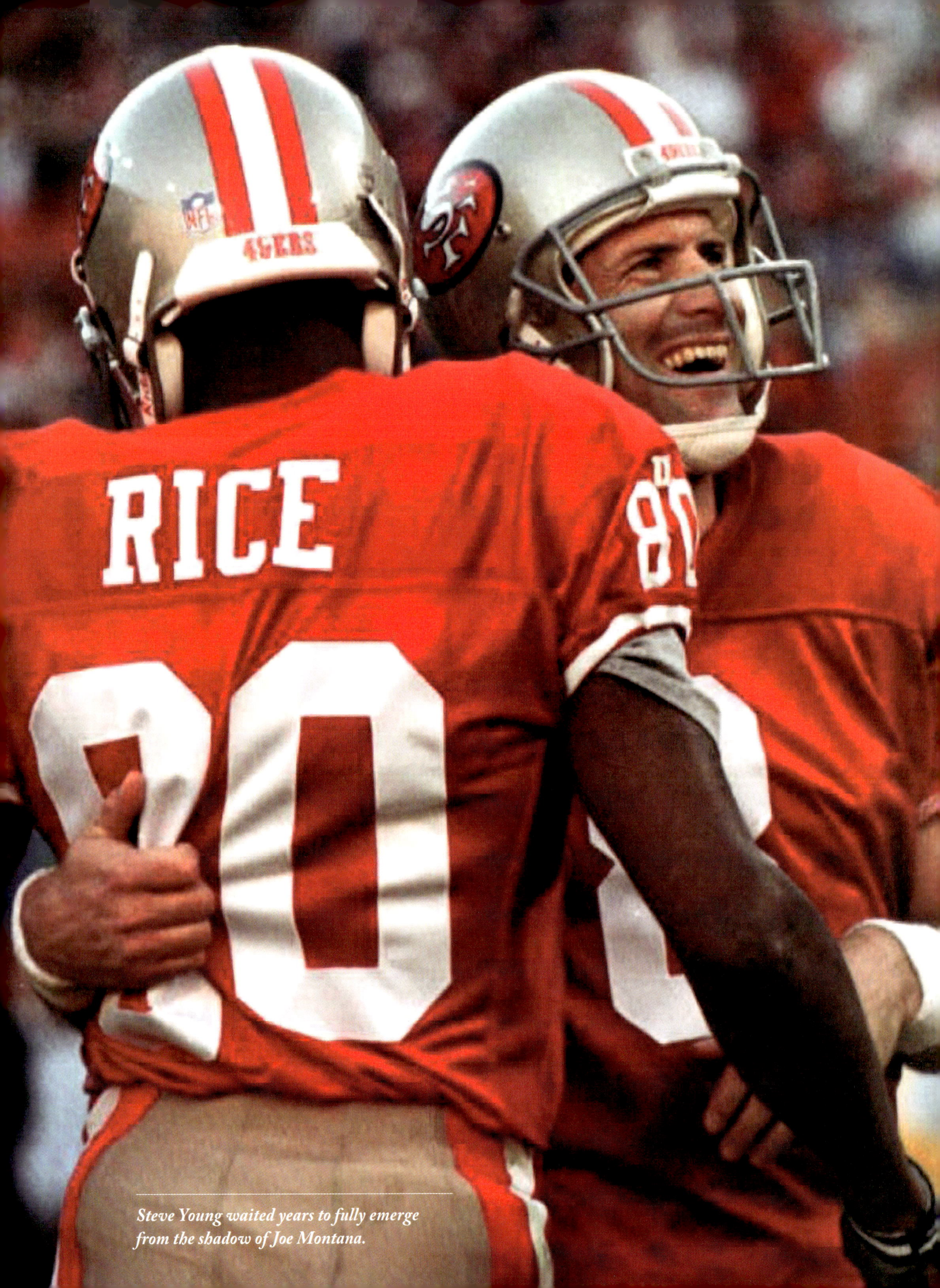

Steve Young waited years to fully emerge from the shadow of Joe Montana.

EXCERPTED FROM SPORTS ILLUSTRATED | FEBRUARY 16, 1995

ON TOP OF THE WORLD

Steve Young has finally completed his long climb from nervous child to proven leader BY MICHAEL SILVER

FOR THE FIFTH TIME IN 13 YEARS, THE SAN FRANCISCO 49ERS HAVE CLIMBED TO THE TOP OF THE FOOTBALL world, forging a path that has brought them to the highest peak of their sport. To stick with that analogy, there is no dispute as to who has been their Sherpa guide. Coach George Seifert calls the shots on the field, owner Eddie DeBartolo Jr. coughs up the cash, and president Carmen Policy cuts the deals. But Super Bowl MVP Steve Young is the leader of the 49ers, the man whose spirit and drive have propelled this team to its lofty perch.

Young is the guy who simultaneously calms and fires up his charges, dispersing harsh words and high fives with equal intensity. Young's the one who rails at teammates for sudden displays of brainlock. In October he even yelled at his coach and got away with it. Young is comfortable as the front man when the locker room door is opened and as the keynote speaker when the door is closed. He's the one who gets the ball to Jerry Rice, who keeps Ricky Watters from spontaneously combusting, who takes fashion tips from Deion Sanders and who shakes off brutal body slams from some of the league's most fearsome defenders.

When 49er fans chanted "Steve! Steve!" as Young took his buoyant victory lap around Candlestick Park following last month's NFC championship victory over Dallas, it was more than a recognition of the 33-year-old quarterback's rigorous quest to escape Joe Montana's shadow. In their delirious state, the Candlestick fans were merely echoing the sentiment that Young's teammates had acknowledged a month earlier when they selected him as the winner of the Len Eshmont Award—given to the most courageous and inspirational 49er player—for the second time in three years.

After four years as Montana's impatient backup, then three more years of starting duty accompanied by constant questions as to whether the 49ers were his team, Young had answered all the skepticism and led his team to victory. The 49ers, winners of four Super Bowls under Montana's guidance, were on their way to a fifth title, and there was absolutely no doubt as to who had led them there.

"I don't think I've had to force anything," Young says of his development as a vocal leader. "I think it has come very naturally. It's funny—so has yelling at people. I used to yell at people in the old days, and now it's coming back."

Perhaps more than any other champion, Young has been defined by the past—by what Montana did that Young, until now, had not been able to do. Young's evolution as a leader has been public and choppy, but contrary to popular perception, it did not begin in the NFL or even when he was starring at BYU. If you go back far enough, you will find that Young, a great-great-great- grandson of Brigham Young, botched his first leadership experience badly.

It happened a quarter century ago, in 1970, the year the Beatles broke up and the Partridge family got together. Young's parents, Grit and Sherry, left their Greenwich, Conn., home and set off on a trip to Philadelphia, bringing in a pair of house sitters to watch eight-year-old Steve and his three younger siblings. Grit, whose real name is LeGrande, is a labor lawyer who traveled often at the time, usually alone. On this special occasion, he and his wife figured they would enjoy an extended weekend of fun and relaxation.

It was a splendid idea. And Steve positively negated it.

"He just ruined the trip," Grit Young recalled in a 1993 interview. "He was afraid (the house sitters) were going to murder him or something. He kept calling, they kept calling, and finally we had to shorten the trip. As a child, he was very nervous, very frightened."

The boy was not exactly suited for prematurely playing the head-of-the-household role. But to his mother, the seriousness with which Young approached his role was prophetic. "He felt a lot of responsibility for his brothers and sisters," Sherry Young said. "I guess that's what it was. He's always been the man in charge." Well, not always. As a child, Steve followed the rule of his father, a serious man of few words. Grit starred as a fullback at BYU in the late '50s and in fatherhood lived up to his nickname. "He didn't care what you chose—from the oboe, to art, to football—but once you did it, he couldn't stand to watch you quit or come up short," Steve says.

According to Grit, Steve was a "worried and intense" child; for example, Steve once failed to show up for class in the second grade, thanks to some still-unexplained fear. But most of that intensity was channeled into athletics. Steve and his peers embraced the four major sports—baseball, basketball, football and hockey—the way Yogi Bear embraces the four basic food groups. He and his younger brother Mike and their friends would play together, often past nightfall. When they didn't play, they watched. Steve remembers tripping off to nearby New York City via train to catch Ranger hockey games and afterward sprinting the 15 blocks from Madison Square Garden to Grand Central Station, hoping to dodge any would-be muggers.

"Most of my friends were Italian Catholics —I'd say 90 percent of them," recalls Young, now the sports world's most famous Mormon. "Very large families, and very athletic. Everyone—everyone—played baseball, basketball and football. We woke up every morning, a group of maybe 10 guys, and we'd just play sports all day long, whatever the game was. And it was just a tremendous way to grow up."

Young's adult life also has been tremendous in many ways. Money never has been an issue, although Young, who says his idea of bliss is "20 bucks and a full tank of gas," continues to live relatively modestly, donating a nice chunk of his wealth to charitable causes. Out of college, he signed what was then the largest contract ever given a pro athlete, a $40 million deal with the Los Angeles Express of the now-defunct United States Football League. Young played two mostly miserable seasons with the Express and bought his way out of the deal, but the contract included an annuity that will kick in two years from now and pay Young a total of $37.2 million by 2027. It was a deal he almost didn't sign. "The money just overwhelmed him," Grit recalls. "The money became his nemesis, and he continued to live as if he didn't have it. He told me before he had to report to camp, 'I don't want to go.' I ended up having to go out to Provo to talk to him. I told him, 'You made a contract; you live up to the contract.'"

Once freed from the USFL, Young went to the next-worst alternative. In 1985 and '86, he played for the hideous Tampa Bay Buccaneers, who owned his NFL rights, and spent most of his time running wildly to escape the stampede of defenders. Critics used to point to the Bucs' 4–28 record over that two-year span as a sign that Young was not a winner; realists understood that quarterbacking the Bucs in

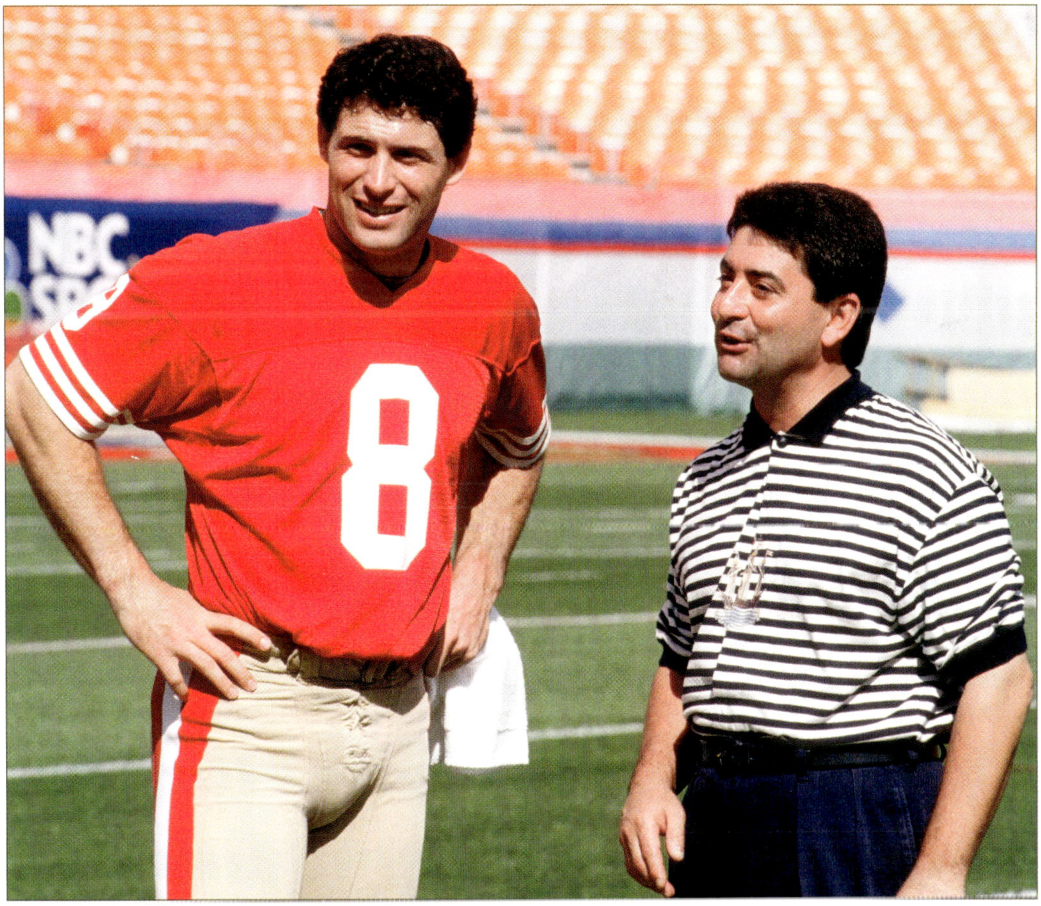

Niners owner Eddie DeBartolo Jr. once promised the starting quarterback job to Montana despite Young being the reigning NFL MVP.

those days was akin to leading ABBA into a Battle of the Bands.

"One time we were playing the Bears," recalls Young, "and one of our coaches looked me right in the eye and said, 'Look, Steve, I know everybody has kind of quit on you here. This is the kind of game where you could really get hurt. Be careful out there.' I couldn't believe it. How can you enter a game thinking like that?"

Finally, in April 1987, then 49er coach Bill Walsh made a trade that will go down as one of the biggest steals in sports history. For a reported $1 million and draft choices in the second and fourth rounds, the 49ers got Young. At the same time, Walsh seemed ready to close the book on Montana, who had won two Super Bowls but was coming off major back surgery. Walsh told Young that a transition was near, and Young said great. The only person who didn't go along with the plan was Montana.

So, though Walsh declared an "open competition" between the two quarterbacks before the 1988 season, Montana never allowed one to develop, blowing Young off the starting line like Ben Johnson on you-know-what. Montana went on to win Super Bowls following the '88 and '89 seasons, won consecutive regular-season MVP awards in '89 and '90 and turned Young into a repressed, impatient mess.

Young's agent, Leigh Steinberg, advised his client to seek a trade after the 1990 season—one that ended with the 49ers losing a 15–13 heartbreaker of an NFC Championship Game to the New York Giants, with only a Roger Craig fumble keeping Young from starting the Super Bowl in place of the injured Montana. As an enticement for Young to stay, Seifert came up with a "handshake agreement" that would guarantee Young three or four starts the following year. Young signed a new deal, and Montana hit the roof. Never a fan of Young's personality, Montana now directed all of his resentment of the organization toward his backup, privately suggesting that Young was not the gracious, supportive understudy many believed him to be.

One example cited by Montana was a training-camp incident in 1991 in which Young, after throwing several interceptions in practice, allegedly persuaded the team's video coordinator to erase the errant throws before the coaches viewed the tape. The fun-loving Montana also came to revile Young as a sort of goody two-shoes, and an extremely pampered one. Whereas most backups in the NFL receive no more than 15%-20% of the snaps in practice, Young typically got about 40% of the practice work during his years behind Montana. It didn't help Montana's mind-set that the 49er offensive coordinator, future Green Bay Packer head coach Mike Holmgren, had coached Young at BYU. The longer Montana remained sidelined by elbow injuries—he would play only one half of one game in the '91 and '92 seasons—the more apparent his dislike for Young became. In one interview, Montana likened Young to

Young's leadership skills flourished. The next season he won respect from his teammates while fighting through a debilitating thumb injury and a series of concussions. He also won his third consecutive passing crown and led the 49ers back to the NFC title game.

"the enemy," adding, "Steve is on a big push for himself."

Though Young continued to take the high road in interviews, he privately became angered by Montana's attitude toward him. And it wasn't just Montana; at times it seemed as if the whole Bay Area, or a large portion of it, was against him. In '91, Young won the first of four passing titles but was only 5–5 as a starter. After going down with a knee injury in November, Young was replaced by Steve Bono, who led the 49ers to five consecutive victories. A good friend of Montana's, Bono also copied the legend's form, as opposed to Young's scrambling style. When the 49ers, despite a 10–6 record, missed the playoffs for the first time in nine years, cries rang out for Young's head: He can't read defenses; he's too impatient; he's a running back in a quarterback's body; and—the doozy—he's not a winner.

The next season, Montana's elbow again forced him onto the injured reserve list, and Young emerged as a star. He led the 49ers to a league-best 14–2 record, won another passing title and was a runaway choice for league MVP. Even Montana admitted that Young deserved the award. But going into the last game of the season, the 49ers activated Montana, and Young became visibly uptight. Montana played splendidly in the second half of the 49ers' 24–6 victory over Detroit that closed the regular season; in the team's playoff opener, a 20–13 victory over Washington, Young played sloppily, fumbling three times and throwing an interception. The next week, in the NFC Championship Game, Young threw a pair of interceptions in the 49ers' 30–20 loss to Dallas. After the game, one radio call-in poll showed that 75% of respondents favored keeping Montana and getting rid of Young. The next day, Steinberg again advised Young to seek a trade, this time through the press, with the agent explaining that Young would never be accepted in the Bay Area. Young again decided to stay, but in the coming months, the 49ers would seriously ponder a scenario in which they would trade Young, retain Montana and Bono and draft Notre Dame's Rick Mirer as the quarterback of the future.

Before the 49ers finally traded Montana to Kansas City in April 1993, the situation became utterly ridiculous. At one point, over beers, DeBartolo offered Montana the starting job, meaning that the league's reigning MVP would be a backup. It turned out that Young was second string for only a day—Montana saw the move as a ploy designed to increase his trade value and rejected the offer—but it was an ugly day. Young, studying for BYU law-school exams, heard about the demotion, and he recalls "throwing things around the house."

But after Montana had departed for K.C., Young's leadership skills flourished. The next season he won respect from his teammates while fighting through a debilitating thumb injury and a series of concussions. He also won his third consecutive passing crown and led the 49ers back to the NFC title game. But again the Cowboys kept Young and the Niners from the Super Bowl.

Then, in 1994, Young put it all together. He had a season that surpassed Montana's 1989 campaign as the best ever, at least according to the league's passer-rating system. He also led the 49ers to the Super Bowl, throwing six touchdown passes to break Montana's record.

Finally, the little boy who couldn't handle his parents' trip to Philadelphia had evolved into the leader of the most successful team in football. He has carried them to the top of the mountain, and as he gazes down at the path below, it suddenly looks straight and sure. •

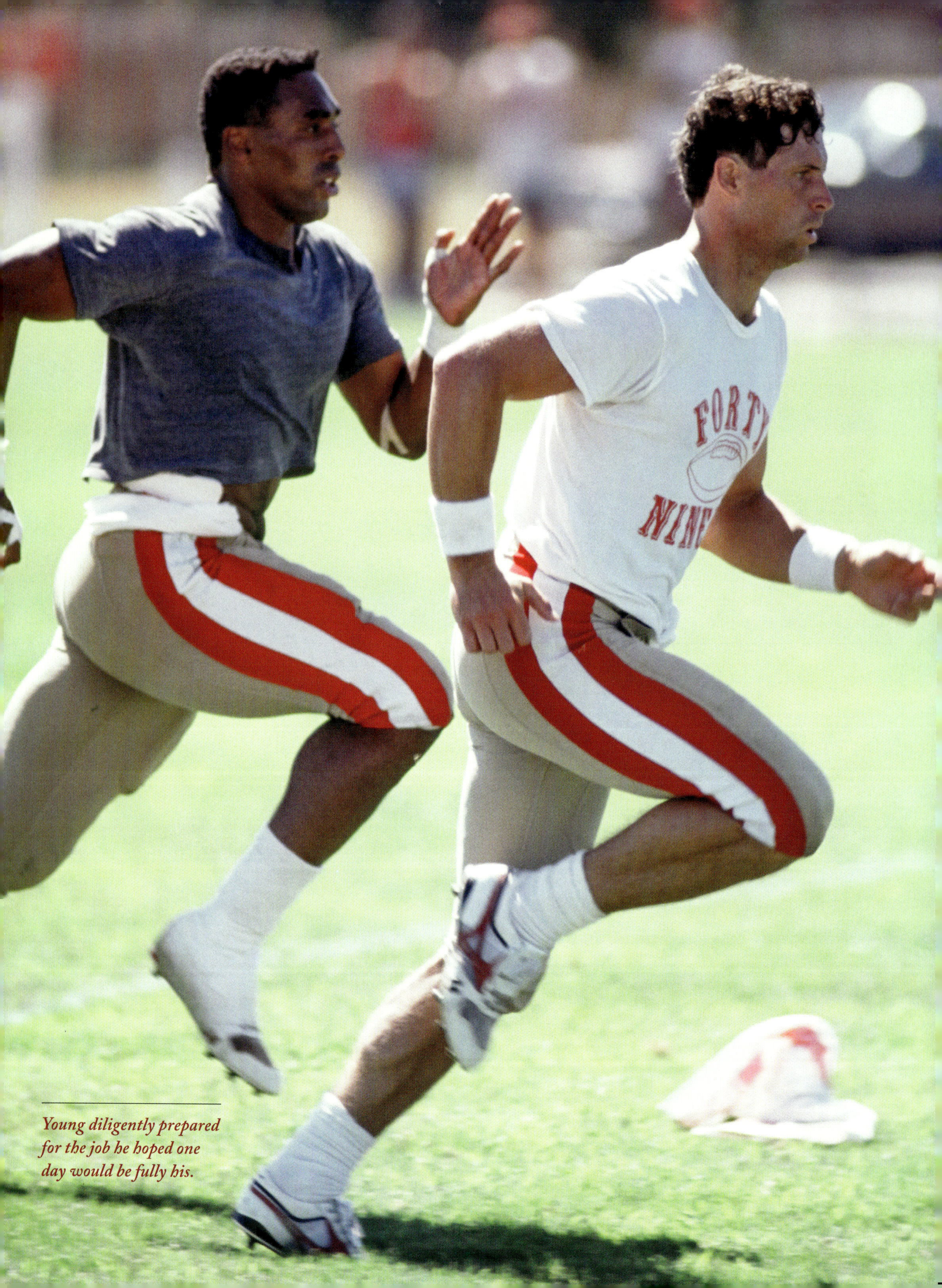

Young diligently prepared for the job he hoped one day would be fully his.

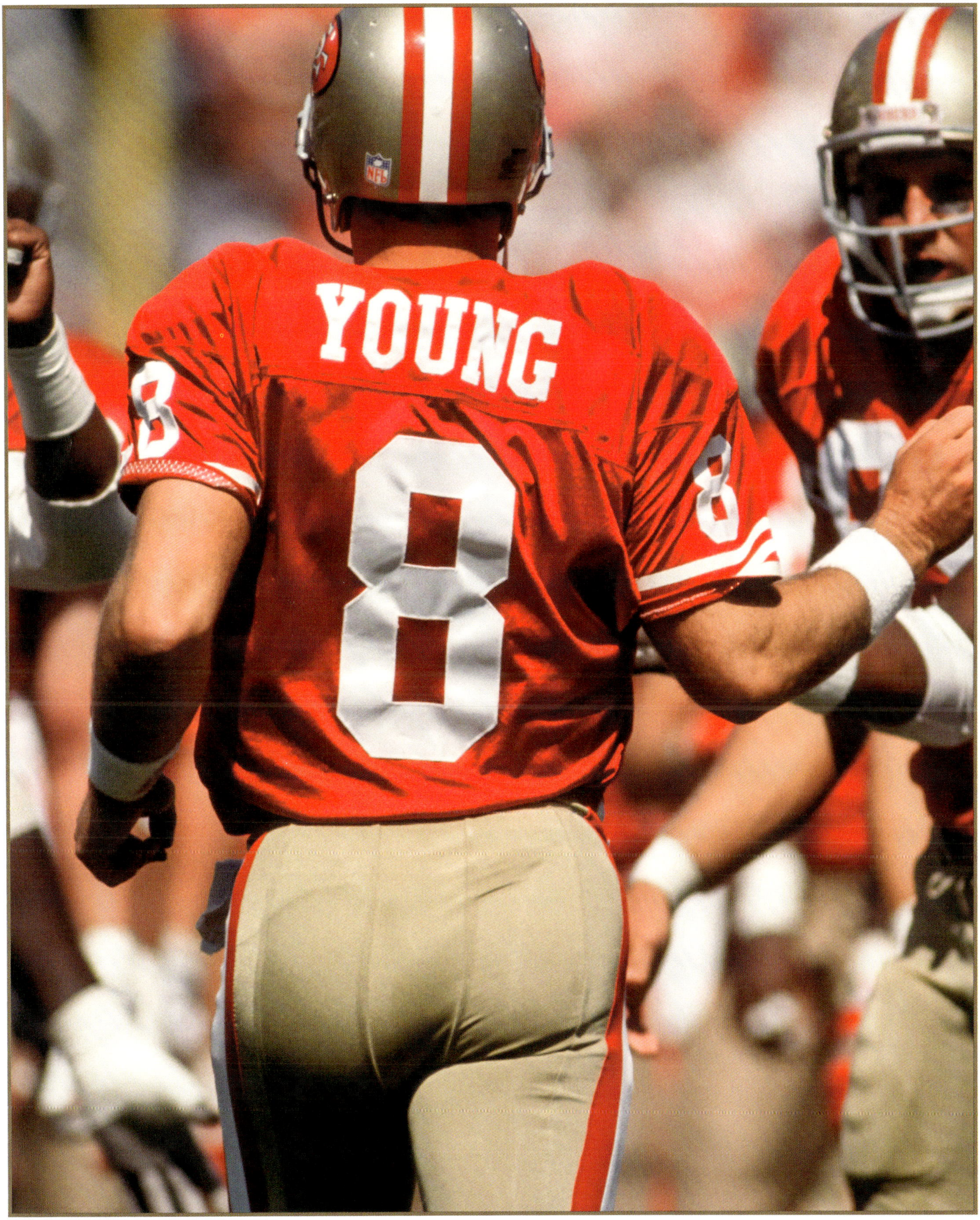

In the end, it was worth the wait.

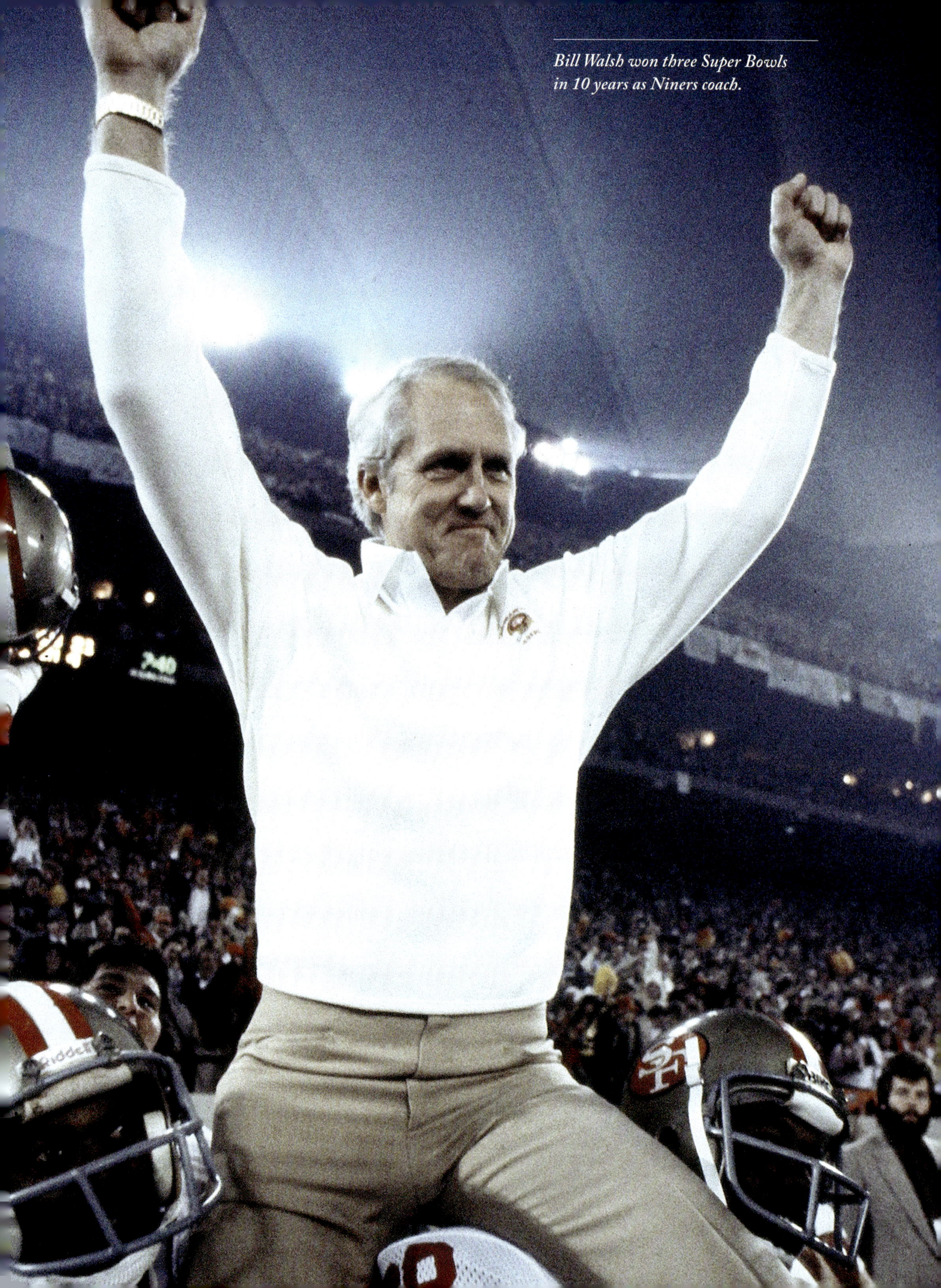

Bill Walsh won three Super Bowls in 10 years as Niners coach.

EXCERPTED FROM SPORTS ILLUSTRATED | MARCH 12, 2007

THE TOP OF HIS GAME

If to ask "What might have been" is the price of genius, Bill Walsh has paid his dues. But as he battles leukemia, the greatest football mind of his era is coming to terms with his considerable legacy BY MICHAEL SILVER

BILL WALSH SITS AT A LACQUERED WOODEN TABLE, THE 18TH HOLE OF THE PRISTINE SHARON HEIGHTS GOLF and Country Club behind him, another blood transfusion and another long, draining day at Stanford Hospital in his immediate future. The Hall of Fame coach is talking about the end of his life—the "final stage," as he calls it—and, at 75, sounds as prepared and unruffled as a man battling leukemia can be. But is he completely without regret? Walsh closes his eyes and furrows his brow, the wrinkles on his prominent forehead becoming more pronounced.

Something is bothering him, something apart from the disease that has left him so vulnerable: a decision he made 18 years ago that he wishes he could take back.

"I should have continued to coach," Walsh says, his words hanging in the air of the country club's nearly deserted dining room. "If I could've taken a month off, or something, to get away … but I had all the other jobs. I couldn't leave. The draft was coming, and I was the general manager. So I didn't see any place to go. I should've turned it over to other guys and taken off. It would've been all right. Of course it would have. But I didn't do it." He sighs and shakes his head.

In January 1989 Walsh—burned out after a decade as coach of the San Francisco 49ers—stepped away from the NFL sideline, never to return. The franchise he'd raised from rubble had just won its third Super Bowl in eight years and was positioned to win more. Under Walsh's coaching successor, George Seifert, the Niners would win their fourth Super Bowl the following year, go to three more NFC title games in the next four years, and win their fifth Super Bowl in January '95. Had Walsh remained as coach, with future Hall of Fame quarterbacks Joe Montana and Steve Young running his avant-garde offense, the man who had been dubbed the Genius knows he could have won four, five, maybe even six Super Bowls. Six! There's a record that might have stood forever. Instead the most influential football man of his era allowed others to bask in the afterglow of his accomplishments.

So now Walsh squints into the descending sun on a clear January afternoon in Menlo Park, Calif., lost in silence, and ponders what might have been. How, after drawing up all those spellbinding game plans, after all that bold draft day wheeling and dealing, could he have so badly botched that one, crucial call?

Eddie DeBartolo Jr. is enjoying Montana—the state where he owns a vacation home, not the quarterback whose excellence helped him become the most successful NFL owner of his era—when the mention of Walsh brings him out of his reverie. A few days earlier, a writer from the Bay Area had called DeBartolo's secretary seeking a phone interview for a story on Walsh. Recounting the writer's message sends DeBartolo into one of his infamous tirades. "He wanted me to give him quotes for an obituary," DeBartolo screams. "A f------ obituary! I said to my secretary, 'Amy, read that to me again because I can't f------ believe what I'm hearing!'"

After DeBartolo calms down, he reminisces about the December 1978 dinner at the Doral hotel in Miami Beach, where he offered Walsh, then the Stanford coach, the job of turning around the franchise DeBartolo had purchased two years earlier. Coming off a 2–14 season that ended the brutal two-year reign of autocratic general manager Joe Thomas, the organization was, in the words of Montana, a third-round draft pick in '79, "a small circus."

After years of being mentored by legendary football men such as franchise builder Paul Brown and offensive guru Sid Gillman, Walsh proved to be a transcendent ringmaster. Hired as coach and G.M., Walsh instituted a system that would revolutionize the game. From his meticulously crafted organization and cerebral practice regimens to his daring personnel decisions and his visionary offensive schemes, he created an enduring model.

But the heavy lifting over those 10 years with the Niners—he was also G.M. from 1979 to '82 and team president from '83 to '87—left Walsh drained, and he chose to walk away. That Walsh now questions the move doesn't surprise his former boss. "Bill was such a competitor, but he was going through such an emotionally tough time," DeBartolo says. "[Quitting] was going through his mind after the fifth or sixth game [in '88], and he held it together."

The two men's relationship had been strained since the 49ers were upset by the Minnesota Vikings in a 1987 divisional-round playoff; afterward DeBartolo stripped Walsh of his title as team president, appointing himself as the replacement. But as early as '82—the season after San Francisco's first Super Bowl victory—Walsh was wearying of the grind and contemplating resigning as coach. The subject was broached to his assistants on a semi regular basis. "There were times we'd be told, 'Go to the East-West [Shrine Game] practices and find a job because Bill's quitting,'" recalls Bill McPherson, a longtime friend of Walsh's who was a 49ers assistant from 1979 through '98. "Then two days later he'd be in his office and we'd say, 'Maybe we still have jobs.'"

In '88 Walsh saw the team through a full-blown quarterback controversy of his own making, angering Montana by inserting Young into the lineup for parts or all of numerous regular-season games. In early November the Niners blew a 23–0 lead at Phoenix and lost to the Cardinals, a game in which Walsh also suffered bruised ribs when he was plowed over during a punt return near the sideline. That evening he was so emotionally and physically sapped that he could barely board the team plane. The next week San Francisco endured a humiliating 9–3 defeat to the Los Angeles Raiders to drop to 6–5. Though Montana rallied the Niners to a 10–6 finish and an improbable Super Bowl title, it didn't improve Walsh's outlook. He was exhausted and disillusioned with coaching.

As furious as Montana was at his coach in the months before Walsh's resignation, he thought the decision to leave was a huge mistake. "I was in shock," Montana remembers. "With the team we had and where we were going, I think he gave up at the wrong time. I know there was a lot of pressure, but he handed over a team that arguably should have won three Super Bowls in a row and might have won who knows how many."

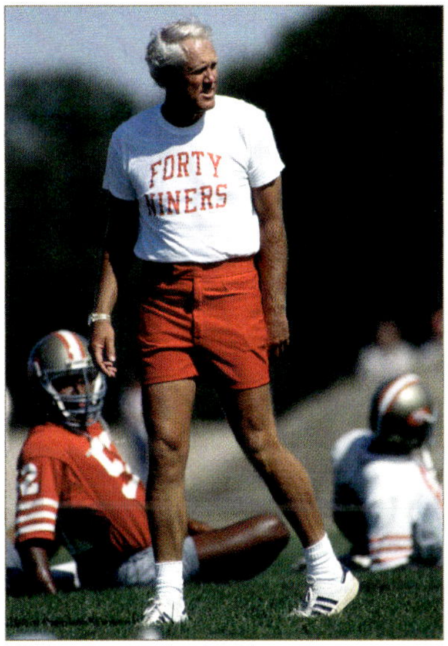

Later in life, Walsh second-guessed his decision to leave the 49ers sideline.

Even as Walsh was making his announcement at a press conference, DeBartolo could sense the coach was having second thoughts. "Bill got better in the next five or six days after the Super Bowl, and then he went to Hawaii and healed even more," DeBartolo says. "But you can't renege on a commitment. He never said to me, 'You know what, I blew it. I shouldn't have resigned.'"

When Walsh acquired Young from the Tampa Bay Buccaneers for second- and fourth-round draft picks before the 1987 season, the left-handed quarterback was the NFL's version of a wild mustang—swift and untamed. It took years for Young's coaches, including Walsh and future offensive coordinators Mike Holmgren, Marc Trestman and Mike Shanahan, to mold him into the precise passer and methodical decision-maker the 49ers' offense demanded. More than seven years removed from his last NFL game, Young now believes that for all the credit Walsh receives, his genius is nonetheless underrated.

"I get the sense that East Coasters don't see the impact [West Coasters] do," Young says. "I don't know if people realize the innovation he has brought to this game on so many levels. From a business perspective, I'd compare it to Silicon Valley—where Andy Grove, Steve Jobs and some of the other pioneers really changed business. Bill Walsh, around that same time, brought the same kind of mentality to football. In terms of how you deal with people and the kind of environment you create, his was a very enlightened approach."

It's not that Walsh wasn't tough on his employees; tales of his authoritarian antics are numerous. "There was the cardboard-box story," says Walsh, smiling at the recollection. Early in his tenure an offensive lineman had become a problem in the locker room. When the player's agent showed up at the Niners' facility demanding a large pay raise for his client, Walsh had enough. "I said, 'Get his stuff, put it in a cardboard box and put it on his doorstep,'" he recalls. "Word got around."

Once, after a rookie defensive lineman smacked Montana during a training-camp drill, Walsh cut the player on the spot. As the newly unemployed behemoth was led off by a team official, in full view of 100 players and thousands of fans at Sierra Community College in Rocklin, Calif., Walsh paced behind them, screaming, "Don't even let him f------ shower!"

Says McPherson, "One time he fired a guy at training camp—I think it was a kicker—because the guy had a dog. Bill was playing tennis, and the dog was running around the courts scaring him, so he yelled, 'Get that guy out of here!' Bill could be mean and tough and as nasty as anyone, but five minutes later he'd turn on the charm. And he is really, really funny."

Mike Walter, an undersized inside linebacker who thrived under Walsh after being waived by the Dallas Cowboys, remembers, "My favorite part of training camp was the 15 minutes we'd meet as a team each night in this big amphitheater at Sierra College, because Bill's dry sense of humor was unbelievable. The night before the first time we were going to be drug-tested, a lot of guys were definitely anxious, and Bill said, 'It's really no big deal. All they're going to do is ask for a little sample …' and he reaches under a desk and pulls out this two-quart Mason jar."

While Walsh's primary job was to win football games, his vision of the coach's role was far more expansive. He had money managers and sociologists counsel his players, delivered speeches on integration and encouraged employees to get involved with charities.

He also seemed aware of the legacy being created by the success of his West Coast offense, the most obvious sign being the wide-open receivers catching Montana's pinpoint passes in stride. Today the West Coast, with its reliance on short passes, precisely timed routes and intricately planned progressions, is the NFL's preeminent scheme. ("Let's call it what it is: the Walshian Offense," Baltimore Ravens coach Brian Billick insists.) But in the early 1980s it merely drove opposing coaches nuts. Old-schoolers, such as the Chicago Bears' Mike Ditka, openly scoffed at the Genius label—a tag Walsh never went to great pains to protest—but his teachings were that innovative. Long before the advent of eBay, copies of his playbooks were being sold on the black market at prices that made him blush.

Walsh was the first coach to script his opening 20 or 25 offensive plays and the first to prowl the sideline with a laminated sheet of plays for specific situations.

Walsh was the first coach to script his opening 20 or 25 offensive plays and the first to prowl the sideline with a laminated sheet of plays for specific situations. He recorded his speeches at team meetings and videotaped new plays being installed, creating an archive as a resource for future Niners coaches and players. And with his blessing, his systems were circulated throughout the league by his former assistants and their protégés. "He was proselytizing," Young says. "He was a missionary. I think Bill realized, I'm way ahead of the league here, and he knew the more people he could touch, the more lasting his impact would be."

Two months ago Walsh sat courtside at Maples Pavilion and watched a Stanford basketball game with Jim Harbaugh, the latest in the long procession of coaches he has mentored. As a member of the school's search committee, Walsh had just helped Harbaugh, 43, a former quarterback at

Michigan and a 15-year NFL veteran, get hired as the Cardinal's coach. In the game they were watching, Stanford had taken an early lead against rival Cal, but Walsh didn't like what he was seeing. "Look at the way Cal's getting back on defense," he told Harbaugh. "They're gaining." Sure enough, the Bears took command and won by four. "His ability to analyze and communicate is unmatched," Harbaugh says of Walsh.

The two men met in the early '90s, when Harbaugh, then with the Bears, was competing in *The Quarterback Challenge*, a made-for-TV event in Hawaii for which Walsh was serving as an announcer. (After staying on as the 49ers' G.M. through the '89 draft, Walsh left the organization for a three-year gig as NBC's lead NFL analyst.) The two began discussing passing mechanics, and soon Harbaugh and another quarterback, Bubby Brister, were behind the centerfield wall of an old baseball stadium getting a 90-minute lesson from Walsh on drops and footwork. "He was just so clear and specific," Harbaugh says, "and I was soaking it up like a sponge."

Late last year, even as his leukemia worsened, Walsh, who twice coached Stanford (1977–78 and '92–94), remained active in the Cardinal's search. In the energetic and enthusiastic Harbaugh, Walsh saw "a nonstop person" who is "as close to Dick Vermeil"—his longtime friend who coached the St. Louis Rams to the Super Bowl XXXIV championship—"as anyone I've seen."

It's a touching storyline—ailing legend guiding protégé—but in Walsh's case so consistent with his past as to be unremarkable. In an era in which many coaches seem to thwart their assistants' opportunities for advancement, restricting their access to the media and discouraging them from interviewing elsewhere, it's instructive to remember how far Walsh went to do just the opposite. "I've never known any coach more tireless in his efforts to help the people around him," says Billick, who worked as a 49ers public relations assistant in 1979 and '80 before beginning his coaching career at San Diego State. "I can never repay Bill, but part of his legacy is that I feel compelled to do it for other coaches, and I think we all feel the same way."

By "we all" Billick means a Who's Who of his profession, from Walsh's former assistants (Holmgren, Dennis Green, Ray Rhodes, Sam Wyche) to a second and third generation who learned the Walsh way (Shanahan, Jeff Fisher, Jon Gruden, Andy Reid and Tony Dungy, who also played for Walsh in '79). Walsh's coaching tree resembles the banyan in Lahaina—and this was by design. While Walsh was a Cincinnati Bengals assistant from 1968 through '75, team founder and coach Paul Brown hindered Walsh's head coaching aspirations. After Brown stepped down and named Bill (Tiger) Johnson as his replacement, Walsh angrily left to become an assistant with the Chargers before moving on to the Stanford job the following season. Last year Walsh told the *Los Angeles Times* that Brown "worked against my candidacy" to be a head coach in the NFL, "and then when I left him, he called whoever he thought was necessary to keep me out of the NFL."

That's why Walsh became a coaching patriarch. And he did so with a social conscience: In 1987, 15 years before the establishment of the Rooney Rule (requiring NFL teams to interview at least one minority candidate for head coaching vacancies), Walsh took the lead in an NFL internship program for minority coaches, bringing prospective assistants into training camp each year and giving them significant responsibility. Among those who served in this capacity were Marvin Lewis, now the Bengals' coach, and Tyrone Willingham, who would go on to be the head man at Stanford, Notre Dame and the University of Washington.

Late in the '88 season Walsh helped Green, his receivers coach, get the Stanford job, then allowed him to begin working there even as the 49ers made another championship run. "Denny had to take on the task at Stanford—that was so critical," Walsh says. "Of course, I had Mike Holmgren to replace him."

And when Holmgren left to become a head coach, he installed Walsh's system first in Green Bay, where he led the Packers to consecutive Super Bowls, and then in Seattle, where he took the Seahawks to another.

"Those coaches were able to be successful because of the blueprint Bill Walsh created," Harbaugh says. "He created the modern-day practice, the modern-day weekly schedule, the way to run a meeting, the way to manage an organization. And when it comes to football expertise, he's the most respected man who's ever coached the game, period."

"I love a parade," composer Harold Arlen wrote in 1931. A half century later, after the 49ers defeated the Bengals in Super Bowl XVI to give San Francisco its first major professional sports championship, Walsh was singing a different tune. "I remember begging [San Francisco city officials], 'Please don't have a parade,'" Walsh recalls. "'Nobody will come.'" Walsh figured he knew the Bay Area well enough. He'd been a local since his days as a student at Hayward High, after his family moved north from Los Angeles in the late '40s. He attended San Jose State in the '50s, where he played split end and competed as a boxer, and began his coaching career at Washington High in Fremont. Later he worked as an assistant at Cal (under Marv Levy), Stanford (under John Ralston) and the Oakland Raiders (under John Rauch and owner-G.M. Al Davis).

San Francisco, Walsh worried, was too sophisticated for a parade. But the city went ahead as planned, and as the flatbed transporting Walsh and some of his players rolled down the Embarcadero, alongside the glimmering bay, the coach felt his worst fears were confirmed. "The road was empty," he recalls. "Nothing. Then we made the turn onto Market Street...."

His voice trails off as he savors the memory. Tens of thousands of fans had turned out to celebrate, and the 49er faithful have retained their affection for Walsh ever since. The feeling is mutual. Despite offers to coach other NFL teams after resigning from the Niners, Walsh refused to stray from his roots and continued to serve the team even when doing so brought indignity: In 1996 Walsh spent a season as a consultant on Seifert's staff, but he was given a windowless office and was largely ignored.

The lesson, as Walsh takes his leave, is clear: In the end a man's relationships matter more than the number of Super Bowl rings in his jewelry box.

Walsh returned again, as vice president and general manager, from 1999 to 2000, and stayed on as a consultant in '01. In that time he helped clean up San Francisco's salary-cap problems and made several astute personnel moves, including the signing of an unheralded former Canadian Football League quarterback, Jeff Garcia, who would be selected to three consecutive Pro Bowls. But Walsh bristled when owner's representative John York lectured him about how to manage an organization, and there was tension between Walsh and coach Steve Mariucci.

(York was the husband of Denise DeBartolo York, the sister to whom Eddie had ceded control of the team after his involvement in a Louisiana gaming scandal in the late '90s.)

So again Walsh stepped away. His health began declining in 2004, and leukemia was the diagnosis. Late last summer a test revealed dangerously low levels of bone marrow, and in Walsh's words, "That's when all hell broke loose." He had two cycles of chemotherapy and in late October took a turn for the worse. For weeks he could eat only crackers, and he had two painful infections on his face that doctors feared he'd be unable to fight off.

As news of Walsh's declining condition spread, his former players and associates rallied to support him. Some, including DeBartolo, flew in from distant cities to visit; others left frequent phone messages. He got a call from Sen. Dianne Feinstein and a home visit from Gov. Arnold Schwarzenegger. Staring at his phone as it rang and rang, unable to muster the energy to answer it, Walsh understood, for perhaps the first time, the true depth of his impact on others—and it caught him off guard.

Among NFL executives, Walsh was revered for proactively releasing popular veterans to keep his franchise thriving, and though he privately anguished over such transactions, he'd act coldly when necessary. Now, years later, even some of the players with whom his relationship had become the most strained—Dwight Clark, Ronnie Lott and Jerry Rice included—were expressing their affection.

Walsh's condition, though incurable, has improved over the past couple of months. Most weeks he spends one or two days receiving blood transfusions; the rest of the time he tries to stay active. Recently, Walsh says, he played "some of the worst golf ever," though he wasn't really complaining. He still has ties to Stanford, serving as a consultant to the athletic director. Last month he visited his beach house near Monterey with his wife, Geri, who suffered a stroke seven years ago and has been largely debilitated since. Walsh and the couple's surviving children, Craig, 47, and Elizabeth, 35 (their oldest son, Steve, died of leukemia in 2002 at age 46), have made arrangements for Geri to receive care if Bill should die first. "She's a courageous and wonderful woman," he says.

Some of Walsh's former players, including Pro Bowl tight end Russ Francis, recently met with him to discuss the possibility of his undergoing experimental treatments that could theoretically keep the leukemia at bay for a prolonged period. Whatever happens, Walsh says, he has steeled himself for the worst.

If anything good has come of this, Montana believes, it's that by steadily reliving the past with friends and visitors, Walsh has been compelled to reflect on his career in a positive manner. "I think there's a lot more feeling there than he ever imagined," Montana says. "He's seeing it now, though it's hard for it to have to come out this way."

As Walsh walks through the country-club parking lot toward his car, he is smiling and unburdened. "I'm at peace with myself," he says softly. In the twilight Walsh stops under a Chinese elm to say goodbye and to make one request. It has nothing to do with the decision he made 18 years ago, and everything to do with the present: "The guy whose belongings we put in the cardboard box—please don't use his name. Since then he has become a deacon in his church. And we have a good relationship now. We really do."

The lesson, as Walsh takes his leave, is clear: In the end a man's relationships matter more than the number of Super Bowl rings in his jewelry box.

It doesn't take a genius to understand why. •

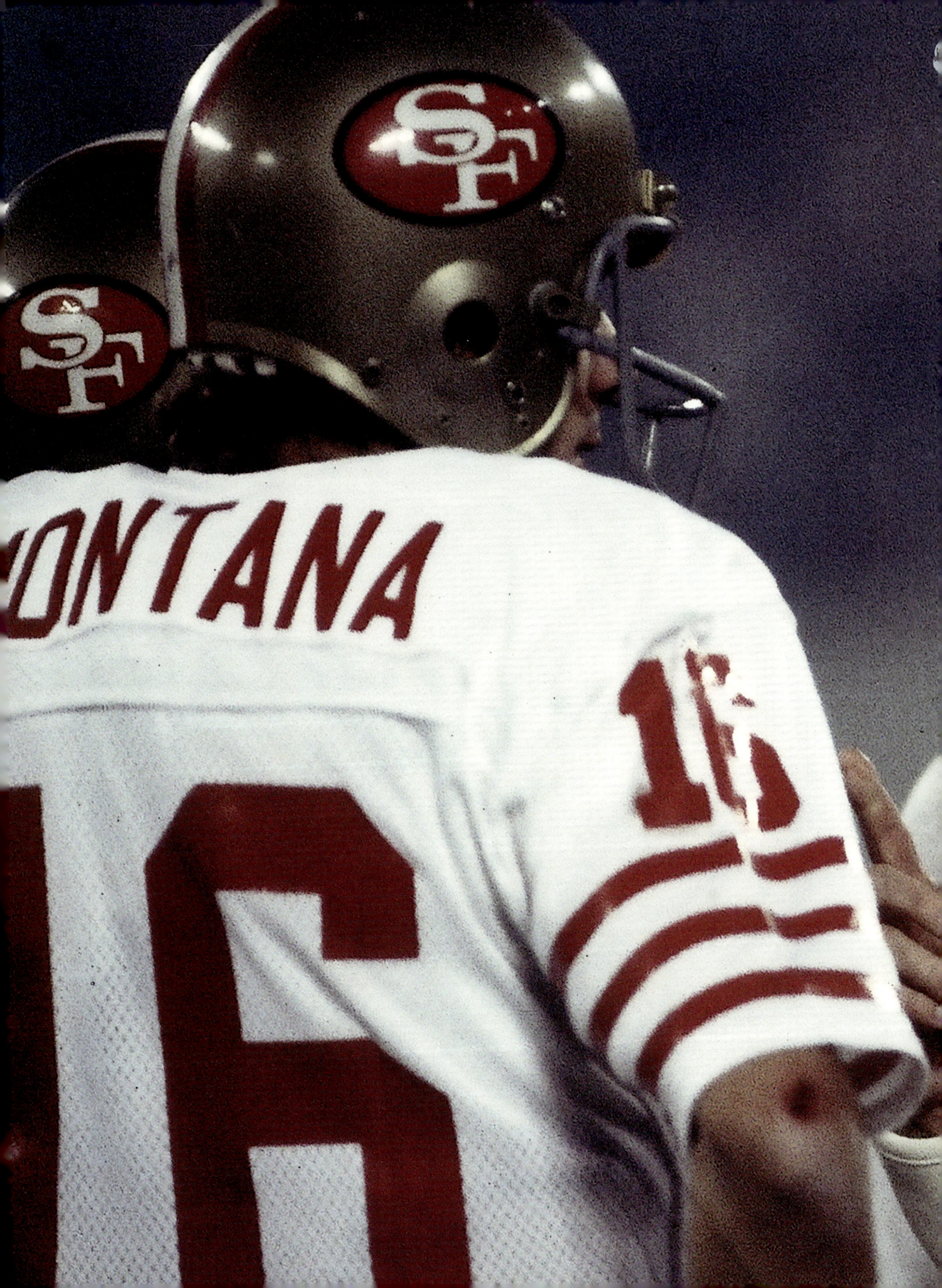

SF
SF
ONTANA
16
16

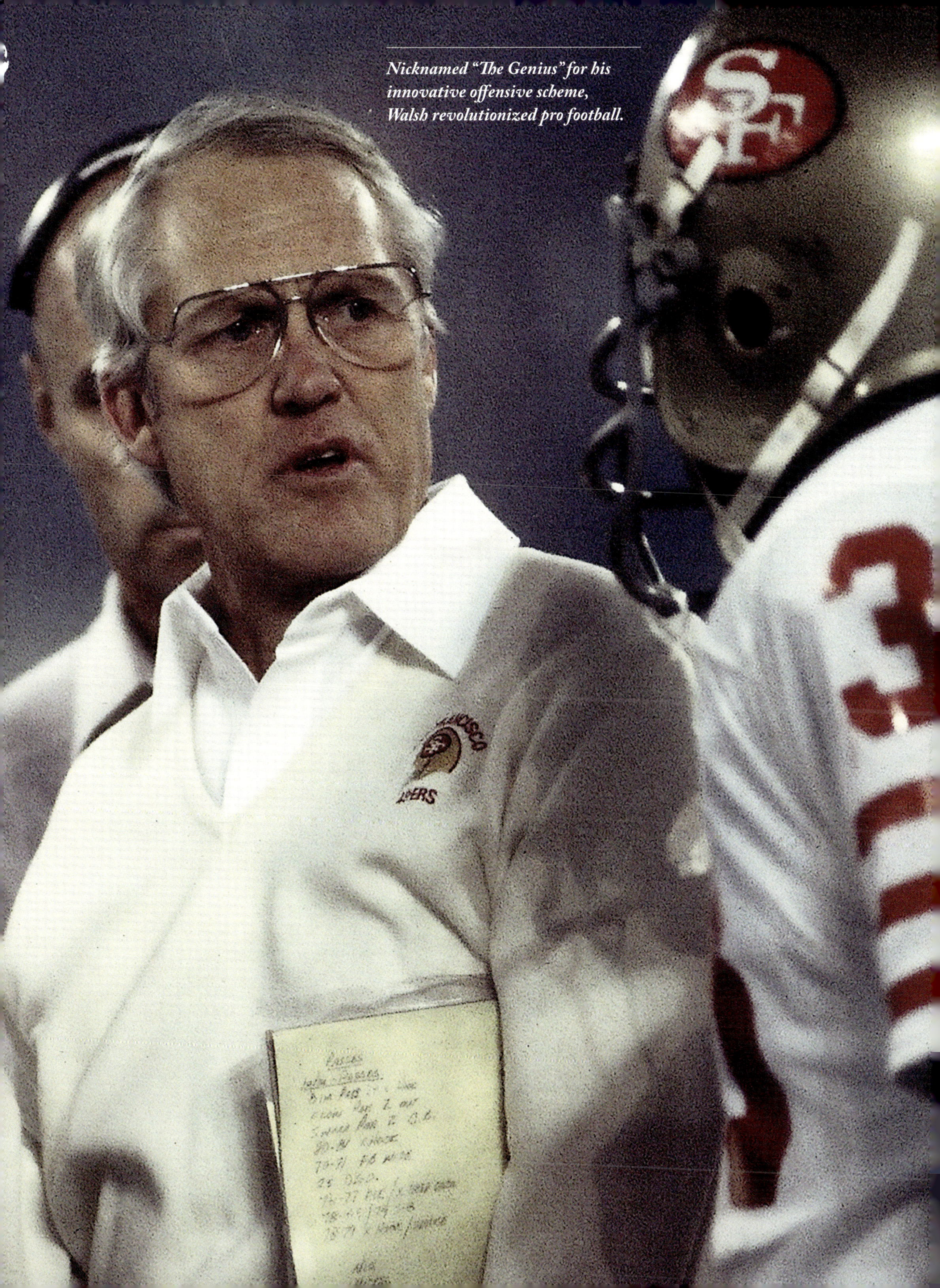

Nicknamed "The Genius" for his innovative offensive scheme, Walsh revolutionized pro football.

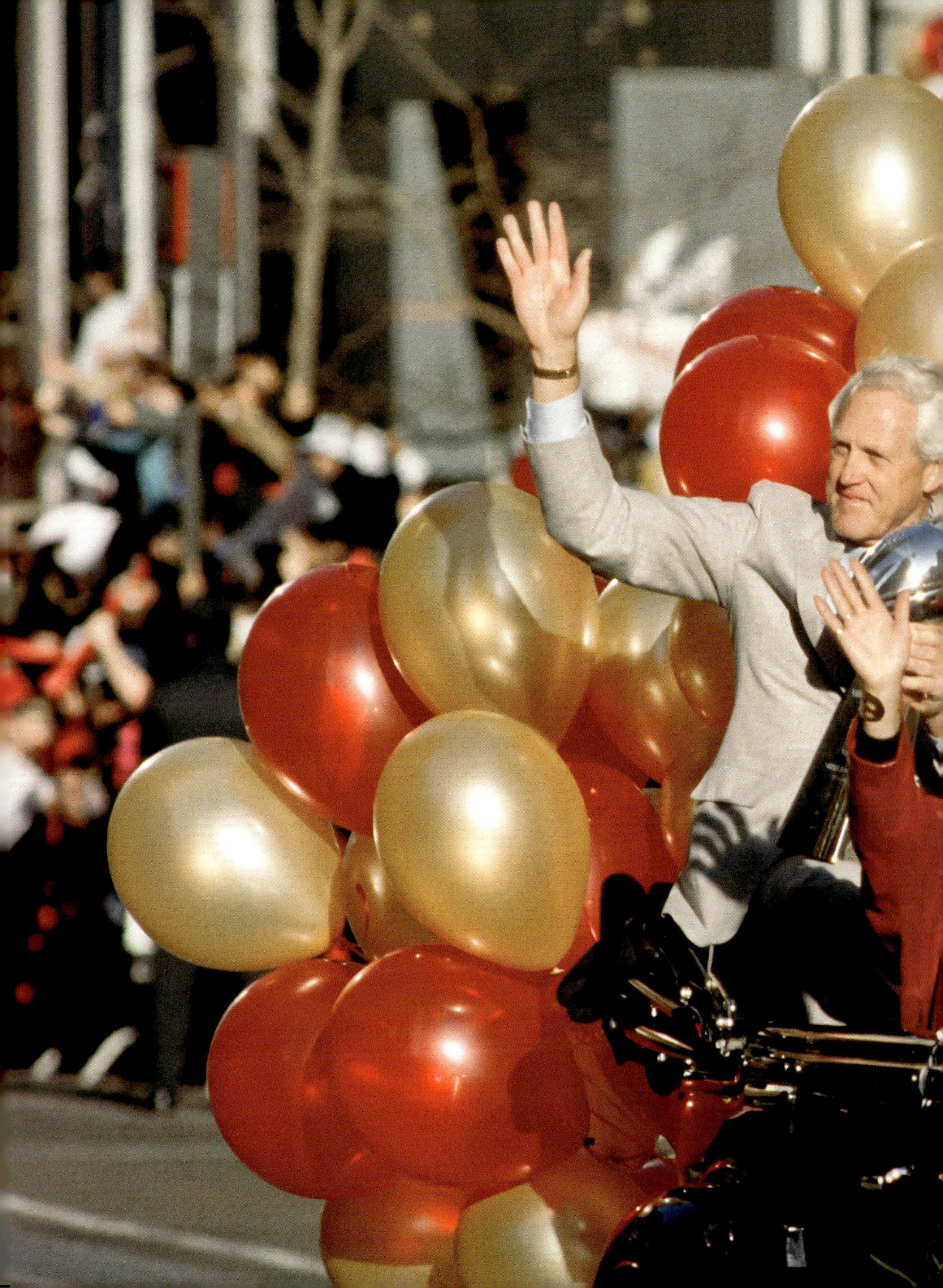

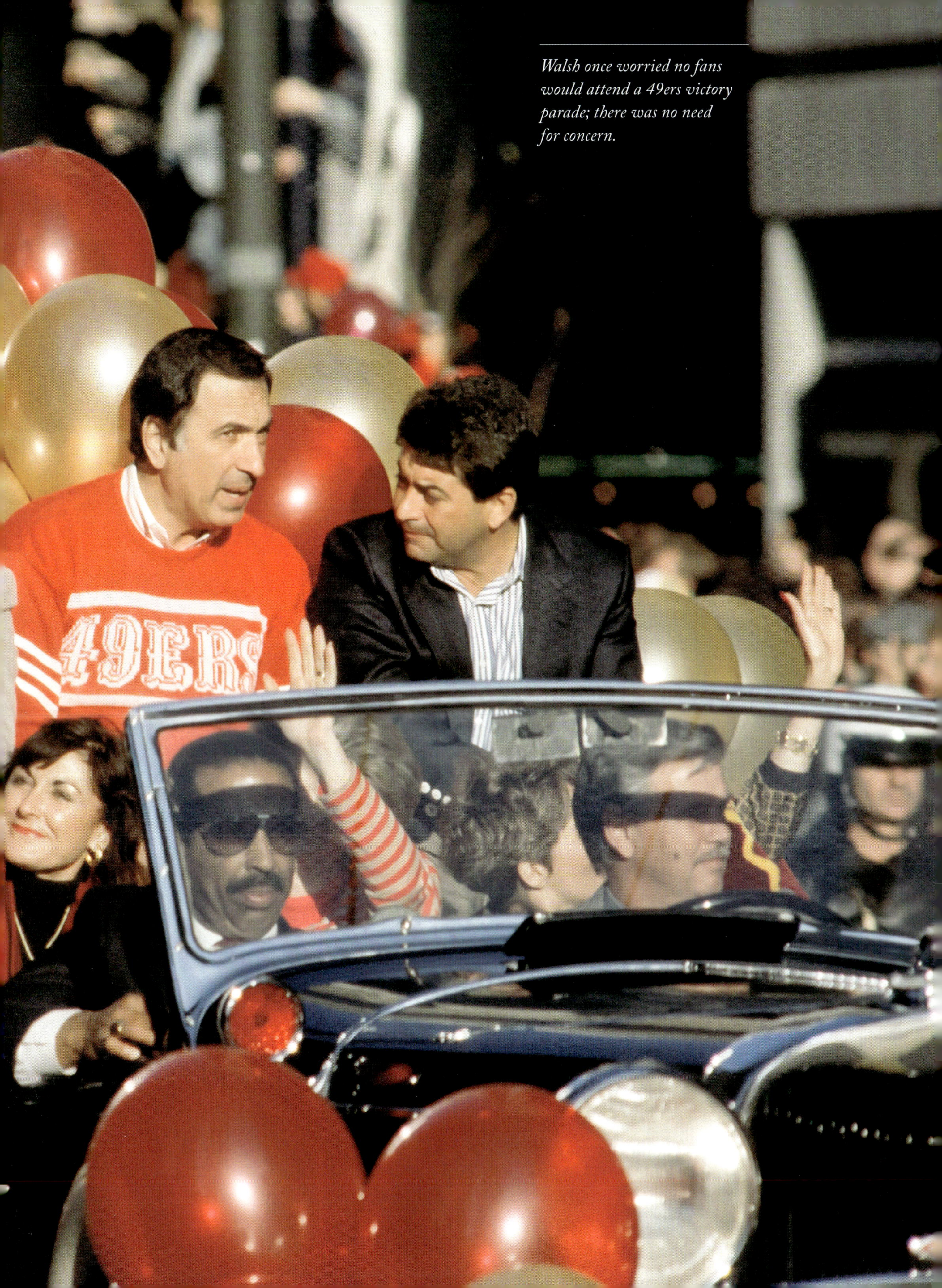

Walsh once worried no fans would attend a 49ers victory parade; there was no need for concern.

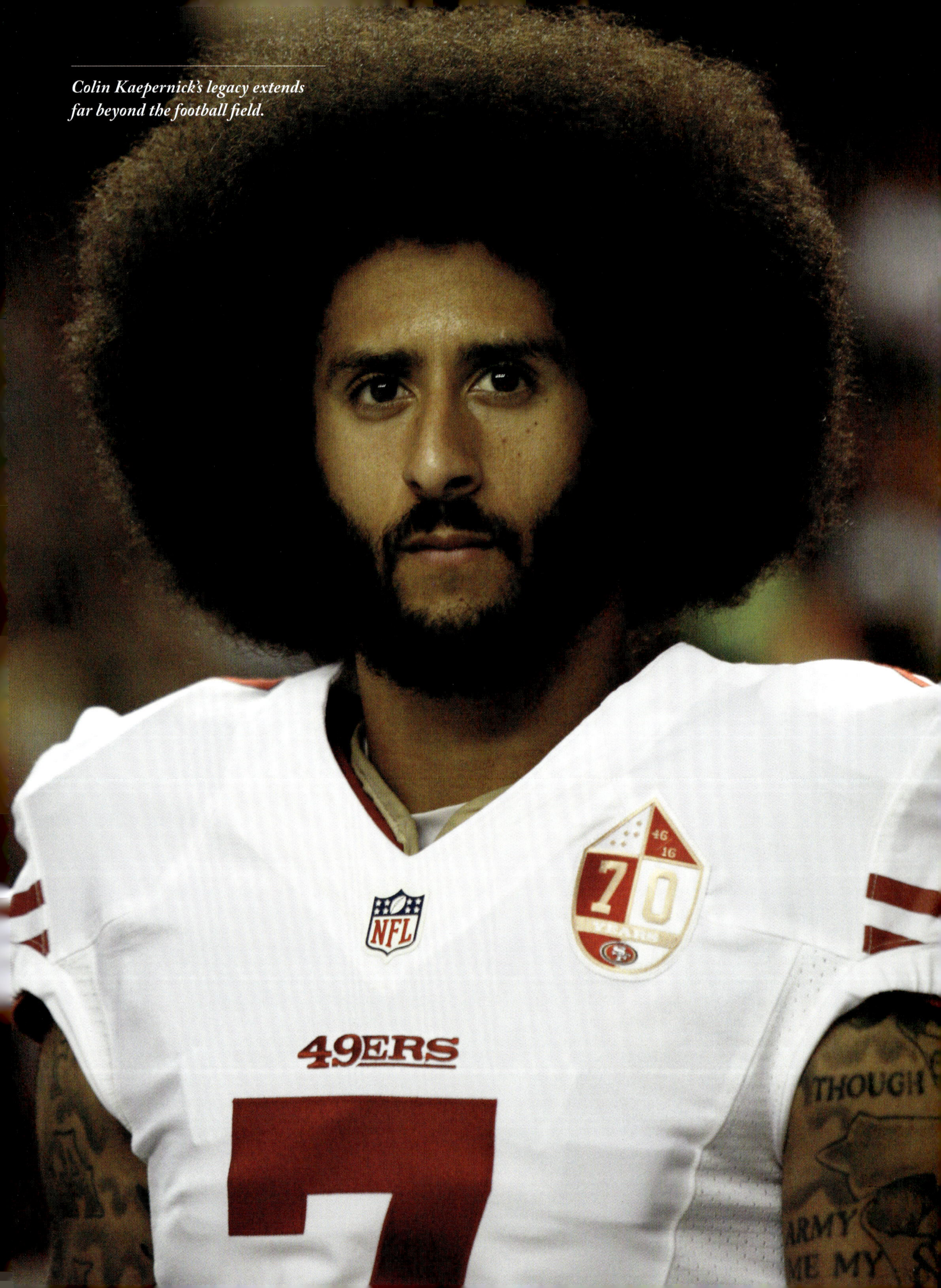

Colin Kaepernick's legacy extends far beyond the football field.

EXCERPTED FROM SPORTS ILLUSTRATED | DECEMBER 11, 2017

THE KAP EFFECT

Yes, the QB took a stand by kneeling. But just as important: he pledged $1 million to the issues that drove him to protest. A close examination of how Kaepernick has given that money away—and to whom—reveals a blueprint for real social change BY GREG BISHOP AND BEN BASKIN

KEVIN LIVINGSTON WAS DRIVING HOME WITH HIS DAUGHTER WHEN HE RECEIVED A RANDOM CALL ONE Saturday morning last April: Colin Kaepernick has something for you. How far away are you?

Livingston runs a charity, 100 Suits for 100 Men, that provides business attire for job seekers who have recently been released from jail or suffered hardship, and after he dropped off his daughter, he raced to the Queens parole office, where he keeps a desk. Kaepernick was waiting for him in his SUV, where he'd been sitting for almost an hour.

The QB stepped out wearing lime-green sneakers and a black T-shirt emblazoned with a panther, lugging two overstuffed cardboard boxes toward a glass door marked STAFF ONLY. He opened a box, pulled out a gray, custom-made three-piece suit, draped a striped tie over the jacket and posed for a few cellphone pics, flashing a smile. One of those photos became an Instagram post, and that post went viral.

The visit marked a rare public sighting for a man defined by contradictions: a quarterback, just four years removed from a Super Bowl appearance, who can't land an NFL roster spot. An activist who has rarely spoken publicly. An athlete who ranks among the most divisive and socially conscious figures in sports. Anyone who wondered what Kaepernick had been up to caught a glimpse that day, but little more. No one saw what happened next.

Of the dozens of suits Kaepernick delivered—some new, some his own—the one in the photo wound up with 26-year-old Mario Lloyde, who had been living month-to-month with his girlfriend in a cramped Baltimore apartment, unable to get more than a temporary gig as a file clerk at a hospital or a cashier at a bookstore. "I was trying to get into real estate," he says, "but I had to dress the part."

The first time Lloyde put on that suit, he says he "felt like Superman." A month later he walked into the offices of Vision Realty Management, where—he swears this to be true—the first thing his interviewer said was, "Well, you already completed step one: You look nice."

Lloyde got the gig, became a full-time clerk and is now studying to become a licensed broker. He also found that suit life suits him well. He has bought nine more ensembles—but nothing that tops the first. "When I put on [that original]," he says, "I feel like I'm representing on behalf of Colin Kaepernick."

That's how Kaepernick, 30, speaks these days: through this kind of work, and then through those he touches. He's the most prominent athlete activist in decades and is close to fulfilling his pledge to donate $1 million to dozens of charities. Much has been made about his choice not to comment on the legions of NFL players protesting during the national anthem—a movement he began last year, kneeling to draw attention to issues like police brutality and racial inequality—or to challenge President Donald Trump's portrayal of his kneeling as unpatriotic. Instead he stays up late, on his laptop, Googling charitable organizations.

Kaepernick declined to comment for this story. But the key information—what, specifically, his donations go toward—is readily available on his website. And yet an odd notion festers, in part because Kaepernick has not addressed one question, the answer to which is both simple and incredibly complex: What, exactly, are you doing to fight for the causes to which you have drawn so much attention?

Much more than one might think.

On Oct. 5, Kaepernick pulled up to DREAM, an East Harlem charter school, where officials whisked him through a back door. He wore a black T-shirt that read I KNOW MY RIGHTS as he strolled through halls decorated with relevant questions painted in red and white: WHAT STORY DO YOUR ACTIONS TELL? WHO ARE YOU GOING TO IMPACT TODAY?

In the front row of the auditorium 14-year-old Kassim Samassi says he sat "hyperventilating" in anticipation. A month earlier he and his ninth-grade classmates had been assigned to read Ta-Nehisi Coates's *Between the World and Me*, an exploration of the nation's racial history, and they had found similarities between Coates's message and Kaepernick's protest. "As a person of color, when you see inequality and police brutality [against minorities], you feel like you don't belong in this world," Kassim says. "And Kaepernick is standing up for all of us."

DREAM's ninth-graders are divided into houses—not unlike Hogwarts, except that here each house is named after an influential American minority. Kassim belongs to the Toni Morrison House, but he foresees a day when there may be one named after Kaepernick as well.

The quarterback's relationship with DREAM began before he ever knelt or pledged a penny. His girlfriend of two years, Nessa Diab, has spoken in the past with the school's female students about self-esteem and body image, and for several years has emceed their Diamond Ball fund-raiser. Kaepernick made a quiet guest appearance at that event in 2015, during a 49ers bye week.

Even with that existing relationship, the QB kept a typically high level of involvement this fall, taking multiple phone calls with the foundation's development group before granting them $25,000 and earmarking much of the money toward college- and career-readiness programs. And in November, 54 DREAM students visited SUNY-Albany, marking the first trip to a college for most of them. Included in that group: Kassim, who wants to attend Stanford and become a software engineer.

The man who enabled those aspirations showed up in Harlem that Thursday in October, flanked only by Diab—no camera crew, no publicist. More than 100 students lined the school's gym in folding chairs as Kaepernick spoke for 45 minutes, mostly answering questions. How does it feel to be at the origin of controversy? What are the specific reasons you decided to protest?

Kaepernick's answers focused on the importance of 1) being "just in unjust places" and 2) confronting "ignorance not with ignorance, but with education." Toward the end, one student asked, Why is it important

> "No matter what I have to sacrifice," he told the students, "if you see wrong in the world, you must say that it is wrong."

for you to stand up for a greater cause, even though you lost your fame and fortune?

Here Kaepernick selected two kids from the audience and brought them up front. "If you," he said to one of them, "saw him," he pointed to the other, "sucker punch someone, and I offered you $20 not to tell anyone, what are you going to do?"

Kaepernick answered his own question. "No matter what I have to sacrifice," he told the students, "if you see wrong in the world, you must say that it is wrong."

Rupa Marya grew up in a 49ers household, but she was never a football fan. For years she waited for prominent athletes to use their platform to address the issues she's devoted her career to fighting—police violence and racism. Then Kaepernick came along. Last August, Marya, 42, wrote a letter to the QB, praising his bravery. She invited him to meet with her fellow volunteers at the Do No Harm Coalition, a San Francisco–based group of 300-plus public health and medical professionals who, rightfully, treat racism and violence as public health emergencies. Forty doctors signed the letter, which ended, "We would like to welcome you into our ranks as a healer."

Marya's still not sure whether Kaepernick saw that note, which she blasted across social media. But a few months later he pledged $50,000 to DNH's Mni Wiconi Health Clinic Partnership, a free clinic being built on the Standing Rock reservation in the Dakotas.

The Lakota Dakota people suffer from a host of ailments at strikingly high rates—from diabetes to depression—and while the main Mni Wiconi clinic will sit on a permanent site, there are remote areas across the 8,000-square-mile reservation that lack resources. Kaepernick focused his support on the creation of a mobile health clinic that will make weekly rounds and deliver medications.

At first glance that donation might seem misaligned with issues like police brutality and racial inequality, but Marya sees the connection. The Lakota Dakota people were one of the fiercest resisters of westward expansion, which she calls the first act of white supremacy in America, and they've faced long-lasting consequences. Today the youth attempted-suicide rate among Oglala Lakota, one of seven Lakota subtribes, is more than seven times the national average.

Kaepernick's Mni Wiconi donation speaks both to the specific nature and the wide breadth of his support. Between October 2016 and December '17 he doled out 31 grants and $900,000 (with $100,000 to be distributed by year's end). He has chosen organizations in big cities (New York, L.A., Chicago) and small ones (Fayetteville, N.C.; Lithonia, Ga.), and he stood behind causes that ranged from police reform to climate change to the need for organic ingredients in community cooking workshops.

In January, Nancy Northup, CEO of the Center for Reproductive Rights, received $25,000 to help finance her outfit's emergency litigation fund, which was created after Donald Trump won the presidency on an anti-abortion platform. (CRR's litigation team, for example, would fight to ensure Planned Parenthood funding.) Northup was initially surprised by that donation—then she, too, saw the connection. "What he's really taking a stance for," she says, "is human rights and equality and fairness and making sure that everybody gets a shot."

Cat Collins, in his role as an informal adviser, helps Kaepernick connect with his charitable partners, and last May he emailed the Arizona office of the American Friends Service Committee, a 100-year-old Quaker organization that advocates for ending mass incarceration. When program director Caroline Isaacs got that email, she reacted as many do when they hear from a stranger with a simple question: If Colin Kaepernick gave you $25,000, what would you do with it? She thought it was a prank. This, roughly, is Step 1 for every Kaepernick donation: the random reach-out.

After that email exchange Isaacs skipped into her office in Tucson. "Colin Kaepernick might be interested in funding us!" she breathlessly told her colleagues. Next she would have to lay out exactly how they'd use the money. Step 2. (Some groups are asked to submit short bullet-pointed proposals; many recount Collins saying, "Keep it simple—and, for the love of God, no PowerPoints!")

Collins and Isaacs lobbed ideas back and forth. He asked if the AFSC needed a van; it didn't. She wanted to film promotional videos; Kaepernick's team felt that was too much like marketing. Eventually they focused on the AFSC's program called Reframing Justice, run by Grace Gamez, which aims to give voice to the formerly incarcerated and ease their transition back into society. Perfect, Collins said.

A week or two later Isaacs's cellphone lit up with text messages. "Holy s---," one read, "we got the Kap money!" Her colleagues had found out on Twitter. Step 3. "It's like we won the lottery," Isaacs says.

Step 4: Spend the money. Gamez decided to hire Glenn Martin, the founder of JustLeadershipUSA, which is trying to cut the U.S. prison population in half by 2030. Martin runs expensive seminars where he trains former inmates (and other volunteers) to assist current convicts in transitioning out of prison. Gamez hopes to bring Martin to Arizona next spring for a session in front of as many as 100 AFSC employees and volunteers. If not for Kaepernick's money, Gamez says, she likely could have sent just one person to the same seminar.

Step 5: Impact. In 2010, Joe Watson was sentenced to 12 years in prison following a string of robberies. Inside, he wrote articles for *Prison Legal News*, and in that work he came across the AFSC. When he was granted early release this year, he volunteered for the outfit, eventually becoming a contracted staff member, and now he'll attend Martin's training session, paid for by Kaepernick.

When Watson recently praised Kaepernick on Facebook, an old prison buddy who'd also served in the U.S. Army commented. "Why do you support him? What does he do for his community?"

"Well, funny you should ask ..." Watson began.

As Kaepernick knelt during the anthem throughout the 2016 season, Adam Jackson, the CEO of a grassroots Baltimore-based think tank, tweeted, "Noble ... Just hope [he] invests money in black people."

Jackson thought back to that post when Collins called in April. He, too, wondered at first if he was being punked. Instead, Jackson submitted a short proposal, then opened the mail one day and there it was: a $25,000 check.

Jackson's subsequent experience embodies the methodology behind Kaepernick's pledges. Leaders of a Beautiful Struggle, Jackson's seven-year-old organization, advocates on behalf of Black Baltimoreans. In this case Kaepernick and Jackson decided to apply the donation to LBS's youth development programs, which train high school students in advocacy and activism. "In the Black community," Jackson says, "we don't have enough voices that are of and from here to speak for ourselves in terms of [policy making]."

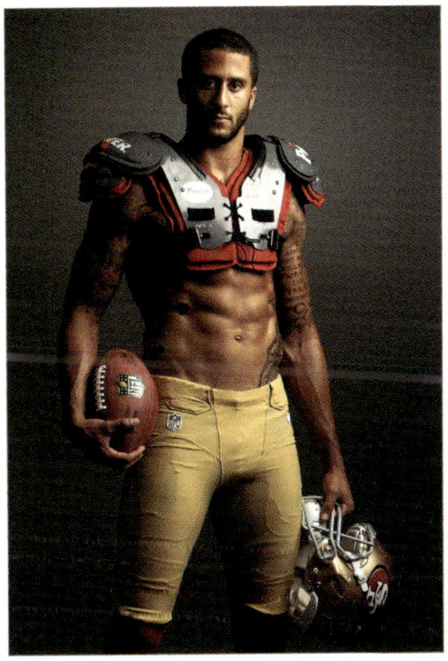

Kap at a photo shoot in 2014.

Kaepernick's work, he argues, is fundamentally different from typical celebrity philanthropy, starting with Kaepernick's view of donations as investments, not just charity. Crucial, too, are the targets (mostly minority-led, grassroots organizations based in communities impacted by the issues he supports) and the intent (resources, infrastructure, trainees who become trainers) of his contributions. What the QB's not doing: feeding large corporate entities (say, March of Dimes) who Jackson says "are basically hustling off suffering poor people and Black folks."

Beyond the cash influx, Jackson points out, Kaepernick's backing can serve as affirmation of the work done by a smaller organization, like his, which makes it easier to obtain further donations, then invest in more infrastructure and so on.

If all athletes took such a specific, targeted approach to their charitable endeavors, Jackson says, they could affect immediate structural change in their communities. "They all tweet, they talk, they wear T-shirts—and that's cool," he says. "But that's cultural. And cultural change can go but so far.

"The purpose of protest is to change the environment that gives everyone else permission not to care about these issues. If there were 100 Colin Kaepernicks—or 2,000!—then you'd be talking about a real social movement.

"Just kneeling," he says, "is a cop-out."

Barbara Fuller isn't interested enough in football (or politics) to have noticed when Kaepernick announced on March 1 that he was opting out of his contract with the 49ers. Besides, Fuller had spent the majority of her 86 years across the Bay, near the Oakland

Coliseum, as the matriarch of a family steeped in Raiders fandom. The news that caught her attention came two weeks later, when President Trump announced his Skinny Budget proposal. That plan (which, ultimately, never made it past the House) called for the elimination of the $3 billion Community Development Block Grant program, a financial feeder for programs such as Meals on Wheels, which delivers food to at-risk seniors. Such organizations, Trump's budget director noted, "sound good but don't show results."

Tell that to Fuller, a retired special education teacher of 46 years who eats more healthily and on a regular schedule through the program, which keeps her food costs down, helping her afford her house in an otherwise unaffordable neighborhood. "I felt angry," she says. "I worked until I was 74, and now that I'm old enough to qualify, the program is going to end?"

There was no TV interview, no ribbon-cutting when, one week later, Kaepernick donated $50,000 to Meals on Wheels. Just a bank transfer. While Kaepernick's charitable aims are not overtly political, they have been colored and driven by the current presidency. In this case his donation was a direct response to the announcement by the President, who one day earlier had stomped deeper into the Kaepernick fray, giddily telling a Louisville rally that the QB hadn't yet found a team because NFL owners "don't want to get a nasty tweet from Donald Trump."

The next afternoon Mary Gregory, the director of development for SOS Meals on Wheels in Oakland, was out delivering food with the city's mayor when she received an unexpected phone call. The organization had seen an uptick in volunteers following the White House announcement, but not an influx in cash—and now her superiors were telling her that Kaepernick wanted his $50,000 earmarked for Oakland residents. Like Fuller.

Kaepernick's money would go toward everything from raw ingredients to packaging to fuel for delivery trucks. And while others could continue to ignore the work he was

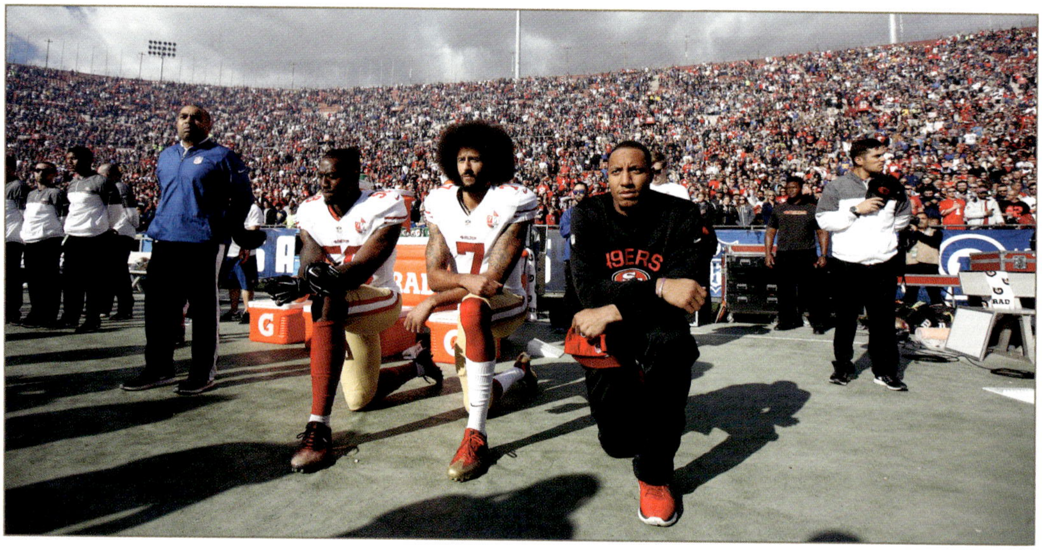

Kaepernick began kneeling during the anthem to protest police brutality and social injustice in 2016. Often, teammates such as Eli Harold (left) and Eric Reid (right) joined him.

doing, that was no longer the case for Gregory. She sees hypocrisy in NFL teams and fan bases that want players to appear charitable—visiting sick children in hospitals, for instance, or cutting ribbons at community center openings—but not actually jump into the fray themselves, especially on thornier issues. Kaepernick's work directly impacts the Barbara Fullers of the East Bay. SOS Meals on Wheels had introduced her to vegetables she'd never heard of; she even came to love couscous. Weren't those direct results?

Says Fuller, "I'm praying for Colin Kaepernick."

Clinton Allen loved football. Two of his uncles played in the NFL, and he grew up obsessing over the Cowboys, working into conversation the names of long-ago stars like (Bullet) Bob Hayes and Drew Pearson. Outside of his team he admired Jim Brown and, in boxing, Muhammad Ali, athletes who stood for racial equality decades before Kaepernick ever knelt.

But in March 2013, when Allen was 25, he was shot and killed by a Dallas police officer. The details of that night remain disputed—the possible presence of drugs in Allen's system, the seemingly high number of gunshots fired—but the incident followed a familiar pattern: an altercation, two drastically different versions of events, another young Black man dead ... and no indictment.

When Kaepernick first took a knee, he clearly (and later frequently) noted the reason for his protest: to draw attention to police brutality and the need for reform. That act meant even more to Collette Flanagan, Allen's mother, than did the $25,000 he donated to Mothers Against Police Brutality, the organization she started in her son's honor. It has pained her to see Trump and other detractors misrepresent the quarterback's initial intentions, to see the meaning of his kneeling shift beneath him. Kaepernick's protest was never about the military or the flag, as the President has suggested. It was always about injustice, specifically young Black men being killed. Men like her son.

As the 2017 season unfolded and Jerry Jones, the owner of Allen's favorite team, demanded that Cowboys players stand for the anthem, Flanagan noticed how police brutality no longer seemed like part of the conversation. When players and owners across the league locked arms on the weekend of Sept. 24, it felt, she says, like a sanitized, gentrified version of Kaepernick's original protest. The impact was less powerful for that very palatability.

"I don't think Colin has lost focus," she says. "Everyone else has, so they can get comfortable. I hear all these crazy things, like 'He was [kneeling] for attention.' Who in the world would want that kind of attention? That's like saying I wanted to be in this club of mothers whose sons were killed."

Kaepernick has gone out of his way to maximize the impact of his philanthropy in a manner that garners minimal attention. He has mostly avoided large organizations. He has empowered those in need, providing them with the infrastructure and the means to build on that momentum. He has stood with those who fight against all varieties of injustice.

Only a scant few of those people who have benefited from Kaepernick's donations have ever met him. Mostly he speaks with the money he gives and the approach he takes to giving. While legions of people argue about his kneeling and whether that disrespects the military, Kaepernick has focused on the issues he originally fought for, using his own money even while remaining unemployed.

Colin Kaepernick may never again play football, but as he has fulfilled his pledge he has said nothing and he has said everything, all at once. •

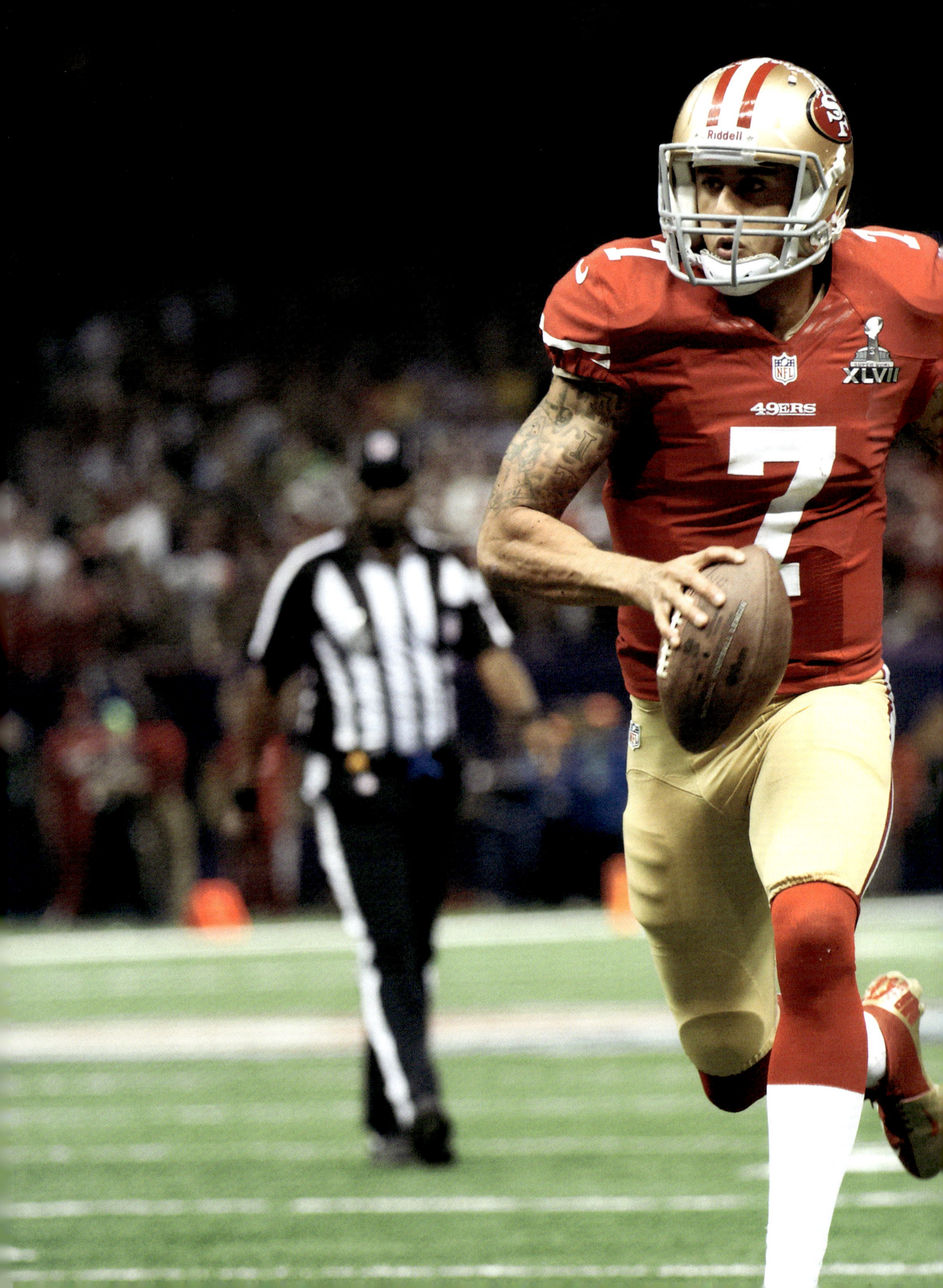
Riddell
49ERS
XLVII

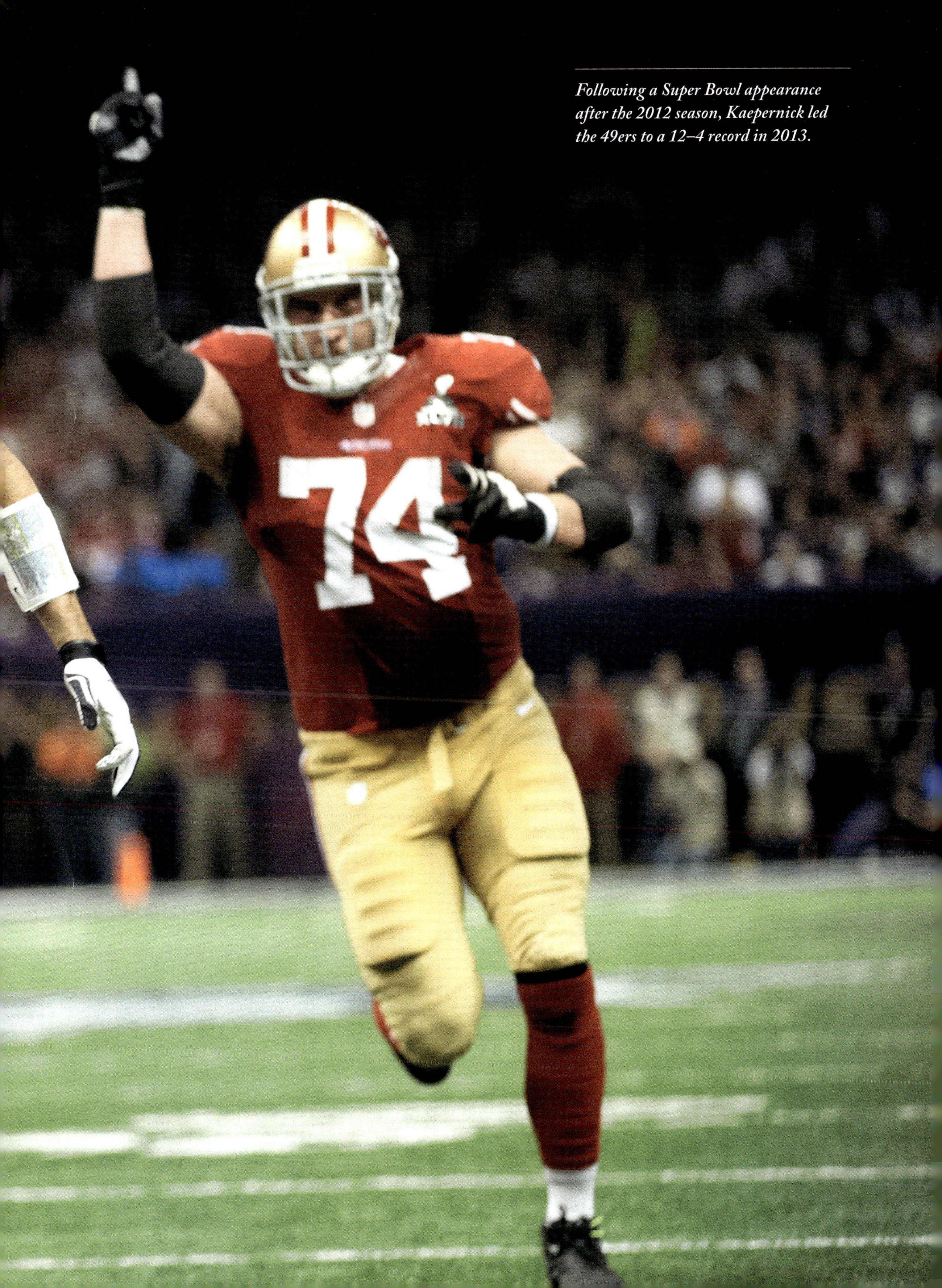

Following a Super Bowl appearance after the 2012 season, Kaepernick led the 49ers to a 12–4 record in 2013.

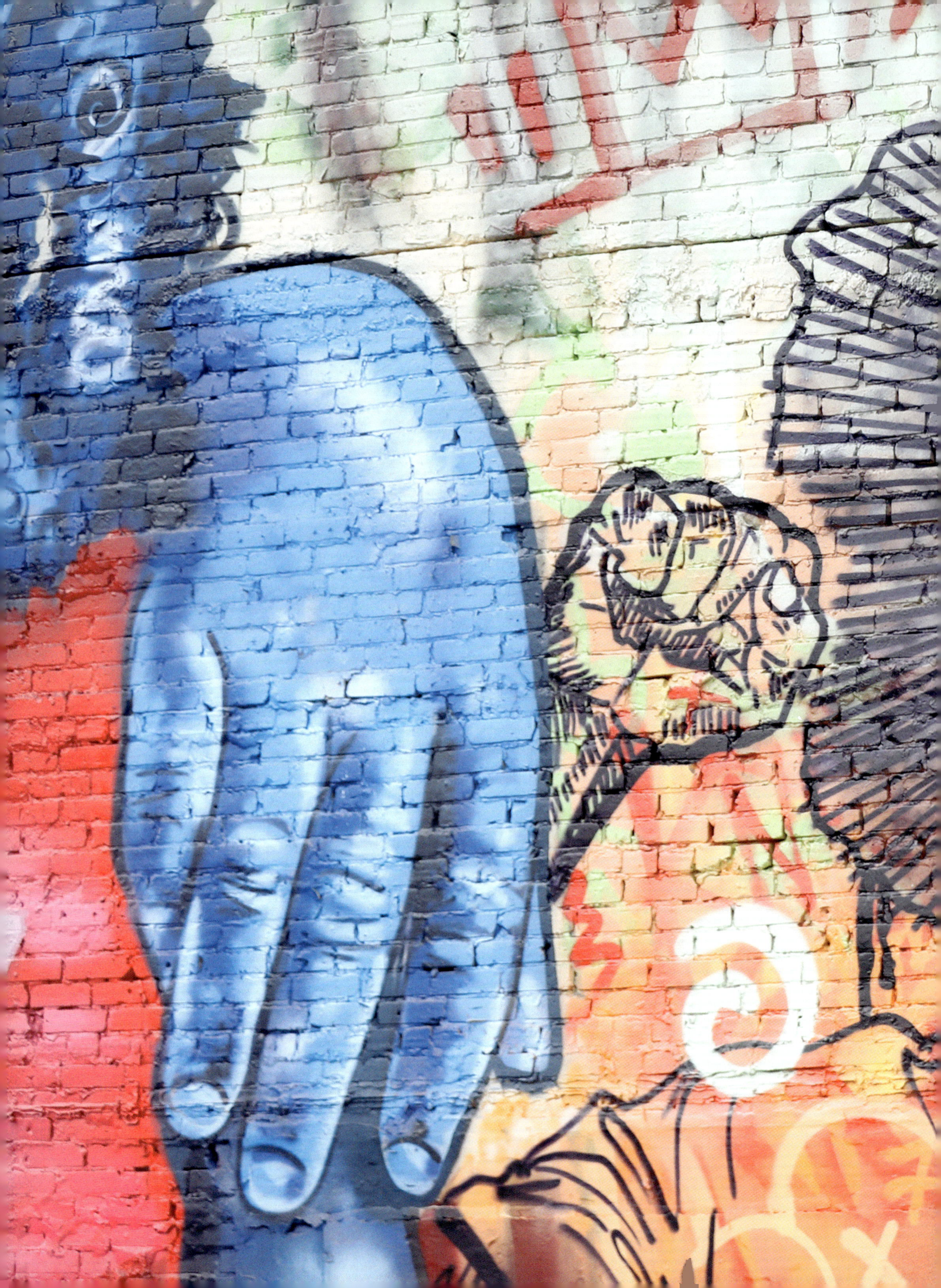

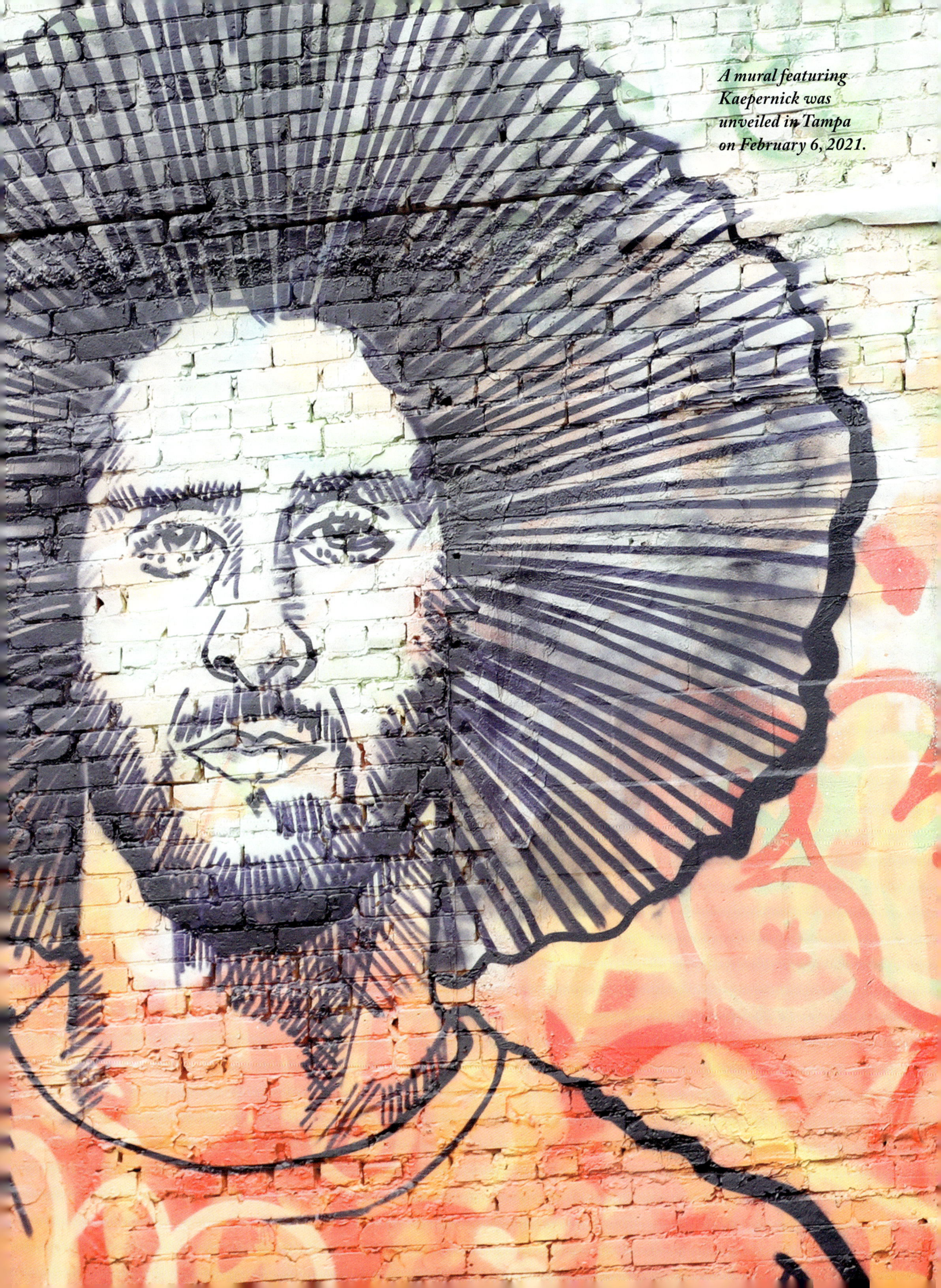

A mural featuring Kaepernick was unveiled in Tampa on February 6, 2021.

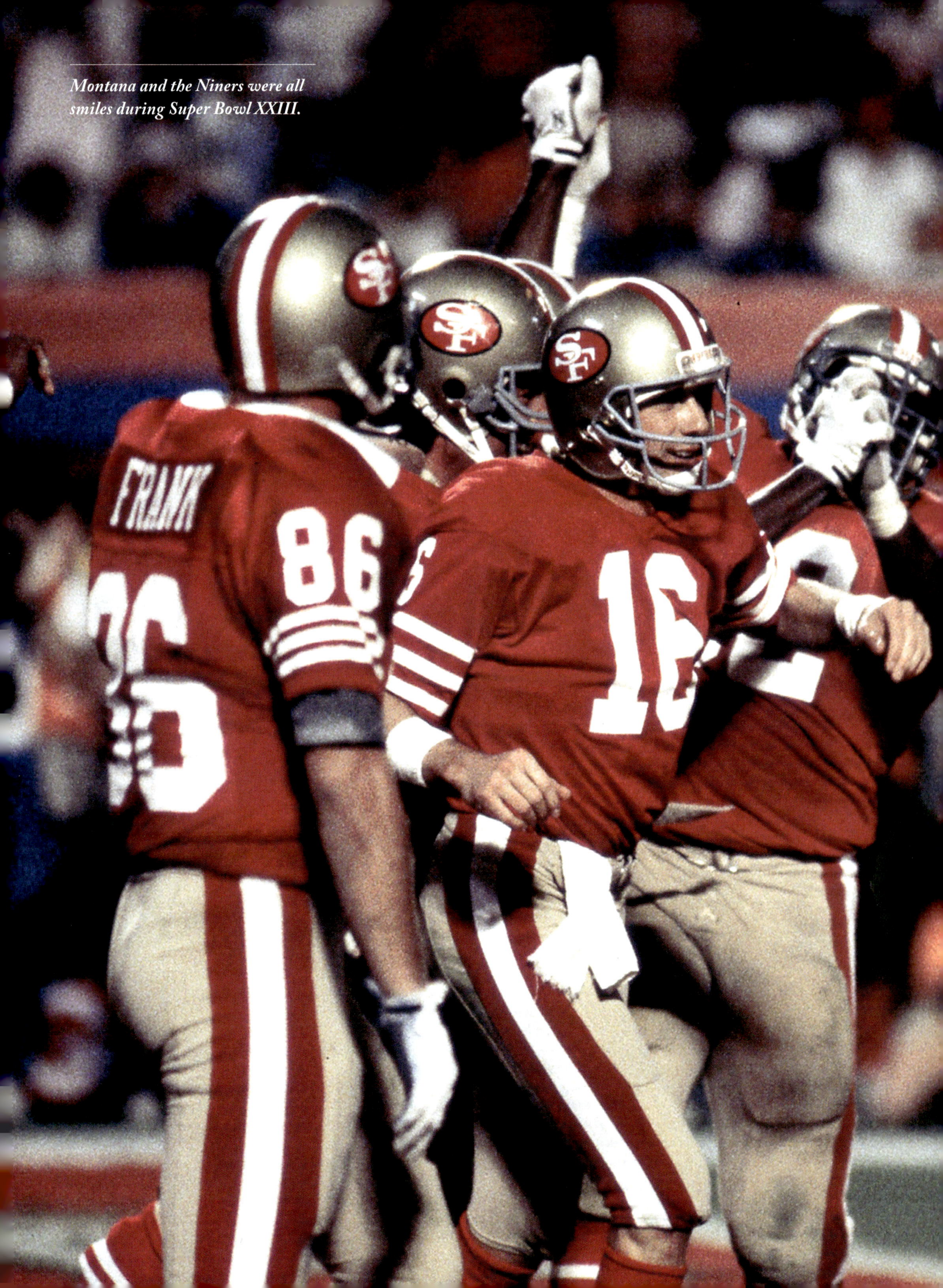

Montana and the Niners were all smiles during Super Bowl XXIII.

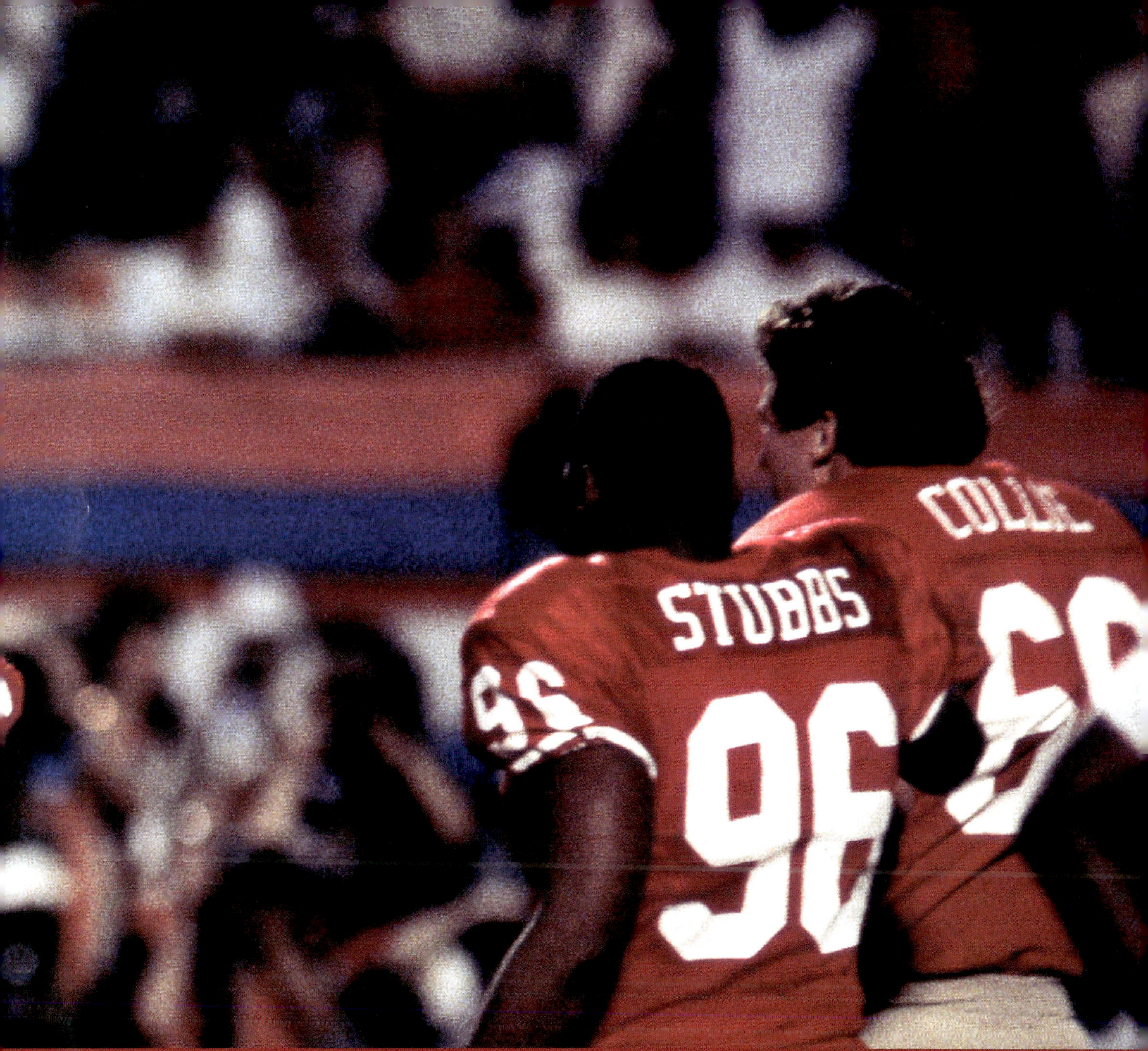

THE SUPER BOWLS

The 49ers have won five Super Bowls, with only the Patriots and Steelers having won more. The games have been full of memorable moments

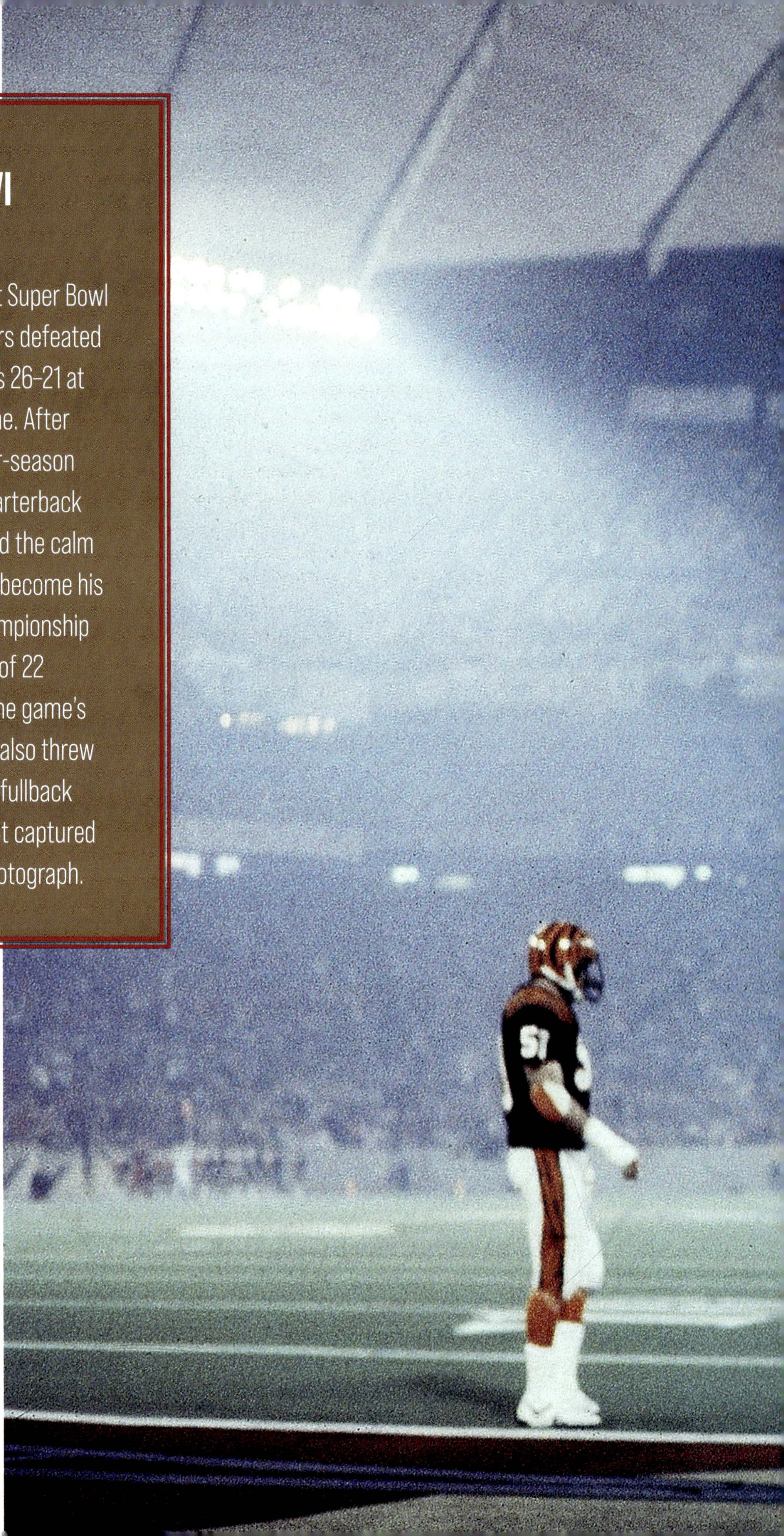

Super Bowl XVI

January 24, 1982

In the franchise's first Super Bowl appearance, the Niners defeated the Cincinnati Bengals 26–21 at the Pontiac Silverdome. After posting a 13–3 regular-season record, third-year quarterback Joe Montana displayed the calm and poise that would become his trademark in the championship game, completing 14 of 22 passes and earning the game's MVP award. Montana also threw a touchdown pass to fullback Earl Cooper, a moment captured in this memorable photograph.

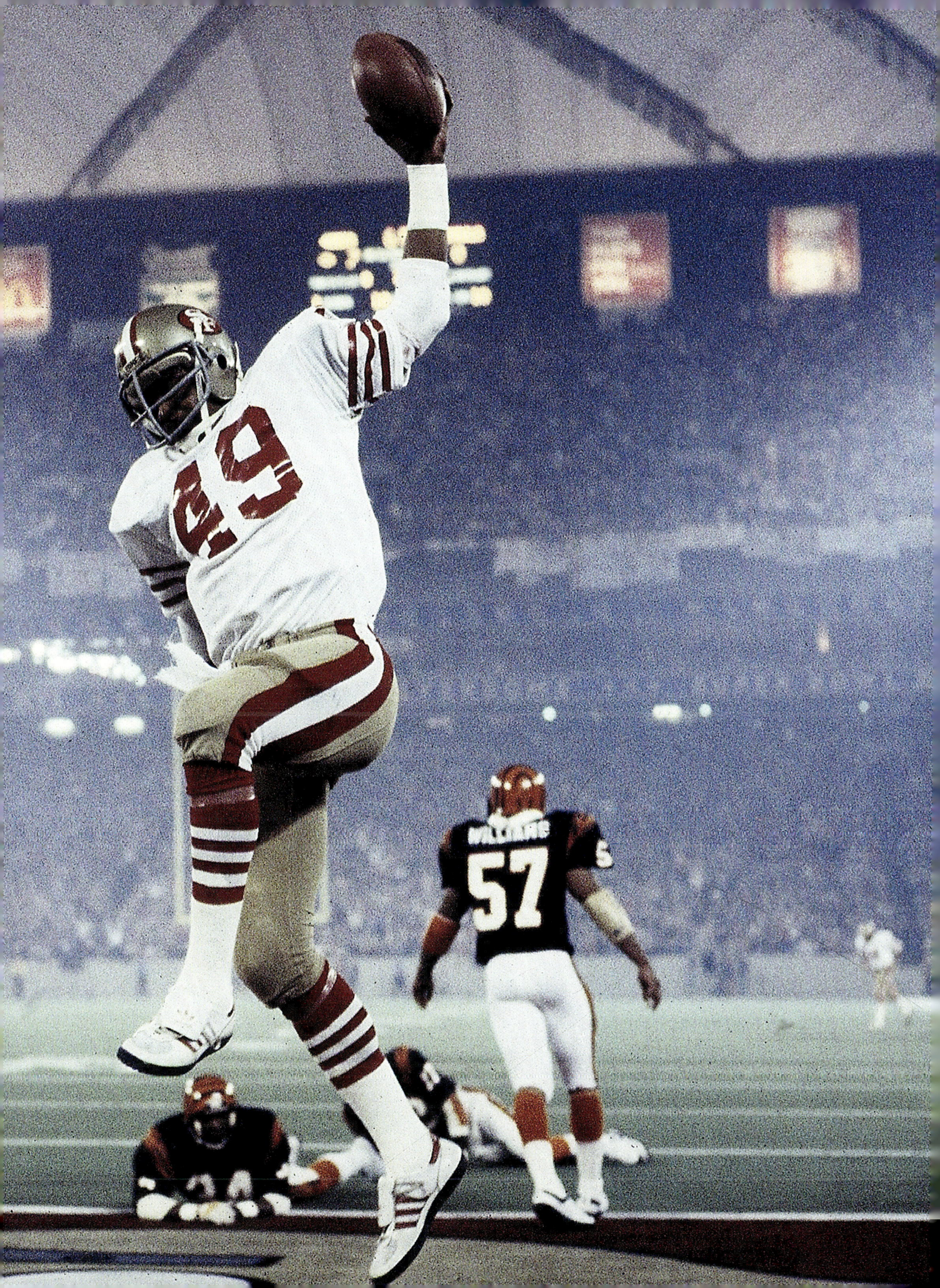
49
WILLIAMS
57

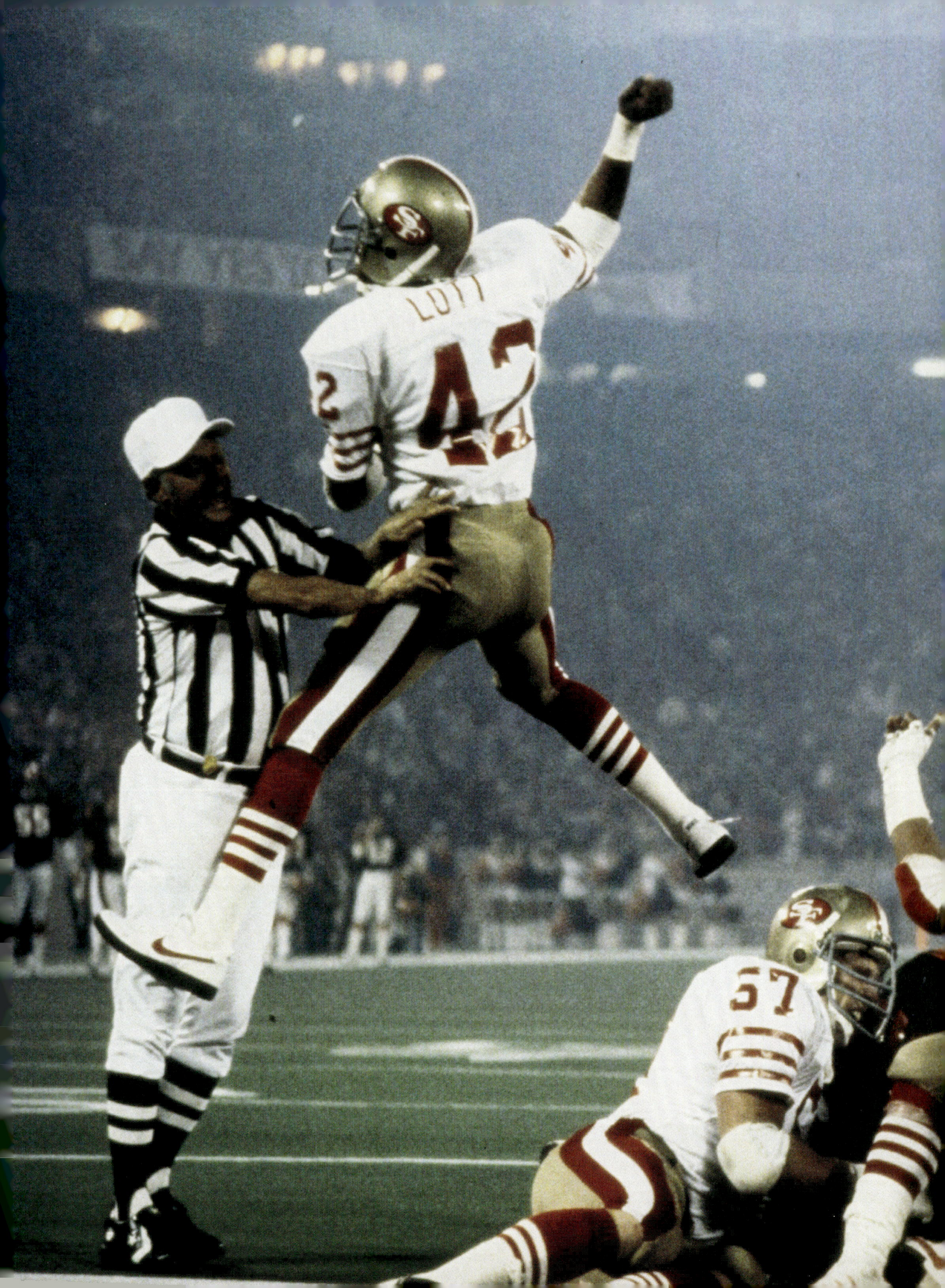

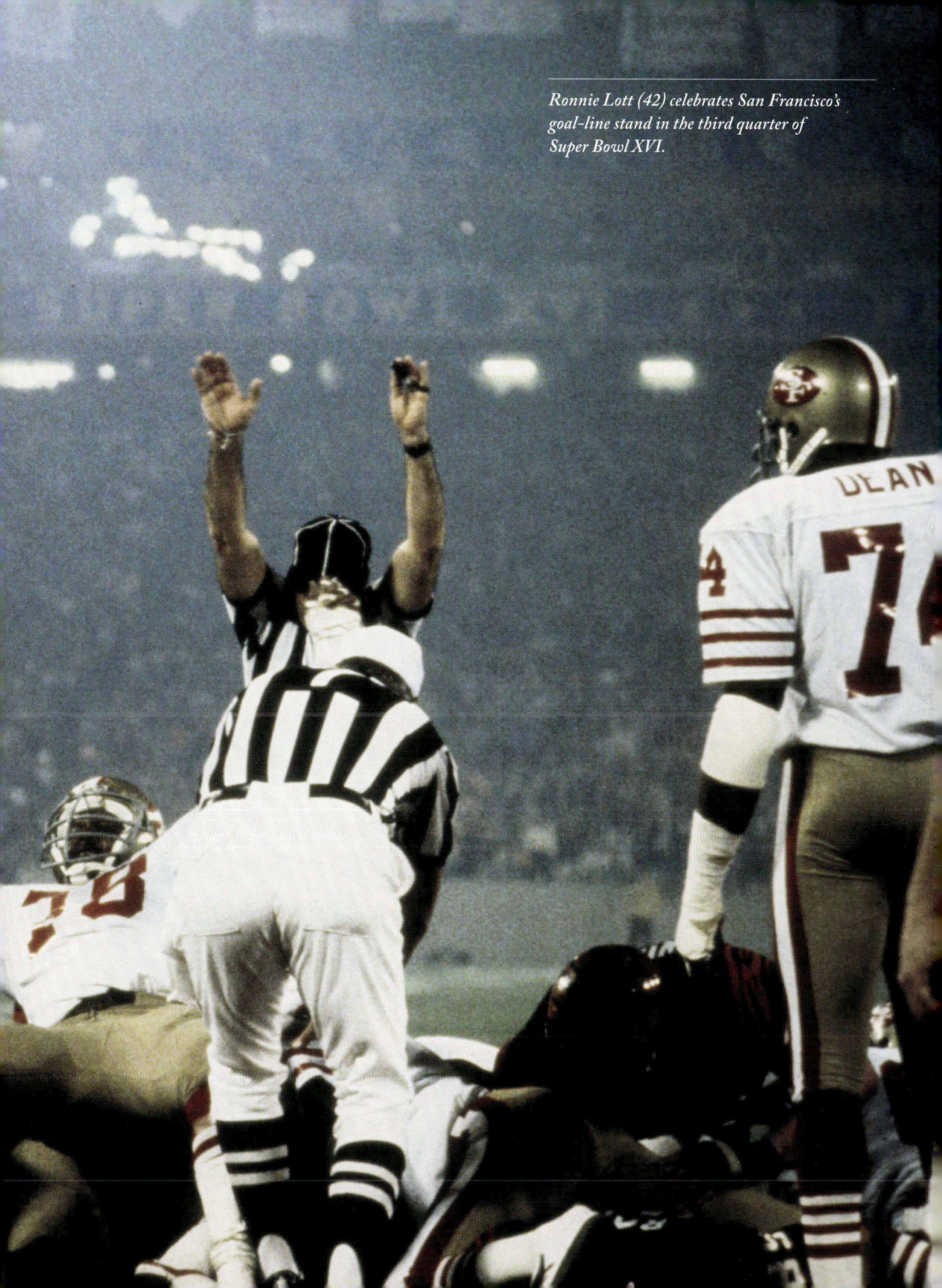

Ronnie Lott (42) celebrates San Francisco's goal-line stand in the third quarter of Super Bowl XVI.

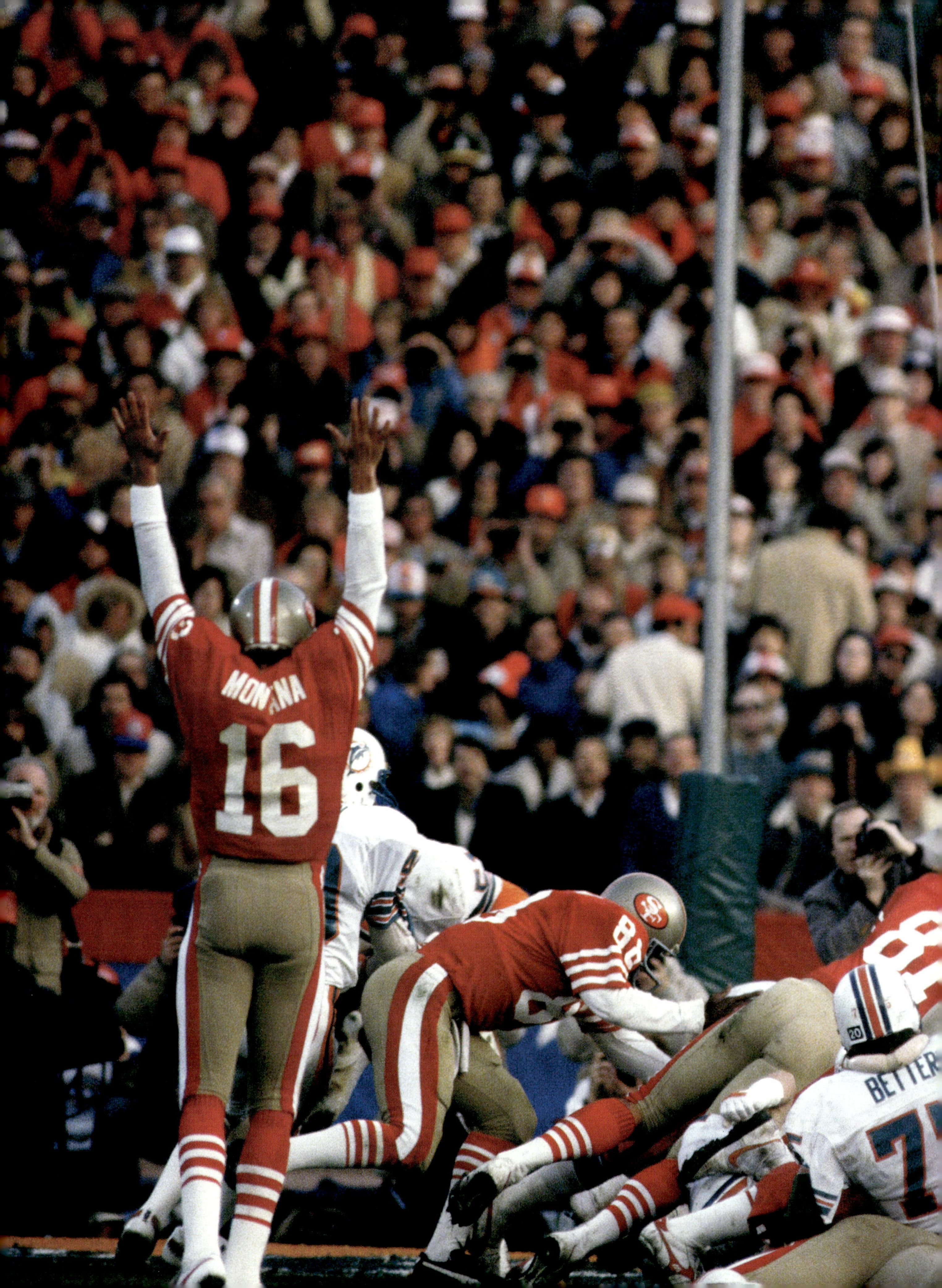

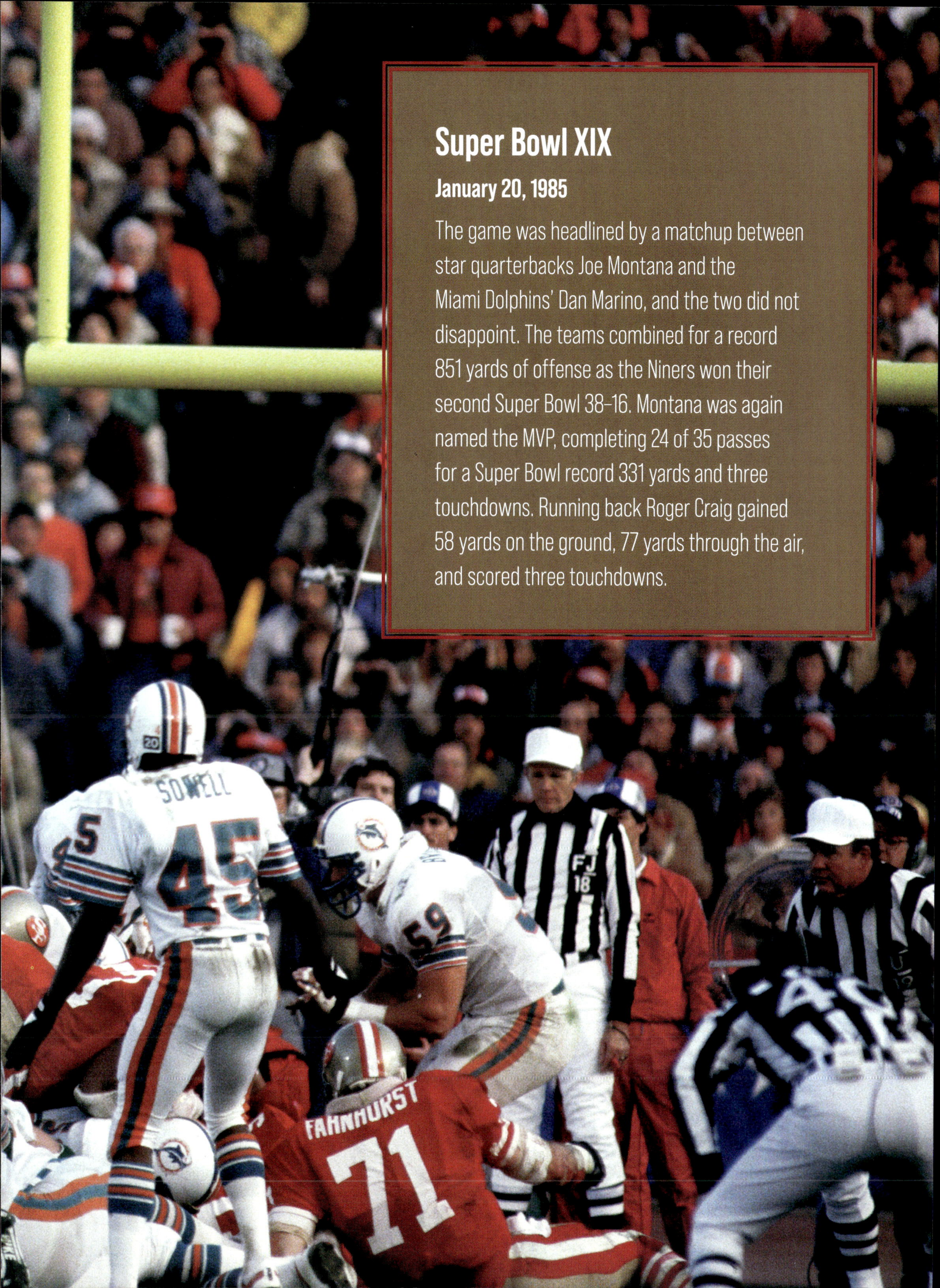

Super Bowl XIX

January 20, 1985

The game was headlined by a matchup between star quarterbacks Joe Montana and the Miami Dolphins' Dan Marino, and the two did not disappoint. The teams combined for a record 851 yards of offense as the Niners won their second Super Bowl 38–16. Montana was again named the MVP, completing 24 of 35 passes for a Super Bowl record 331 yards and three touchdowns. Running back Roger Craig gained 58 yards on the ground, 77 yards through the air, and scored three touchdowns.

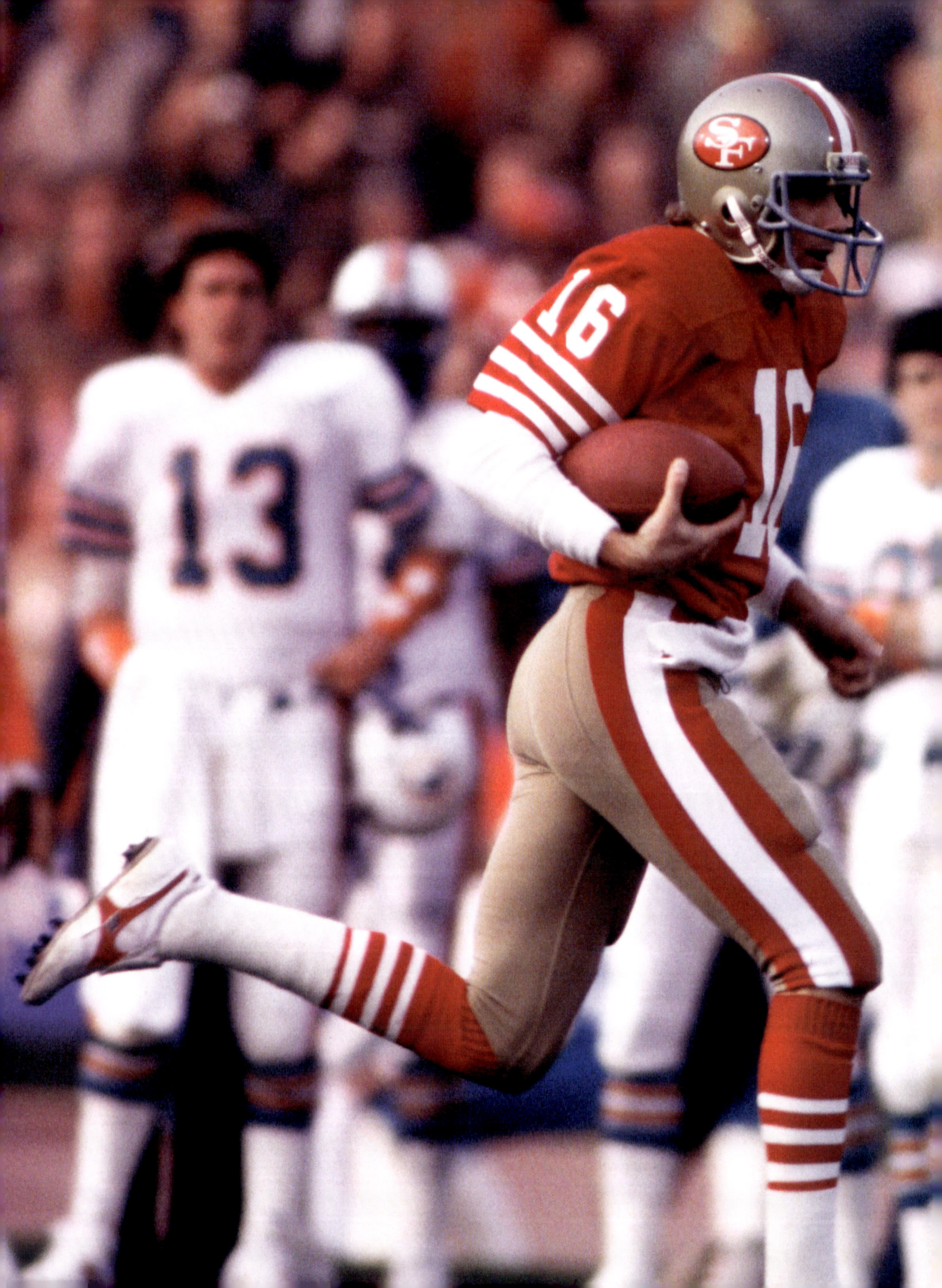

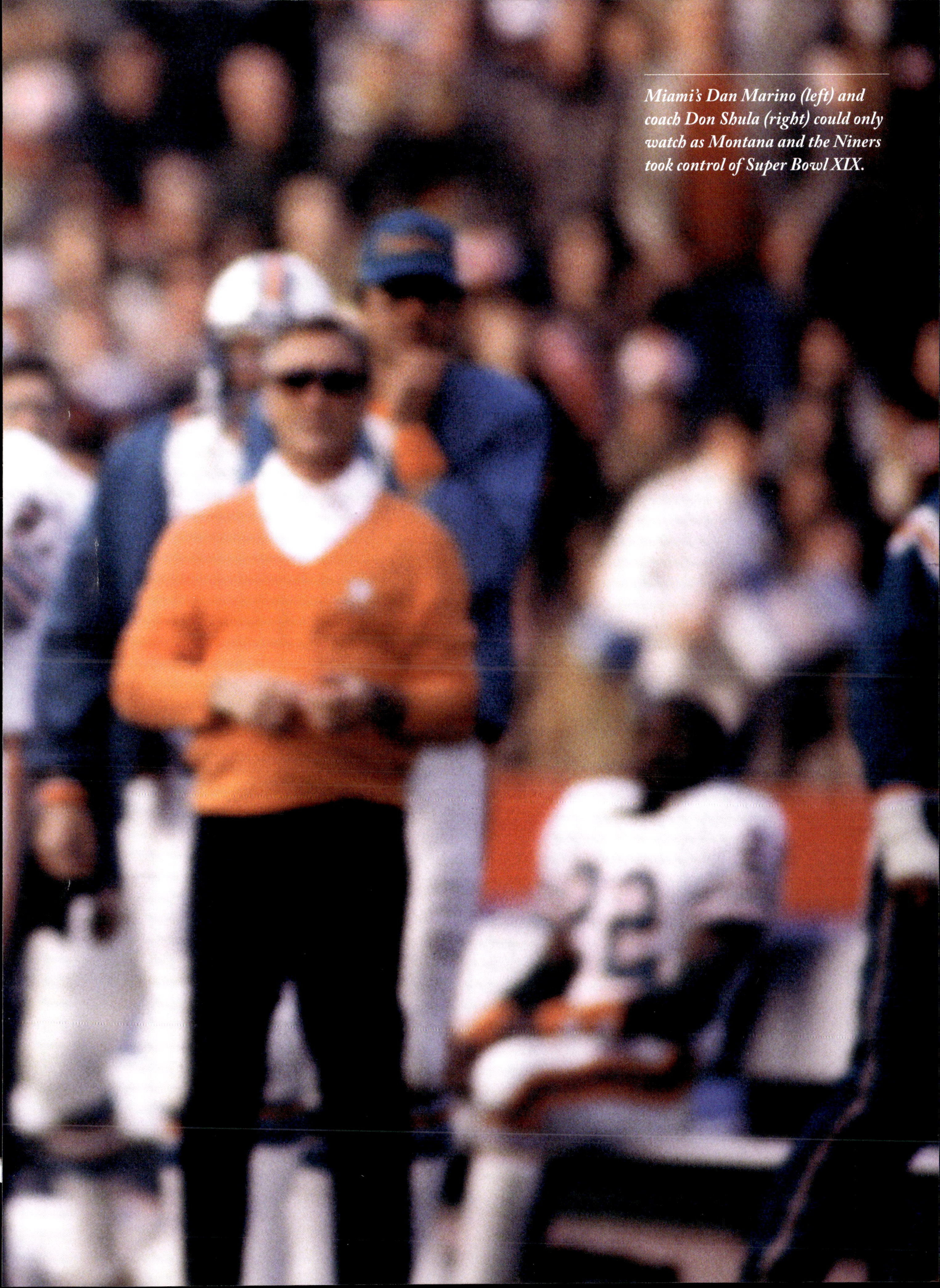

Miami's Dan Marino (left) and coach Don Shula (right) could only watch as Montana and the Niners took control of Super Bowl XIX.

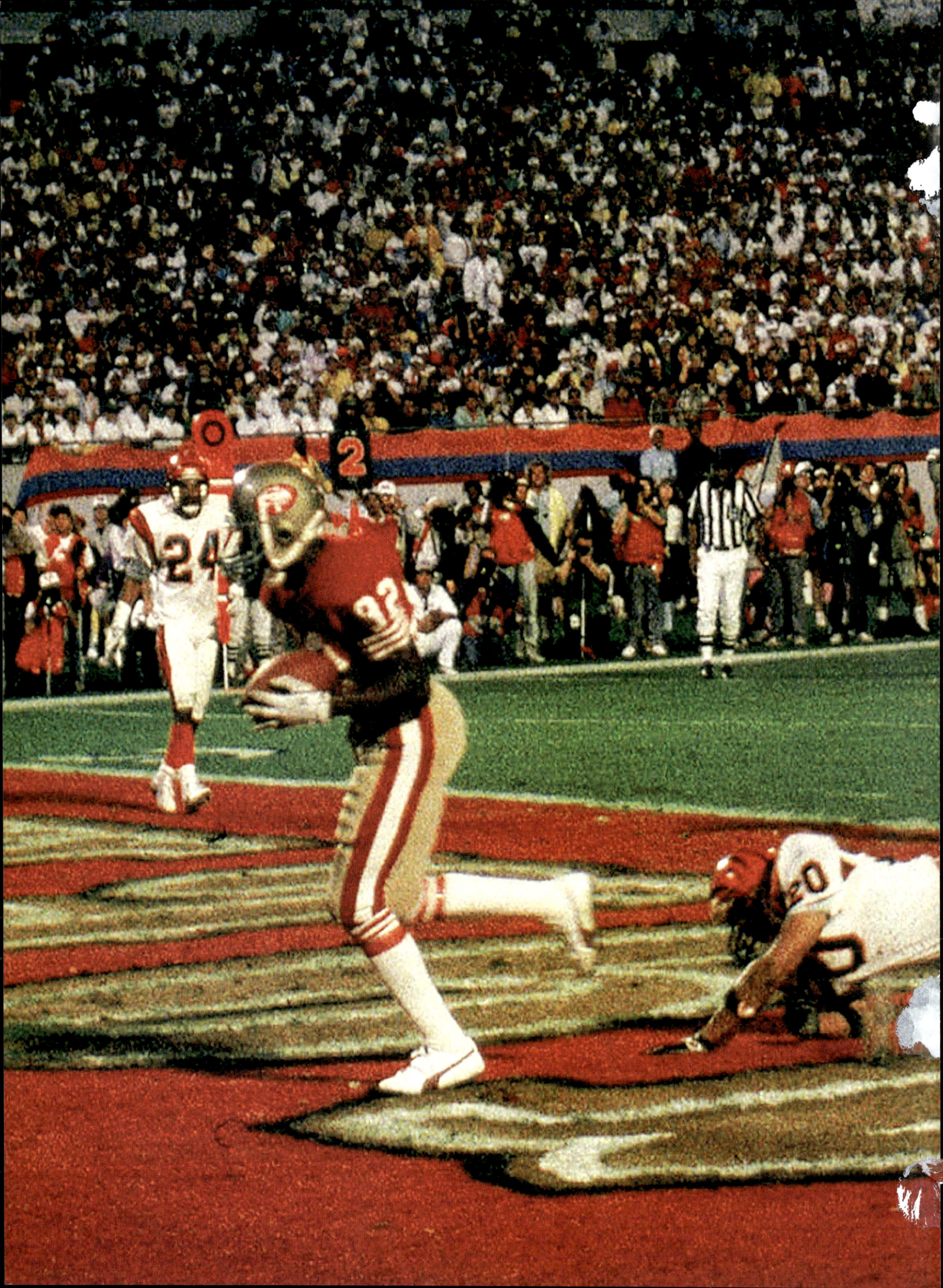

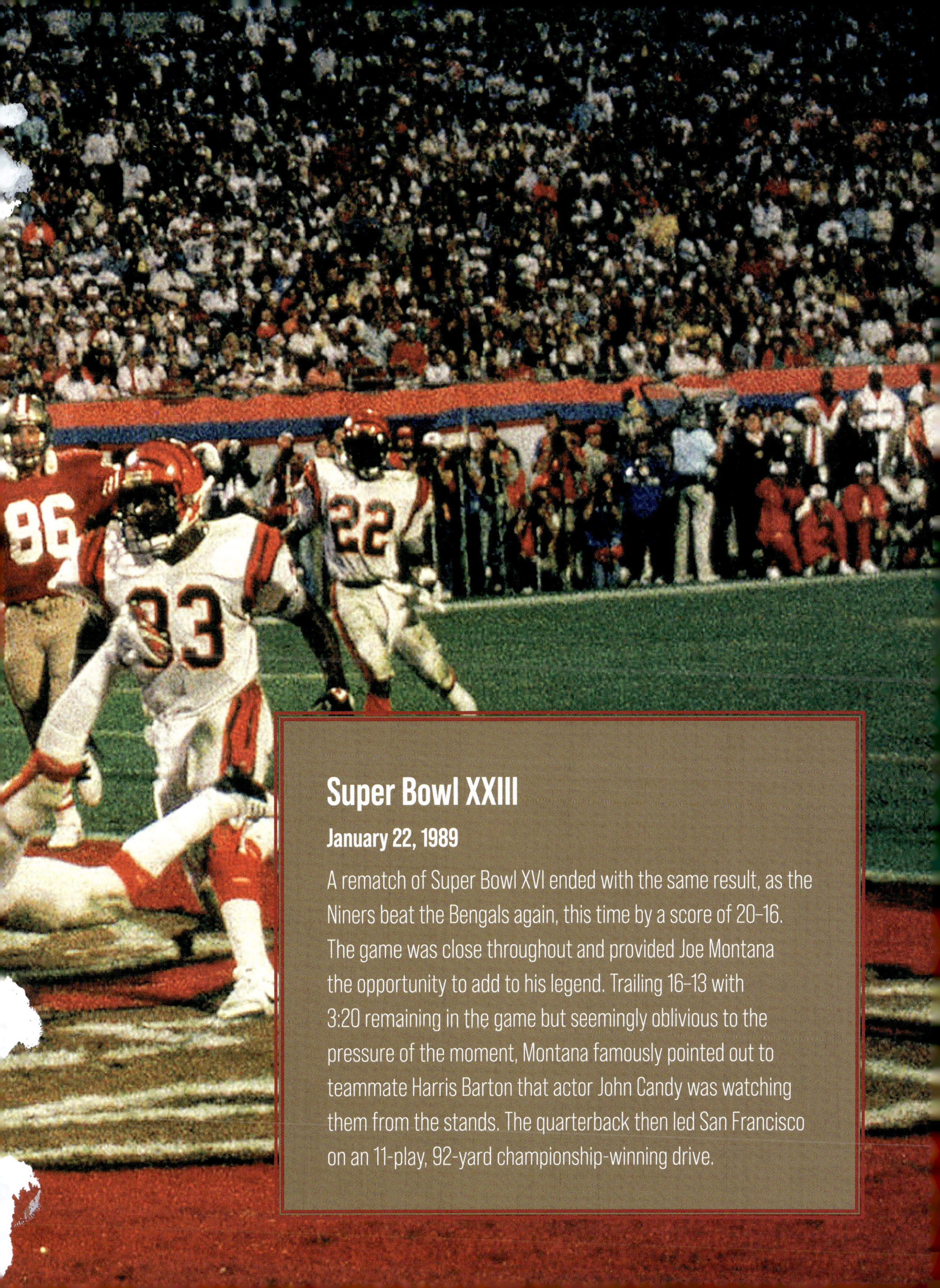

Super Bowl XXIII

January 22, 1989

A rematch of Super Bowl XVI ended with the same result, as the Niners beat the Bengals again, this time by a score of 20–16. The game was close throughout and provided Joe Montana the opportunity to add to his legend. Trailing 16–13 with 3:20 remaining in the game but seemingly oblivious to the pressure of the moment, Montana famously pointed out to teammate Harris Barton that actor John Candy was watching them from the stands. The quarterback then led San Francisco on an 11-play, 92-yard championship-winning drive.

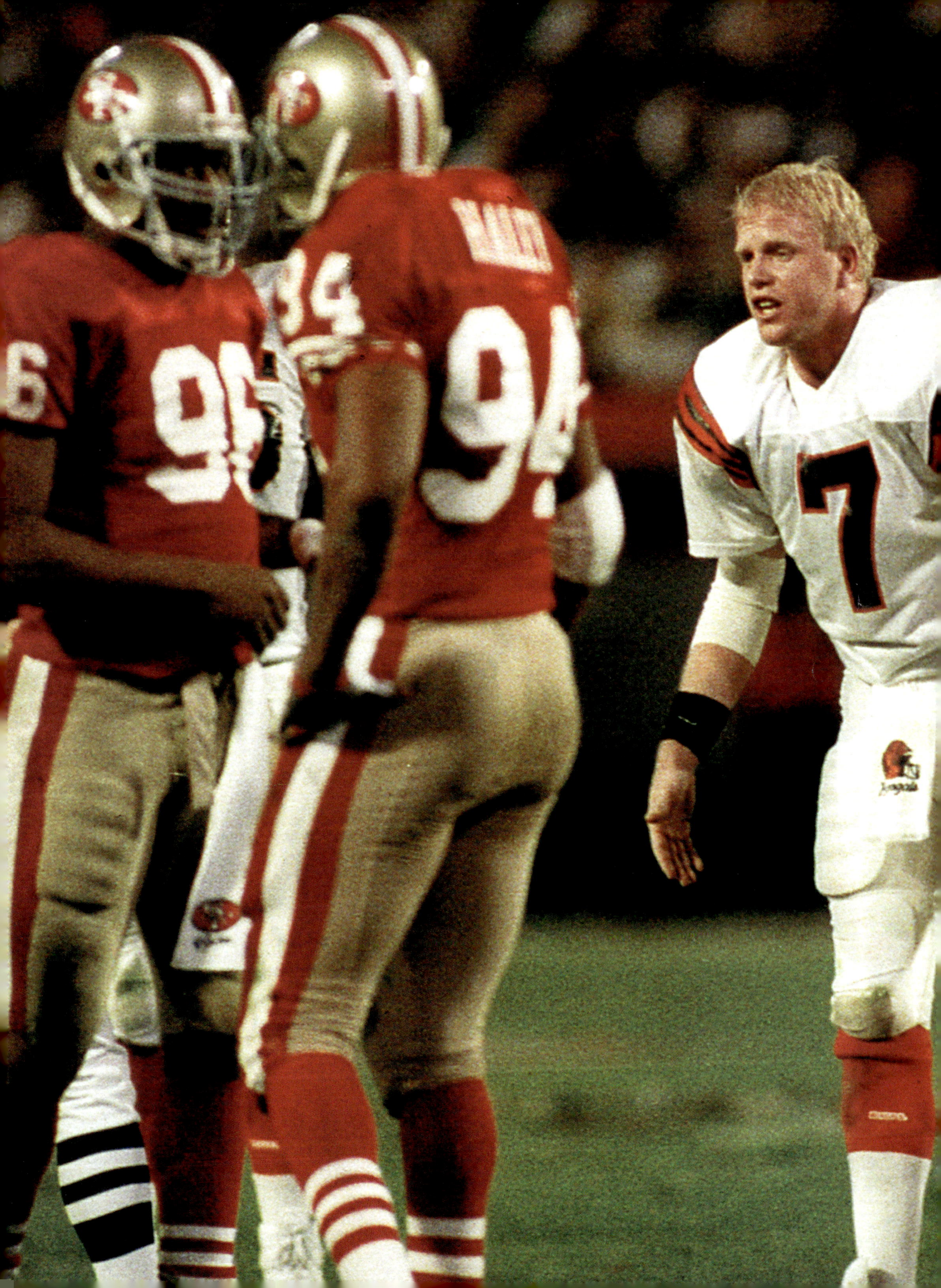

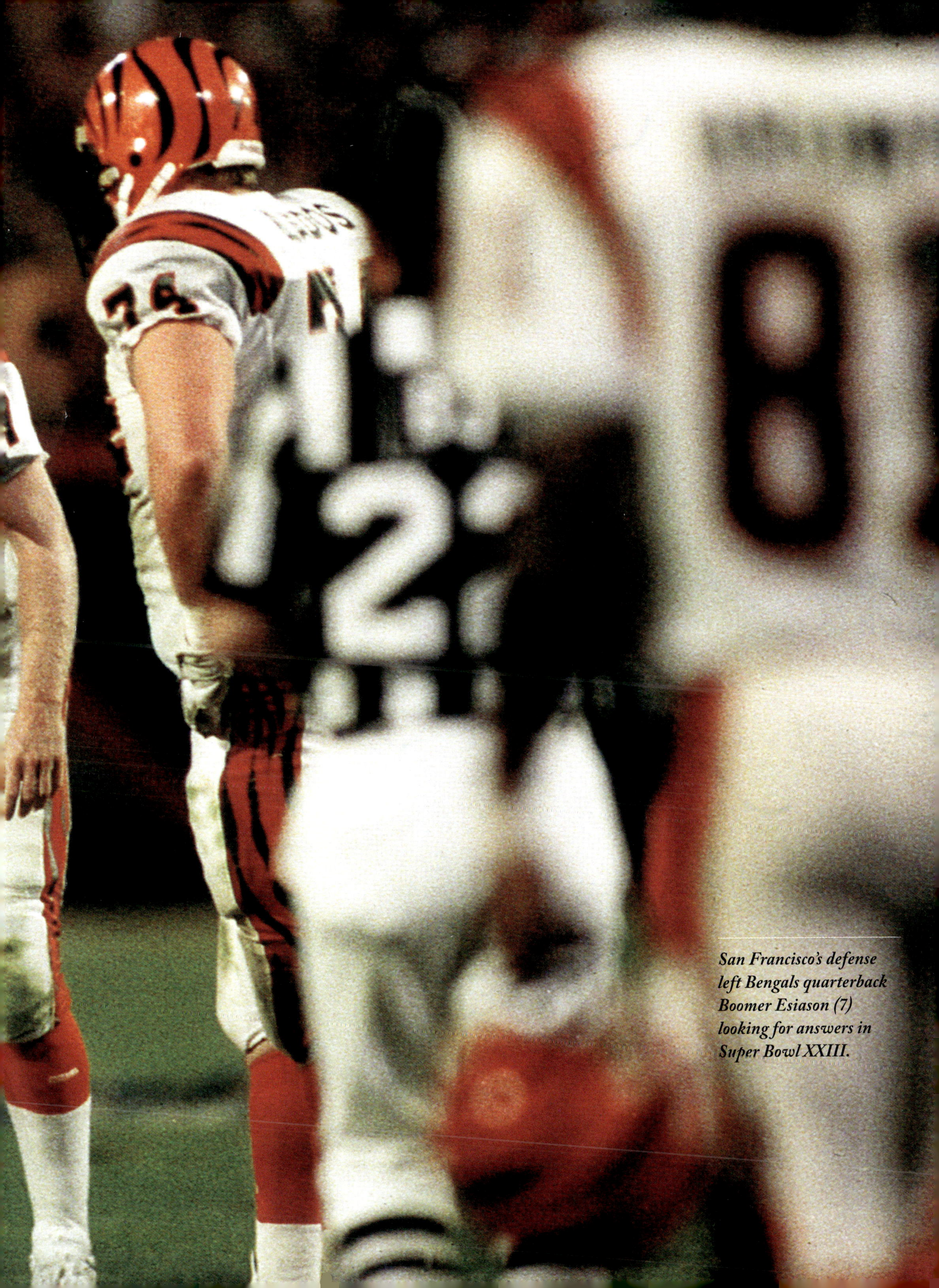

San Francisco's defense left Bengals quarterback Boomer Esiason (7) looking for answers in Super Bowl XXIII.

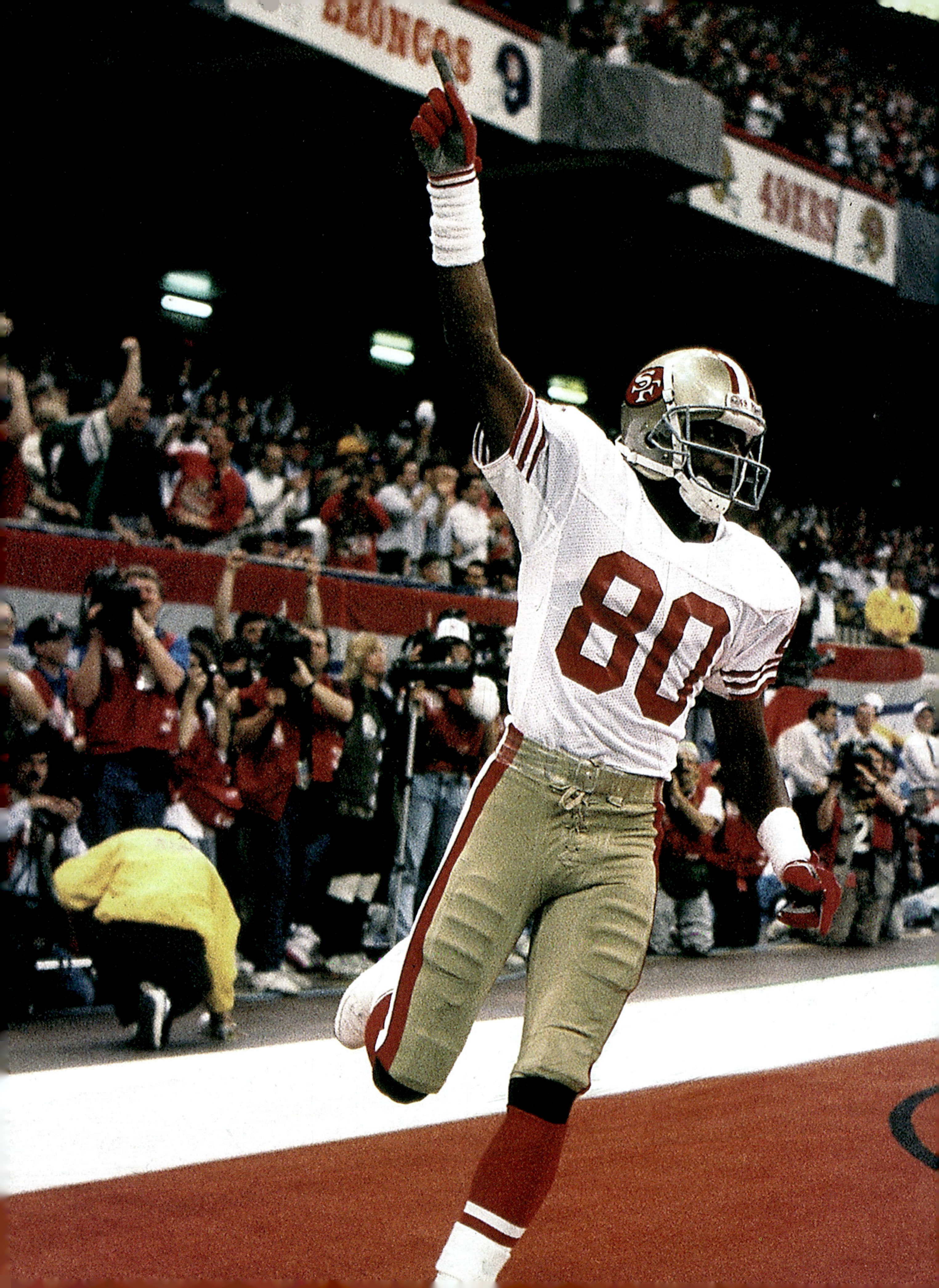
BRONCOS
9
49ERS
80

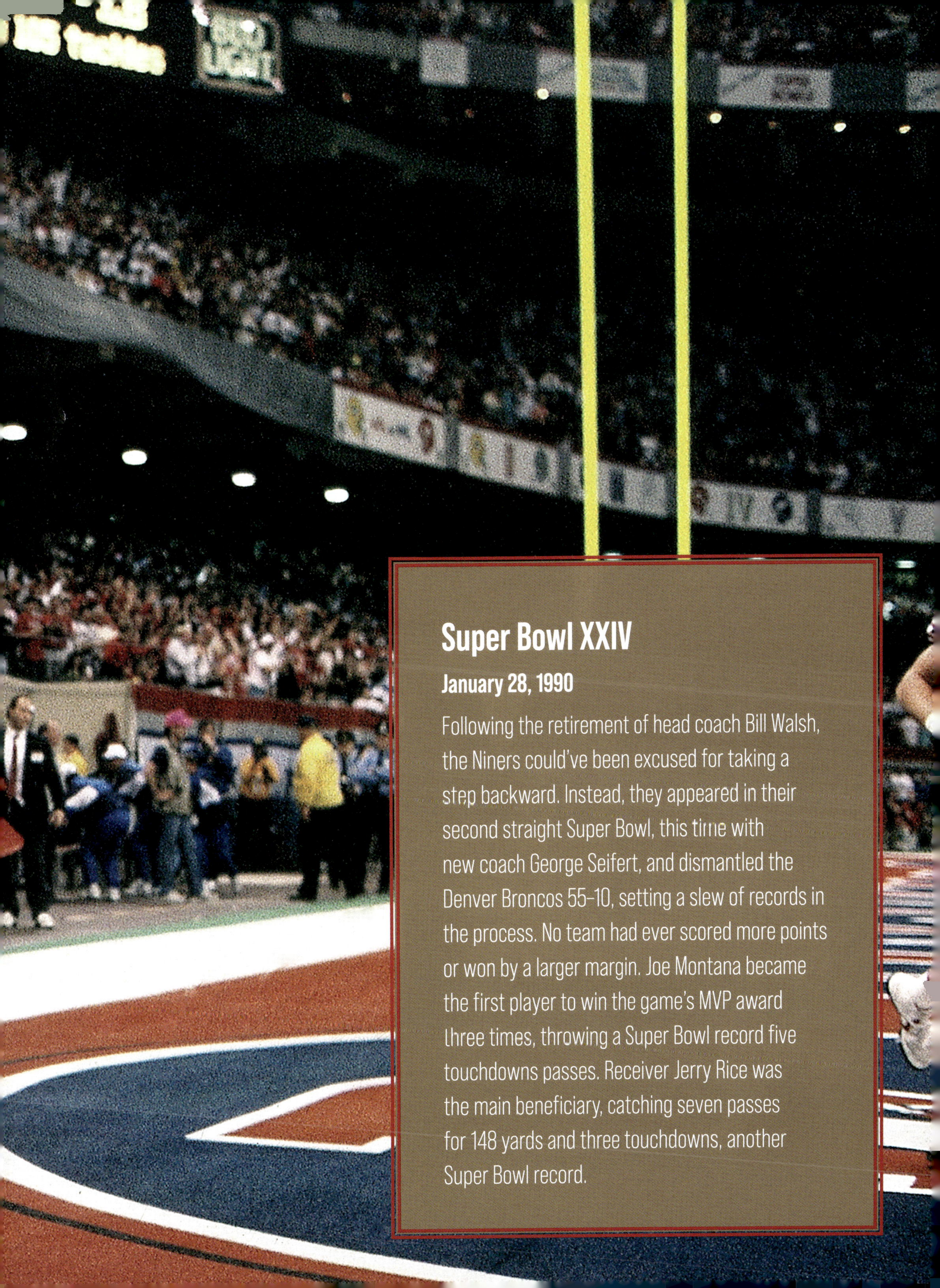

Super Bowl XXIV

January 28, 1990

Following the retirement of head coach Bill Walsh, the Niners could've been excused for taking a step backward. Instead, they appeared in their second straight Super Bowl, this time with new coach George Seifert, and dismantled the Denver Broncos 55–10, setting a slew of records in the process. No team had ever scored more points or won by a larger margin. Joe Montana became the first player to win the game's MVP award three times, throwing a Super Bowl record five touchdowns passes. Receiver Jerry Rice was the main beneficiary, catching seven passes for 148 yards and three touchdowns, another Super Bowl record.

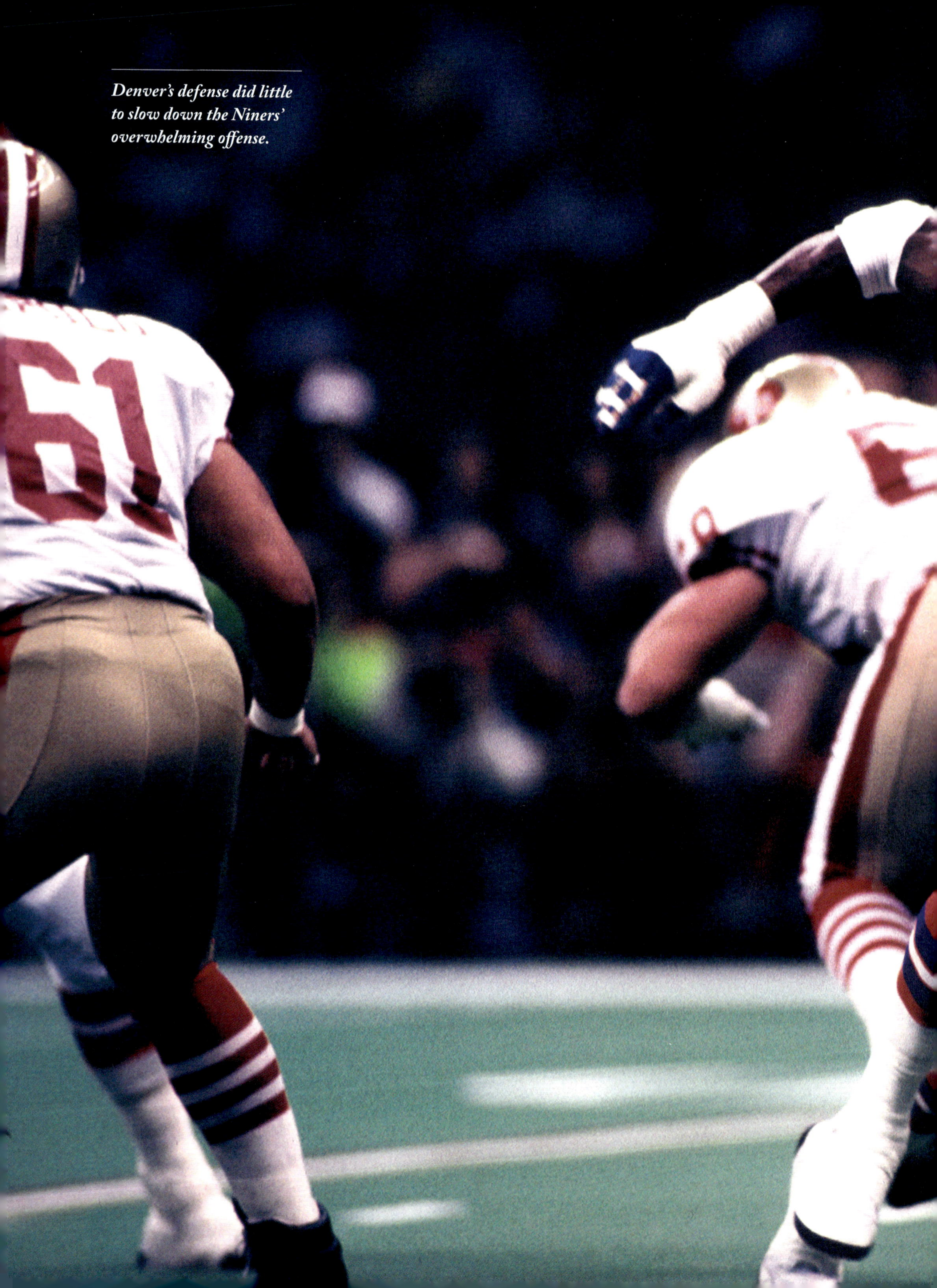

Denver's defense did little to slow down the Niners' overwhelming offense.

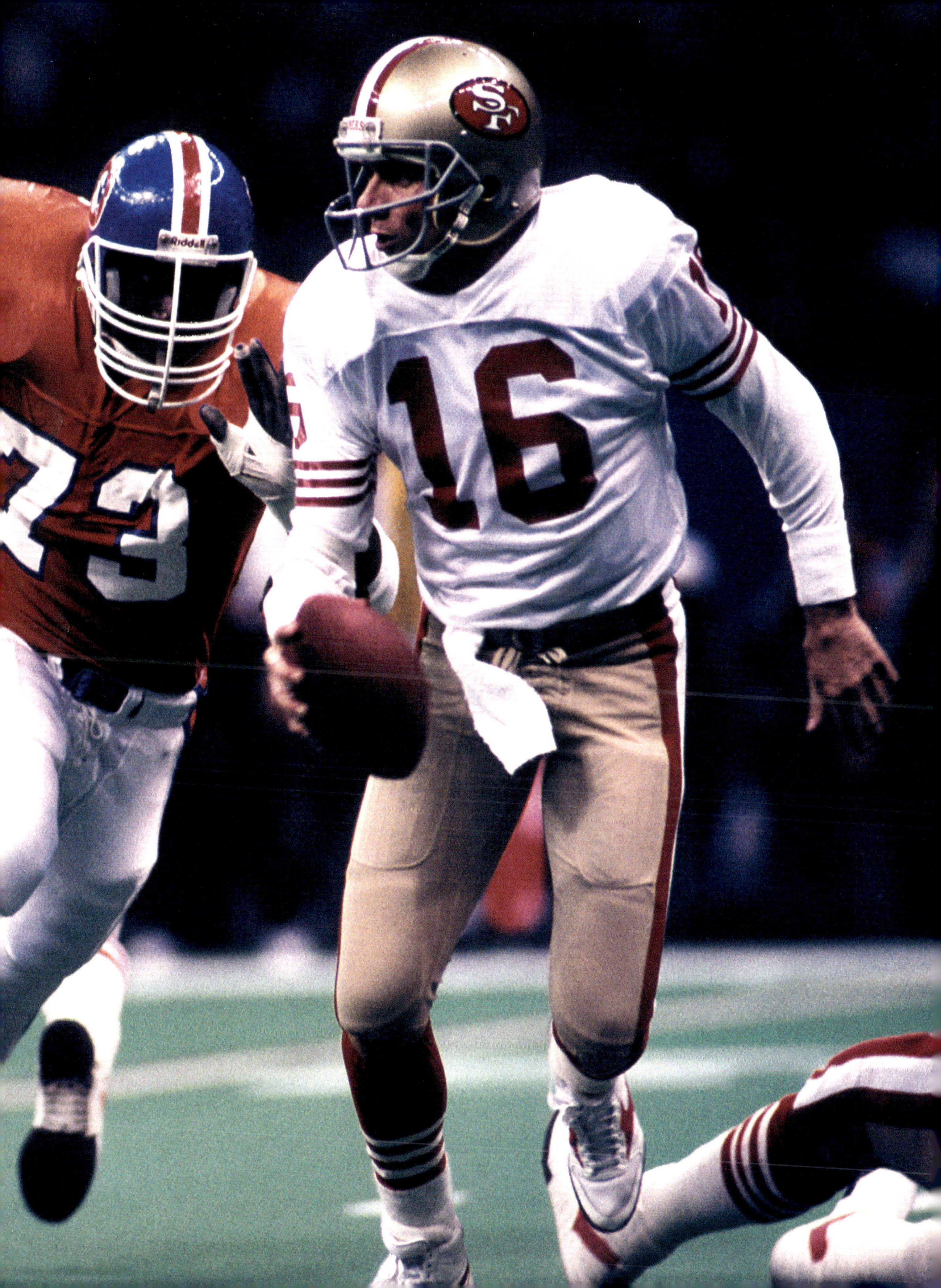
SF
16

Super Bowl XXIX

January 29, 1995

After spending much of his career in the shadows, Steve Young stepped fully into the light in Super Bowl XXIX, leading the Niners to a 49–26 victory over the San Diego Chargers. Young completed 24 of 36 passes for 325 yards and six touchdowns, breaking the record set five years earlier by Joe Montana. Jerry Rice and running back Ricky Watters each scored three touchdowns as San Francisco became the first franchise to win five Super Bowls.

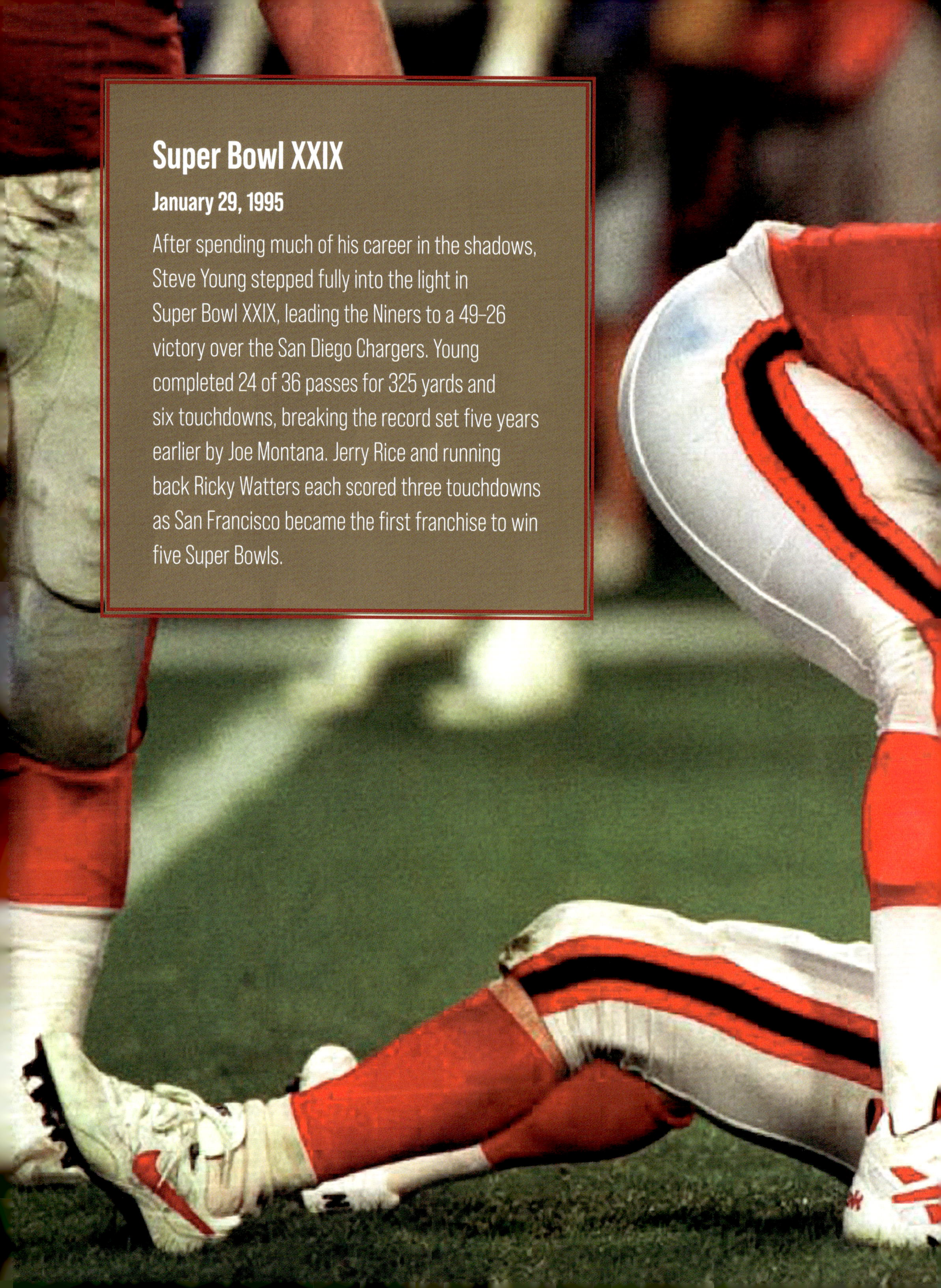

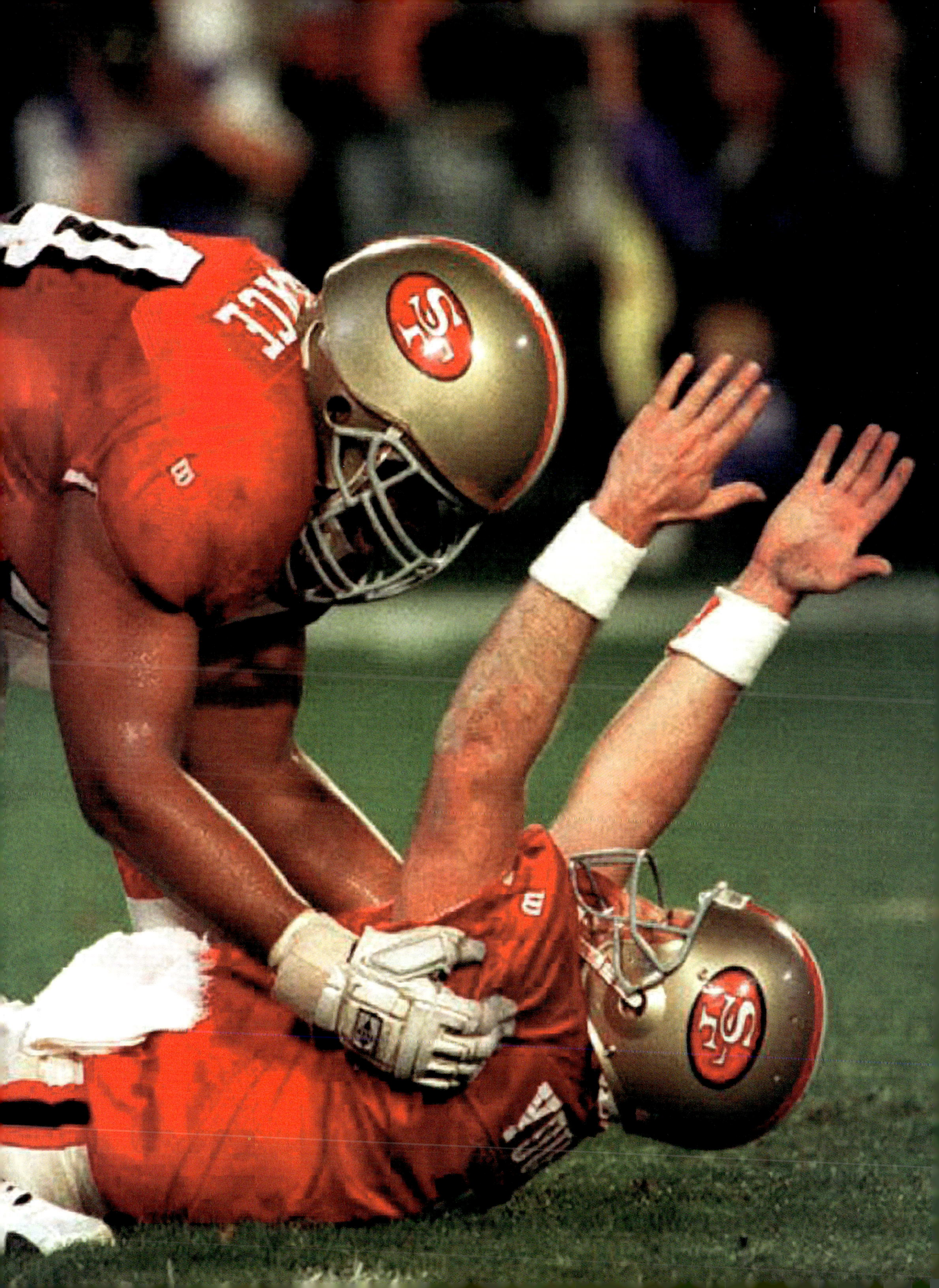

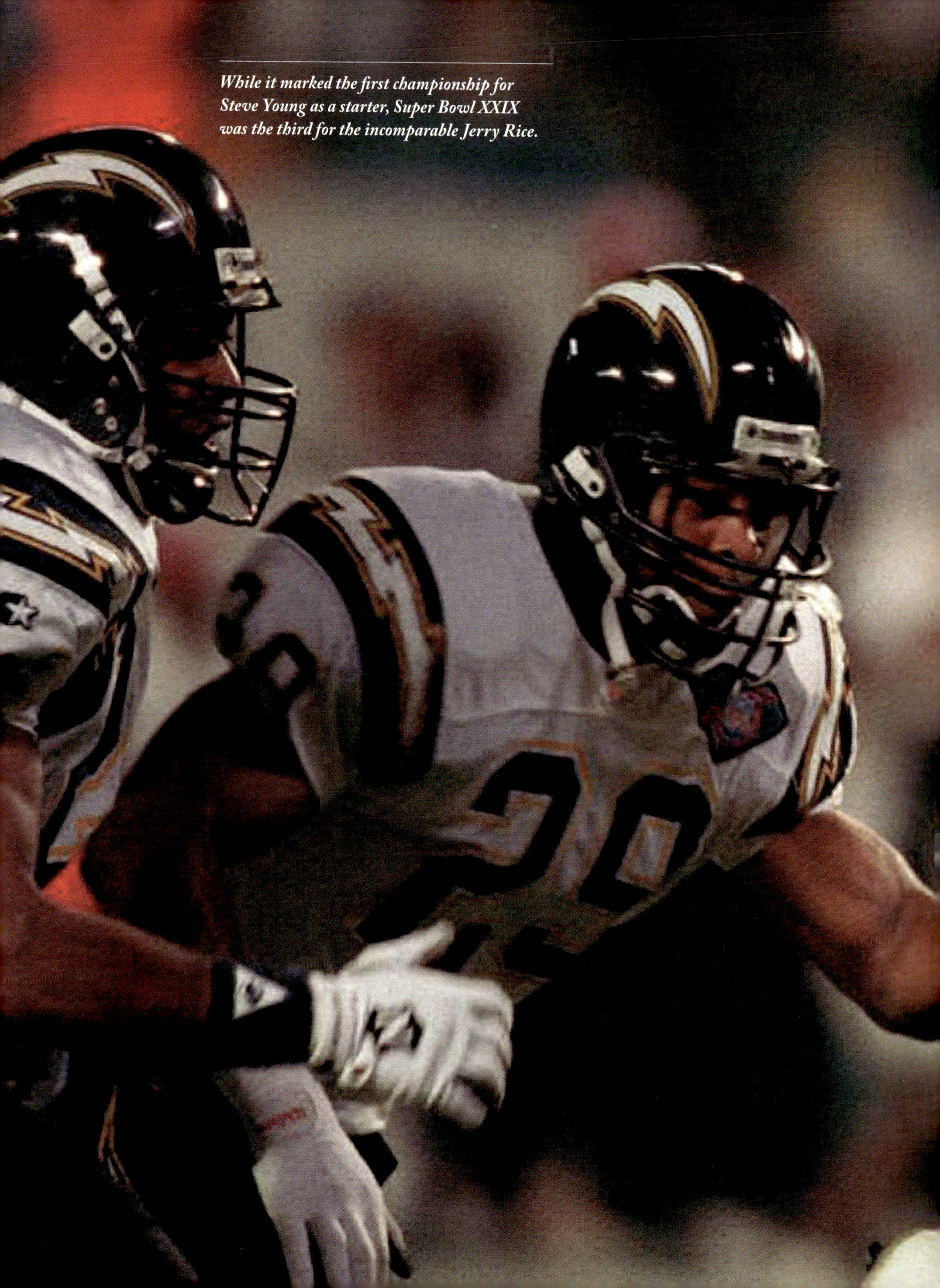

While it marked the first championship for Steve Young as a starter, Super Bowl XXIX was the third for the incomparable Jerry Rice.

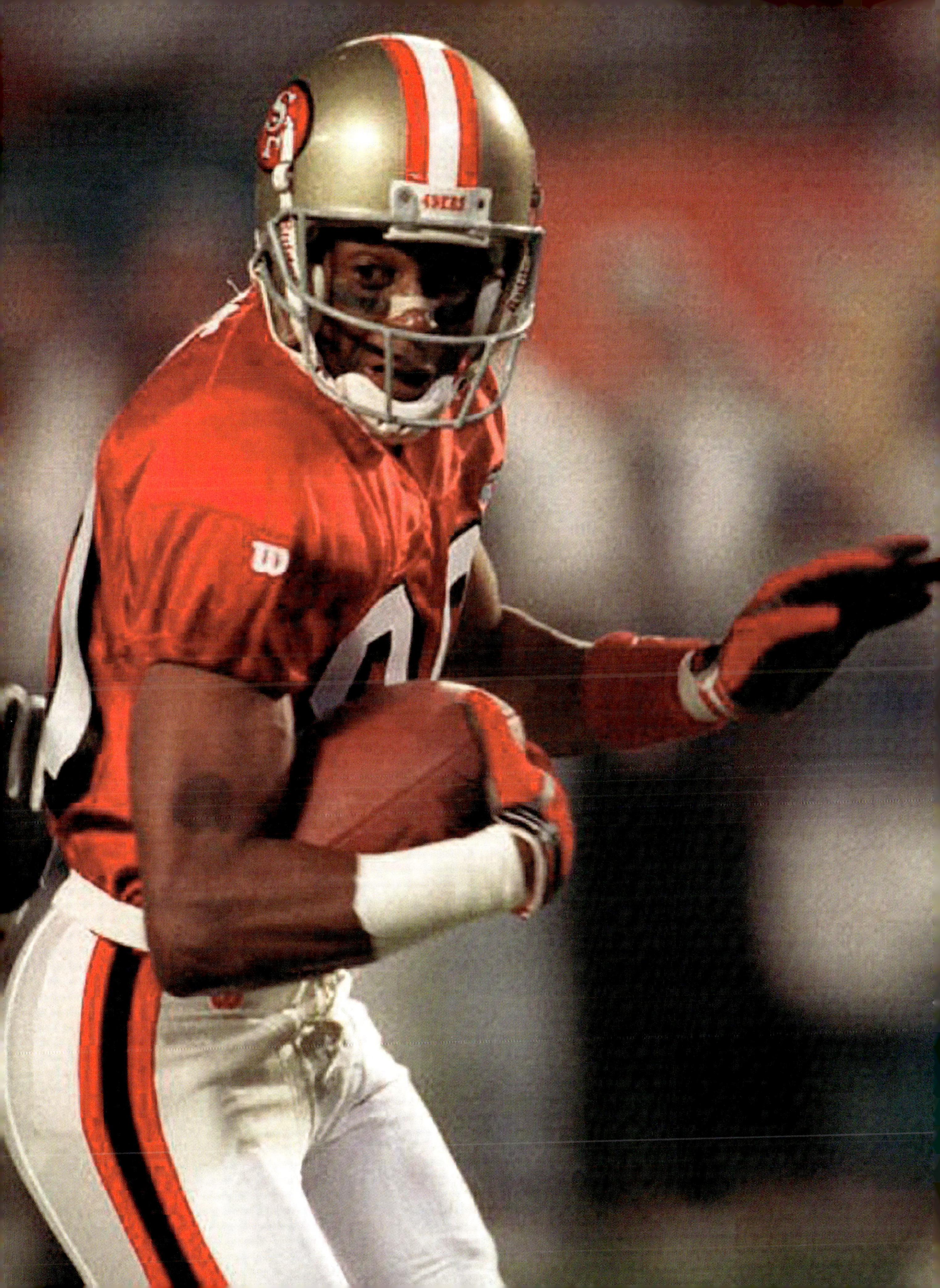
49ERS

49ERS BY THE NUMBERS

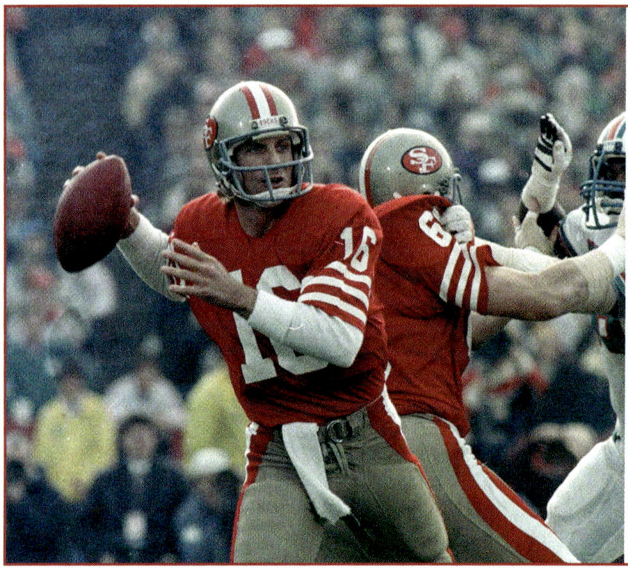

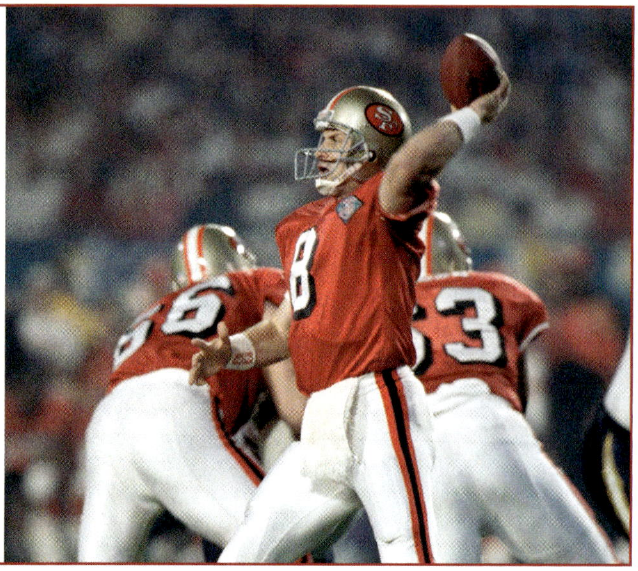

JOE MONTANA vs. STEVE YOUNG

Joe Montana		Steve Young
13	Years	13
139	Games Started	124
100-39-0	Record	91-33-0
2,929	Completions	2,400
4,600	Attempts	3,648
63.7	Cmp %	65.8
35,124	Yards	29,907
244	TDs	221
123	INTs	86
23	4Q Comebacks	12
25	Game-Winning Drives	15

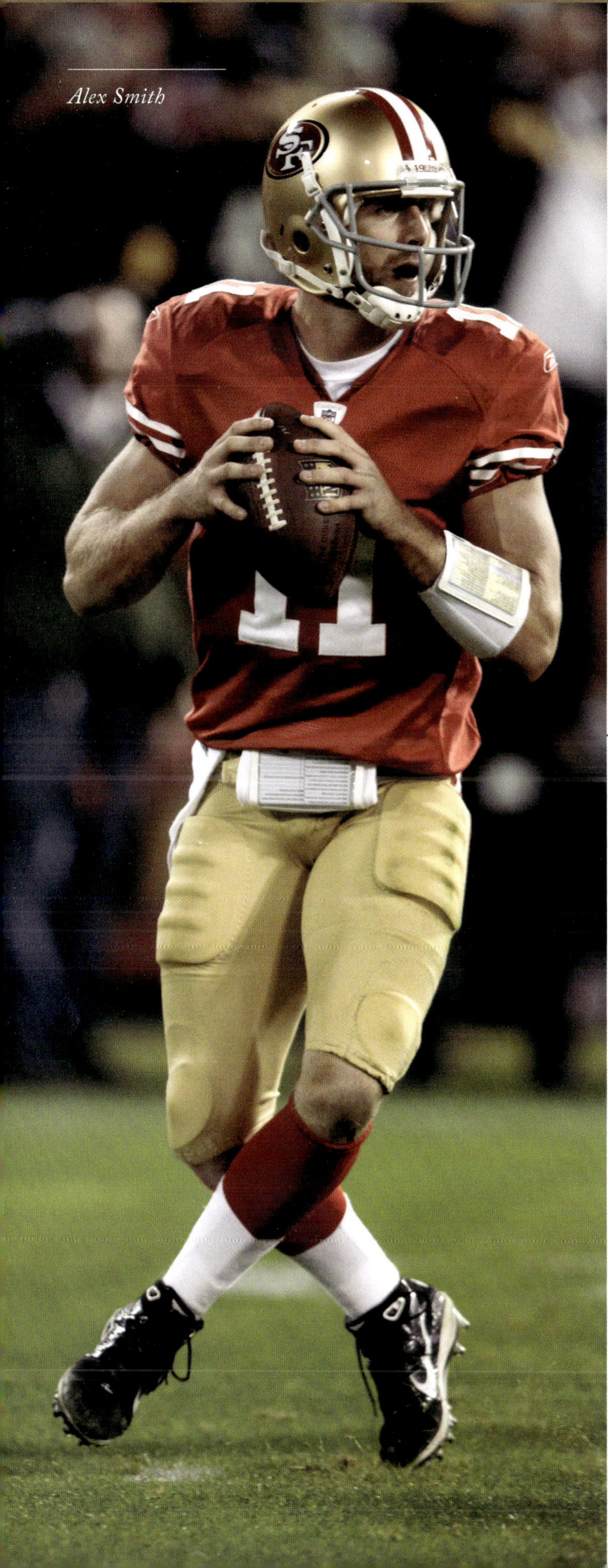

Alex Smith

CAREER PASSING YARDS

1. Joe Montana **35,124**
2. John Brodie **31,548**
3. Steve Young **29,907**
4. Jeff Garcia **16,408**
5. Y.A. Tittle **16,016**
6. Alex Smith **14,280**
7. Colin Kaepernick **12,271**
8. Frankie Albert **10,795**
9. Jimmy Garoppolo **7,352**
10. Steve DeBerg **7,220**

CAREER PASSING TDs

1. Joe Montana **244**
2. Steve Young **221**
3. John Brodie **214**
4. Frankie Albert **115**
5. Jeff Garcia **113**
6. Y.A. Tittle **108**
7. Alex Smith **81**
8. Colin Kaepernick **72**
9. Jimmy Garoppolo **46**
10. Steve DeBerg **37**

CAREER RECEIVING YARDS

1. Jerry Rice **19,247**
2. Terrell Owens **8,572**
3. Dwight Clark **6,750**
4. Gene Washington **6,664**
5. Billy Wilson **5,902**
6. Vernon Davis **5,640**
7. John Taylor **5,598**
8. Brent Jones **5,195**
9. Freddie Solomon **4,873**
10. Roger Craig **4,442**

CAREER RECEIVING TDs

1. Jerry Rice **176**
2. Terrell Owens **81**
3. Gene Washington **59**
4. Vernon Davis **55**
5. Billy Wilson **49**
6. Alyn Beals **49**
7. Dwight Clark **48**
8. John Taylor **43**
9. Freddie Solomon **43**
10. Brent Jones **33**

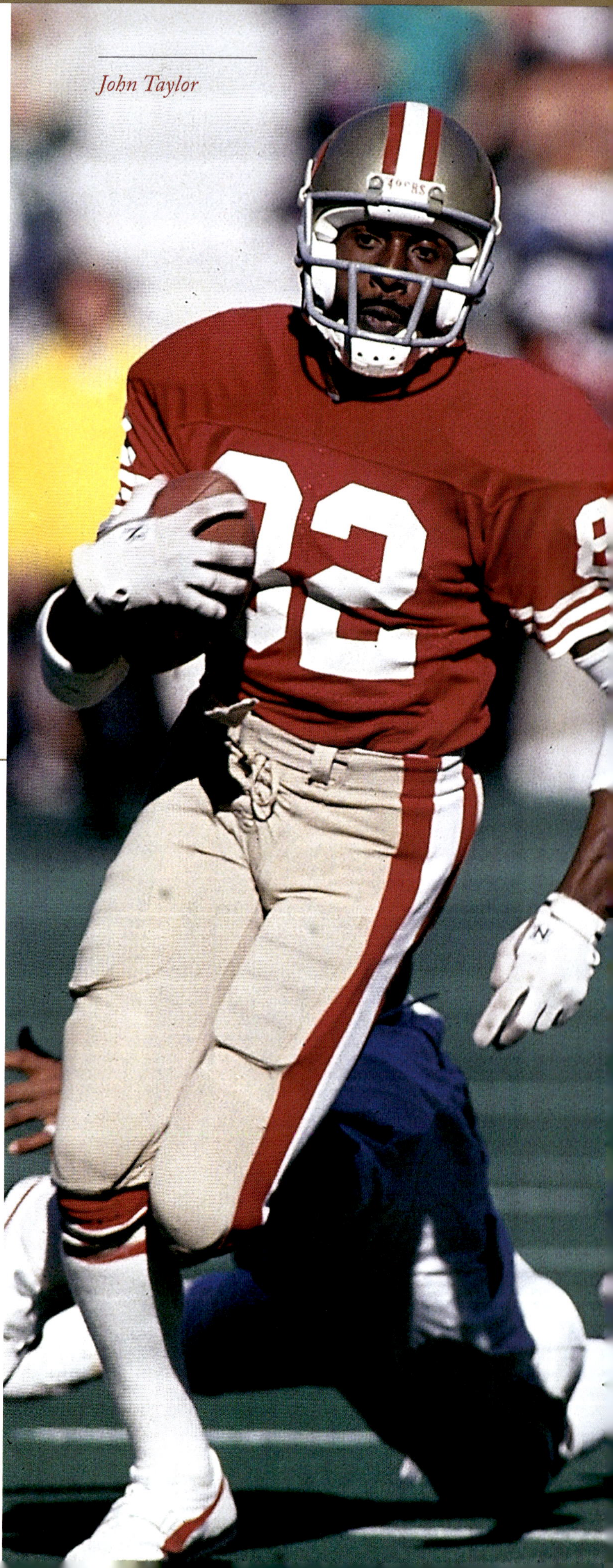

John Taylor

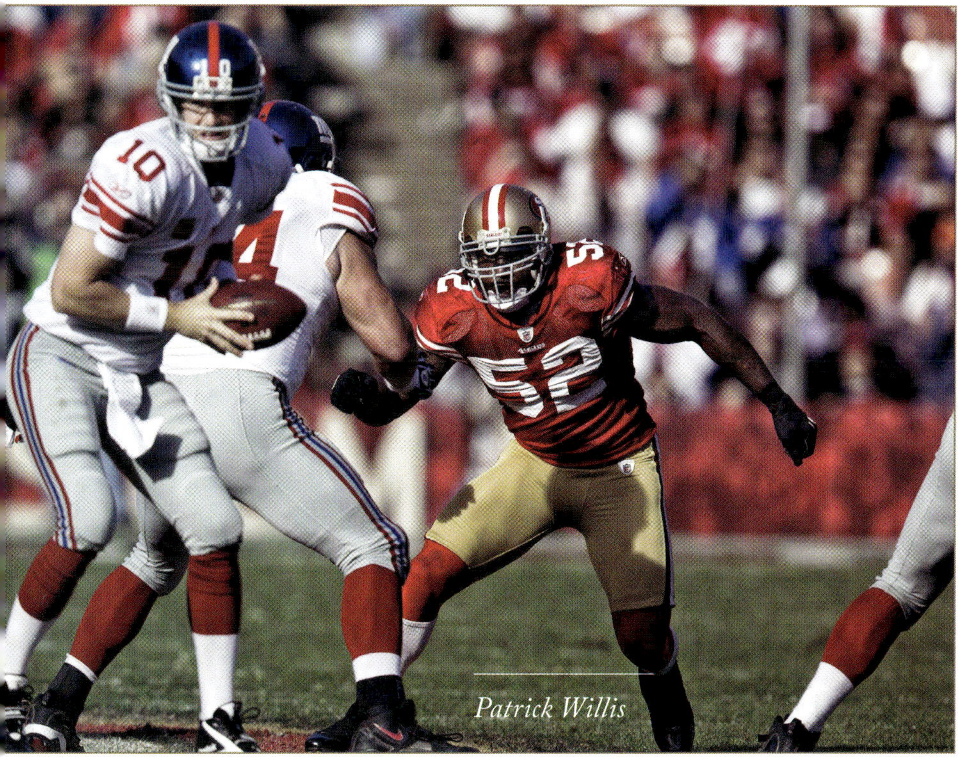

Patrick Willis

CAREER SOLO TACKLES

1. Patrick Willis **733**
2. Ronnie Lott **721**
3. Ken Norton Jr. **549**
4. NaVorro Bowman **527**
5. Derek Smith **521**
6. Bryant Young **519**
7. Tim McDonald **471**
8. Bill Romanowski **445**
9. Merton Hanks **433**
10. Jeff Ubrich **366**

CAREER INTERCEPTIONS

1. Ronnie Lott **51**
2. Jimmy Johnson **47**
3. Kermit Alexander **36**
4. Merton Hanks **31**
5. Lowell Wagner **31**
6. Dwight Hicks **30**
7. Jim Cason **25**
8. Rex Berry **22**
9. Don Griffin **22**
10. Tony Parrish **22**

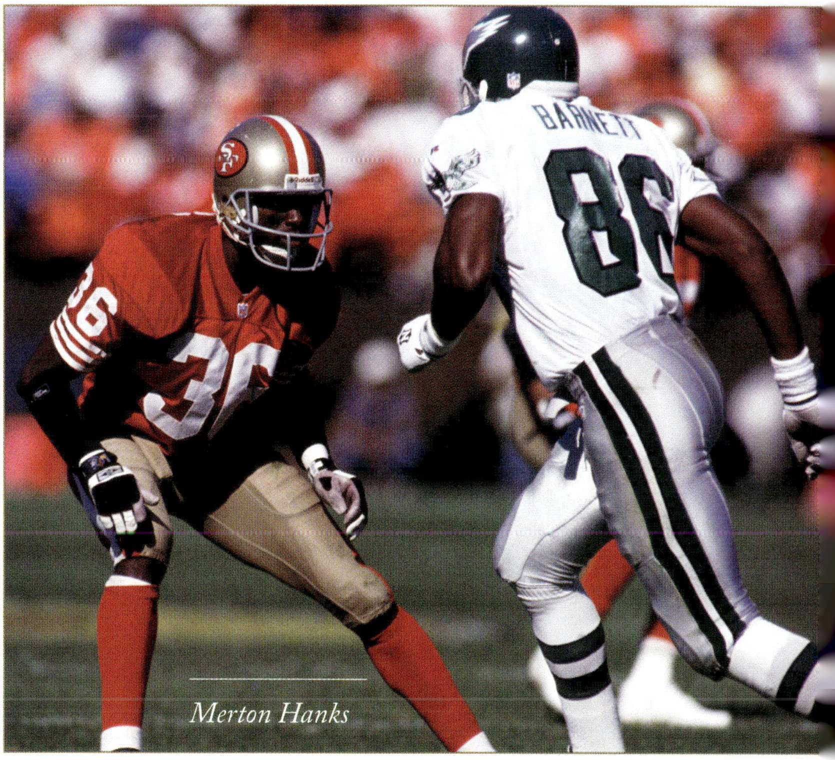

Merton Hanks

CAREER COACHING VICTORIES

1. George Seifert **98**
2. Bill Walsh **92**
3. Buck Shaw **71**
4. Steve Mariucci **57**
5. Dick Nolan **54**
6. Jim Harbaugh **44**
7. Kyle Shanahan **29**
8. Red Hickey **27**
9. Jack Christiansen **26**
10. Frankie Albert **19**

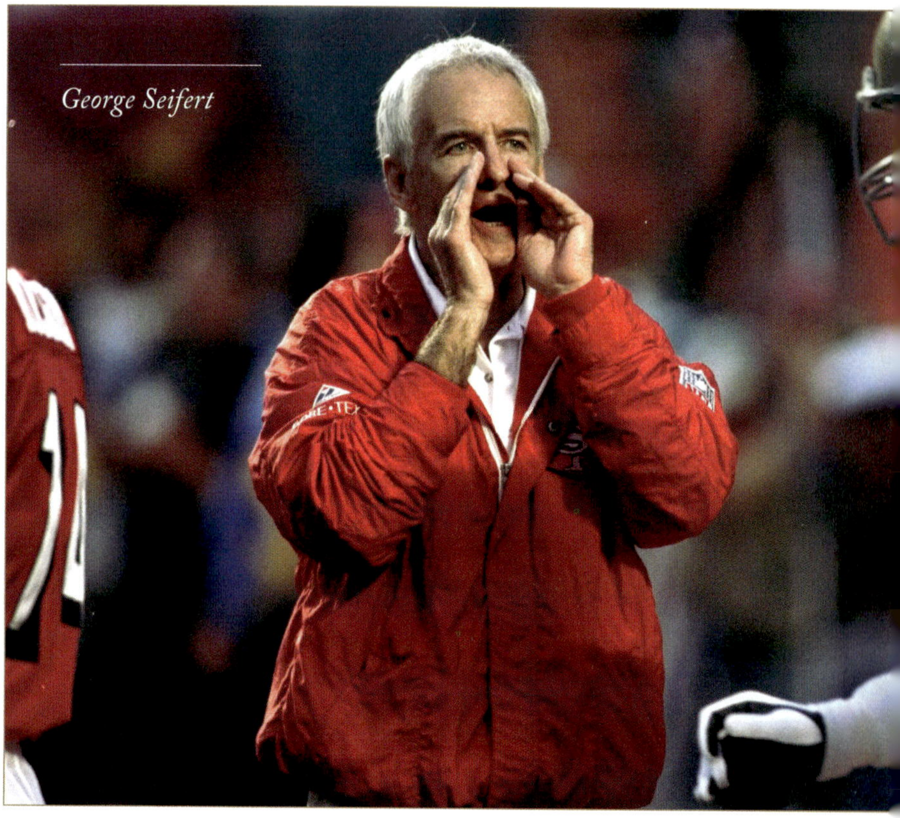

George Seifert

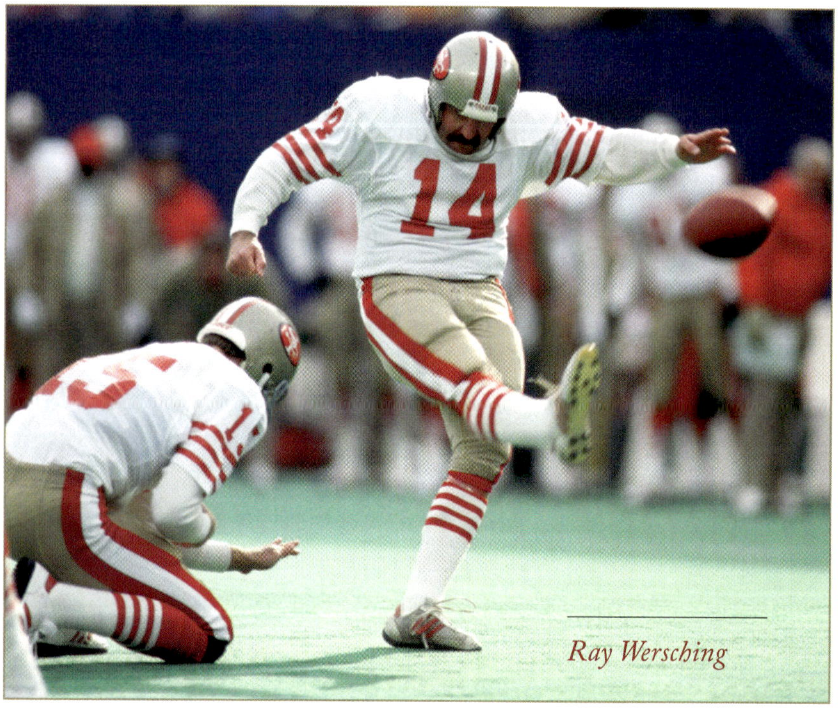

Ray Wersching

CAREER FIELD GOALS MADE

1. Ray Wersching **190**
2. Tommy Davis **130**
3. Joe Nedney **129**
4. Mike Cofer **128**
5. Robbie Gould **114**
6. Phil Dawson **99**
7. Bruce Gossett **99**
8. David Akers **73**
9. Gordon Soltau **70**
10. Wade Richey **54**

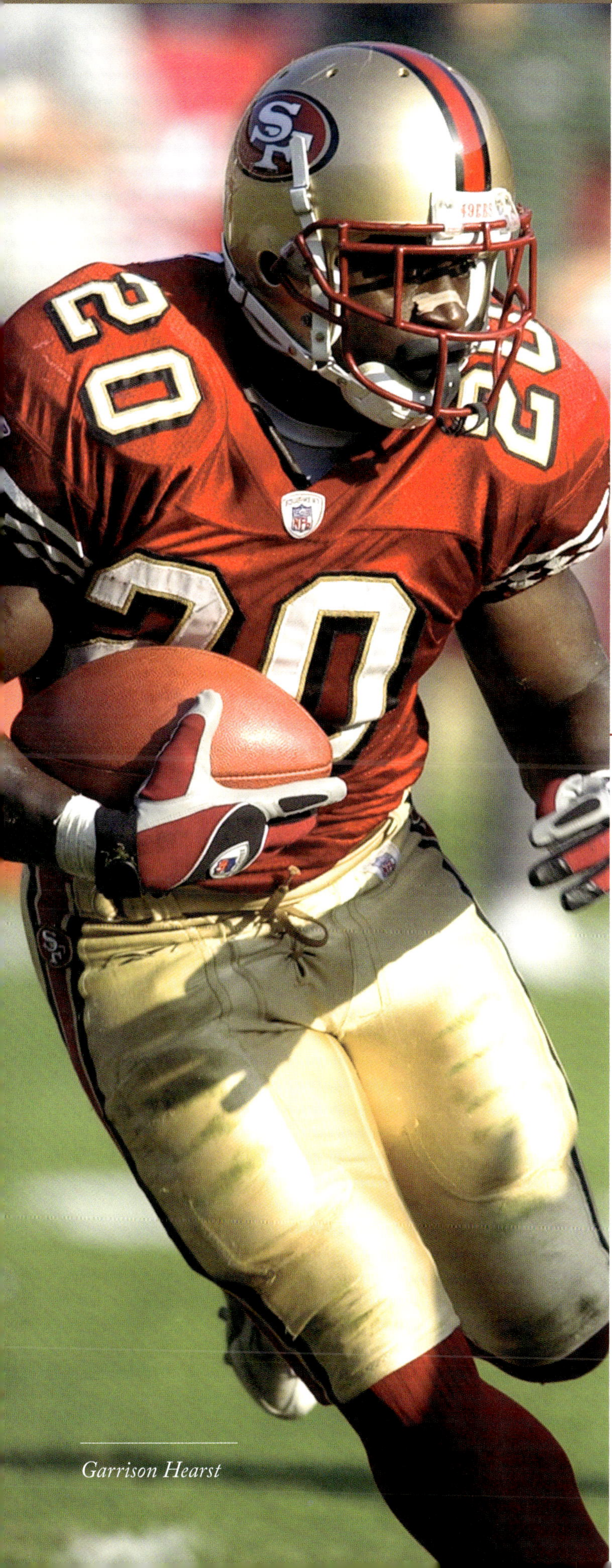

Garrison Hearst

CAREER RUSHING YARDS

1. Frank Gore **11,073**
2. Joe Perry **8,689**
3. Roger Craig **7,064**
4. Ken Willard **5,930**
5. Garrison Hearst **5,535**
6. J.D. Smith **4,370**
7. Hugh McElhenny **4,288**
8. Kevan Barlow **3,614**
9. Steve Young **3,581**
10. Johnny Strzykalski **3,415**

CAREER RUSHING TDs

1. Joe Perry **68**
2. Frank Gore **64**
3. Roger Craig **50**
4. Ken Willard **45**
5. J.D. Smith **37**
6. Steve Young **37**
7. Hugh McElhenny **35**
8. Frankie Albert **27**
9. Garrison Hearst **26**
10. Tom Rathman **26**

THE COVERS

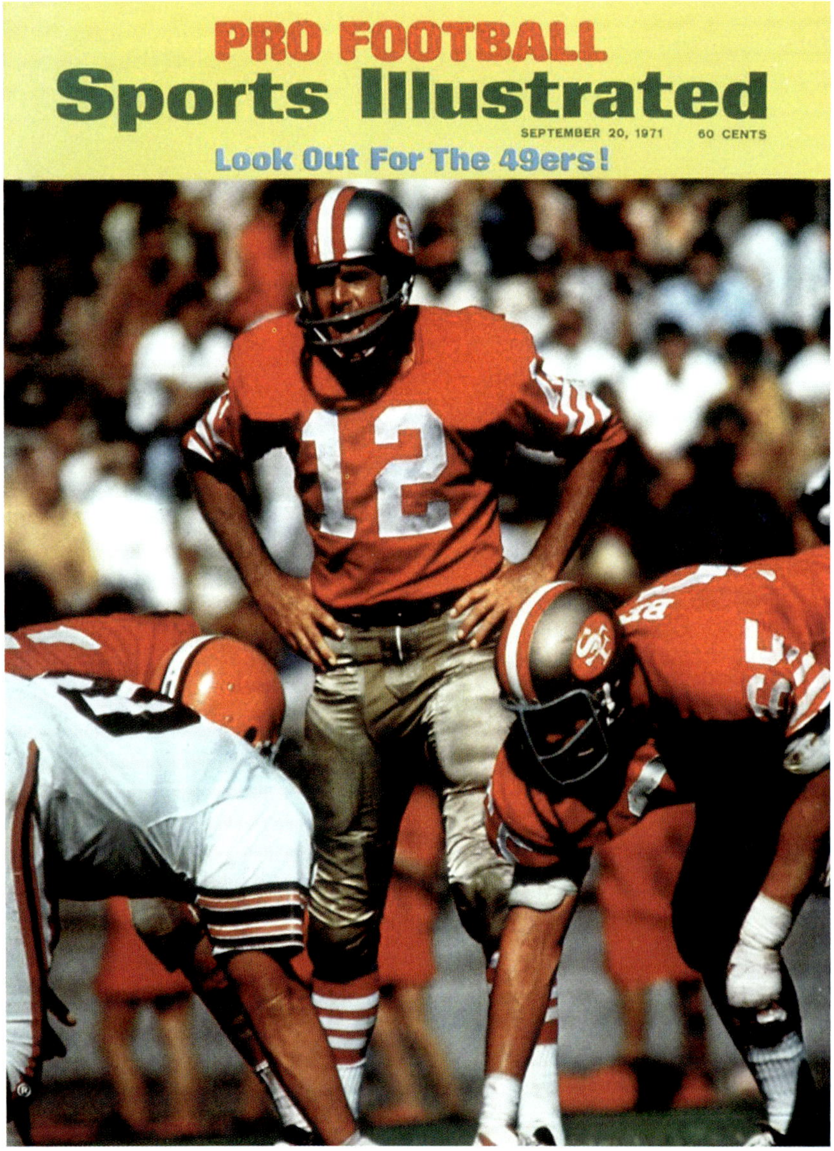

September 20, 1971

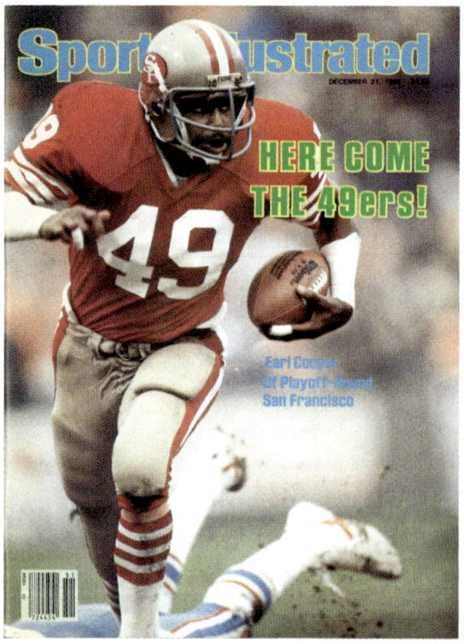

December 21, 1981

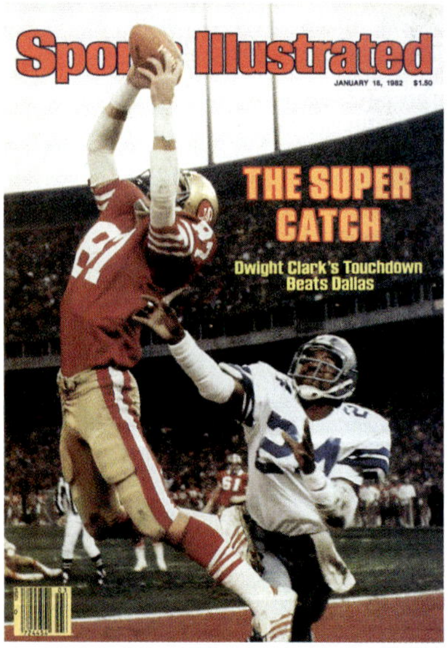

January 18, 1982

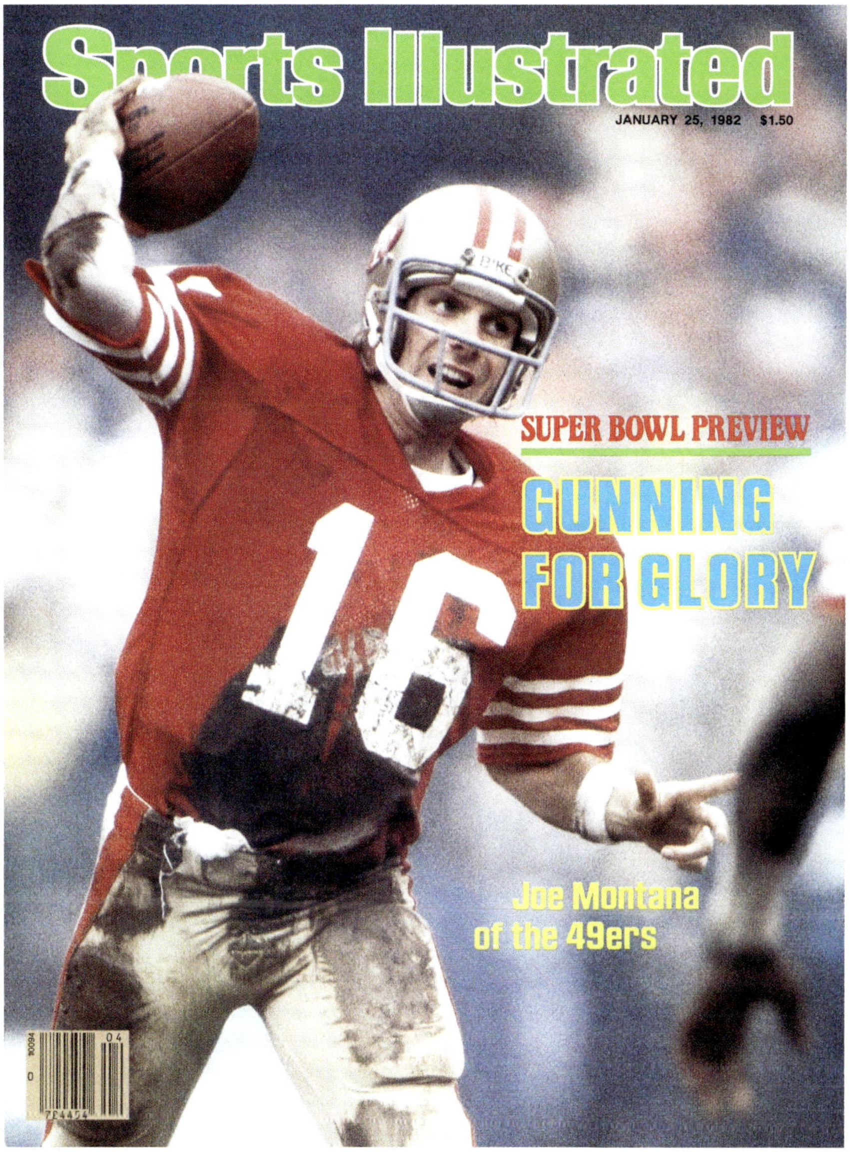

January 25, 1982

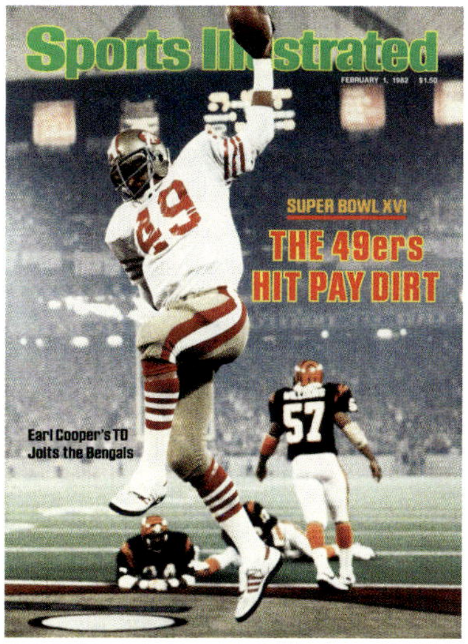

February 1, 1982

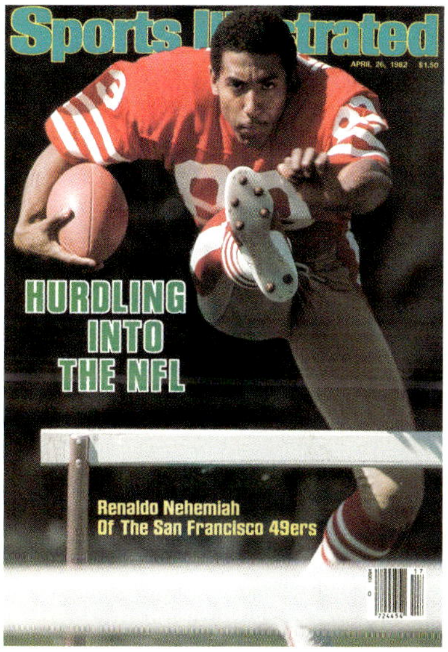

April 26, 1982

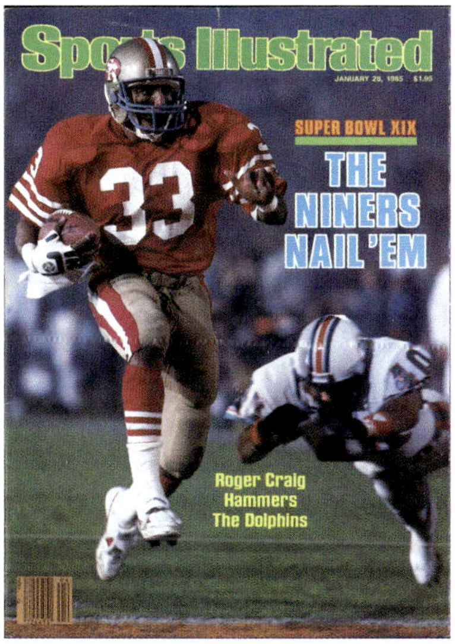

January 28, 1985

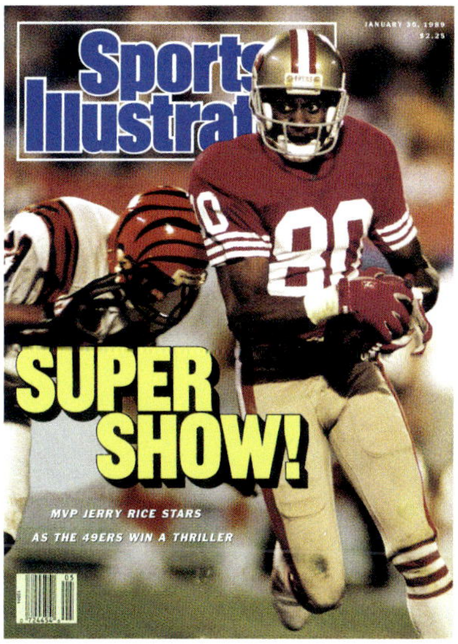

January 30, 1989

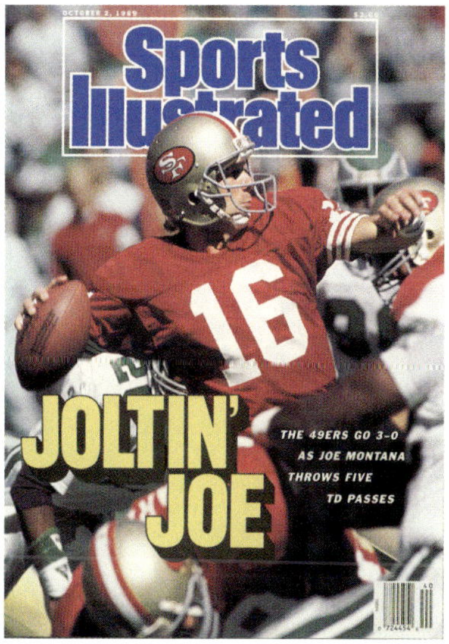

October 2, 1989

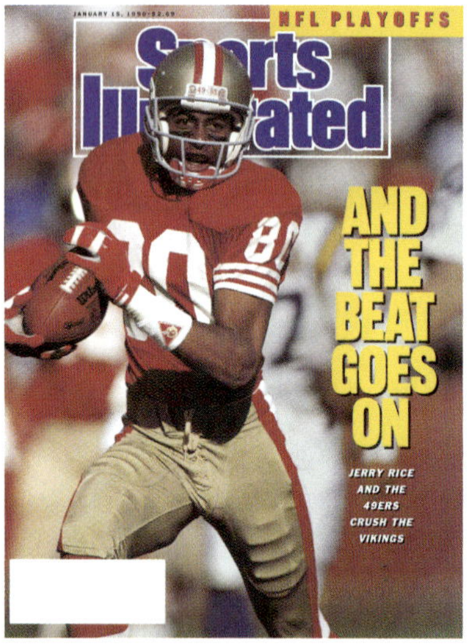

January 15, 1990

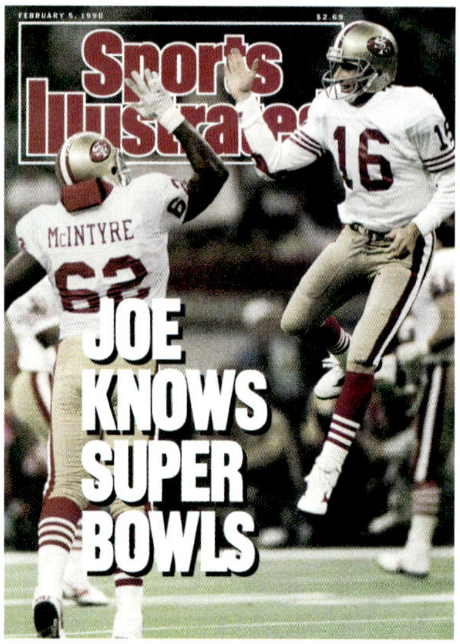

February 5, 1990

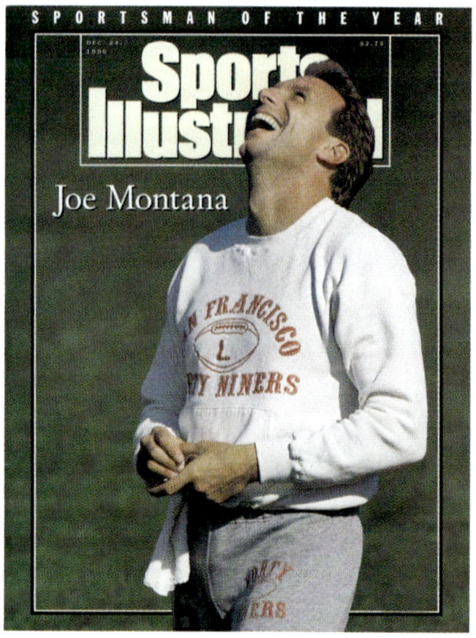

December 24, 1990

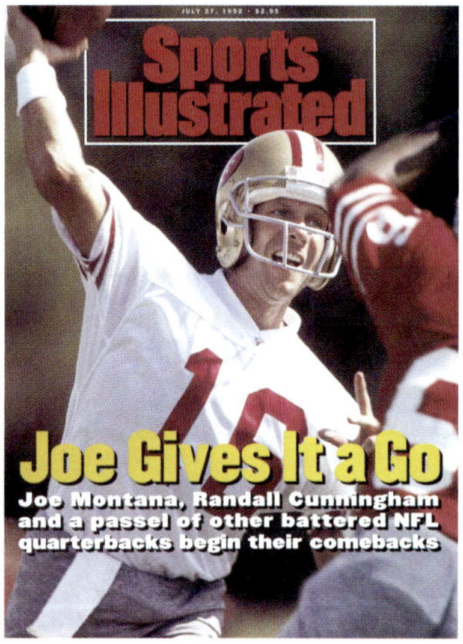

July 27, 1992

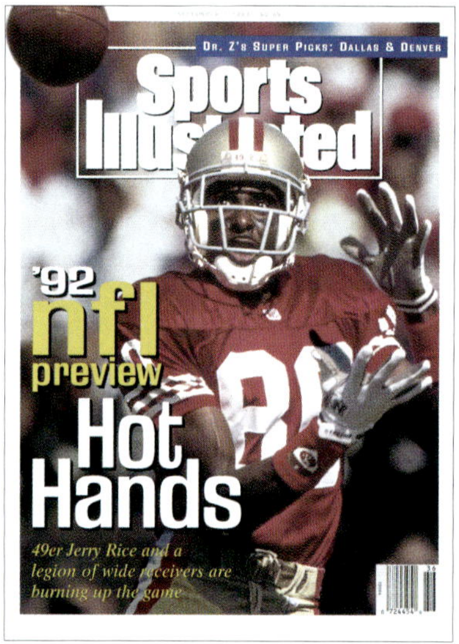

September 7, 1992

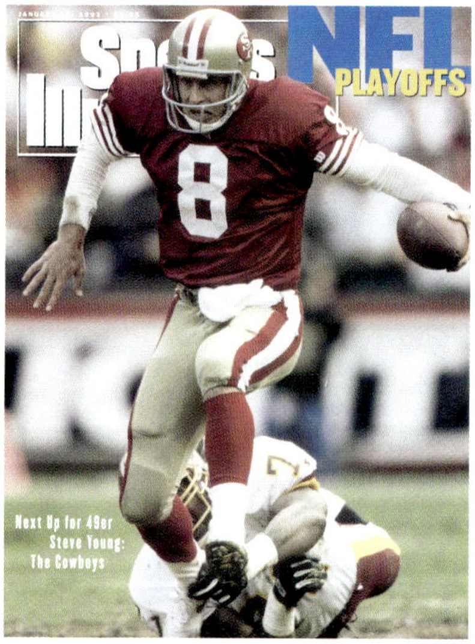

January 18, 1993

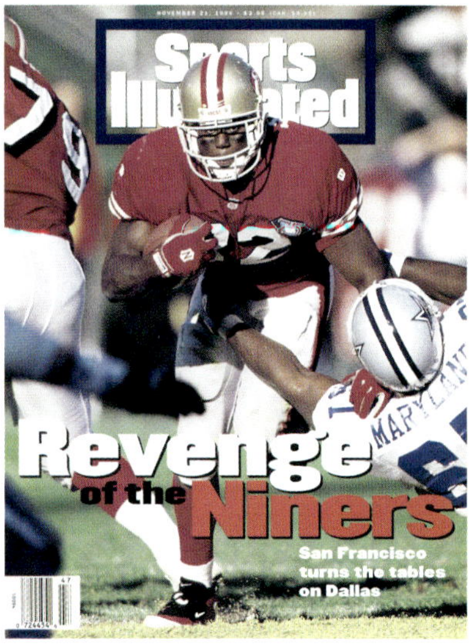

November 21, 1994

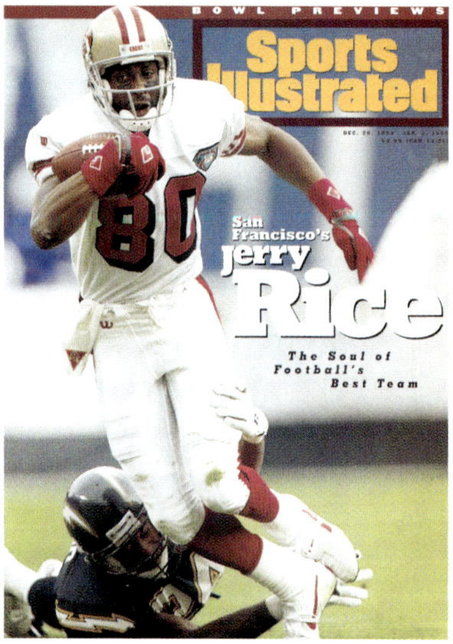

December 26, 1994

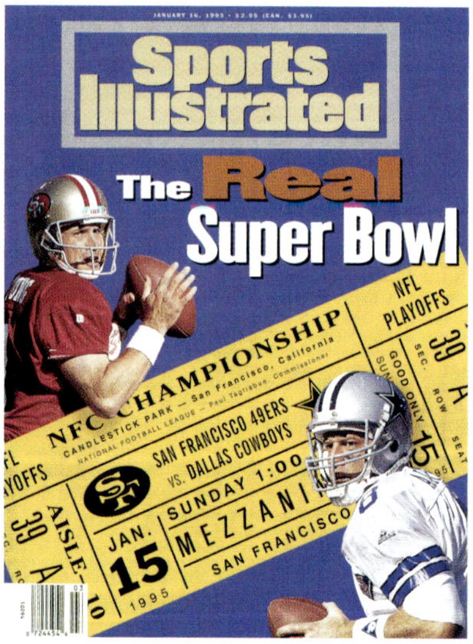

January 16, 1995

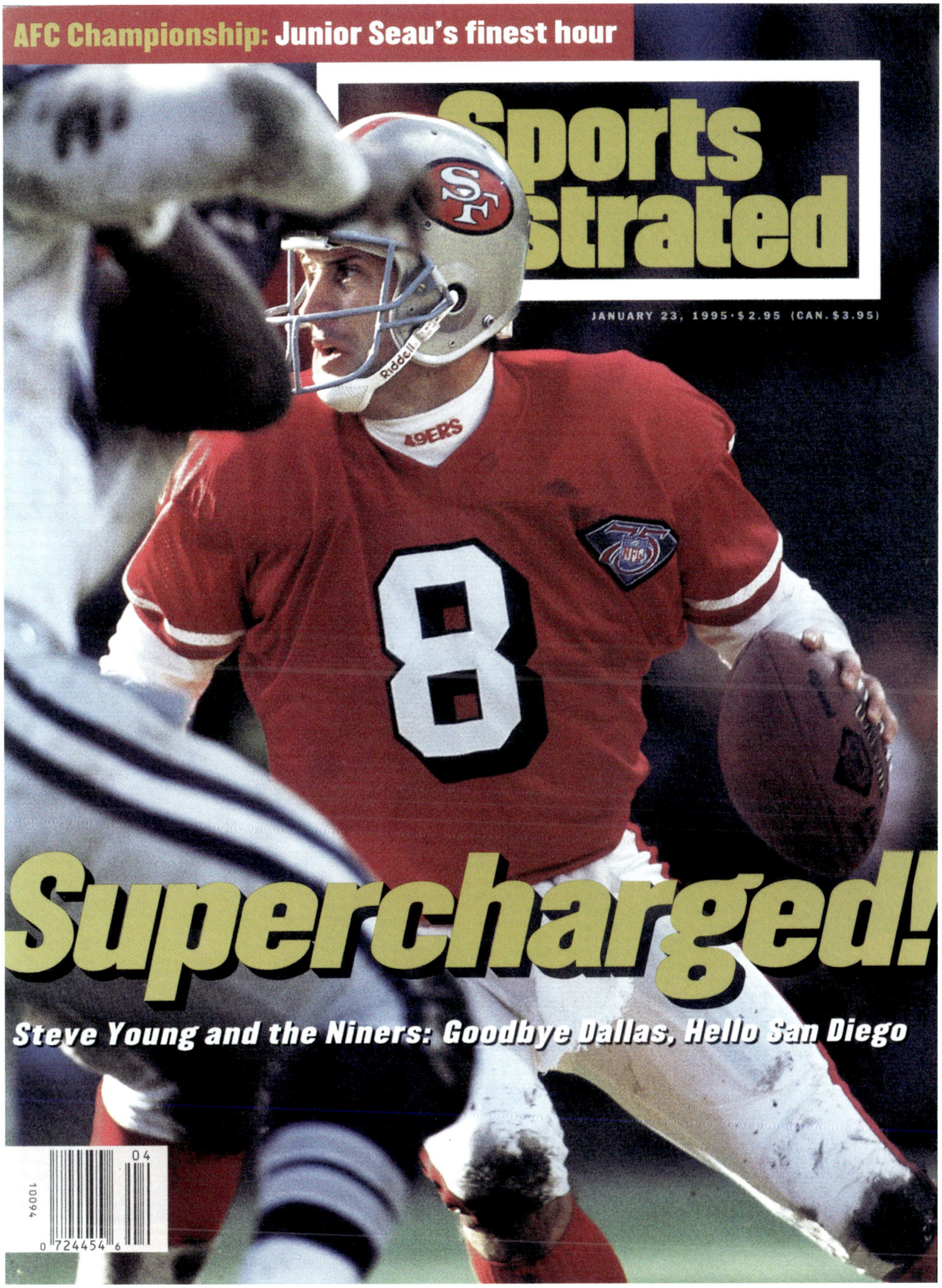

January 23, 1995

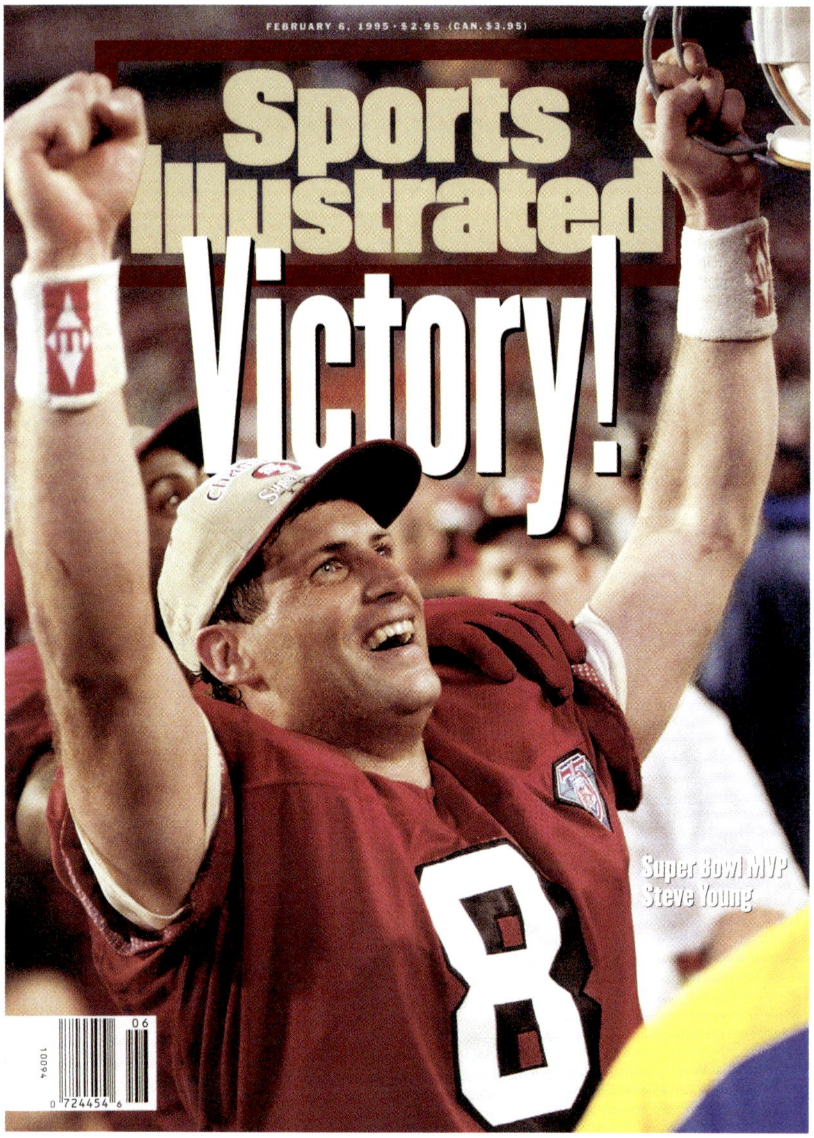

February 6, 1995

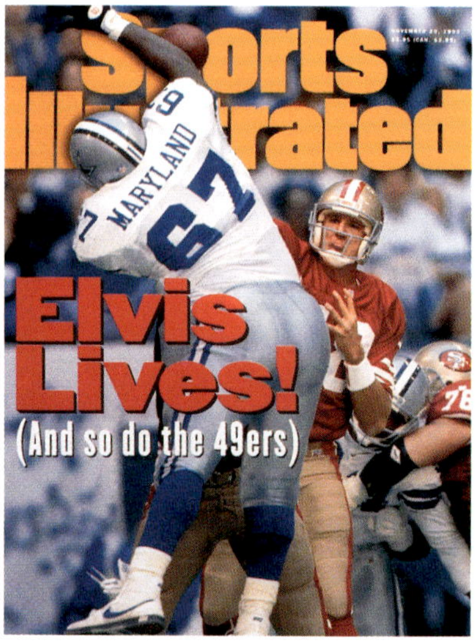

November 20, 1995

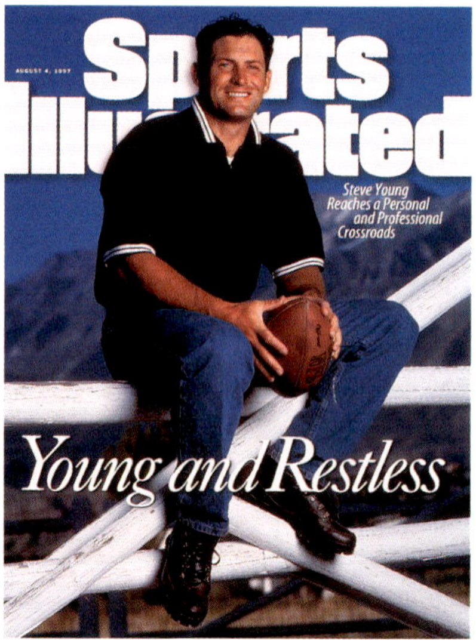

August 4, 1997

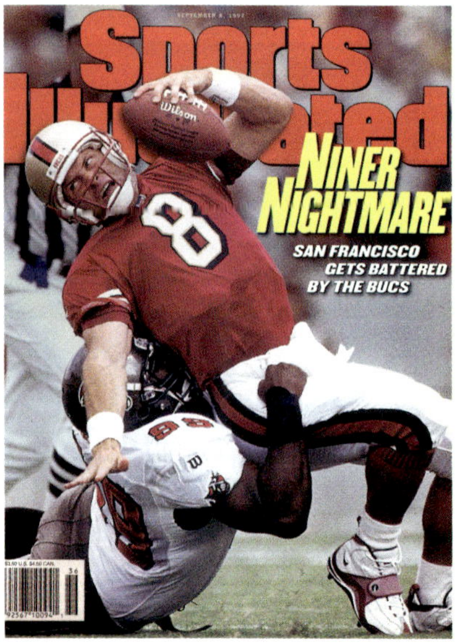

September 8, 1997

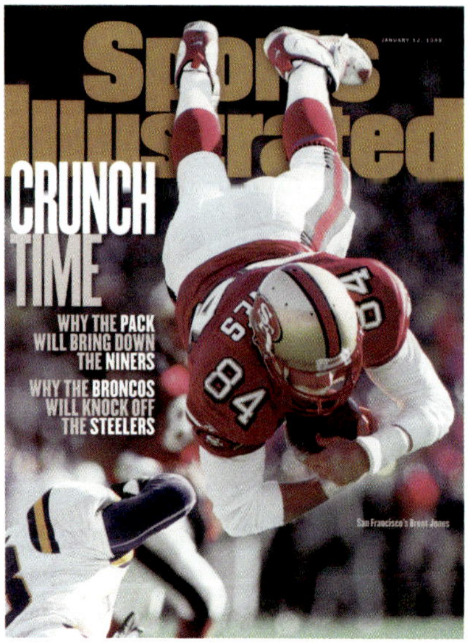

January 12, 1998

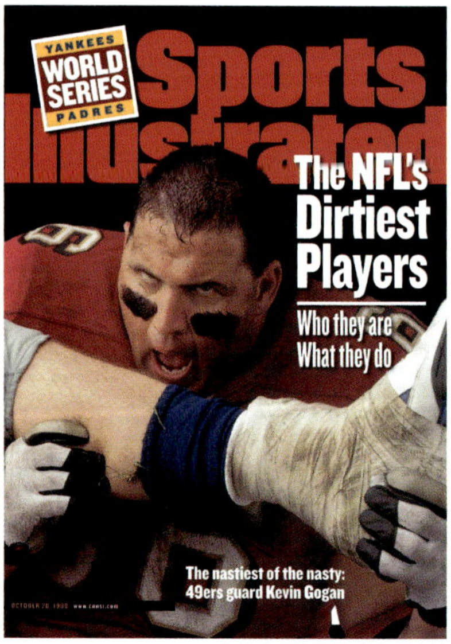

October 26, 1998

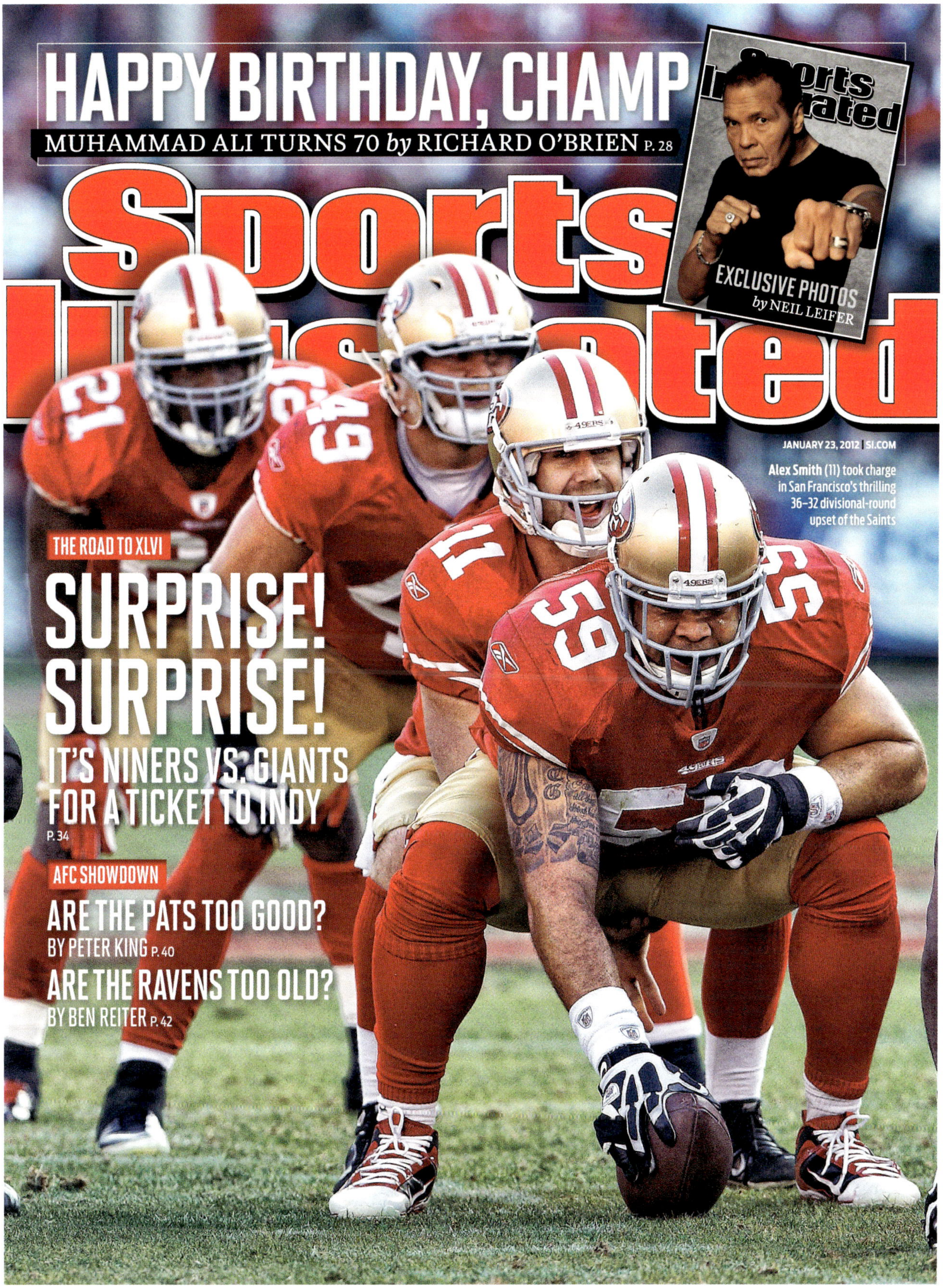

January 23, 2012

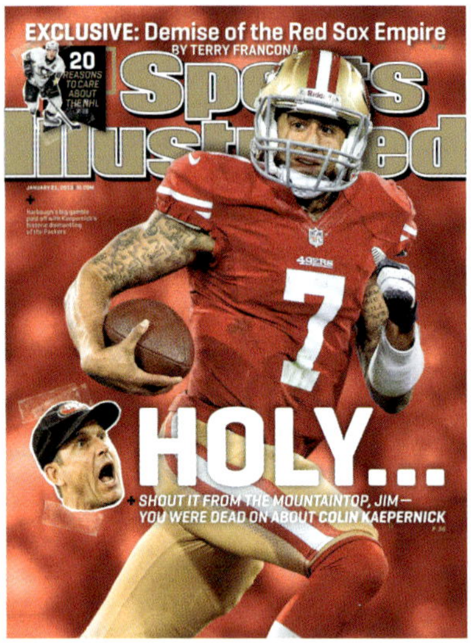

January 21, 2013

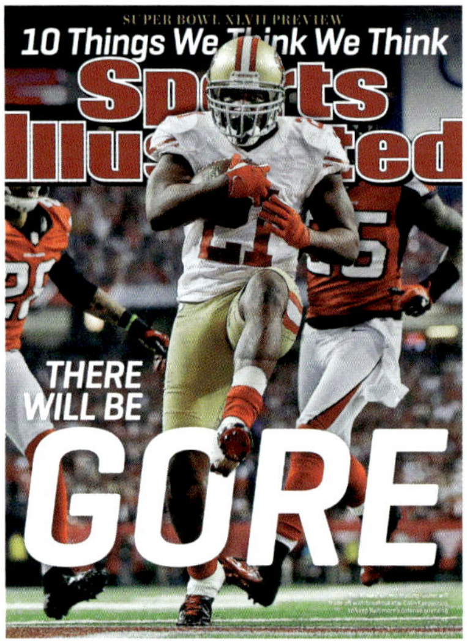

January 28, 2013

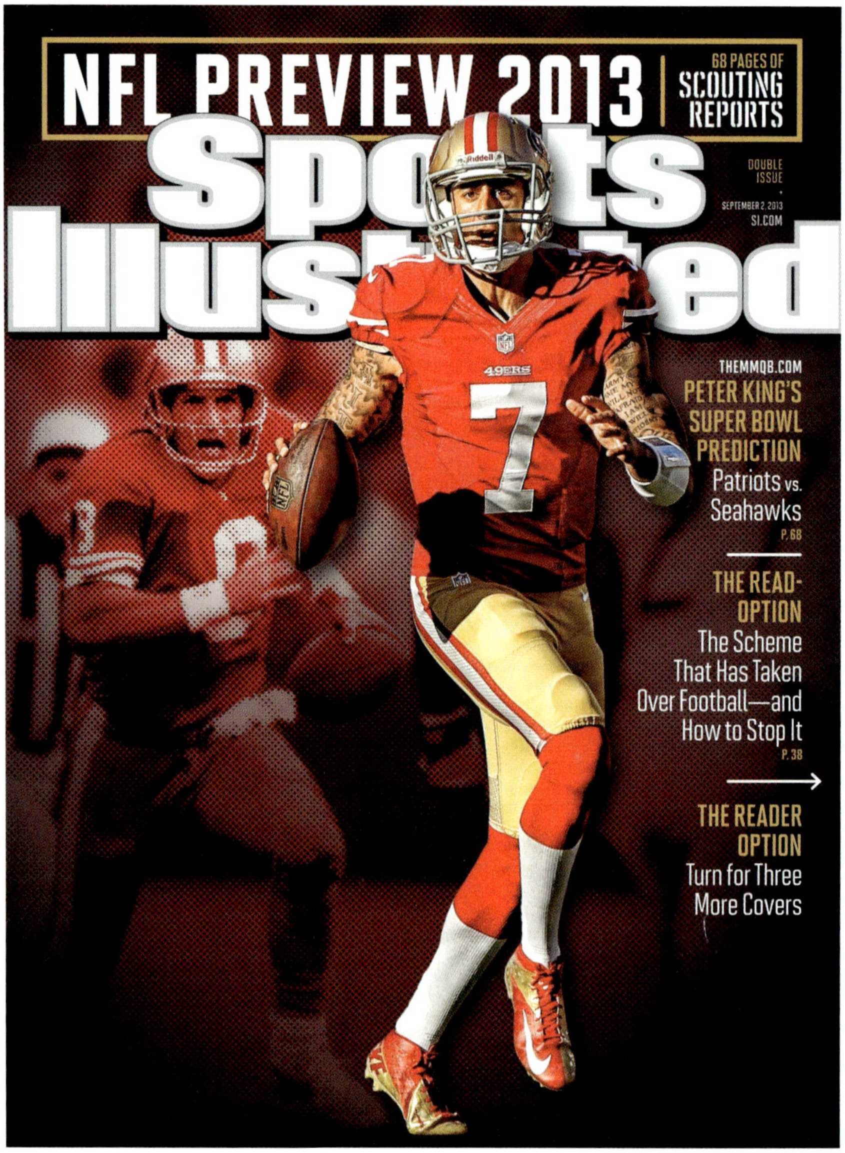

September 2, 2013

Photo Credits

Al Tielemans: Page 194; Andy Hayt: Pages 16, 28, 59, 68, 81, 201; Bob Rosato: Page 92; Heinz Kluetmeier: Pages 30, 156, 212; John Iacono: Pages 182, 222, 224; John W. McDonough: Page 114, Mark Kauffman: Pages 34, 64; Neil Leifer: Pages 18, 20, 22, 23, 49, 50, 51, 63; Peter Read Miller: Pages 94, 97, 106, 110, 221, 223; Robert Beck: Pages 112, 191; Walter Iooss Jr.: Pages 67, 163, 174.

Additional photography: AFP: Page 218; AP Photos: Page 220; Arthur Anderson/AP Photos: Pages 15, 60; Bettman: Pages 47, 53, 54, 70, 74, 130, 144; Bob Verlin/Getty Images: Page 124; David Madison/Getty Images: Pages 12, 87, 153, 172, 173, 184; Dino Vournas/AFP: Page 166; Donald Miralle/Getty Images: Page 98; Doug Collier/AFP: Page 216; Focus on Sport: Pages 56, 58, 75, 78, 85, 86, 88, 90, 91, 118, 134, 162, 169, 177, 204, 225; George Gojkovich/Getty Images: Pages 132, 146, 148, 224; George Rose/Getty Images: Page 223; Greg Trott/AP Photos: Page 138; Harry How/Getty Images: Page 73; Icon Sportswire: Pages 206, 214; James Flores/Getty Images: Pages 158, 164; Jed Jacobsohn/Getty Images: Pages 100, 155; Michael Zagaris/Getty Images: Pages 44, 46, 102, 104, 107, 186, 192; Octavio Jones/Getty Images: Page 196; Otto Greule Jr./Allsport: Page 105; Owen C. Shaw/Getty Images: Pages 80, 210; Peter Read Miller/AP Photos: Page 137; Rob Brown/Getty Images: Pages 43, 208; Rob Carr/Getty Images: Page 116; Robert Daemmrich/AFP: Page 161; Robert Houston/AP Photos: Page 26; Robert Riger/Getty Images: Pages 33, 39, 52; Tony Tomsic/AP Photos: Pages 36, 126; Vernon Biever/AP Photos: Pages 25, 198, 202.

Library of Congress Cataloging-in-Publication Data available upon request.

This book is available in quantity at special discounts for your group or organization.
For further information, contact:
Triumph Books LLC
814 North Franklin Street, Chicago, Illinois 60610
(312) 337-0747
www.triumphbooks.com

Printed in U.S.A.
ISBN: 978-1-62937-954-8